Governing Codes

LEXINGTON STUDIES IN POLITICAL COMMUNICATION

Series Editor: Robert E. Denton Jr., Virginia Tech

This series encourages focused work examining the role and function of communication in the realm of politics including campaigns and elections, media, and political institutions.

TITLES IN SERIES:

Governing Codes: Gender, Metaphor, and Political Identity
By Karrin Vasby Anderson and Kristina Horn Sheeler

Governing Codes

Gender, Metaphor, and Political Identity

Karrin Vasby Anderson and Kristina Horn Sheeler

LEXINGTON BOOKS

A Division of
ROWMAN & LITTLEFIELD PUBLISHERS, INC.
Lanham • Boulder • New York • Toronto • Oxford

LEXINGTON BOOKS

A division of Rowman & Littlefield Publishers, Inc.
A wholly owned subsidary of The Rowman & Littlefield Publishing Group, Inc.
4501 Forbes Boulevard, Suite 200
Lanham, MD 20706

PO Box 317
Oxford
OX2 9RU, UK

British Library Cataloguing in Publication Information Available

Library of Congress Cataloging-in-Publication Data

Governing codes : gender, metaphor, and political identity / by Karrin Vasby Anderson
and Kristina Horn Sheeler.
    p. cm.
    Includes bibliographical references and index.
    ISBN 0-7391-1022-5 (hardcover : alk. paper)—ISBN 0-7391-1199-X (pbk. : alk.
paper)
    1. Women in politics—United States. 2. Feminism—United States. 3. Sex role—
Political aspects—United States. I. Anderson, Karrin Vasby. II. Sheeler, Kristina K.
Horn.
    HQ1236.5.U6G68 2005
    305.43'32'0973—dc22   2005011741

Printed in the United States of America

♾™ The paper used in this publication meets the minimum requirements of American
National Standard for Information Sciences—Permanence of Paper for Printed Library
Materials, ANSI/NISO Z39.48–1992.

Dedicated to our parents

Kay and Arnold Horn
Owen and Patricia Vasby

Contents

Acknowledgements

In addition to a complementary research agenda, we share a strong friendship that developed as graduate students at Indiana University. There we were lucky enough to meet other graduate students who were always supportive of our research efforts. In particular, we'd like to thank "the girlfriends" for their support and encouragement as we completed this project. Also to Irwin, you were always on the lookout for articles about women in politics—thanks for your eternal vigilance. Our professors were instrumental in helping us develop our critical perspectives. We'd like to thank Robert Ivie for his guidance as he saw us through the very beginnings of this manuscript. In addition, our colleagues at Colorado State University and Indiana University Purdue University Indianapolis (IUPUI) have been wonderfully supportive as we have worked on this project, encouraging our efforts, serving as readers and collaborators, and inspiring us with their own research.

A special thank you goes to our families. Kari would like to thank Thad Anderson. I'm so glad we can share our lives and dreams with each other. Jaret and Joshua, being your mom is the best and most meaningful job I will ever have. Thanks for giving me an excuse to ditch my computer for the sandbox once in a while. I also want to acknowledge my parents, Owen and Patricia Vasby. Not only did you give me the confidence to do what I do, but your continued presence in my family's life is a blessing. Thanks, too, to my brother Kyle, whose example always has inspired me to do my best. I appreciate the support of my oldest and dearest friends—Amy McLean, Stacy Phillips, Linda Baldini, and Tammy Kerr. Thanks for encouraging me as a writer, commiserating with me as a mother and teacher, and proving that friends *can* talk politics and religion and remain friends. Finally, Kristy, I appreciate your generous spirit, your professional excellence, and your impeccable taste.

Kristy would like to thank Ian Sheeler for putting up with many late nights and for helping me laugh at the little things. Thank you also for helping me take time away from the office. You're the reason behind my success. My parents, Arnold and Kay Horn, and my sister, Beth Cohagan, were tireless cheerleaders as the manuscript came together. Thank you for asking how it was progressing and especially for reading it when asked. To my niece and nephew, Abigail and Evan, I appreciate your visits and our trips to the fair. I hope you will continue to be inspired by the strong women and men in your lives. And finally to my co-author, thank you for being one of many inspirational women in my life.

Finally, we would like to acknowledge that this book was a completely co-authored project. Each author contributed equally and we chose to list our names alphabetically. We would also like to acknowledge that portions of our work have appeared before in the following:

Anderson, Karrin Vasby. "'Rhymes with Rich,' 'Bitch' as a Tool of Containment in Contemporary American Politics." *Rhetoric & Public Affairs* 2 (1999): 599–623. Copyright Michigan State University Press. Used with permission. All rights reserved.

Anderson, Karrin Vasby. "From Spouses to Candidates: Hillary Rodham Clinton, Elizabeth Dole, and the Gendered Office of U.S. President." *Rhetoric & Public Affairs* 5 (2002): 105–32. Copyright Michigan State University Press. Used with permission. All rights reserved.

Anderson, Karrin Vasby. "Hillary Rodham Clinton as 'Madonna': The Role of Metaphor and Oxymoron in Image Restoration." *Women's Studies in Communication* 25 (2002): 1–24. Used with permission of the Organization for Research on Women and Communication. All rights reserved.

Anderson, Karrin Vasby. "The First Lady: A Site of 'American Womanhood'" in *Inventing a Voice: The Rhetoric of American Twentieth Century First Ladies*, edited by Molly Meijer Wertheimer (Lanham, Md.: Rowman & Littlefield, 2004): 17–30. Used with permission. All rights reserved.

Sheeler, Kristina Horn. "Marginalizing Metaphors of the Feminine," in *Navigating Boundaries: The Rhetoric of Women Governors*, edited by Brenda DeVore Marshall and Molly A. Mayhead. Copyright © 2000 by Brenda DeVore Marshall and Molly A. Mayhead. Reproduced with permission of Greenwood Publishing Group, Inc., Westport, Conn.

Preface

As we look forward to completing this project in the summer of 2004, a friend forwarded to us an opinion piece titled "In Praise of Unruly Women" by Arianna Huffington. In it, Huffington recounts the antics of the latest woman who refuses to be contained by the media: Teresa Heinz Kerry. It seems that Heinz Kerry is unruly because she is "too outspoken," "too opinionated," "slightly zany," and, heaven forbid, has hair that is "unkempt." Huffington laments that "we may have come a long way baby" but a double standard still exists for women in politics, and especially for political wives. We couldn't agree more, which was the motivation behind this book project.

In our study of women in politics, we discovered that diverse groups of political women (women candidates, political executives, and political spouses) often are affected by the same gendered strategies—tactics used by political opponents and the media alike to contain them. This book identifies four women prominent in the contemporary U.S. political scene: Democrats Ann Richards and Hillary Rodham Clinton and Republicans Christine Todd Whitman and Elizabeth Dole. Each woman is in a unique position with respect to gender and public leadership and helps to illustrate the ways in which metaphor plays a central role in the construction of public identity in contemporary U.S. politics. Our thesis is that metaphors function both as constraints and rhetorical resources for political figures. On one hand, familiar narratives and stereotypes about women and power often govern media portrayals of public women, containing and constraining them. Conversely, however, the women we examine mine the metaphorical landscape for rhetorical strategies they can use to accomplish their pragmatic goals.

To begin, we briefly recount the heritage of the study of metaphors, noting that we approach metaphor not simply as a stylistic device but as a way into and of understanding the political process. To this end, metaphors suggest possibilities for and limitations of women's political agency. Next we discuss the linguistic barriers that historically have been salient for women candidates and leaders: the metaphor of containment and the notion of the double bind. To illustrate the prevalence of metaphor in media portrayals of public women, we identify four clusters of metaphors that are primary in their characterizations: pioneer, puppet, beauty queen/hostess, and unruly woman/"bitch."

With this metaphorical discussion in place, we move to an analysis of each of our four case studies. Former Texas Governor Ann Richards is the sassy grandmother governor who transformed leadership in Texas. Richards capitalized on the metaphor of the unruly woman, moving Texas forward even as she appealed to its pioneer foundations. As a transitional figure, she illustrates how to gain credibility from a liberal frame within a weak governorship. In contrast, former New Jersey Governor Christine Todd Whitman illustrates how to govern credibly as a conservative within a strong governorship. As a conciliator, Whitman's leadership was gendered feminine in that she deferred to the state and her party. Primary for Whitman was the need for cooperation in order to accomplish her goals. Our analysis of former first lady and current New York Senator Hillary Rodham Clinton details her transformation from "bitch" to Madonna, illustrating that the unruly woman metaphor does not hold as many opportunities for political spouses and senators as it does for women executives. Finally, Elizabeth Dole's journey from political spouse to presidential candidate to U.S. Senator from North Carolina indicates that the U.S. electorate accepts women in representative positions more easily than in executive positions. In the first two of Dole's three nationally-prominent campaigns, a distinct narrative is drawn. In 1996, Elizabeth Dole was depicted as the hostess/beauty queen during her husband's bid for the presidency. That image lingered over her 2000 bid for the Republican presidential nomination, combining with the narrative of Dole as a pioneer. When Dole campaigned for the U.S. Senate, a single news narrative failed to emerge. Instead, the media portrayed a more complex candidate who appealed to voters as a potential partner in governance, rather than as a leader.

To conclude, we discuss the theoretical implications of our analysis for the study of gender, metaphor, and political identity. While it is possible for political women to manage their public personae in ways that afford them political advantages and challenge age-old stereotypes, the prevalence of metaphor and the clustering effect in news narratives makes the task of identity formation much more difficult. Each woman illustrates the potential to turn a containing metaphor on its head, capitalizing on the political resources at her disposal. Further, each woman in this study illustrates the importance of place, political affiliation, and political style when using the resources of the political culture to negotiate public identity. We acknowledge that the women in this study cannot stand in for all political women, but instead call for many more analyses of public women and the constraints that affect credibility, women's power, and identity formation.

Introduction

The Role of Language in Politics

November 21, 1994. *Newsweek*'s Jonathan Alter reported that "Democrats got clobbered, crushed, dissed, demolished—you pick the verb—at the polls last week."[1] Republican gains were attributed to a host of missteps taken by the Clinton administration, not the least of which was said to be the appointment of First Lady Hillary Rodham Clinton as the head of the president's key domestic initiative: health-care reform. When that bill went down in defeat, Rodham Clinton remarked, "I've been re-zoned," and a British journalist observed that the first lady's "well-ordered phrases and rounded paragraphs" were interwoven with "deliberate and subtle hints to suggest she is the model of tradition, the perfect wife, mother, hostess, and God-fearing American citizen."[2] The first lady had become the essence of the traditional Madonna, a metaphor that would encapsulate her public persona both as she presented it in speeches and as it was covered in the media. This supposed "retreat" to tradition was howled at by critics who thought it underscored Rodham Clinton's penchant for phoniness, and by some feminists who lamented the loss of an activist first lady. But the British journalist interpreted the changes to Rodham Clinton's image differently, stating, "Mrs. Clinton is not simply giving herself a new image. By doing so she is attempting to reposition herself politically."[3] Indeed, the Madonna-figure so publicly chastised for bucking tradition used the traditional duties of the first lady to spread a women's rights message abroad, garner public favor at home, defend herself and her husband against numerous public scandals, and eventually launch a successful bid for the U.S. Senate.

The case of Hillary Rodham Clinton's public failures and successes helps to illustrate the role that metaphor plays in contemporary U.S. politics. But Rodham Clinton is not alone. Many political women have struggled with the media's attempts to confine them in stereotypical images and simplistic narratives. A number have turned these images on their heads, using them to political advantage. This book examines four such cases. We identify four women prominent in the contemporary U.S. political scene: two Democrats and two Republicans. Each woman is in a unique position with respect to gender and public leadership. Former Texas Governor Ann Richards was the "pioneering" first woman to win the Texas governorship "in her own right." Former New

Jersey Governor Christine Todd Whitman was a tough-on-taxes moderate who rose in the Republican ranks through strategies of conciliation. Elizabeth Dole took a star turn stumping for her husband's presidential aspirations, but became the first Republican woman to make a so-called "credible" run for the top office herself. Two years later she secured a U.S. Senate seat representing the state of North Carolina and became that state's first female senator. Hillary Rodham Clinton was the first first lady to seek and win elective office as the U.S. Senator from New York.[4] What is striking about each of these cases are the ways in which metaphor played a central role in the construction of a public identity for each woman. The thesis of this book is that metaphors function both as constraints and rhetorical resources for political figures. On one hand, familiar narratives and stereotypes about women and power often govern media portrayals of public women, containing and constraining them. Conversely, however, the women we examine mine the metaphorical landscape for rhetorical strategies they can use to accomplish their pragmatic goals.

Before exploring each case in detail we first must outline the theoretical heritage and critical vocabulary that shape our discussion of the codes that govern us and how public women use them. The literature on gender, metaphor, and political identity is vast. Our intent here is not to provide an exhaustive analysis of important academic discussions surrounding each of those topics. Instead, we summarize what became for us analytical touchstones shaping our critical assessment of gender, metaphor, and political identity. When considering the functions of metaphor in a rhetorical/political context we underscore that metaphor is more than a stylistic device. George Lakoff and Mark Johnson have argued that "metaphor is pervasive in everyday life, not just in language, but in thought and action. Our ordinary conceptual system, in terms of which we both think and act, is fundamentally metaphorical in nature."[5] I. A. Richards explains that metaphor is a "borrowing between and intercourse of thoughts, a transaction between contexts."[6] It is a way to call up a particular meaning in the mind of an audience through the relationship between tenor and vehicle, the relationship between the idea or subject being expressed, and the image through which this idea is conveyed.[7] Metaphors in political media function enthymematically, encouraging the audience to supply premises about subjects that remain unstated, yet agreed upon.[8] Kenneth Burke points out that the pattern of vehicles in a body of discourse "necessarily directs the attention into some channels rather than others," influencing one's terministic perspective.[9] Through this expression we have not only a linguistic device, but also a perspective that evokes particular attitudes and actions. Robert L. Ivie explains that all "human motives [are] entangled in metaphor's linguistic web."[10] Through the use of metaphor, reality is conceived in a particular way because of the linguistic vehicles employed in its construction, and this reality can change as we use different vehicles to structure that reality. F. C. T Moore argues that "Today's metaphor is tomorrow's literal sense."[11]

Since metaphors are foundational to language, perception, and persuasion, critically assessing their function in a particular body of discourse lends useful insight into how that discourse affects people. Ivie offers a model for metaphoric criticism, encouraging the identification and analysis of metaphoric clusters that share similar entailments of meaning, each subgroup representing a first approximation of one of the rhetor's principal conceptual images. As these clusters of vehicles become more refined, the critic begins to examine their interaction throughout the text to determine how they function as a system of conceptual metaphors—where clusters co-occur, how they accommodate one another, which dominates the others, and what lines of argument they inspire."[12]

The approach taken in this book is to examine metaphoric clusters both within media coverage of political figures *and* in the rhetorical performances made by the individuals themselves. This provides a view of each woman's public identity as it was crafted and contested in the media. The importance of considering the impact of media coverage on public image is underscored by Shawn Parry-Giles, who notes that often a rhetor's own style and strategies will be erased by the larger narrative that shapes media coverage. She advocates the "recognition of the media's role in the complex process of image-making."[13]

Although sensitivity to the mediated nature of contemporary political communication informs this study, our primary focus on metaphor allows us to see moments where the political women we have studied react strategically to the media frames that encapsulate their public personae. Even when the frames seemed designed to constrain the candidates' actions or identity, each woman sometimes managed to employ metaphor in creative and liberating ways. An examination of speech texts, public appearances, and campaign discourse revealed the ways in which metaphors can serve as inventional tools.

Robert Ivie's procedure for identifying key metaphors served as a useful guide in this project.[14] First the critic familiarizes herself with the context in which discourse occurs as well as texts by speakers under study. This helps the critic to create a sense of the overall picture before noting particularities in the texts that are the focus of analysis. To establish this context we assessed discourse by and about women governors and first ladies before focusing specifically on the rhetoric (speeches and appearances) and media coverage (newspaper and magazine articles, transcripts of television broadcasts) of the women featured in this study.[15] Second, the critic notes problematic vehicles within their immediate verbal (or, more generally, symbolic) contexts. To do this, the critic performs a series of close readings of representative texts, marking vehicles in each reading until reaching the point where no new images are uncovered. This procedure of identifying vehicles with texts reduces the original discourse to a set of highlighted terms that can be analyzed for their relationships to one another.

Once the context is established and key vehicles identified, the critic's third step is to cluster marked vehicles that share similar "entailments." Following Lakoff and Johnson, "metaphorical entailments can characterize a coherent system of metaphorical concepts and a corresponding coherent system of meta-phorical expressions for those concepts."[16] Thus, each cluster represents the "metaphorical concepts" of the discourse and the clusters as a whole note the larger "system of metaphorical concepts." Fourth, with the clusters identified, the critic compiles vehicles and immediate contexts within each cluster. This step displays the specific applications of vehicles within each "metaphorical concept." Finally, the critic analyzes the clusters to note the overall system or patterns of metaphorical concepts for the purpose of assessing the limits or unre-alized potential of the metaphorical system guiding our understanding, in this case, of women political executives and political spouses.

We particularly were interested in messages that contributed to the public persona or political identity of each woman. Our goal was not simply to produce a typology of metaphors salient to contemporary political discussion (although the set we identify is instructive for anyone interested in the dynamics of politi-cal campaigns), but to use our critique to explicate and perhaps improve women's agency in contemporary U.S. politics. Ivie asserts that "Knowledge as the result of critical inquiry serves to enhance our ability to act upon the world with positive effect. . . . Rhetor-scholars proceed carefully, rigorously, and hon-estly toward a serviceable language of discovery, a language that lends insight from the critic's perspective, motivates a response, and requires reconsideration when its ends no longer are salient or well served."[17]

With regard to women's political agency in the contemporary U.S. context, there are two generally accepted premises: 1) Women have made great gains in terms of public leadership and representation in the last half–century, and 2) despite recent progress, women have a long way to go to achieve parity with men in the U.S. political system. Other studies offer sociological, economic, and political support for the preceding claims.[18] This study examines the role lan-guage plays in either impeding or fostering women's agency in the contempo-rary U.S. political sphere. Although we do not discount the economic and socio-logical forces that have brought about change in the political landscape, we emphasize that no one has access to political processes apart from language. Jean Bethke Elshtain put it this way: "I do not think language *creates* the world. There is a there there. But language is importantly constitutive of the world as we come to know it. . . . [W]ords are our entry point into worlds. The repertoire of words available to us, as persons and as citizens, helps to forge and to shape our possibilities for action and reaction in the world."[19] In order to appreciate the limitations of and possibilities for women's political agency, we first must un-derstand the linguistic barriers that historically have been salient for women candidates and leaders. Two that are critical for the cases examined in this book are the metaphor of containment and the notion of the double bind.

The role of women political leaders has been constructed within a culture of "containment," a metaphor that resonated in U.S. politics and culture during the Cold War. Alan Nadel argues that the containment metaphor was the defining trope of post-war American culture, claiming that popular discourse in the 1950s "constantly tr[ied] to make impossible distinctions between Other and Same, partner and rival, for the purpose of acquiring or excluding, proliferating or containing proliferation."[20] He notes that sexual containment was particularly powerful during this time, and demonstrates the ways in which political demonization of the Soviet Other during the Cold War was transformed into cultural demonization of female and racialized Others. Similarly, Elaine Tyler May documents the ways in which containment was translated from political strategy to domestic ideology, noting that the family and gender roles were located "within the larger political culture, not outside it."[21]

Although containment became the central trope of U.S. politics during the Cold War, rhetorics of containment have informed the nation's identity and practice since colonial times. David Campbell explains that America, as an imagined community, utilized the dichotomy between "civilized" and "barbarian" to justify its colonization of the New World. The impulse to colonize was further legitimated by the myth of American exceptionalism which originated with the Puritans and suggested that the "American self was the product of divine intent." These two discourses, the civilized/barbarian dichotomy and the myth of American exceptionalism, combined to foster a culture which strove to contain "barbarism" wherever it was found. Campbell explicates the ways in which containment metaphors surfaced in Puritan doctrines of civility (the need to contain the internal barbarian), in frontier structures designed to keep Native Americans out of settled areas (the need to contain the pagan barbarian), and in colonial slave codes (the need to contain the racialized barbarian). Campbell argues that fear of the Other is inscribed into U.S. identity, and the strategy of containment historically has been the mode of operation for combating that fear.[22]

Like other containment rhetorics, sexual containment has roots in early American discourse. Most notably, containment metaphors emerged in the debates over women's suffrage, with opponents to suffrage arguing that women should remain cloistered in the private sphere.[23] Not only did they object to women voting, they deemed any woman who spoke to "promiscuous" audiences composed of women and men to be "masculine, unwomanly, aggressive, and cold."[24] Sexual containment strategies did not disappear after women won the vote in 1920. The fear of outspoken, politically active women has informed much of popular culture and political discourse throughout the twentieth century. In fact, the discursive strategies of nineteenth-century anti-suffragists reemerged during the debate over women's liberation and the Equal Rights Amendment (ERA) in the 1970s. Susan Douglas notes the ways in which "radical feminists" of the 1970s were castigated in the media as "ugly, humorless, disorderly man-haters in desperate need of some Nair."[25] The image of the desexed women's rights advocate was subsumed into popular culture and political discourse almost as easily in the late twentieth century as it had been one hundred years earlier.

As a result of this culturally-pervasive containment logic, women leaders often are placed in a double bind. Kathleen Hall Jamieson has documented the ways in which conflicts between role expectations trap women in double binds that curtail their options and circumscribe their power. For example, women's roles as mothers and caregivers historically have been cast in opposition to men's role as rational thinkers, thus "women have been identified as bodies not minds, wombs not brains."[26] Women also have experienced disjunction between the demands of femininity and social definitions of competence and leadership.[27] Prior to the twentieth century, these double binds were enforced culturally and legally, through prohibitions against women's public speech, suffrage, and access to the workplace. Although most of those laws have been dismantled, the social and psychological traces of double binds endure. Jamieson's work illustrates not only how various double binds are rhetorically instantiated in Western culture, but also how women have worked to circumvent the authority of double binds and, in some cases, have "den[ied] others the power to define and as a result confine them in false options."[28] The cases discussed in this book reveal the variety of ways in which the double bind can influence a political persona. On one hand, it serves as the context for the candidacy of any woman—a rhetorical constraint that must be negotiated. Yet, our assessment suggests that the double bind affects different individuals in different ways. A candidate's own party affiliation, geographical location, and personal style influence the rhetorical options at her disposal for challenging the double bind.

The question of style is more than an aesthetic one. Robert Hariman calls political style the "artistry of power" and asserts that "to the extent that politics is an art, matters of style must be crucial to its practice."[29] Hariman illustrates the ways in which a leader's political style is an articulation of the types of power available to him in a given context.[30] The fact that Ann Richards exhibited "down-home" sensibilities, a quick wit, and a combative approach to politics was not just a matter of personal style. Richards mined the Texas political landscape for rhetorical strategies that would garner her political power. That Christine Todd Whitman's approach was radically different from Richards's illustrates not just a personality difference between the two women, but a distinction in the rhetorical situation each faced. The exigencies to which they responded and the constraints they faced were different. Thus, the power they ultimately were able to enact rhetorically differed as well. This book extends Hariman's investigation into political style not only by applying his hypothesis to women leaders, but also by exploring the ways in which political power is situated within particular contexts—contexts that produce a host of rhetorical strategies that may be of use to others. Generalizations about how to engage and manage masculine culture can only be meaningful in particular experiences—that is, we can only understand and test generalizations by exploring how specific women have acted. We examine the rhetoric of public women in the face of gendered imagery. It is not enough, however, to identify the containing language or even the attitudes motivated by such metaphoric constructions. Instead, we must focus on how women leaders perform metaphoric imagery, recasting perceptions either to empower or undermine the credibility and perceived success of women leaders.

The case studies developed in this book are not meant to stand in for all women leaders but to illustrate the important role metaphor plays in contemporary U.S. politics. Although our texts reflect diversity in terms of political party, age, geographic region, and political role, we lack representation of many important types of women leaders: women of color, women of various economic classes, and political leaders operating outside the mainstream of U.S. national politics. It also was not our intent, as we selected our particular cases, to choose an exhaustive or even representative list of women. There are a number of books and anthologies that examine systematically the rhetoric and/or political identity of public women.[31] Instead, we chose four women who have reached prominence in the public mind, have achieved unique political successes, and have faced significant rhetorical challenges. We did not limit ourselves to elected officials, but opened our analysis up to political spouses since, as we explain later in the study, first ladies occupy a unique symbolic position in U.S. culture, and assessing their political identity is particularly fruitful ground for research on metaphorical frames and rhetorical strategies.

We hope that this initial foray into the topic of gender, metaphor, and political identity will spur further discussions that could encompass the issues omitted here. We contend, however, that our exclusive focus on women should not lead the reader to conclude that our exploration of metaphor in U.S. political culture has no relevance for male politicians. Karlyn Kohrs Campbell points out that "[b]ecause members of the largely white male political elite face fewer rhetorical challenges, their discourse is a less fertile field for rhetorical research. Those who must discover ways to subvert popular belief and to overcome unusually significant persuasive obstacles, such as prohibitions against speaking itself and stereotypes that reject them as credible or authoritative, must be more inventive than their advantaged counterparts."[32] The notion that political identities often are constructed and disseminated through metaphor is equally instructive for male and female leaders. Uncovering the rhetorical ingenuity of women politicians casts the critical net wider than it would be if our focus was limited to those who require the least amount of creativity.

When Hillary Rodham Clinton shed the weight of the failed health-care reform campaign, averted the shadow of scandal and Congressional investigation, shook the shame of a philandering husband, and escaped even the strictures of the first ladyship to nab a seat in the U.S. Senate, many were left wondering "how did she do it?" The answer lies not in shady back-room politicking, but in public rhetorical maneuvering. Metaphor was both the lock and key to the shackles that encompassed Rodham Clinton's public identity. This book examines four such cases that illustrate how metaphors serve as constraints and rhetorical resources for contemporary political individuals.

Notes

1. Jonathan Alter, "How He Could Recover," *Newsweek*, November 21, 1994, Lexis Nexis Academic Universe (accessed July 17, 2002).

2. Bridget Kendall, "The First Lady's Not for Turning?" *The Independent*, November 11, 1994, Lexis Nexis Academic Universe (accessed July 17, 2002).

3. Kendall, "The First Lady's Not for Turning?"

4. When we refer to these women throughout our book, we use the name that the woman herself most often used. For example, we refer to Christine Todd Whitman as Whitman and Hillary Rodham Clinton as Rodham Clinton. This is not an inconsistency, but rather acknowledgement of the ways the women represented themselves to the public.

5. George Lakoff and Mark Johnson, "Conceptual Metaphor in Everyday Language," in *Philosophical Perspectives on Metaphor*, ed. Mark Johnson (Minneapolis: University of Minnesota Press, 1981), 287.

6. I. A. Richards, *The Philosophy of Rhetoric* (London: Oxford University Press, 1936), 94.

7. Richards, *The Philosophy of Rhetoric*, 96.

8. Robert L. Ivie observes that "[Ernesto] Grassi underscores the metaphorical origins of rhetorical invention generally when he reminds us that the middle terms (or topoi) of enthymemes are grounded in analogies. Metaphors, as the source of arguments and first principles, provide the linguistic mechanism for grasping similarities among dissimilarities." See Robert L. Ivie, "Cold War Motives and the Rhetorical Metaphor: A Framework of Criticism," in *Cold War Rhetoric: Strategy, Metaphor, and Ideology*, eds. Martin J. Medhurst, Robert L. Ivie, Philip Wander, and Robert L. Scott (New York: Greenwood Press, 1990), 73–74.

9. Kenneth Burke, *Language as Symbolic Action: Essays on Life, Literature, and Method* (Berkeley and Los Angeles: University of California Press, 1968), 45.

10. Ivie, "Cold War Motives and the Rhetorical Metaphor," 72.

11. Quoted in Ivie, "Cold War Motives and the Rhetorical Metaphor," 73.

12. Ivie, "Cold War Motives and the Rhetorical Metaphor," 74. Also see Robert L. Ivie, "Metaphor and the Rhetorical Invention of Cold War 'Idealists,'" *Communication Monographs* 54 (1987): 166–68.

13. Shawn Parry-Giles, "Mediating Hillary Rodham Clinton: Television News Practices and Image-Making in the Postmodern Age," *Critical Studies in Media Communication* 17 (June 2000): 206.

14. Ivie, "Metaphor and the Rhetorical Invention," 166–68.

15. Specific methodological details such as the time-frame for each analysis and sources for texts are detailed in the case studies themselves.

16. Lakoff and Johnson, "Conceptual Metaphor," 292.

17. Ivie, "Cold War Motives and the Rhetorical Metaphor," 76, 77. See also Ivie's editorial statements in the *Quarterly Journal of Speech* 79 (1993)–81

(1995), and James F. Klumpp and Thomas A. Hollihan, "Rhetorical Criticism as Moral Action," *Quarterly Journal of Speech* 75 (1989): 84–97.

18. James Devitt, *Framing Gender on the Campaign Trail: Women's Executive Leadership and the Press* (Women's Leadership Fund, 1999). Devitt reports that women have made gains in terms of column space in newspaper stories reporting on political races. However, women are less likely than men to be reported as supporting their campaign promises with evidence and more likely to be the subject of personal stories about appearance, personality, or personal life. See also Barbara Brotman, "Courting Votes," *Chicago Tribune*, November 3, 1999, 2. Brotman quotes two pollsters, Linda DiVall and Celinda Lake, who appeared at a Women in Business, Politics, and Power conference in Chicago, Illinois. While women are gaining credibility on issues "where being a woman is a plus," they are still perceived as less credible on issues that require toughness. "Only 46 percent of voters are very comfortable with having a woman as president. . . . Men prefer a man as president by a 21-point margin." Similar conclusions are detailed in *Keys to the Governor's Office* (Brookline, Mass.: Barbara Lee Family Foundation, 2001); See also Nancy E. McGlen and Karen O'Connor, *Women, Politics, and American Society*, 2d ed. (Upper Saddle River, N.J.: Prentice Hall, 1998); Kim Fridkin Kahn, "Does Gender Make a Difference? An Experimental Examination of Sex Stereotypes and Press Patterns in Statewide Campaigns," *American Journal of Political Science* 38 (1994): 168–70. Numerous studies are cited in Shanto Iyengar, Nicholas A. Valentino, Stephen Ansolabehere, and Adam F. Simon, "Running as a Woman: Gender Stereotyping in Women's Campaigns," in *Women, Media, and Politics*, ed. Pippa Norris (New York: Oxford University Press, 1997); Susan J. Carroll, *Women as Candidates in American Politics* (Bloomington: Indiana University Press, 1994).

19. Jean Bethke Elshtain, *Real Politics at the Center of Everyday Life* (Baltimore, Md.: Johns Hopkins University Press, 1997), 46.

20. Alan Nadel, *Containment Culture: American Narratives, Postmodernism, and the Atomic Age* (Durham, N.C.: Duke University Press, 1995), 6.

21. Elaine Tyler May, *Homeward Bound: American Families in the Cold War Era* (New York: Basic Books, 1988), 10.

22. David Campbell, *Writing Security: United States Foreign Policy and the Politics of Identity* (Minneapolis: University of Minnesota Press, 1992), 116, 121, 127.

23. See Karlyn Kohrs Campbell, *Man Cannot Speak for Her*, vol. 1 (New York: Greenwood Press, 1989), 9–12. For a discussion of prohibitions against women speaking before "promiscuous audiences" see Susan Zaeske, "The 'Promiscuous Audience' Controversy and the Emergence of the Early Woman's Rights Movements," *Quarterly Journal of Speech* 81 (1995): 191–207.

24. K. K. Campbell, *Man Cannot Speak*, 12.

25. Susan J. Douglas, *Where the Girls Are: Growing Up Female with the Mass Media* (New York: Random House, 1994), 189.

26. Kathleen Hall Jamieson, *Beyond the Double Bind: Women and Leadership* (New York: Oxford University Press, 1995), 53. That contemporary female politicians felt the weight of that dichotomy was illustrated by Patricia Schroeder, former U.S. Representative from Colorado, who quipped, "I have a uterus and a brain and they both work."

27. Jamieson, *Beyond the Double Bind*, chapter 6.

28. Jamieson, *Beyond the Double Bind*, 8.

29. Robert Hariman, *Political Style: The Artistry of Power* (Chicago: University of Chicago Press, 1995), 3. Hariman situates his study between the extremes of political realism and poststructuralism. His rationale bears repeating here for it guides our study as well. Hariman states, "Consideration of the artistry of civic life goes against the norms of realism dominant in the social sciences, while it seems to fall short of the powerful critiques of literary autonomy and political privilege ascendant in the humanities. Yet, even if realist or poststructuralist attitudes prevail, they leave too much unsaid. The modern human sciences have not yet produced a strong account of what every successful politician knows intuitively: Political experience, skill, and result often involve conventions of persuasive composition that depend on aesthetic reactions. As long as this account is not available, theoretical understanding of the dynamics of political identity will remain detached from ordinary personal experience."

30. We use the male pronoun here because Hariman's study is exclusive to male political figures. The extension of this theory to women in politics is an expansion of Hariman's original work.

31. See Karlyn Kohrs Campbell, ed., *Women Public Speakers in the United States: A Bio-Critical Sourcebook*, 2 vols. (Westport, Conn.: Greenwood Press, 1994); Molly Mayhead and Brenda DeVore Marshall, eds. *Navigating Boundaries: The Rhetoric of Women Governors* (Westport, Conn.: Praeger, 2000); Molly Meijer Wertheimer, ed., *Inventing a Voice: The Rhetoric of American First Ladies of the Twentieth Century* (Lanham, Md.: Rowman & Littlefield, 2004); Molly Mayhead and Brenda DeVore Marshall, *Women's Political Discourse* (Lanham, Md.: Rowman & Littlefield, forthcoming).

32. Karlyn Kohrs Campbell, "The Sound of Women's Voices," *Quarterly Journal of Speech* 75 (1989): 212.

Chapter 1

Gender, Metaphor, and Political Identity

Research on candidate image has focused primarily on traits that make candidates appealing to voters.[1] Candidate image includes both a political image (party affiliation, issue identification, and links to other political individuals and groups) and a personal image (age, ability, speaking style, etc.).[2] It has been argued that voters are most concerned that a candidate be trustworthy and that honesty ranks at the top of the list of characteristics voters desire their candidates to display.[3] Research on how voters assess whether a candidate is trustworthy or honest suggests that political image has more to do with communicative elements than with a candidate's "record on the issues." Thomas Hollihan asserts that "[w]ith regard to trust and integrity, research suggests that voters are very sensitive to a candidate's physical appearance."[4] One often-noted observation regarding the importance of physical appearance to political image is the disparity between voters who viewed the 1960 presidential debate between John F. Kennedy and Richard M. Nixon versus those who heard the debate on the radio. A more contemporary example would be Vice-President Al Gore's physical transformation during his 2000 presidential bid. On the advice of handlers, Gore switched from formal dark business suits to less formal shirts and pants in earth tones—a switch that was meant to challenge his "stodgy" persona.[5]

Evaluating the political image of women candidates and leaders is more complex because gender influences people's perceptions of character traits. Kathleen Hall Jamieson explains:

> [T]he same cues are evaluated differently in men and women. Assertiveness is valued in men, but not in women. Where attractive men in managerial positions are assumed to have achieved their status through native ability and hard work, attractive women are assumed to have slept their way to the top. When women use qualifiers in their statements, their credibility suffers; not so for men. The same cues (e.g., poor eye contact, vocalized pauses) are interpreted differently in men and women. Men with poor eye contact are seen as shy; women are deemed incompetent. Female professors have to pass a higher threshold test as well. Male teachers who are

responsive are 'really good guys'; women who are responsive are just being women.[6]

Kim Kahn and Ann Gordon echo Jamieson's claim, noting that "[r]eliance on sex stereotypes . . . leads people to view women as less competent overall than men."[7] A potential explanation for the difference in trait evaluation is offered by the resonance model of campaigns, which suggests that "campaign communication is most persuasive when it plays upon—or interacts—voters' prior predispositions."[8] Shanto Iyengar, Nicholas A. Valentino, Stephen Ansolabehere, and Adam F. Simon contend that

> [c]ulturally ingrained expectations about the strengths and weaknesses of candidates serve as important filters for interpreting and understanding campaign communication. The typical voter lacks the motivation to acquire even the most elementary level of factual knowledge about the candidates and campaign issues. In low information environments, expectations based on visible cues—including a candidate's gender—take on special importance. Messages that confirm rather than cut against these expectations are more likely to be noticed, assimilated, and retained.[9]

To date, the vast majority of research on candidate image and campaign strategy has focused on candidate traits and voter evaluation; however the trait perspective accounts for only a portion of the rhetorical situation faced by a candidate. On a deeper, perhaps even subconscious level, the metaphors that shape the vocabulary of the campaign and corresponding media coverage influence the impressions that voters form of candidates. Women leaders do not simply appear on the scene, but appear among a complex set of images and expectations that have evolved as our country has elected and will continue to elect women public officials. The prevailing metaphors are significant in that they frame expectations concerning what is appropriate for public office holders who are women and the impact they may have on leadership culture. The metaphors themselves can be problematic for thinking about women in positions of leadership, or they can serve as rhetorical resources in the creative task of helping candidates achieve resonance with voters. The purpose of this chapter is to introduce the metaphoric clusters salient to our four case studies and to describe the ways in which those clusters have influenced women politicians historically.

The case studies addressed in this book focus on two specific types of women politicians: governors and political spouses. Although the women we study have held other political positions (Christine Todd Whitman's appointment to President George W. Bush's cabinet and both Hillary Rodham Clinton's and Elizabeth Dole's election to the U.S. Senate), they entered the political spotlight either as gubernatorial candidates or political spouses, and those personae colored later impressions of each woman. Our choice to focus on these two classes of politicians was deliberate, because examining women in these unique roles has the potential to reveal more about gender, metaphor, and political identity than if we had confined our examination to elected representatives.

At the time of this writing, our country has elected or appointed twenty-seven women to the position of state governor (See Table 1.1. Women Governors).[10] More women have risen to the ranks of Congress and the Supreme Court; however, none functions with the individual, executive power afforded to the position of governor. Yet, while increasing numbers of women are filling representative positions, women in gubernatorial positions are not growing so steadily. Several scholars and political analysts suggest that we may be more likely to accept "women who represent us" than women who take charge and run things on their own.[11] It follows that for women, representing is less a violation of the masculine political culture than leading. After all, (in stereotypical terms, at least) leading requires aggression, initiative, expertise, and reason.

Table 1.1. Women Governors

Governor	Political Party	State	Years Served
Nellie Tayloe Ross	Democrat	Wyoming	1925–27
Miriam "Ma" Ferguson	Democrat	Texas	1925–27; 1933–35
Lurleen Wallace	Democrat	Alabama	1967–68
Ella Grasso	Democrat	Connecticut	1975–80
Dixy Lee Ray	Democrat	Washington	1977–81
Martha Layne Collins	Democrat	Kentucky	1984–87
Madeleine Kunin	Democrat	Vermont	1985–91
Kay Orr	Republican	Nebraska	1987–91
Rose Mofford	Democrat	Arizona	1988–91
Joan Finney	Democrat	Kansas	1991–95
Ann Richards	Democrat	Texas	1991–95
Barbara Roberts	Democrat	Oregon	1991–95
Christine Todd Whitman	Republican	New Jersey	1994–2001
Jeanne Shaheen	Democrat	New Hampshire	1997–2003
Jane Dee Hull	Republican	Arizona	1997–2003
Nancy Hollister	Republican	Ohio	31 Dec 1998–10 Jan 1999
Judy Martz	Republican	Montana	2001–2005
Ruth Ann Minner	Democrat	Delaware	2001–
Jane Swift	Republican	Massachusetts	2001–2003
Jennifer Granholm	Democrat	Michigan	2003–
Linda Lingle	Republican	Hawaii	2003–
Janet Napolitano	Democrat	Arizona	2003–
Kathleen Sebelius	Democrat	Kansas	2003–
Olene Walker	Republican	Utah	2003–2005
Kathleen Blanco	Democrat	Louisiana	2004–2005
M. Jodi Rell	Republican	Connecticut	2004–
Christine Gregoire	Democrat	Washington	2005–

Representing requires concern and deference to the public good, connection and concern for humane rather than personal interests. This makes the twenty-seven women who have occupied the governor's mansion an interesting study in the characterizations of leadership. Not only have some of these women made an impact on the state level, but on the national level as well, suggesting that they may be able to affect leadership culture productively on a larger scale.

The public personae of political spouses are interesting insofar as they highlight cultural assumptions about women's "proper" role in society. Karlyn Kohrs Campbell points out:

> wives of candidates challenge the public and press differently than do women candidates for public office. Women candidates ask voters to revise the relationship between women ard public power. By contrast, the candidates' wives raise the more problematic issue of the relationship between women, *sexuality*, and power. That is, spouses exert their power by virtue of their sexual and marital relationship to the candidates, their influence is indirect and intimate, a subtle intrusion of the private into the public, political sphere.[12]

In the year 2000, however, the distinction between spouse and candidate was blurred when both Hillary Rodham Clinton and Elizabeth Dole ran for public office, highlighting tensions between public vs. private power and male vs. female roles. In order to assess the role that metaphor played in shaping recent debates over women's public power and political identity, we must examine metaphoric clusters that historically have influenced media coverage of political women. The four that emerged in our research were pioneer, puppet, hostess/beauty queen, and unruly woman.[13]

Pioneer

With respect to women governors, the first and probably most obvious metaphoric cluster used to characterize them is "Pioneer." A pioneer is someone who is a trailblazer or groundbreaker in the sense that most of these women were the first elected female governor of their state and have many other "firsts" lining their biographies. Their determination, practical wisdom, perseverance, and hard work characterize pioneers. Miriam Ferguson, for example, was called "a stalwart, this pioneer woman Governor-in-prospect" after her successful run in the Democratic primary,[14] and *The Literary Digest* of November 1924 claimed the pioneering efforts of Ross and Ferguson certainly meant that "women have taken a step toward the White House" smoothing the way remarkably for women.[15]

Similarly, one of Dixy Lee Ray's advisers likened her campaign to a Lewis and Clark expedition[16] and in Ella Grasso's obituary her husband is quoted, calling Grasso "'a pioneer. If she succeeds, she makes it easier for thousands of women in future generations.' Succeed she did."[17] Even Christine Todd Whitman's pioneering qualities were used to encourage her to run for the vice-presidency where she could do the same pioneering work she did in the governorship, and Bob Dole noted her "virtually unlimited potential."[18]

Pioneers also are known for their "pioneering spirit," an appeal to "common folks" working hard side by side, demonstrating that you do not have to be exceptional to possess pioneering qualities and underscoring the "grassroots" appeal of many of these women. In particular, this spirit is reminiscent of the populist rhetoric of the late nineteenth century that appealed to the honest laborer who had been "forgotten" by the government. This spirit was especially evident in the characterizations of western and southwestern women of Texas, Wyoming, Kansas, and Nebraska. *The Nation* explained "Ma" Ferguson's appeal to "common folks" and called the Fergusons "self styled champions of the forgotten man."[19] Following her election, *The Woman Citizen* claimed that Ross was "devoted to the rights of the common people"[20] and in March 1925 called Ross a "well-rounded, able and engaging woman" after her attendance at the presidential inauguration.[21] In commenting upon the ability of Wyoming women to handle themselves with political responsibilities such as suffrage, the article proceeded to explain: "Hardy and intelligent women in the old days came to Wyoming and pitched in with the men."[22]

The pioneering spirit of the women governors enabled them to appeal to the "common people," "the forgotten man." Nancy Bocskor, Nebraska's Republican Party Executive Director, explained that the woman versus woman 1986 gubernatorial race in Nebraska came about because of the state's "'pioneer spirit— women and men working hard side by side.'"[23] Joan Finney, the first woman governor of Kansas, "attributed her victory to having drawn on her own reservoir of goodwill . . . by espousing populist ideas . . . giving the people more control."[24] Her "grassroots support" was credited with upsetting her opponent.[25]

The grassroots appeal of these pioneering politicians allowed them in some cases to distance themselves from the "woman question" and later feminism, since feminism was characterized as radical, aggressive, and extreme—not mainstream or the focus of common hard working folks. Ferguson insisted she ran for governor for her husband and not to advance women's issues. When asked if she had any advice for women, she responded, "'Why certainly not! Why should I?' in plain surprise."[26] Ella Grasso of Connecticut downplayed the feminist issue, calling herself "'just an old shoe,'"[27] and Ray of Washington state demanded to be called Chairman of the Atomic Energy Commission, not Chairperson, insisting she was not a "feminist crusader—'I'm not a joiner type.'"[28]

However, because there are only twenty-seven women who have served as governors, their pioneering achievements can easily be chalked up to their status as symbolic rather than serious leaders. *The Progressive* considered Ella Grasso "symbolic of what the American Woman could achieve through hard work, perseverance, intelligence, and political toughness rather than through sexuality and appeals to the male sense of justice. Her symbolic position has not changed. But the question is whether she has the courage and the ability to be a first-rate governor."[29] Madeleine Kunin of Vermont was direct about the "symbolic element to her campaign. 'Let's face it, I'm charting a new course,' Kunin says. 'So far there are no portraits in the statehouse which look like mine.'"[30] Even *The Woman Citizen* pointed out that the achievements of Ross and Ferguson may have been remarkable, but "neither case is an all-wool feminist triumph" since neither succeeded "wholly on [her] own records."[31] They were merely anomalies, "unusual" achievements, the exception that proved the rule.[32] Although these pioneering women could be congratulated, skepticism underlies their ability to govern successfully until such time as they are able to prove themselves. Once again, women are easily marginalized because they are symbolic, not serious or courageous leaders. They may work hard, but often beside men, not on their own. The norms of U.S. political culture are suspicious of women's achievements, causing their capability as executive leaders to be dismissed and further reifying the patriarchal expectations of the political sphere.

Puppet

Although women governors often were hailed as pioneers, political spouses (and in particular U.S. first ladies) sometimes have been cast in the role of puppet—extensions of their husbands' political careers who, if they spoke publicly at all, acted as political mouthpieces for the candidates to whom they were married. The term "first lady" appears in journalistic references to the president's wife as early as 1870, although its use hearkens back to 1789 when "crowds accustomed to the pomp of royal persons heralded the wife of their new president as 'Lady Washington.'"[33] During the nineteenth century it was assumed that the first lady would occupy a position "at the head of the female society of the United States."[34] Today, although phrases like "female society" sound arcane, the first lady continues to stand as a symbol of American womanhood, reflecting, as Betty Boyd Caroli states, "the status of American women of their time while helping shape expectations of what women can properly do."[35]

The United States historically has "expected first ladies to reflect ideals of home, family and womanhood," with the term "lady" connoting "middle- and upper-class respectability and suggest[ing] a certain kind of demeanor."[36] Margaret Carlson calls the first ladyship "the most tradition-bound and antiquated model of American womanhood."[37] Germaine Greer concurs, quipping that the first lady "is the archetypal lipstick-skirt-high-heels beside the archetypal suit."[38] Caroli explains that norms of femininity were inscribed into the role of first lady in the eighteenth century, since the majority of early first ladies "acquiesced in limiting themselves to a supportive role reflecting the predominant attitude about femininity."[39] This standard continued through the mid–nineteenth century, when "[y]outhful surrogates [as first ladies] became a tradition because they evidently fit in with prevailing ideas about femininity—womanliness could be exemplified in obsequious, smiling mannequins who showed little evidence of thinking for themselves."[40]

Certainly, not every early first lady reacted to cultural norms of femininity by declining to think for herself. Abigail Adams, Sarah Polk, and Mary Lincoln each were vocal, independent presidential spouses. Edith P. Mayo notes, however, that "virtually every First Lady who has used her influence has been either ridiculed or vilified as deviating from women's proper role or has been feared as emasculating."[41] Historian Simon Schama attributes America's resistance to assertiveness in the first lady, in part, to cultural *mythos*, stating, "Haunting the West is the ancient myth of women as swallowers of virile men. In the White House, the choice is to be a dutiful reflection of the husband's virtue or to devour the husband's strength. And this Delilah image is so deeply rooted that it's incredibly difficult to transcend."[42]

This cultural fear of feminine strength is complicated by the expectations of masculinity tied to the presidency.[43] Assertive presidential wives may fare better if their husbands are viewed as strong and effective (i.e., as the "man in charge"), whereas presidents lacking overtones of masculinity and strength can be perceived as too easily swayed by the opinions of politically involved wives. Caroli asks, for example, "[c]ould Eleanor Roosevelt have broken so many precedents if Franklin had accomplished less? Did Rosalynn Carter's determination make Jimmy look less decisive?"[44] Even in the face of FDR's popularity, many contemporary journalists derided Eleanor Roosevelt's political activism. After criticizing her propensity for travel, which resulted from Roosevelt taking on the role of FDR's "eyes and ears," journalist Malcolm Bingay advised the first lady to "light somewhere and keep quiet."[45] Former President Richard Nixon echoed Bingay's admonition, warning that "[i]f the wife comes through as being too strong and too intelligent it makes the husband look like a wimp."[46]

To say that first ladies have been cast as puppets does not mean that the puppet metaphor accurately captures the historical role played by presidential spouses. Scholarship on the U.S. first ladyship has expanded in recent years, casting new perspectives as to how first ladies, in a variety of ways, have challenged this stereotype and achieved political agency within presidential administrations.[47] Mayo comments, "It is sad and telling that the press and public alike are unaware that Presidential wives since Abigail Adams have been wielding political influence."[48] Denise M. Bostdorff traces the historical evolution of the first lady and notes that "even in the earliest administrations, the first lady served as a political partner."[49] Caroli chronicles key political contributions of first ladies, noting, for example, that Dolley Madison's famous "parties" were strategically orchestrated political events, one of which has been credited with James Madison's victory in the 1812 election.[50] First ladies like Abigail Adams, Sarah Polk, Eleanor Roosevelt, and Edith Wilson served as gatekeepers for the president, keeping their husbands informed of public sentiment and (in Wilson's case) even monitoring access to the president. Other first ladies such as Nancy Reagan, Rosalynn Carter, and Hillary Rodham Clinton were recognized as policy advisors to the president. First ladies also historically have championed political causes. Although the causes often are characterized in benignly feminine terms ("beautification" or "historic preservation"), the causes, themselves, frequently are highly political endeavors such as promoting environmentalism and preserving women's history. But the fact remains that first ladies who exercised their influence in private fared better in terms of their public persona than did spouses who challenged publicly the puppet role.

The puppet metaphor affected women governors as well. For the woman executive, the puppet is the most passive of the metaphoric clusters, exemplified in Governors Miriam "Ma" Ferguson of Texas and Lurleen Wallace of Alabama. Both Ferguson and Wallace ran for governor because their husbands could not. Jim Ferguson had been impeached in 1917 in Texas and George Wallace could not run for a consecutive term in Alabama in 1966. Many sources were very direct when reporting this situation. For example, *The Outlook* explained that "Mrs. Ferguson was selected to run . . . not as a woman, but as a wife. Her supporters would have chosen her husband . . . if they could."[51] A caption at the beginning of an article in *The Saturday Evening Post* declared that "Wallace is running in his wife's name."[52] However, Wallace assured the voters there would be no "petticoat government. If [Lurleen] were elected she would be governor in name only. He would run the state as he always had."[53]

The governor as puppet is an instrument, an object, a token to be manipulated by some more powerful other—most often a man, and more specifically a husband. This is most clearly demonstrated by a cartoon in *Collier's* of April 1926 with "Pa" seated and a little "Ma" on his lap with Pa moving her mouth. The caption read, "'Now sing us a little song,'" and the article itself suggested Ferguson acted "merely as the puppet" of a man. "When anybody calls at the governor's office, he must see GOVERNOR Jim first. And Mrs. Ferguson cannot open her mouth until he speaks. He is the ventriloquist, and she is the dummy. She admits it."[54] Not only was Mrs. Ferguson a ventriloquist's dummy, but she was also "the only weapon" Texas voters "could put their hands on" to defeat the Ku Klux Klan.[55] In other words, she would do. The article continued by stating that the voters of Texas "gave no thought to the quality or merit of the weapon employed, reasoning that in two years they could dispose of Mrs. Ferguson and supplant her with a more worthy instrument."[56] Clearly Ferguson did not win the election so much as the Ku Klux Klan lost. At best, her admission to the governorship was passive, fitting for a woman. She gave "little distinction to the office she" held.[57]

Without the aid of a cartoon, Lurleen Wallace was aptly depicted as a showpiece that her husband could wield from town to town in *his* re-election bid. An article in *The Atlantic Monthly* of August 1967 began:

> Through the spring and fall campaigns last year, she tagged after him
> as he scuttled, with the tense urgency of a squirrel, across the map of

Alabama. They put her, with one female companion, in a separate car behind his, and she was reverently borne from town to town like some irreplaceable ceremonial fixture, a token to lend the dubious enterprise a measure of legitimacy and sanction. . . . She submitted to it with an air composed, patient, somewhat inert and remote—a small, quiet figure, smiling pleasantly and a little uneasily, with an expression sometimes, as she squinted in the sun, faintly perplexed.[58]

Clearly Lurleen Wallace was considered George's token to show from town to town, often called his "proxy,"[59] "a distinctive footnote," and his "appendage."[60] She was described in passive terms, all appropriate characterizations of a woman in patriarchal leadership culture.

At best, the governor as puppet is simply "a stand-in," "proxy," "surrogate," or "follower," dutifully submitting to her husband. The implication is that there are appropriate and natural roles for women in relation to men, specifically their husbands, and more importantly, the role of governor comes in direct opposition to the role of wife. Thus, wife must take precedence over politician, allowing a woman to maintain her proper subservient role.

In an article titled "Can a Wife be Governor?" *Collier's* drew the distinction between Ma Ferguson's marriage vow "to love, cherish and to OBEY" her husband and the oath that she took as governor to "faithfully and impartially discharge and perform all the duties incumbent upon me as governor of Texas."[61] According to *Collier's*, "If she turns a deaf ear to reform measures and the pleas of other women, she does it not as a traitor to the cause of women's rights, which she never espoused, but in traditional feminine loyalty to one man." And so in running for governor she obeyed her husband. "Only as a matter of wifely duty does Miriam A. Ferguson serve her term, a political prisoner in her own office." If she wanted to act on her own, she could not, *Collier's* pointed out; "she'd just break up her home"[62] Furthermore, the Norfolk *Virginian-Pilot* suggested that the puppet imagery undermined any power that women governors may gain through simultaneous characterization as a pioneer. Ferguson's "apparent surrender of power to her husband dims the luster of Mrs. Ferguson's accomplishment as one of the women pioneers in State politics."[63] The metaphoric clusters characterizing women in politics simultaneously keep women in their proper place and reinforce the masculine rational norms of control that have long characterized domestic politics.

Many women governors had to contend with similar criticisms. For example, Ella Grasso, often called the first woman governor who did not follow in her husband's footsteps, had to battle criticisms that she was not a serious governor. When her legislature passed a budget despite her warnings that it could create a huge debt for Connecticut, and then she refused to veto or amend it, the media labeled her "an 'invisible governor,' who was 'governing by default' and 'playing politics' by setting up members of her own party for attack in the 1978 elections."[64] *Newsweek* claimed that Ann Richards was selected to deliver the keynote address at the 1988 Democratic convention simply "to score points in the

South and to exploit George Bush's gender-gap woes."[65] And according to the *New York Times*, Christine Todd Whitman had to contend with "persistent rumors" that her husband had "undue influence" over her policy decisions and her campaigns.[66] Whitman also had to deal with attacks that she was simply a token woman delivering the response to President Clinton's 1995 State of the Union address. Jay Severin, a Republican consultant, acknowledged, "'If she were Christopher Whitman and not Christie Whitman, she wouldn't be giving the response.'"[67] It is not uncommon for women governors to have to contend with criticisms undermining their political clout or leadership ability, suggesting they are merely tokens to be used by their parties. These images keep gender relations in check while dismissing any rhetorical sensitivity on the part of women governors who attempt to negotiate the prevailing masculine political norms. As a result women continue to be marginalized as serious contributors to liberal democratic politics.

Hostess/Beauty Queen

The governor and political spouse as puppet cluster suggests that there is a proper role for women in relation to men. They are invisible, follow behind, and are available to be used and manipulated for whatever cause. If women are to become public figures, then how might they do so? One avenue is seemingly to praise women for their "proper talents," thus leading to characterizations of women politicians as "hostesses" and "beauty queens" and continuing to keep gender relations in bounds. The political woman as hostess and beauty queen encapsulates a cluster of metaphors representing all things that traditional women are allowed praise in public: they are sometimes giddy, attractive social creatures who win popularity contests and enjoy playing hostess and caretaker as a wife, mother and/or grandmother. Significantly, the political woman as beauty queen must be married, contrary to the typical Miss America who is a single woman.[68] Martha Layne Collins exemplifies this governor as beauty queen, being a former Kentucky Derby queen herself. Although this metaphoric cluster appears to allow women a more active role than governor as puppet does, it still underscores women's femininity and attention to beauty and appearance as appropriate and reinscribes women's traditional role in a hierarchical family structure. These are the reasons for her appeal. The rhetorical sensitivity that goes along with playing hostess is completely overlooked, for example. As Martha Layne Collins will admit, she poured many cups of coffee and hosted many dinners to get to the governor's mansion.

Consider this description of Nellie Tayloe Ross, our country's first "Governor Lady"[69]—a title noting her proper upbringing—regarding her attendance at the presidential inauguration in 1925: "Governor Ross delighted the capital. Her poise was excellent, her appearance splendid, her stories good, and her speeches modest but full of fact as well as spirit. . . . A medium-sized, pleasant, smiling, youthful woman with a delightful voice in which there were tones of restraint, authority and geniality—and a good-looking face with soft lines."[70] This sounds like the description of the Miss America pageant winner, excelling in poise, beauty, speaking, and congeniality.

The connection is much more direct with Martha Layne Collins, who was compared with the outgoing Kentucky governor's wife, Phyllis George, a former beauty pageant winner herself: "The two women have much in common. Both were reared in small towns and influenced by strong mothers. Both became cheerleaders, sorority members and beauty queens," but unlike George, Collins "sometimes wears homemade clothes and buys off the rack" and often does her own hair. "She backed the Equal Rights Amendment but has done little for it. . . . 'She doesn't threaten anyone. Small-town women like her and men think she looks like a nice wife and mother,'" claimed former FDR adviser Edward Prichard. She and her husband also enjoy entertaining. According to a friend, "'If you don't let her wait on you, she won't be happy.'"[71]

Collins described her gubernatorial duties as "'the state's official hostess.'"[72] A *McCall's* article quoted Collins explaining her entertaining hints, such as choosing flowers, and "her formula of making each event special." She likes "'simplicity and elegance—nothing too showy or intimidating'" when planning and has a tradition of "presenting each guest with a party favor at meal's end." She encourages "all hostesses [to] nurture their creative spirit" and includes a few of her favorite recipes for Kentucky Quiche, Cheese Grits, and Cinnamony Fried Apples.[73]

As long as the woman governor is a beautiful hostess and entertainer, she upholds the traditional feminine expectations of her gender role. We are not forced to reconsider what it means to be a woman in a position of leadership nor are we allowed to reflect on the leadership activities that go into a dinner party and playing hostess—allowing masculinity to become reinscribed as the norm in the political sphere.

The giddy beauty queen image did not bypass Madeleine Kunin, known as a tough governor. However, her toughness was not the issue in this popular press story: "In the cramped backseat of what passed in unpretentious Vermont for an official limousine sat slender, blue-eyed, 51-year-old Madeleine Kunin, who giggled. 'Isn't this fun?' she whispered to a companion. 'You have to remember this is still a bit new to me.'"[74] Commenting after she replaced Vermont's agricultural commissioner with an appointment of her own, "'I felt like such a meanie.'"[75] Here Kunin is reported as childlike, not as governor.

Kunin also was presented as a hostess in *McCall's*, introducing readers to some "'very Vermont' delicacies."[76] Perhaps in an effort to upstage her "aggressive" "hardball" image,[77] Kunin the hostess opened her own door to greet journalists; she served coffee in a room that was "warm and informal (just like the governor)"; she was called by her first name. She balances her time between official duties, family, and friends, and "does make sure to gather with her friends over coffee and maple upside-down cake [recipe included] at least once a month." She likes cooking with Vermont produce and was pictured with "some of her favorite cooking utensils."[78]

Even in 2002, the *New York Times* seemed unsure of how to report the results of Michigan's Democratic gubernatorial primary, and so resorted to familiar gendered imagery. After an opening paragraph explaining that "the giants of the Michigan Democratic Party were quiet," the woman who silenced them is introduced: "Glowing at the center table was Jenni the giant-slayer, a former beauty queen turned Phi Beta Kappa lawyer who ran for office the first time only four years ago."[79] Whereas her male political opponents are referred to as Governor James J. Blanchard and Representative David E. Bonier, she is beauty queen "Jenni," and, as if an afterthought, a member of Phi Beta Kappa and a lawyer. Whereas her upcoming opponent in the general election is a "tough conservative" with an "act-first, ask-later approach," she has "made-for-television looks and on-the-stump charisma."[80] To make matters worse for her political credibility, the article offers the following explanation of her preparation for the office:

> She long ago abandoned the nickname Jenni, which she used when she was an aspiring actress, became Miss San Carlos, Calif., and appeared on 'The Dating Game' (she picked a bachelor but did not go out with him because he had a girlfriend). Now, Ms. Granholm's focus is on politics, where she alternates between sincere whispers and dynamic declarations. A mother of three, she offers a fierce handshake followed by a soft shoulder touch, and appeals to voters by looking directly into their eyes with her clear blue ones.[81]

Concluding, the *New York Times* declares her the "perfect" alternative to her opponent: "She is the perfect un-Engler. Blond, trim, articulate, intelligent. Who could ask for more?"[82] Who could ask for more indeed.

The beauty queen trains for public office through traditional means: she is a schoolteacher and homemaker, or if in public, the secretary of state,[83] reflecting the stereotypical notion of woman as secretary. *The Literary Digest* quoted Arthur Rex Graham, a Consolidated Press Association correspondent: "Mrs. Ross yet is the perfect type of homemaker. She plans to 'keep house' for the State as she did for William Ross, practising [*sic*] the homely virtues of rigid economy, neatness, orderliness and efficiency."[84] The *Digest* also quoted the Birmingham *News*: "'The majority of women being natural-born housekeepers, why shouldn't the infinite detail of a Governor's office appeal to the female of the species? . . . [E]very woman who ever filled her job fully as head of a home has had excellent training to be Mayor and Governor.'"[85] An AP Candidate Bio profiled Martha Lane Collins as "a former teacher and beauty queen"[86]; Jane Hull of Arizona was "a fiscally conservative former schoolteacher,"[87] and Rose Mofford also of Arizona was a lifetime "state employee who took a caretaker approach."[88] An AP Candidate Bio on Jane Hull further highlighted her elementary education degree and public school teaching experience[89] and Jeanne Shaheen was identified as a high school teacher and "consensus-builder."[90]

In the hostess and beauty queen we have the traditional stereotypical woman, a beautiful mother who is active in public within certain parameters. What is evident in many of the descriptors of the beauty queen is the obsessive focus on appearance, clearly reinforcing the myth that to be valued, a woman must be beautiful. Additionally, beauty and leadership are seen as dichotomous terms. The beautiful woman can never be trusted for she will arouse the passions, not the intellect, of those around her, or she is too irrational herself. Also, a woman is more often at home dealing with children as a teacher or caretaker, not a leader who deals with adults. The metaphoric imagery creates a suspicion of the feminine and underscores women's proper role in the family, reinforcing the masculine rational norms of political culture.

If governors were cast as hostesses because of implicit cultural norms, first ladies had a quasi-official mandate to serve as national hostesses. Although the duties and responsibilities of the first lady are not prescribed in the Constitution, presidents' wives always have assumed a prominent position in American politics, due, in part, to the unique nature of the American presidency. Caroli points out that the office of the president combines two jobs which typically are distinct in other governmental systems: "a head of state who presides over ceremonial functions, and a head of government who makes major appointments and takes a decisive role in legislation."[91] Because the president is occupied with responsibilities as the head of government, presidential spouses often have assumed many of the ceremonial functions performed by the head of state. Since the inception of the role, first ladies have been expected to perform social and ceremonial functions. The political power that inhered in this social role historically has been occluded, but even a brief examination of the actions of first ladies reveals the impact of what we (following Robert Hariman) term a "social" political style.[92] The exemplar for first ladies' social style is Dolley Madison, a presidential spouse typically remembered for "throwing great parties" (and wrongly credited with introducing the U.S. to ice cream). Madison's "parties," however, were strategically orchestrated political events designed to facilitate the political aims that Dolley Madison shared with her husband, James Madison. Mayo and Meringolo cite one example of Madison's social style as follows:

> She invited James Madison's enemies in Congress to dinner, and with her warmth and gregariousness won support for him before the 1812 election. So charming and hospitable was she at these gatherings that Congressman Jonathan Roberts observed, "You cannot discover who [are] her husband's friends or foes." Her sixteen years as a leader of Washington society established Dolley Madison as the most dominant force in the social life of the early republic.[93]

Not only did Madison's social prowess earn her the reputation as a "dominant force in the social life of the early republic," it also promoted her and her husband politically. Caroli observes that Madison's dinner for members of Congress during the 1812 campaign led politician James Blaine to "credi[t] Dolley with a large share in her husband's 1812 victory."[94]

This version of social style is grounded in Hariman's theory of political style, which posits that style is connected to power in intimate and fundamental ways. He defines political style as "a coherent repertoire of rhetorical conventions depending on aesthetic reactions for political effect," and identifies four styles prominent in male-dominated political spheres: realist, courtly, republican, and bureaucratic. According to Hariman, political style operates through rules for speech, interaction, and performance. It functions to shape identity, generate consensus, and distribute power. For example, the realist style is exemplified in Machiavelli and instantiates the political actor as strategist. Speech is devalued in the realist style, artlessness is professed, and text is sublimated for a focus on "unencumbered experience."[95] Conversely, the republican style, which is premised on the Ciceronian citizen-orator, privileges rhetoric, operates from consensus, and draws power from heroic *mythos*.

Hariman presents his four political styles as androgynous, equally employable by women and men. Yet, the archetypes used to generate each style are male and the gendered nature of political power is not a question tackled by Hariman. He does suggest, however, that his typology of four political styles is just a beginning, and he urges other scholars to explore additional versions of political style.

Dolley Madison was not the first presidential spouse to enact the social style. The social obligations of first ladies began to be defined in the nineteenth century, when Louisa Adams "traveled around Washington, calling on as many as twenty-five women in a single day from a list her husband drew up for her."[96] The fact that John Quincy Adams took the time to prescribe who his wife should call on testifies to the political import of social interactions.

The political nature of private sphere activities routinely is downplayed, particularly in reference to the activities of political wives. For example, when First Lady Edith Roosevelt held weekly meetings with wives of cabinet members, presidential aide Archibald Butt assumed that the women did little more than "take tea and compare crochet patterns." Yet, when Helen Taft, wife of the secretary of war, referred to the gatherings she described them as something other than a "social affair."[97] Taft's assertion indicates an understanding of "social affairs" as innocuous and apolitical; however, we contend that Roosevelt's gatherings were an enactment of a social style that fosters accomplishment of political goals.

Grace Coolidge facilitated her husband's political achievements by using social style to temper Calvin Coolidge's interpersonal uneasiness. Caroli notes that "[a]t official receptions, the president curtly nodded to the people and quickly passed from one obligatory handshake to the next while Grace's exceptional memory for names and her genuine concern for guests' comfort made them feel at ease."[98] Mamie Eisenhower also achieved political advancement for

Ike by embodying hospitality. Mayo and Meringolo explain that "[t]hroughout the nation's history, advancing a husband's career through social entertainment has been a traditional female role, and Mamie saw her primary duty as first lady as that of a successful White House hostess."[99] Similarly, Lady Bird Johnson fulfilled the "responsibilities" of a "political wife" early in her marriage to Lyndon Johnson by accommodating "any of Lyndon's political friends," as well as "those he hoped to bring into that category," whom he frequently brought home unannounced.[100] Barbara Bush testifies in her autobiography about George Bush's propensity to bring home guests with virtually no notice, both before and after their arrival to the White House.[101]

These examples illustrate how the social style of first ladies functions to support the political achievements of United States presidents, deflating the myth that politics historically has been transacted only by men in the public sphere. As early as the eighteenth century, women participated in politics through their social interactions. One assumption underlying the social style is that political power is rooted not just in the public sphere but also in private interactions. Consequently, one implication of defining political power in this manner is the collapse (or, at least, intermingling) of public and private spheres.

Abigail McCarthy notes that political wives contribute to their husbands' careers by providing "status maintenance, intellectual contributions, and public performance."[102] The social style, however, has not been used exclusively to further the political agendas of male politicians. Some first ladies employed the social style in service of their own political or personal goals. Florence Harding garnered favorable journalistic coverage by "invit[ing] newspaperwomen to cruise down the Potomac with her on the presidential yacht."[103] Eleanor Roosevelt invited young African-American women from the National Training School for Girls to a White House garden party, using a feminine medium of entertaining to make a progressive statement about race.[104] Mayo and Meringolo note that many first ladies extended their role as the "nation's hostess" in order to act "as diplomats," identifying Eleanor Roosevelt, Jacqueline Kennedy, Pat Nixon, and Nancy Reagan as examples of first ladies who used the social style in this manner.[105]

A key characteristic of social style is that it enacts political power while disguising its nature as political. First ladies have been forced to disguise their political power by professing apoliticism. Some of the most political first ladies, such as Barbara Bush, have been the most insistent about their disconnection from political matters.[106] Social style is defined by the constraint of conforming to norms of femininity while, at the same time, developing a tacit ability to employ femininity in order to achieve political agency.

Hostess is one component of the hostess/beauty queen metaphoric cluster— one that has potential for helping political spouses (more so than governors) achieve political agency without sacrificing "resonance" with the public. A more damaging aspect of this image, however, is the political spouse as beauty queen. First ladies have long stood as icons for style and beauty in U.S. culture—from

Mamie Eisenhower's bangs to Jacqueline Kennedy's pill-box hat. The emphasis on style is exemplified by the Smithsonian Institute's display of first lady gowns in its exhibit that chronicles the history of the U.S. first ladyship. Both the amount of money first ladies spend on their clothes and the designers whom they frequent routinely are paid significant media attention.

Although physical attractiveness benefits male and female politicians (attention to men's physical appearance has increased in modern campaigns), media accounts still focus on women's physical attributes more than on men's[107] and this trend is particularly evident with respect to political spouses. Take, for example, the two political spouses studied in this book. A *Washington Post* essay published during the 1996 presidential campaign characterized Elizabeth Dole, wife of Republican presidential nominee Bob Dole, as follows:

> Despite all the progress women have made, the mantel of presidential spouse remains largely ornamental. And Elizabeth-as-object glitters. She glides around the room on slim calves, a pair of green contact lenses jewelling her eyes, plum lipstick freshly applied before she steps onstage. Her intelligence is noted, but it has always been her charm that earns applause.[108]

Focus on Dole's physical appearance was the norm for coverage of her, even though she rose to prominence in Washington as a cabinet member in several Republican presidential administrations, rather than as a politician's wife. The *Washington Post* article continues:

> The *New York Times* wrote of her in 1980 "At 44, she is one of the most stunning women in Washington—slender, blue-eyed, fair skinned, with dark hair worn in a flippy style that she says is 'my first blow-dry hairdo; I'm worried that it might be too flat on top.'" And *Business Week*, in 1983: "She is to the Reagan administration what Jacqueline Kennedy was to Camelot—a glamorous, feminine presence, draped on a frame of steel."[109]

Not only is the popularity of political spouses tied to their appearance in media accounts, reports also link the candidates' success or failure to their spouses' ability (or willingness) to fulfill the beauty queen role. Campbell chronicles the case of Hillary Rodham Clinton's repeated physical transformations:

> In 1978, at the start of Clinton's first term as Arkansas governor, his wife reportedly "rejected makeup, glared through thick glasses, drowned herself in big shapeless fisherman's sweaters, and adamantly stuck to her maiden name." When Clinton lost his re-election campaign in 1980, [journalist and biographer Gail] Sheehy wrote, "Hillary determined to do whatever it took to put her husband back in power. So, without a word from Bill, she shed her name for his. She also dyed her hair, traded her thick glasses for contacts, and feigned an interest in fashion." . . . Hence, although she stopped wearing

headbands and restyled her hair in 1992, the transformation into a more conventional political wife had begun more than a decade earlier.[110]

The hostess/beauty queen metaphoric cluster is the most traditional and probably most recognizable stereotype that emerges in media accounts of political women. It encompasses issues of power, sexuality, and publicity. Given the increasing significance of image and appearance for both men and women in the current U.S. political landscape, it is likely that this cluster is not a vestige of the sexist past, but a lingering influence on how the media and the electorate make sense of politicians.

Unruly Woman

Focus on appearance carries over into the fourth and final cluster of metaphors. Whereas the beauty queen is beautiful, the fourth cluster emphasizes reversal, pointing out how some political women simply do not measure up in the poise and appearance category. The final cluster is complex and significant, for successful management contributes to the leadership successes of recent women governors. It incorporates a range of gendered images emphasizing disruption, dichotomy, and reversal—often reversal of the hostess/beauty queen cluster's emphasis on appearance and family structure. This reversal ranges from the masculine, "bitchy" Dixy Lee Ray to "female governor" Kay Orr who was elected governor while her husband stayed home to bake meat loaf and write cookbooks. Additionally, the reversal creates the sense that the woman elected to the masculine office is somehow unfitting, disorienting, the butt of humor, or just an unlikely candidate for the position. The juxtaposition accomplishes a variety of purposes. It may be to point out the lack of a necessary feminine quality in a biologically-sexed female who has allowed the masculine to over-characterize her—perhaps a woman is "bitchy," a political "maverick." Or, it may be to provide the appearance of balance for political actions required by the situation—perhaps a woman is fulfilling the masculine expectations of leader, but she is also compassionate and caring, doing her job as woman. Yet, the result is dichotomous thinking in which gendered terms are seen as opposites that do not fit together or fit together awkwardly. Or, it may be to emphasize an inappropriate or comical relationship between the governor and her "First Man," created as a result of the woman's election to public office. Whatever the gendered incongruity, the characterization of the woman official is seen as strange, humorous, ungenuine, and especially disruptive to the social hierarchy, and ultimately undermines the power and authority of the woman politician who is not following the prescribed expectations of the masculine political sphere.

This cluster, in which gender construction and reversal are at issue, encompasses what Kathleen Rowe calls the "Unruly Woman." According to Rowe, the

unruly woman is found in a range of examples from Mae West, Barbara Stan-
wyck, and Katharine Hepburn to Miss Piggy and Roseanne Barr. More importantly, the unruly woman opens the possibility for "recoding and reauthoring the
notion of 'Woman.'"[111] The unruly woman creates a spectacle of herself, emphasizing the social construction of gender. In addition, the unruly woman:

1.   creates disorder by dominating, or trying to dominate, men. She
     will not confine herself to her proper place.
2.   is excessive physically, she may be fat, and excessive in speech,
     in quantity, content, or tone.
3.   makes jokes, or laughs herself.
4.   may be old or a masculinized crone.
5.   is associated with thresholds, borders, or margins, and taboo.[112]

These characteristics result when women disrupt the expectations of femininity
and the social hierarchy inscribed in the hostess/beauty queen cluster of metaphors. Even though the political individual as unruly woman disrupts boundaries, the metaphor also tells us that the woman has transgressed. Such a spectacle becomes problematic when thinking about women public officials, unless the
woman can find a way to use it to her advantage to advance a more productive
metaphor.

Turning the negative stereotype on its head is a challenge, in part, because
of the pervasiveness of the term "bitch" in U.S. social and political culture. In
one word, "bitch" becomes a metaphor for women leaders who transgress
boundaries and disrupt expectations in ways the media and general public resist.
The term "bitch" is used frequently in the public sphere. Famous women earning
the moniker "bitch" are a diverse lot, including Jeane Kirkpatrick, Roseanne
Barr, Margaret Thatcher, Leona Helmsley, Bette Davis, Pat Schroeder, Nancy
Reagan, Geraldine Ferraro, Cher, Kim Basinger, Diana Ross, Whitney Houston,
Barbara Streisand, Madonna, Marsha Clark, and Shannon Faulkner.[113] Margaret
Carlson, contributor to *Time* and panelist on CNN's *Capital Gang*, recounts her
experience with the term:

> I know something about this because of the stack of hate mail that ar-
> rives if I so much as frown at Robert Novak on CNN's *Capital Gang*.
> He can shout me down, insisting I don't know what I'm talking about
> and be deluged with fan mail. If I go so far as to say "Let me finish,"
> letters arrive about how strident and shrill I am—and, yes, what a
> bitch.[114]

Calling a woman a bitch is not a new phenomenon. As early as 1400, a bitch
was defined as "a malicious, spiteful, promiscuous or otherwise despicable
woman." The term shed its connotation of sexual promiscuity in modern times
and became a synonym for an "uppity," "vocal," or "pushy" woman.[115] Film star
Bette Davis summed it up when she said, "When a man gives his opinion, he's a
man. When a woman gives her opinion, she's a bitch."[116] Laurel Sutton points

out that the "word *bitch* is the prime example of a subclass of terms for women-as-sex-objects, that of women as animals."[117] C. Robert Whaley and George Antonelli explain that an examination of animal metaphors applied to women reveals "a basis for the concept of woman as male chattel, themes of male conquest, domination, and exploitation."[118] Animal metaphors dehumanize women and often highlight their relationship to males. Labels like "kitten" and "bunny" characterize women as domesticated sexual playthings, while "fox" and "wildcat" suggest an exotic and appealing female to be tamed or hunted. "Bitch" represents "the domesticated animal that has gone wrong, that bites the hand that feeds it. A female dog in heat or protecting her young will growl, threaten, or even bite her owner; she has reverted to her wild state; she is a *bitch*, uncontrollable."[119] When the "bitch" metaphor is invoked in popular culture it unleashes the myth of women's power as unnatural and threatening. Whaley and Antonelli conclude, "Men flee from bitches because they have reverted to wild animals, usurped the master's control, and taken over his territory."[120]

In contemporary America, "bitch" routinely is employed in everyday dialogue. On the news we heard that when "Mayor Marion Barry was caught smoking crack in a sting operation mounted by the male-dominated FBI, his first reaction was, 'Bitch set me up.'"[121] O. J. Simpson was recorded on a 911 tape shouting at his former wife Nicole Brown, "I don't want you in my house, you bitch!"[122] Women in the military have been assaulted with the epithet for years. Kathleen Hall Jamieson notes that "early female West Point cadets . . . were mocked by their male peers. 'Good morning sir,' She would say with the prescribed deferential salute. 'It was a good morning until you got here, bitch,' he would mimic, in falsetto."[123] Shannon Faulkner, the teenager who won admittance to The Citadel (whose mascot is the bulldog) was, upon her arrival, greeted by T-shirts that characterized the student body as "1,952 BULLDOGS AND 1 BITCH."[124] Barbara Donlan sums up the culture of denigration as follows:

> [T]urn on the TV or the radio, or just tune in to the guy on the next barstool talking about his ex-wife and you would be forced to conclude that bitches are everywhere. She wants child support? She's a bitch. She's 16 and she won't "give it up"? That bitch. (If she does, she's promoted to a "ho.") She runs for national office instead of staying home in Queens ironing her husband's shirt? Bitch. She "takes over" the meeting? Hey, you know what that makes her.[125]

Since "bitch" is used so commonly in everyday dialogue, it is not surprising that it also turns up in political discussions. Officials on Capitol Hill testify to the frequency of the term's connection with women in politics. Jean Dugan, a Senate staffer who co-chairs the Capitol Hill Women's Political Caucus was quoted as saying, "You do hear the term 'bitch' applied to women while their male counterparts are simply called 'aggressive.'"[126] Mike Kennedy states, "The word [bitch] hurts, but women concede that those kinds of insults and labels go with the territory."[127] The *Sacramento Bee* reports that "[i]n Washington and elsewhere, veteran female politicos agree, scarcely a week passes that the epithet isn't uttered about some woman in some important position somewhere."[128] Maureen Downey states that "most powerful women have heard the word 'bitch' before."[129] Rob Morse concurs, claiming that "[p]olitical women all have heard 'bitch' before."[130] When George Bush ran against Geraldine Ferraro for the vice-presidency, Barbara Bush summarized her opinion of Ferraro as follows: "I can't say it but it rhymes with 'rich.'"[131] Bush was furious when her comment was circulated nationwide. She tried to cover her tracks by claiming that the word she had in mind was "witch,"[132] and later apologized to Ferraro, saying "I certainly didn't mean anything by it."[133]

The Bush/Ferraro incident was not an isolated case of "bitch" being used (whether explicit or implied) to describe a female political figure. In February 1996 *The New Republic* noted that the "majority leader of the Washington State Senate apologized for calling Congresswoman Linda Smith 'a self-promoting miserable bitch.'"[134] According to *The Atlanta Journal and Constitution*, Janelle Edwards, a Georgia state Democratic activist, "counted bitch among the milder sentiments in anonymous letters she received after her party's November defeat."[135] The *Sacramento Bee* reports that Sacramento television anchor Stan Atkinson experienced "considerable embarrassment" in October 1992 when he was recorded "[m]outhing the word 'bitch' as a news story about U.S. Senate candidate Barbara Boxer had finished."[136] Kay Orr, the Republican candidate for governor of Nebraska in 1986, initially was labeled a "bitchy woman candidate."[137] Pat Schroeder, the long-time U.S. Representative from Colorado, was labeled the "Wicked Bitch of the West" after she pressed for an investigation of the Tailhook scandal,[138] and following her visit to the Miramar Naval Base one retired pilot stated his intention to return to his home in Schroeder's district and post a sign reading "Ditch the bitch."[139]

Labeling political women "bitches" is a common and rhetorically effective way of casting them in the role of unruly woman. A closer look at two governors, Dixy Lee Ray and Kay Orr, illustrates the force of the unruly woman metaphoric cluster. Ray is the bitchy extreme, overly masculine, while Orr has apparently switched gender roles with her husband, causing a concern about his masculinity. As a result, descriptions of Ray focus on her inappropriately unfeminine, radical qualities that somehow make her less of a woman and by extension an inappropriate, eccentric governor. Descriptions of Orr focus on her husband, attempting to give him a voice that justifies his non-traditional gender role.

Ray was a well-educated woman, yet media descriptions often put her education secondary: "Dr Ray, who is single, has degrees in zoology and biology."[140] Other descriptions note: "Ray, who never married, lives with her sister."[141] *Time* claimed, "Her manner is brisk and candid. Her taste in clothes runs to blazers and tweed skirts with knee socks and 'sensible' shoes. A sturdy, affable spinster of 59, Dixy Lee Ray lives in an 8-ft.-by-28-ft. motor home."[142] Even in her obituary, the *Los Angeles Times* described her as "a short, chunky woman with cropped hair and tailored clothes. . . . she was called Dick as a child—short for 'that little Dickens'" and later changed her name to Dixy Lee, "after a favorite region and a Civil War General."[143]

Newsweek encompassed many of the image issues leveled at Ray: "the major newspapers opposed her, her foes chuckled and just about everyone predicted the state was not ready for an unmarried woman who gave herself a chain saw for Christmas."[144] She lived in the governor's mansion with her sister and had a very straightforward style, firing all appointees of the previous governor. Quoting Ray, "'So I said if they needed it, I'd send them a box of Kleenex—along with their pink slip.'"[145] *Newsweek* continued to describe her as "a short woman with gray hair, plump, rosy cheeks, an engaging smile—and a sharp wit." She "has no real program of her own" and "pads around the governor's mansion in Hush Puppies and keeps her poodle, Jacques, at her feet under her desk in the governor's office."[146] As Ray countered, "'If I don't conform to the image of what a governor should be or act like, I'm sorry,' she says. 'But I'm not going to spend hours agonizing over it. I grew up before self-analysis became a popular indoor sport.'"[147]

Ray's political approach was considered "maverick."[148] She had "the subtlety of a Seattle stevedore" that doesn't walk but "stalks" or "bulldozes."[149] Yet she was described with a warm side: "radiat[ing] a charm that makes her seem like a benevolent pixie, a chubby (5 ft. 4 in., 165 lbs.) Peter Pan."[150] "'She has a streak of Golda Meir in her'" according to a former AEC member, and her aides were intimidated by her and named "yes-yes-yes people."[151] Her opponents promoted bumper stickers saying "Ditch the Bitch," and her 1976 campaign manager claimed she had a "highhanded style," that "ridiculed" and "antagonized people."[152] As a *Time* article concluded: "Dixy Lee Ray relishes too much delivering thunderbolts from the Olympia of her own Washington."[153]

Ray clearly was no beauty queen and her example illustrates the difficulties the media has with a political woman who does not uphold the traditional feminine expectations of beauty and family. Her unmarried status led to many whispers about her sexual orientation, though at the time the word lesbian was never used to describe her. Because of her unruly performance she was neither a proper woman nor a competent governor. Yet her policies did not discredit her executive potential so much as her overly-masculine demeanor. Thus, it is not enough for a woman executive to lead "just like a man."

The other prototype of this final cluster is Kay Orr. Orr's persona was not that of the over-masculinized leader, but it is clear that with a woman in a leadership position there is also a problem concerning who "wears the pants" in the family. The focus of her characterizations is on the disruption that her position creates within her family structure; however, it is cast as humorous and as something one would find in a sitcom. It is certainly not something to see in the world of politics. Further, the reversal casts her husband in the starring role because of his identity crisis and paints the governor as a "female" governor so that she does not appear overly masculine and as a result efface her husband's masculinity.

The following headline encapsulated the problem: "While Nebraska Governor Kay Orr Makes Policy, Husband Bill, Her 'First Gentleman,' Bakes Meat Loaf."[154] The article proceeded:

> It sounds like the premise for a sitcom: When his wife becomes Governor of a midwestern state, a hotshot insurance executive has to find ways of coping on the home front. Forthcoming episodes deal with husband learning to cook, husband (henceforth to be known as First Gentleman) being seated with the wives at the Governors' conference, and husband deploring the décor of the Governor's mansion.
>
> Turn off the laugh track, folks, this is no sitcom. It's the very happy real-life story of Nebraska's first female Governor. . . . Her husband . . . suddenly had to worry about the house while Kay worried about the senate.[155]

The article explained that Orr's transformation began when Kay became state treasurer and "housekeeping would have to be an either Orr proposition." Kay said that she "'taught Bill that being patient and understanding about my job was not simply waiting for me to come home and fix his meal. . . . That was very nice of him, but he had to take it one step further and fix himself his own meal.'" Bill finds he is a veteran meat loaf maker and "is comfortable with the role of consort and official spouse." Bill and Madeleine Kunin's husband "seek each other out at gubernatorial gatherings. 'We sit in the back corner and talk. . . . Sometimes they have to shush us.'" Bill also put together *The First Gentleman's Cookbook* and used the royalties from the book to renovate the Governor's mansion, previously decorated in "early Holiday Inn" according to Mr. Orr.[156]

The Lincoln *Journal* also captured this odd reversal, praising Mr. Orr's good sense of humor as he defined "'how the state's First Man should act.'" Orr responded that he has a good sense of humor and that he has "'nothing to be embarrassed about here. I'm just as proud as I can be about my wife.'" He admitted "he has taken his share of ribbing" about being the "First Man"—his friend told him he should change his name to Adam. Another friend called him "The Governor's Bagman" when a picture of Bill holding Kay's purse ran in newspapers.[157]

Such concern over the apparent masculinity of a husband or a state that would elect a woman governor was even expressed with Miriam Ferguson's election in 1925 with a cartoon depicting a very small Texas tied to a very large Ma's apron strings.[158] Additionally, Shana Alexander writing in *Life* magazine likened the 1966 Alabama gubernatorial election to Al Capp's "Li'l Abner" comic strip. As Alexander wrote: "When Governor Wallace said Lurleen was to be the candidate, a Southern newspaper commented, 'It's as difficult to imagine her running for governor as it is to imagine Helen Hayes butchering a hog.' Not, evidently, for the people of Alabama. And not for us *Li'l Abner* fans, either."[159]

Exaggerating the incongruity between traditional gender roles and their reversal focuses attention on the construction of gender while it also disrupts the social hierarchy. What we are left with is trying to make sense of women leaders using dichotomies that can be equally as problematic since they are rooted in mutually exclusive expectations. *The Atlantic Monthly* described Lurleen Wallace as: "A small tidy woman with a fondness for blazers and turtleneck blouses, which make her look like the leader of a girls' college glee club, she is attractive in that hard, plain, small-faced somewhat masculine way that Deep Southern women tend to be attractive—in fact, over the years, she has even acquired a certain resemblance to her husband."[160] Bringing together oppositional terms only serves to make the woman governor appear unnatural or ungenuine, reinforcing the norm that she is acting outside appropriate borders, taboo, unruly.

Newsweek pointed out Ella Grasso's "cropped brown hair is frequently a mess," her spectacles are frequently on her head, and her "baggy beige pantsuit . . . [and] lace-up shoes" contribute to her "rumpled image" in which she "looks as if she was left behind by a tornado." The article goes on to note: "the larger irony is that Grasso, 55, happens to be a woman much as Babe Ruth happened to have spindly legs; it is a minor but much dwelt-upon characteristic that sometimes obscures the true stamp of a tough, tenacious professional . . . [who] can plot, coerce, compromise and charm with the best of her masculine peers." But apparently that did not stop some of her party aides' worries over how they could go into the office of a woman governor "'and swear at her.'"[161]

Rose Mofford, according to the *New York Times*, wore a "trademark . . . platinum beehive hairdo" and was "dangerous with a one-liner. She is a raucous quipster who antagonizes almost no one and disarms almost everyone with political barbs."[162] "She was a star athlete, winning national honors in softball. She was also a prize-winning typist."[163] *Newsweek* also claimed that Mofford was "not exactly the classic picture of a politician, what with a doll collection in her office and her name in the phone book . . . the improbable 'grandmother of Arizona.'"[164] She was described as a "Mae West look-alike, or 'Tammy Faye in 10 years.'"[165] In the Kansas gubernatorial race, *Newsweek* claimed that Joan Finney's candidacy was disorienting. She "is not only an ardent right-to-lifer but a Democrat and a woman to boot. . . . The role-reversing contest has dismayed many voters."[166]

Newsweek claimed that Ann Richards "looks like a suburban matron, talks like a good ole boy and works a crowd like a trench-savvy politician." Despite her reputation "as an able manager . . . she seems an unlikely governor of Texas."[167] Molly Ivins explained: "Ann Richards is smart and tough and funny and pretty, which I notice just confuses the hell out of a lot of people." Ivins continued, saying that what makes men uncomfortable is "seeing a pretty woman be bitingly funny. You can tell they think it's an extremely dangerous combination."[168] She "is living proof that appearances can be dangerously deceptive. She seems, well, like somebody's grandmother . . . [and] also a hard-nosed politician."[169] And not to be outdone, several sources point out that Jane Hull is more likely known as the "Iron Lady" of Arizona than by her official title of governor.[170]

What these descriptions emphasize is that even though women can be all these things, there is something unfitting, unlikely, or disorienting going on. Instead of confronting the masculine norms of political culture that work to contain women, the woman governor is the one who is out of bounds. Instead of acknowledging the ways that political practice works every day—rhetorically—the rationality guiding political participation takes precedence.

These four clusters of metaphors: pioneer, puppet, hostess/beauty queen, and unruly woman, provide the constructions that current women political figures must negotiate. If recent women politicians were to transform some of these metaphors successfully, the resultant image would not be one that attempted to fuse together two dichotomous and gendered terms, but rather one that is transformative, seeing political leaders as chief executives without the necessity of a feminine qualifier or fear of appearing overly masculine or effacing a husband's masculinity. Such stretching would give male politicians more latitude as well.

This is an issue that women like Christine Todd Whitman and Madeleine Kunin acknowledged. Whitman was quoted in the *Chicago Tribune*: "'Where a man is considered strong, a woman is considered bitchy. Where a man is decisive, a woman is shrill. There is a double standard, but if you're spending your entire time railing against it, you won't get anything done.'"[171] And according to Kunin:

> At some gut level, the art of politics—combative, competitive, self-asserting—is sometimes difficult to integrate with our feminine selves. . . . Each step builds a new self-image, enabling us to move from the passive to the active voice. . . . We will not accept that there is a permanent dichotomy between being in charge and being feminine. Our goal is to humanize this world by combining both; let us begin.[172]

Notes

1. See, for example, Edward A. Hinck and Shelly S. Hinck, "Politeness Strategies in the 1992 Vice Presidential and Presidential Debates," *Argumentation & Advocacy* 38 (2002): 234–50; Spiro Kiousis, Philemon Bantimaroudis, and Hyun Ban, "Candidate Image Attributes: Experiments on the Substantive Dimension of Second Level Agenda Setting," *Communication Research* 26 (1999): 414–28; K. L. Hacker, *Candidate Images in Presidential Elections* (Westport, Conn.: Praeger, 1995); T. M. Harrison, T. D. Stephen, W. Husson, and B. J. Fehr, "Image Versus Issues in the 1984 Presidential Election," *Human*

Communication Research 18 (1991): 209–27; and P. H. Tannenbaum, B. S. Greenberg, and F. R. Silverman, "Candidate Images," in *The Great Debates*, ed. S. Kraus (Bloomington: Indiana University Press, 1962): 271–88.

2. W. Husson, T. Stephen, T. M. Harrison, and B. J. Fehr, "An Interpersonal Communication Perspective on Images of Political Candidates," *Human Communication Research* 14 (1988): 397–421.

3. S. Keeler, "The Illusion of Intimacy: Television and the Role of Candidate Personal Qualities in Voter Choice," *Public Opinion Quarterly* 51 (1987): 344–58. S. A. Hellweg, "An Examination of Voter Conceptualization of the Ideal Political Candidate," *Southern Speech Communication Journal* 44 (1979), 373–85.

4. Thomas Hollihan, "Nurturing Political Images," in *Uncivil Wars: Political Campaigns in a Media Age* (Boston, Mass.: Bedford/St. Martin's, 2001), 66. For research on appearance, nonverbal communication, and political image see S. W. Rosenberg and P. McCafferty, "The Image and the Vote," *Public Opinion Quarterly* 51 (1987): 31–47 and H. S. Friedman, T. I. Mertz, and M. R. DiMatteo, "Perceived Bias in the Facial Expressions of Television News Broadcasters," *Journal of Communication* 30 (1980): 103–111.

5. See, for example, Helen Kennedy, "Gore's a Bore No More: Makeover Having its Effect," *New York Daily News*, January 19, 2000, Lexis Nexis Academic Universe (accessed August 1, 2002); Maureen Dowd, "The Alpha-Beta Macarena," *New York Times*, November 3, 1999, Lexis Nexis Academic Universe (accessed August 1, 2002).

6. Kathleen Hall Jamieson, *Beyond the Double Bind: Women and Leadership* (New York: Oxford University Press, 1995), 123. Jamieson cites a number of studies to support her contention, as follows: Norma Costrich, Joan Feinstein, Louise Kidder, Jeanne Marecek, and Linda Pascale, "When Stereotypes Hurt: Three Studies of Penalties for Sex-Role Reversals," *Journal of Experimental Social Psychology* 11 (1975): 520; M. L. MacDonald, "Assertion Training for Women," in *Social Skills Training*, ed. J. P. Curran and P. M. Monti (New York: Guilford, 1981); Madeline E. Heilman and Melanie H. Stopeck, "Attractiveness and Corporate Success: Different Causal Attributes for Males and Females," *Journal of Applied Psychology* 70 (1985): 379–88; P. H. Bradley, "The Folk-Linguistics of Women's Speech: An Empirical Examination," *Communication Monographs* 48 (1981): 73–90; A. Bridges and H. Hartman, "Pedagogy by the Oppressed," *Review of Radical Political Economics* 6 (Winter 1975): 75–79.

7. Kim Fridkin Kahn and Ann Gordon, "How Women Campaign for the U.S. Senate: Substance and Strategy," in *Women, Media, and Politics*, ed. Pippa Norris (New York: Oxford University Press, 1997), 62.

8. Shanto Iyengar, Nicholas A. Valentino, Stephen Ansolabehere, and Adam F. Simon, "Running as a Woman: Gender Stereotyping in Political Campaigns," in *Women, Media, and Politics*, ed. Pippa Norris (New York: Oxford University Press, 1997), 79.

9. Iyengar et al., "Running as a Woman," 79.

10. See Kristina Horn Sheeler, "Marginalizing Metaphors of the Feminine," *Navigating Boundaries: The Rhetoric of Women Governors*, eds. Molly Mayhead and Brenda DeVore Marshall (Westport, Conn.: Praeger, 2000), 15–30.

11. Sue Tolleson-Rinehart and Jeanie R. Stanley, *Claytie and the Lady: Ann Richards, Gender, and Politics in Texas* (Austin: University of Texas Press, 1994), 3.

12. Karlyn Kohrs Campbell, "Shadowboxing with Stereotypes: The Press, the Public, and the Candidates' Wives," Research paper R–9 (President and Fellows of Harvard College, 1993), 1.

13. These four metaphoric clusters emerged after examination of magazine and newspaper, and, more recently, broadcast media accounts of both women governors and political spouses, particularly first ladies. While not a definitive survey of all media, this survey considers major publications with large national audiences such as the *Associated Press Political Service*, the *New York Times*, *Newsweek*, *Time*, and *The Nation*, local, historical, and women's magazines such as *Current Opinion*, *The Literary Digest*, and *The Woman Citizen*, and broadcast sources such as CNN, MSNBC, and the broadcast networks. Our survey of these sources was thorough to the point of being indicative of the main metaphoric patterns used to characterize women executives and political spouses.

14. "Miriam Amanda Ferguson: Soon to Take Office as the First Woman Governor of Texas," *Current Opinion*, October 1924, 436.

15. "Woman's Bigger Dent in Politics," *The Literary Digest*, November 22, 1924, 17.

16. Daniel Chu with William J. Cook, "Governors: Whistling Dixy," *Newsweek*, October 4, 1976, 47.

17. "Connecticut's Favorite Daughter: Ella T. Grasso, 1919–1981," *Time*, February 16, 1981, 20.

18. B. Drummond Ayres, Jr., "Whitman, in California, Fields the Vice-Presidency Question," *New York Times*, April 30, 1995, late edition, 37, Lexis Nexis Academic Universe (accessed October 29, 1999).

19. Harold Preece, "Ma Ferguson Wins Again," *The Nation*, September 21, 1932, 255.

20. "Women Who Won on November 4th," *The Woman Citizen*, November 15, 1924, 9.

21. Elizabeth K. Phelps Stokes, "Your Business in Washington," *The Woman Citizen*, March 21, 1925, 8.

22. Stokes, "Your Business in Washington," 8.

23. Michael Doan and Michael Bosc, "Kay Orr and Helen Boosalis: Woman Power on the Prairie," *U.S. News & World Report*, May 26, 1986, 8.

24. "Joan Finney," AP Candidate Bios. *The Associated Press Political Service*, Lexis Nexis Academic Universe (accessed October 20, 1998).

25. "Joan Finney."

26. Max Bentley, "'I'll Be Governor, Not Jim,' Says Ma Ferguson," *Collier's*, September 27, 1924, 12.

27. "Grasso: Piedmont Spoken Here," *Time*, November 18, 1974, 10.

28. "Dixy Rocks the Northwest," *Time*, December 12, 1977, 31.

29. Alexander Burnham, "The Testing of Ella Grasso," *The Progressive*, April 1976, 34.

30. "Vermont: Statehouse Stakes," *Newsweek*, October 29, 1984, 44.

31. "Women Who Won," 9.

32. "Women Who Won," 9.

33. Betty Boyd Caroli, *First Ladies*, expanded edition (New York: Oxford University Press, 1995), xv.

34. Caroli, *First Ladies*, 38.

35. Caroli, *First Ladies*, xxi.

36. Edith P. Mayo and Denise D. Meringolo, *First Ladies: Political Role and Public Image* (Washington, D.C.: Smithsonian Institution Press, 1994), 8.

37. Margaret Carlson, "All Eyes on Hillary," *Time*, September 14, 1992, Expanded Academic ASAP (accessed October 27, 1995).

38. Germaine Greer, "Abolish Her: The Feminist Case Against First Ladies," *New Republic*, June 26, 1995, 20, Expanded Academic ASAP (accessed October 27, 1995).

39. Caroli, *First Ladies,* 32.

40. Caroli, *First Ladies,* 57.

41. Edith P. Mayo, "The Influence and Power of First Ladies," *Chronicle of Higher Education*, September 15, 1993, A52.

42. Jesse Kornbluth, "Free Advice: Five Historians Comment on Hillary's Dilemma," *New Yorker*, January 30, 1995, 34.

43. Suzanne Daughton, "Women's Issues, Women's Place: Gender-Related Problems in Presidential Campaigns," *Communication Quarterly* 42 (1994): 106–19; Michael Kimmel, *Manhood in America: A Cultural History* (New York: Free Press, 1996), 36–38.

44. Caroli, *First Ladies*, 65.

45. Maureen Beasley, *Eleanor Roosevelt and the Media: A Public Quest for Self-Fulfillment* (Urbana: University of Illinois Press, 1987), 103.

46. Scott Steele, "A Man of Hope (Ark.)," *Maclean's*, November 16, 1992, 43.

47. Molly Meijer Wertheimer, ed., *Inventing a Voice: The Rhetoric of American First Ladies of the Twentieth Century* (Lanham, Md.: Rowman & Littlefield, 2004).

48. Mayo, "The Influence and Power of First Ladies," A52.

49. Denise M. Bostdorff, "Hillary Rodham Clinton and Elizabeth Dole as Running 'Mates' in the 1996 Campaign: Parallels in the Rhetorical Constraints of First Ladies and Vice Presidents," in *The 1996 Campaign: A Communication Perspective*, ed. Robert E. Denton (Westport, Conn.: Praeger, 1998), 201.

50. Caroli, *First Ladies*, 15.

51. "'Me for Ma,' Says Texas," *The Outlook*, September 3, 1924, 5.

52. Harold H. Martin, "'The Race of The Thousand Clowns,'" *The Saturday Evening Post*, May 1966, 25.

53. Martin, "'The Race of The Thousand Clowns,'" 26.

54. "Petticoat Politics," *Collier's*, April 17, 1926, 19.

55. Robert M. Field, "Will 'Ma' Ferguson Be Impeached?" *The Outlook*, December 9, 1925, 554.

56. Field, "Will 'Ma' Ferguson Be Impeached?" 555.

57. Field, "Will 'Ma' Ferguson Be Impeached?" 555.

58. Marshall Frady, "Governor and Mister Wallace," *The Atlantic Monthly*, August 1967, 35.

59. "In the First Big Test of the Negro Vote," *U.S. News & World Report*, May 16, 1966, 39.

60. David Margolick, "Lake Lurleen Journal," *New York Times*, June 19, 1991, A16.

61. Willson Whitman, "Can a Wife be Governor?" *Collier's*, September 5, 1925, 5.

62. Whitman, "Can a Wife be Governor?" 6.

63. Quoted in "Is Pa or Ma Governor of Texas?" *The Literary Digest*, April 11, 1925, 15

64. Alexander Burnham, "Governor Grasso's Troubles," *The Progressive*, January 1978, 36.

65. Daniel Pedersen, "Richards: 'I Like to Make People Laugh,'" *Newsweek*, July 25, 1988, 22.

66. Brett Pulley, "The 1997 Elections: Profile—Born With Politics in Her Veins," *New York Times*, October 29, 1997, late edition, B1, Lexis Nexis Academic Universe (accessed August 20, 1999).

67. "Christine Whitman Seen as Vice Presidential Material," *Chicago Tribune*, January 25, 1995, evening update edition, 2, Lexis Nexis Academic Universe (accessed October 20, 1999).

68. Never having married or being divorced complicates the imagery for the woman executive. See the next section titled "Unruly Woman."

69. "The Governor Lady Finds that in the East as in the West Americans Are 'Mine Own People,'" *Good Housekeeping*, July 1928, 67.

70. Stokes, "Your Business in Washington," 8.

71. Leah Rozen and Elinor J. Brecher, "Kentucky's New First Family Includes Another Beauty Queen—But Martha Layne Collins is the Governor," *People Weekly*, November 28, 1983, 59–60.

72. Janet Sirotu, "*McCall's* Goes to a Party: Derby Day Breakfast for 12,000!" *McCall's*, April 1987, 109.

73. Sirotu, "*McCall's* Goes to a Party," 109–110.

74. Marge Runnion, "Once a Refugee From Nazi Europe, Madeleine Kunin Takes Charge as Vermont's First Woman Governor," *People Weekly*, April 1, 1985, 105, Lexis Nexis Academic Universe (accessed October 20, 1998).

75. Runnion, "Once a Refugee From Nazi Europe," 105.

76. Colette Rossant, "A Visit With Vermont's Governor," *McCall's*, January 1988, 82.

77. "Second Time Around," *Time*, September 24, 1984, 31; "Vermont: Statehouse Stakes," 42.

78. Rossant, "A Visit With Vermont's Governor," 82–83.

79. Jodi Wilgoren, "A Nominee with Vigor Gives Michigan Democrats Hope," *New York Times*, August 8, 2002, <http://www.nytimes.com/2002/08/08/politics/08MICH.html?tntemail1> (accessed August 8, 2002).

80. Wilgoren, "A Nominee with Vigor."

81. Wilgoren, "A Nominee with Vigor."

82. Wilgoren, "A Nominee with Vigor."

83. If a woman holds a public office at the state level, it is more likely to be secretary of state than any other elected office. As of July 2004, 10 women serve as secretary of state at the state level, more than any other elected office with the exception of lieutenant governor, which may or may not be elected independently of the governor. See "Gender Gap in Government," <http://www.gendergap.com/governme.htm#STATE%20GOVERNMENT> (accessed July 21, 2004).

84. "Wyoming's Woman Candidate," *The Literary Digest*, November 1, 1924, 13.

85. "Woman's 'Bigger Dent in Politics,'" 17.

86. "Martha Layne Collins," AP Candidate Bios, *The Associated Press Political Service*, Lexis Nexis Academic Universe (accessed October 20, 1998).

87. Todd S. Purdum, "Once Again in Arizona, Secretary of State is Suddenly Thrust into the Job of Governor," *New York Times*, September 5, 1997, late edition, A20.

88. Purdum, "Once Again in Arizona," 20.

89. "Jane Dee Hull," AP Candidate Bios, October 1, 1998, *The Associated Press Political Service*, Lexis Nexis Academic Universe (accessed October 20, 1998).

90. "Cynthia Jeanne Shaheen," AP Candidate Bios, November 7, 1996, *The Associated Press Political Service*, Lexis Nexis Academic Universe (accessed October 20, 1998).

91. Caroli, *First Ladies*, xviii.

92. Robert Hariman, *Political Style: The Artistry of Power* (Chicago: University of Chicago Press, 1995).

93. Mayo and Meringolo, *First Ladies*, 16–17.

94. Caroli, *First Ladies*, 15.

95. Hariman, *Political Style*, 13–49.

96. Mayo and Meringolo, *First Ladies*, 18.

97. Caroli, *First Ladies*, 121–22.

98. Caroli, *First Ladies*, 168.

99. Mayo and Meringolo, *First Ladies*, 21.

100. Caroli, *First Ladies*, 232–33.

101. Barbara Bush, *A Memoir* (New York: St. Martin's, 1994).

102. Abigail McCarthy, "ER as First Lady," in *Without Precedent: The Life and Career of Eleanor Roosevelt*, ed. Joan Hoff-Wilson and Marjorie Lightman (Bloomington: Indiana University Press, 1984), 215.

103. Caroli, *First Ladies*, 162.

104. Maureen Beasley, *Eleanor Roosevelt and the Media*, 101–02.

105. Mayo and Meringolo, *First Ladies*, 23.

106. Andrew Sullivan, "Sacred Cow," *New Republic*, June 22, 1992, 42.

107. James Devitt, *Framing Gender on the Campaign Trail: Women's Executive Leadership and the Press*, Women's Leadership Fund, 1999.

108. Laura Blumenfeld, "And One of Them Shall Be First," *Washington Post*, April 8–14, 1996, national weekly edition, 6.

109. Blumenfeld, "And One of Them Shall Be First," 6.

110. Campbell, "Shadowboxing with Stereotypes," 5.

111. Kathleen Rowe, *The Unruly Woman: Gender and the Genres of Laughter* (Austin: University of Texas Press, 1995), 31.

112. Rowe, *The Unruly Woman*, 31.

113. The list was compiled from several sources: Chris Bynum, "Defining the B-Word; Hillary Clinton Isn't the Only Woman in Authority Who is Dogged by a Particular Label. The Question Is, What Does It Mean?" *Times-Picayune*, January 17, 1995, F1, Lexis Nexis Academic Universe (accessed February 2, 1996); Melinda Back, "The Voice of the Victims," *Newsweek*, January 23, 1995, 48; Richard Leiby, "TO B OR NOT TO B.; Reflections on a Word That Rhymes with Glitch," *Washington Post*, January 12, 1995, final edition, C1, Lexis Nexis Academic Universe (accessed February 2, 1996); and Barbara Brotman, "1995: One Step Forward, One Back; The Year of Any Woman Brought Out the Best in Us—and the Worst," *Chicago Tribune*, December 31, 1995, final edition, C1, Lexis Nexis Academic Universe (accessed February 2, 1996).

114. Margaret Carlson, "Muzzle the *B* Word," *Time*, January 16, 1995, 36.

115. Rob Morse, "Rhymes with Gingrich," *San Francisco Examiner*, January 5, 1995, fourth edition, A1, Lexis Nexis Academic Universe (accessed February 2, 1996); Katherine Lanpher, "Women Should Make Newt's Term Work for Them," *Dayton Daily News*, January 6, 1995, city edition, 11A, Lexis Nexis Academic Universe (accessed February 2, 1996); and Beverly Gross, "Bitch," *Salmagundi* (Summer 1994): 146, Expanded Academic ASAP (accessed February 2, 1996).

116. Maureen Downey, "It Rhymes with Gingrich: Remark by Mother of the House Speaker Sparks Debate on Use of 'Bitch' to Describe Women with Power," *Atlanta Journal and Constitution*, January 5, 1995, D1, Lexis Nexis Academic Universe (accessed February 2, 1996).

117. Laurel A. Sutton, "Bitches and Skankly Hobags: The Place of Women in Contemporary Slang," in *Locating Power*, ed. Kira Hall, Mary Bucholtz, and

Birch Moonwoman (Berkeley: Berkeley Women and Language Group, 1992), 561.

118. C. Robert Whaley and George Antonelli, "The Birds and the Beasts: Woman as Animal," *Maledicta: International Journal of Verbal Aggression* 7 (1983): 220. See also Julia Wood, *Gendered Lives: Communication, Gender, and Culture* (Belmont, Calif.: Wadsworth, 1994), 133 for a discussion of the ways in which animal and food metaphors trivialize women.

119. Sutton, "Bitches," 562.

120. Whaley and Antonelli, "The Birds," 225.

121. Carlson, "Muzzle," 36.

122. Carlson, "Muzzle," 36.

123. Jamieson, *Beyond the Double Bind*, 121.

124. Brotman, "1995."

125. Barbara Donlan, "'B' Word Still Hangs in the Air Like a Bad Vapor," *Boston Herald*, January 22, 1995, second ed. 49, Lexis Nexis Academic Universe (accessed February 2, 1996).

126. Leslie Phillips and Patricia Edmonds, "Women in Congress: Fighting the Old Boy Network; Getting Voice Heard a Daily Balancing Act," *USA Today*, April 1, 1992, final edition, 1A, Lexis Nexis Academic Universe (accessed February 2, 1996).

127. Mike Kennedy, "'B-word' Used in Arsenal of Hate," *Kansas City Star*, January 6, 1995, metropolitan edition, A1, Lexis Nexis Academic Universe (accessed February 2, 1996).

128. "Gingrich Cries Foul Over Mom's Whisper," *Sacramento Bee*, January 5, 1995, A1, Lexis Nexis Academic Universe (accessed February 2, 1996).

129. Downey, "It Rhymes."

130. Morse, "Rhymes with Gingrich."

131. Gross, "Bitch."

132. Karen DeWitt, "The 104th Congress; The Speaker's Mother; Quick Indignation After CBS Interview," *New York Times*, January 5, 1995, late edition, A23, Lexis Nexis Academic Universe (accessed February 2, 1996).

133. Gross, "Bitch."

134. "Notebook," *The New Republic*, February 19, 1996, 10.

135. Downey, "It Rhymes."

136. "Gingrich Cries Foul."

137. David E. Proctor, Roger C. Aden and Phyllis Japp, "Gender/Issue Interaction in Political Identity Making: Nebraska's Woman vs. Woman Gubernatorial Campaign," *Central States Speech Journal* 39 (1988): 196.

138. Carlson, "Muzzle," 36.

139. Gregory Vistica, "Schroeder Hopes Navy Vitriol Has Faded," *San Diego Union-Tribune*, February 20, 1993, Lexis Nexis Academic Universe (accessed February 2, 1996).

140. "AEC Gets a Female Boss," *Senior Scholastic*, March 5, 1973, 17.

141. Eileen Keerdoja with Pamela Abramson, "Dixy Lee Ray is Still Speaking Out," *Newsweek*, June 8, 1981, 16.

142. Sam Iker, "Changes in Dixyland," *Time*, November 5, 1973, 98.

143. "Dixy Lee Ray, Former Head of U.S. Atomic Agency, Dies," *Los Angeles Times*, January 3, 1994, A3.

144. Tom Mathews with Paul S. Greenberg, "Washington: Lady with a Chain Saw," *Newsweek*, April 11, 1977, 45.

145. Mathews, "Washington: Lady with a Chain Saw," 45.

146. Mathews, "Washington: Lady with a Chain Saw," 45.

147. Mathews, "Washington: Lady with a Chain Saw," 45.

148. "Surprises from Nation's Two Woman Governors," *U.S. News & World Report*, October 10, 1977, 45; "Dixy Rocks the Northwest," 27, 31.

149. Chu, "Governors: Whistling Dixy," 47; "Dixy Rocks the Northwest," 26.

150. "Dixy Rocks the Northwest," 27.

151. "Dixy Rocks the Northwest," 31.

152. Dennis A. Williams with Michael Reese, "Can Dixy Rise Again?" *Newsweek*, July 14, 1980, 28; "Defeat for Dixy Lee Ray," *Time*, September 29, 1980, 25.

153. "Dixy Rocks the Northwest," 35.

154. Joanne Kaufman and Barbara Kleban Mills, "While Nebraska Governor Kay Orr Makes Policy, Husband Bill, Her 'First Gentleman' Bakes Meat Loaf," *People Weekly*, December 12, 1988, 189.

155. Kaufman and Mills, "While Nebraska Governor Kay Orr Makes Policy," 189.

156. Kaufman and Mills, "While Nebraska Governor Kay Orr Makes Policy," 189, 191, 192.

157. Quoted in William E. Schmidt, "Lincoln *Journal*: Nebraska's First Man Enjoys the Last Laughs," *New York Times*, October 21, 1988, late city final edition, A14.

158. "Texas Tangled in 'Ma's' Apron-Strings," *The Literary Digest*, September 24, 1932, 11.

159. Shana Alexander, "On the Lookout for Lurleen," *Life*, July 22, 1966, 19.

160. Frady, "Governor and Mister Wallace," 37.

161. "On the Run with Ella," *Newsweek*, November 4, 1974, 21.

162. Lindsey Gruson, "A Familiar Role for Acting Governor," *New York Times*, February 7, 1988, late city final edition, 26.

163. Gruson, "A Familiar Role for Acting Governor," 26.

164. Jennifer Foote, "Arizona's 'Rosie' New Boss," *Newsweek*, February 22, 1988, 27.

165. Foote, "Arizona's 'Rosie' New Boss," 27.

166. Eloise Salholz with Karen Springen, "Are We in Kansas Anymore?" *Newsweek*, October 8, 1990, 34.

167. Pedersen, "Richards," 22.

168. Molly Ivins, "A Texas Treasure," *Ms*, October 1988, 26.

169. William Plummer and Anne Maier, "After Mudslinging Primary, Victor Ann Richards Sets her Sights on the Lone Star Statehouse," *People Weekly*, April 30, 1990, 85.

170. "Jane Dee Hull."

171. "Quotes of the Day," *Chicago Tribune*, April 4, 1995, evening update edition, 2, Lexis Nexis Academic Universe (accessed October 20, 1998).

172. "On Political Courage, Witches, and History," *Ms*, November 1987, 84.

Chapter 2

Ann Richards

Ann Richards, Texas Governor 1991–1995, is one of the most easily recognized female political figures with her "Dairy Queen lady" hair and her wise-cracking stories. Richards is an important figure for study because of the strategies she used to perform executive leadership competently in the state of Texas. Her case demonstrates how other political women operating from a liberal frame may secure power in a weak political structure by relying on the rhetorical resources at their disposal.

Richards negotiated the constraining metaphors of Texas political culture to advance her goals for a new Texas of inclusion and diversity. Texas political culture, rich in history and tradition, projects larger-than-life images of tough and outspoken politicians. Asserting power in the Texas governorship means lobbying and appointing members to boards and the legislature, shucking and jiving, spinning a yarn, and har-de-harring with the best of Texas "good ol' boys." The governor must use the identity and community-building function of storytelling to her advantage, joining populist and progressive appeals that are deeply embedded in Texas's history. The most immediate result for Richards was the metaphoric and literalized characterization of her as something of a pioneer. She was cast in the image of a pioneer not only because of her gender and trail-blazing manner, but also because of the folksy appeal of her rhetoric.

The news media attempted in vain to contain the power of Richards's pioneer image by portraying her in more traditional ways, as a puppet and beauty queen. To compete in Texas political culture, any candidate must hold her own ground and come out fighting. In fact, Richards participated in one of the most negative campaigns in Texas history that reinforced her pioneering spirit with images of an unruly woman, marked by her boisterous laughter and other excesses: her joking, storytelling, quips, high visibility, and general refusal to be contained by traditional gender roles. She drew attention to those very gender stereotypes, sometimes productively and sometimes in ways that reinscribed them.

This chapter considers the rhetorical challenges that Richards negotiated as candidate and governor in the state of Texas.[1] Ultimately she redefined leadership through the power of visibility, capitalizing on the rhetorical resources of the unruly woman metaphor. As the architect of the new Texas, Richards was an active transitional figure between the old and new Texas. Her vision of a new Texas, with its doors opened to all, was an everpresent source of political tension to which she responded with the language of cooperation as her main form of rhetorical leadership toward achieving more inclusive politics. In this way, Richards continued to narrow the gap between perceptions of women and political leadership, transcending the old and new Texas, but she also reinscribed some of those same gendered expectations, contributing in part to her reelection defeat in 1994 to George W. Bush.

The Lone Star Mystique

The first rhetorical challenge that Richards met head-on was the gendered nature of Texas political culture. As Elizabeth Fox-Genovese explains, Texas is not an easy place to characterize. The state's history and culture are extraordinarily complex, "with its multiple nationalities . . . farming, ranching, and urbanizing sectors, its religious and cultural diversity, and its indomitable sense of its own destiny and power."[2] Yet, a story finds its way into any discussion of Texas politics, one that metaphorically retains and perpetuates what some call the "Lone Star mystique," defining what it means to be Texan in masculine (Anglo) terms highlighting the frontier experience.[3] Ann Richards opened her 1993 remarks to Sweet Briar College with the following observation: "Someone asked me to begin by giving you some insight into 'the unique nature of the Texas political environment.' Well, let me put it this way. I come from a short line of women governors."[4] Similarly in 1994 to the Conference on Women's History, she noted "that the history of Texas is the history of things men do outdoors."[5] Even though some people might disagree, "the truth is that Texans don't mind having a reputation as a state where men are men and women are governor. Nor do we mind being thought of as the native habitat of the good ol' boy. And you all know what I'm talking about."[6] Governor Richards was no exception when it came to perpetuating the mythos of the Texas frontier experience. It was one of the many ways she used the resources at her disposal to create identification with her audience.

This mythos is in direct contrast to the powers of the Texas governor who actually shares executive power with five other office holders elected independently of the governor: the lieutenant governor, attorney general, comptroller, treasurer, and commissioner of the general land office. The power of the governor's office is weak compared to other states, but weak is not the image of Texas politicians to whom Richards often pays homage. In her speech before Executive State Agency Heads early in her term, Richards remarked that "these strong, handsome buildings are named for Texas heroes . . . for men who . . . gave their lives to the people of Texas. Inside this building and its neighbors, the people's work is being done. . . . That work must be as strong and durable as 'Texas sunset red' granite; the men and women doing the work must be as selfless and trustworthy as our Texas heroes."[7] Richards more specifically paid tribute to Sam Houston in remarks at Sam Houston State University. She compared Houston to George Washington and recalled "a man of conscience and courage . . . the man who signed himself 'I am Houston' . . . the man who his Cherokee brothers and sisters called the Raven and Big Drink . . . who the Mexicans called General Goddamn . . . who the historians called the Great Designer and the Sword of San Jacinto. Today, we recall him by the name he loved best. Texan. And proud of it."[8] Rhetorically Richards reinforced the power of the Lone Star mystique as represented by its leaders and by extension her inclusion in that group.

As a result, a "larger-than-life" image of Texas politicians was perpetuated, and this image clearly applied to Richards during her campaign for governor. In the words of David Maraniss discussing the 1990 Texas gubernatorial campaign, "Everything American is here, yet it is all somehow enlarged and distorted. Texas doesn't invent things, it transforms them: cliché into reality and reality into myth. Which brings us to the 1990 campaign for governor between Republican Clayton Wheat Williams Jr. and Democrat Dorothy Ann Richards. All distorted. All American. All true. All myth."[9]

This mythical edge worked to frame the Richards-Williams campaign. The following news analysis was typical:

> The Old West may be gone but it's not forgotten in the Texas governor's race, where Clayton Williams, the Republican nominee, is casting himself as John Wayne. From his white ten-gallon hat down to his polished boots, this West Texas entrepreneur is intent on convincing voters that he can gun down the state's problems the way the legendary actor gunned down the bad guys. Though no popcorn is served, the drama is playing on small screens statewide via television advertisements. Williams talks tough and, literally, rides a horse. So far, his campaign show seems to be a hit. State Treasurer Ann Richards, an elegant scrapper familiar to national audiences . . . is struggling to rewrite the script before Williams rides off into the governor's mansion. . . . More than usual is riding on this Texas showdown.[10]

The race was a drama that could be viewed on television, much like a John Wayne movie, and was generating a potential showdown of mythical proportions that underscored the masculine edge of Texas politics.

Larger-than-life language worked to characterize Texas political campaigns, not simply thought of as "races" between candidates. The guiding metaphors more clearly reflected the rowdy image of Texas politicians. Even as early as 1987, speculations were mounting regarding Richards "cross[ing] paths" with

Attorney General Jim Mattox and their "potential head-on battle for the Democratic nomination."[11] But the campaign wasn't going to be easy, especially for a woman. As Billy Porterfield asked, "How can Ann Richards prevail against two tough, hard-eyed hombres? Not by duking it out with them, that's for sure. The woman has a hard row to hoe."[12]

Gender issues complicated media discussions of the campaign, which began to feature both gender and the rowdy nature of politics in Texas. As the *Austin American-Statesman* headline aptly claimed, "Gender Issue Cutting in on Williams-Richards Political Dance."[13] The *Texas Monthly* cover of October 1990 capitalized on the "dance" metaphor, complete with a computer-generated cover of Williams and Richards doing the tango. Next to the picture appeared the caption "Dirty Dancing. Stepping Out with Ann and Claytie as They Stomp Across Texas—and Each Other."[14] Similarly, in noting the negative tone of the campaign, the *Austin American-Statesman* explained that Richards "danced to Williams' tune during the summer, responding to attacks."[15] Richards was characterized not as taking the lead, but rather as following Williams's lead, allowing him to determine the steps. Ultimately the race became characterized as a "battle of the sexes."[16] "Before Ann Richards and Clayton Williams began their gubernatorial slugfest," noted the *Houston Chronicle*, "men and women in this state were fairly harmonious in their political views. While they're not warring yet, the classic standoff between a good-ol'-boy Republican and a good-ol'-gal Democrat is highlighting differences between the sexes."[17]

Richards did little to shed her fighting image during the primary or the final leg of the campaign. The *New York Times* reported that Richards "was prepared for a negative fight if Mr. Williams began one and would respond in kind, just as she did in the Democratic primary."[18] According to Richards, "The reality is that you can't fight fire with anything but a back fire because it just takes one candidate in a race to begin it."[19] Richards even called her campaign "rowdy" and "rough-and-tumble," noting in the *Austin American-Statesman* that "politics is a contact sport. . . . It's not for the weak or lily-livered."[20] As a result, the campaign became a "dogfight," a "battle. . . . one of the longest and meanest political contests in the state's history," and "fighting a war on horseback."[21] One headline read, "Williams, Richards playing 'chicken'";[22] another read, "Williams, Richards fuss over newest negative ad."[23] Richards and Williams had to "duke it out," "spar," and engage in "mudslinging" in a "raucous," "dirty campaign" of "cow-patty-tossing-style politics."[24]

When it was all over, Richards didn't just win, but one headline declared, "She Whups Him!"[25] In summing up the campaign, the *Houston Chronicle* explained, "All Ann Richards had to do to make it to the Governor's Mansion was defeat a former governor and one of the toughest bare-knuckled brawlers in Texas political history in the democratic primary and then beat a near-instant folk hero in the general election."[26] Even a magazine traditionally marketed to female audiences was not exempt from masculine fighting metaphors as early on as the primary. According to *Vogue*, "It was down and dirty from day one. Rich-

Rowdy Good ol Gal while Fighting for office [handwritten annotation]

ards crippled White with a series of brilliantly misleading ads. . . . Then she got her bell rung by Mattox. . . . They slugged it out."[27] Newspaper stories were equally as "battle-focused." According to the *San Diego Union Tribune*, Richards "gave as good as she got during slash-and-burn primary and gubernatorial races in which all participants displayed such impressive capacity for vitriol, innuendo and attack advertising that they attracted national attention."[28]

Running for political office in Texas is "a brutal marathon, a street fight with no time-outs, no rules," a "nasty brawl."[29] As *Vogue* noted, "Texas politicians are expected to be able to defend themselves. Nobody gets to be governor or senator who doesn't have a pretty thick skin, Olympian stamina, and lots of money."[30] This was quite a struggle for an office with "few powers other than those of appointment and persuasion, [but] Richards . . . doesn't buy those constraints on her power."[31] As the governor told the *Fort Worth Star Telegram*, it "has to do with the personality and drive of the person of the chair."[32] Richards certainly had the personality and drive in a race that became a battle of personalities. In another article, the *Fort Worth Star Telegram* called it "Texas's larger-than-life race for governor" and "a battle of personalities. Depending on your preference, it was Claytie vs. the Lady or Ann and the Man."[33] Outside Texas it became not just a battle of personalities, but a battle of "symbols—the rugged cowboy and the spunky lady duking it out. This, after all, is Texas, where politics is blood sport, where down-and-dirty tactics are a tradition."[34]

The fact that the election was characterized as a battle is not necessarily news. However, Richards winning the "down-and-dirty" battle as a woman is significant. She prevailed in the tough election, notably one of the nastiest in the state's history. She successfully used the resources of the rowdy political culture to her advantage when taking on her opponents. She was a good ol' gal who came out fighting just as the culture required. But once in office, Richards had to rely on other facets of the political culture.

Storytelling on the Political Trail

In Texas the most effective governors have enacted power implicitly and leadership strategically through the power of the story and Richards certainly had an arsenal of stories at her disposal. Storytelling performed the important function for Richards of building relationships in a state where "political participation is viewed as a series of personal relationships" and the party is the place where these relationships are formed.[35] Some would call this the "good ol' boy" network. Yet, during the 1980s the Democratic Party could no longer guarantee success for a Democrat, much less a liberal Democrat, and especially a female liberal Democrat like Ann Richards.[36] Her progressive tendencies put her at odds with more conservative Texans, yet her populist appeals and stories endeared her to them.

Beverly Stoeltje argues that what identifies someone as a Texan is "the ability to tell a story, respond to, and understand a story."[37] Such a skill is learned informally through social interactions in traditional settings. It requires that the storyteller not just speak or listen appropriately, but also the ability "to judge what stories to pass on and to whom, to assess what constitutes a valid subject for a story, and to interpret the message of the whole act of storytelling."[38] Richards is a keen storyteller. Suzanne Coleman, the governor's speech writer, explained to *Texas Monthly* that "Nobody is a better judge of an audience than Ann Richards."[39] "Unlike Williams, whose road managers delight in reeling off his next line before he does, Richards tailors her speeches to the audience. . . . At each speech, it is as if she flicks a switch and the words come out just so."[40]

Richards credits her father with her storytelling ability.[41] Cecil Willis was a bawdy "raconteur in the grand old Texas domino-parlor tradition, a man who can still spin a yarn for five or ten minutes with exquisite timing and a half-dozen accents, hitting his punch line with the lazy cunning of a vaudeville pro."[42] As Willis told *Vogue*, "I was a salesman, you know, so I'd pick up a few every day and bring 'em home, tell 'em to Dorothy Ann. Before long, she'd start bringin' 'em home from school. So we'd swap. I'd give her a couple to take back to school, and she'd give me some to go to work with."[43] It wasn't long until "Dorothy Ann" learned that "'people liked you if you told stories, if you made them laugh.' Her parents were always urging her to 'tell the one about' . . . an injunction she has followed ever since."[44]

Storytelling has an identity-defining and community-building function, identifying the teller as a part of the group and validating the nature of the community at large, in this case as a Texan validating the Lone Star mystique. The centrality of the story to everyday interactions "contributes considerably to the mystique of Texas and serves to distinguish the insiders from the outsiders."[45] Richards was powerful in her storytelling ability to establish identification with an audience. For example, she told a story of the "old boy" driving in the country who heard the "god-awful commotion" of hogs. It seemed the local farmer lost his voice and the only way he could call his hogs was by beating on the fence. The farmer's voice got better, but "the dang woodpeckers are drivin' [those hogs] crazy." As Richards explained, "There are a lot of Texans who can identify with those crazy hogs."[46] We "are so starved for good news" about the economy that we'll listen to "any bird" out there.

And then there's the story about the freezing bird she told many times, but for particular effect to the Cattle Ranchers Association. As the story goes, someone walked by and covered the freezing bird in cow chips. The bird finally warmed up and started singing. But when the bird started singing someone heard and uncovered it and the bird froze to death. There were three morals to the bird story: "One: It isn't necessarily your enemies who put you in it. Two: It isn't necessarily your friends who get you out. And, three: When you're in it up to here, for God's sake, don't sing."[47] That was one of Richards's favorite stories and one that "anyone in public office can identify with . . . especially in the

Pioneer (Texas?)

middle of legislative session—which is definitely 'in it.' And I know that anyone in the cattle industry identifies. . . . No one would blame us if most of the
time we weren't sure whether to hunker down and wait it out or holler as loud as
we could. And of course, as governor, I'm paid to holler."[48]

Not only did Richards holler, but she spun a yarn with the best of any Texas
storyteller and in the process validated what it meant to be a Texan. Harry Ransom explained that the "Spirit of Texas" is often contradictory and unpredict-
able: Texans' "bifocal attention to what is behind and what is ahead accounts for
much of the vitality and most of the contradictions in Texas."[49] Yet the contradictions have a way of rapidly unifying the people "as Texans" with a particular
spirit that is unmatched.[50]

Richards often recaptured that Texas spirit in her own stories immortalizing
the myth of Texas's past even as she hoped to build a "new Texas" of the future.
This was really the hallmark and challenge of Richards's rhetoric. Just as Ransom discussed the contradictions that are the "Spirit of Texas," Richards was
clearly a woman of contradictions. On the one hand she embraced the populist
frontier image of Texas's past; on the other she hoped to move that past forward.

When Richards declared her administration progressive, she meant "progressive in the proud tradition of Sam Houston." In that tradition she spoke often
of "building a New Texas" together, one "worthy of the people's trust," "open,"
"fair and equitable and stable," "safer and more secure."[51] She emphasized that a
progressive outlook was required in government rather than just responding to
problems, for "as many a Texas armadillo has learned, that's too late to leap."[52]
However, her progressive new Texas always had one foot in the traditional
Texas of Sam Houston so as not to alienate the portion of her audience who
identified with a pioneer heritage. Progressive in that sense relied on paradox.
When describing the new Texas, Richards's active language included archetypal
metaphoric vehicles such as "light" and "open," signaling her forward approach,
as well as construction metaphors to emphasize the building of the future on the
foundation of the past.

Nearly two years after taking office, Richards's admirers gave her positive
marks for her progressive administration. According to delegates interviewed
during the 1992 Democratic convention, Richards was "a powerful woman in a
state regarded by much of the country as controlled entirely by men, . . . [a
woman who] brought progressive leadership to a conservative state."[53] Richards
was well on her way to moving Texas forward and her stories were one resource
that served her political goals well.

Pioneering New Ground in Texas

As Richards negotiated Texas political culture she represented herself
metaphorically and literally as a Texas pioneer. The pioneer can be a metaphor
that works to contain woman governors. Even though they are the "first," their

ability to lead is suspect until they are able to prove themselves. In Richards's case, the image worked to her advantage as a storyteller advancing populist and progressive appeals to move Texas forward for the people and simultaneously validate its pioneer past. Her "folksy charm and down-home humor" showed she was not afraid to "roll up her sleeves" and work with all citizens.

Richards was certainly a pioneer in the sense that she was the first woman elected Texas governor "in her own right." To make this point, Richards was sometimes compared with Texas's other woman governor, Miriam Ferguson, noting that Richards was "the first woman to be elected to the post in her own right. Ferguson openly served as a proxy for her husband."[54] The *Houston Chronicle* noted that "Richards became the state's second woman governor and the first to win the chief executive officer's job in her own right, without a husband who had previously held the office."[55] In winning the office "in her own right," Richards "blazed her own trail to the mansion," "forged a path for women," and "marched into office."[56] In assessing her term in office during her reelection bid, she was hailed as "the pioneer of modern women in statewide politics. But this year the door she kicked open has swung wide."[57] That was because "Richards appointed more women and minorities to state agencies . . . than any other governor," earning her the label "precedent-setting."[58] Richards as pioneer was portrayed as clearing new ground, in the image of pioneers during the country's westward expansion.

In 1991 Richards was chosen as one of *Glamour* magazine's "Women of the Year" for her pioneering work as a woman political figure. According to former Vermont governor Madeleine Kunin, a member of the nomination committee, in the *Dallas Morning News*, "She is just one of the role models for women in politics. . . . There are not too many members of that club—yet."[59] Carol Bellamy, also on the committee, explained in the same article, "This year shows Ann Richards is not just a pretty picture. . . . This isn't just somebody who gives a good speech—this is a person who leads."[60]

Ann Richards as governor was a complex web of populism and progressivism, allowing her to court the frontier myth as well as a progressive new Texas as she negotiated Texas political culture. Trying to undermine that complexity, some media descriptions attempted to contain Richards in more traditional ways, using metaphors that limited women governors before her. However, Richards's performance was not one that could be controlled easily. Rather than allowing herself to be merely defined by such metaphors, she engaged them actively and redirected their focus in empowering ways.

Containing Ann Richards's Image

Ann Richards did not easily conform to stereotypes. She felt that fitting the stereotypes would cause her to lose her "verve" for politics.[61] Media representations, the criticism of opponents, and her own colorful comments created a complex image of a tough campaigner and governor who was not afraid of battle. However, the puppet and beauty queen imagery used by the media and her critics attempted to contain her in ways that women executives often encounter. While the puppet imagery simply did not account for Richards's public persona—she was no passive executive—the beauty queen image further complicated Richards's status, especially as she relished herself as a grandmother and a very public public figure.

Let Someone Else Pull the Strings? Not Governor Richards

One often-used metaphor to contain women executives is the image of the puppet. Here women executives are contained as passive objects to be used by men generally, their husbands specifically, and/or their political parties. Puppet executives do not lead, but follow, unable to make decisions on their own.

Attempts were made to contain Richards as a puppet in two ways. First, she did not win her election. Instead, her opponent lost. Even in the Democratic primary, Richards simply "picked up a sympathy vote."[62] Once the primary was over, she was characterized as not having any ability to affect the outcome of the election. Brian Eppstein, a Republican with the Eppstein Group, blamed Williams for losing his lead. "Ann Richards has not done anything extraordinary. All she's done is avoid blunders . . . so it is up to the error-prone Williams to win or lose the race."[63] Outgoing governor Bill Clements put it succinctly, "She didn't win the election, Clayton lost it."[64] These images attempted to frame Richards as ineffectual and passive, as someone who did not play an active role in her campaign, whereas her male rival was the one calling the shots.

Second, once in office Richards's critics attempted to characterize her leadership as "hidden," passive, and absent, rather than directive and decision making. For example, "Her detractors say the new governor has hidden from the state's problems."[65] According to Tom Craddick, a state Representative and chair of the House Republican Caucus, Richards was "AWOL—Absent Without Leadership."[66] Each of these comments suggested leadership required being seen. According to James Leonard, the chair of a Republican group, "We can't afford a governor who rolls over and plays dead."[67] State Republican chairman Fred Meyer, one of Richards's staunchest critics, asserted that Richards was "a master politician" who "has avoided decisions everyplace she could."[68]

Ann Richards was in fact no puppet governor, metaphorically or literally. The criticism was an easy one to place on a woman in masculine-motivated political life, but it was not believable enough to contain Ann Richards. Whether she won or Williams lost did not explain her active, visible leadership once in office. In fact, Richards was a master of political visibility. Thus, her critics' attempt to undermine her leadership with traditional metaphoric characterizations that have contained women governors in the past simply did not extend to the active Governor Richards.

There She Is . . . Richards as Beauty Queen

While there was no way a sassy brawler from Texas could be contained metaphorically as passive, another traditional outlet for characterizations of women governors is the metaphor of the beauty queen. The beauty queen cluster brings together imagery of the traditional woman. She is a caretaker (mother, grandmother, wife) and hostess, a winner of popularity contests, who focuses on appearance over everything else. She is active in public life, but only within certain boundaries, and she reinforces the myth that to be valued, a woman must be beautiful. Further, beauty and leadership are constructed as mutually exclusive. The beauty queen is comfortable with home and family, caring for children, reinforcing the rhetorical separation between the public and private spheres. However, Richards's image as beauty queen was more complex than such characterizations of previous women governors, for Richards prided herself on being a caretaker and homemaker before she entered public office and she was frequently seen with her granddaughter Lilly. In addition, she realized there are rhetorical advantages to be gained by plying your opponents with flowers or cookies. As *Texas Monthly* noted, "In Richards's hands, cookies were proof of self-assurance."[69]

The beauty queen's metaphorical focus is on appearance, and the media were all too interested in Richards's clothing and personal appearance above everything else. In discussing her first day on the job, the *Houston Post* highlighted what Richards chose to wear after she "got out of bed Wednesday as the newly elected governor of Texas . . . a hot pink suit, a pink and blue silk scarf and brown leather shoes—Richards set off to prove that she has the courage to push for changes in state government and the wisdom to lead Texas one day at a time."[70] As the preparations began for Richards's inaugural, discussion was mounting about her appearance. "Ann Richards may shorten her signature bouffant hairdo, her feet will be properly attired, and she won't be carrying weapons at her inauguration less than a month away. Instead, Richards will arm herself with a suit and coat made of Texas mohair and designed by a fashion professor from Texas Women's University in Denton."[71] On inauguration day, "Dressed in a white mohair two-piece suit, Richards said she envisions a Texas free from racism or sexism."[72] Her attire took precedence over her message.

Richards's hair had a life of its own and was the subject of many articles. The *Houston Post* thought it important to report on inauguration day that "strong winds buffeted the platform, rippling flags and, at their peak, causing Richards's now-famous bouffant hairdo to quiver slightly."[73] Not to be outdone, the *Fort Worth Star Telegram* reported: "Wearing a yellow ribbon in remembrance of U.S. troops, Richards briskly walked the 13 blocks to the Capitol, flanked by her family. A stiff north wind didn't rustle her trademark white helmet of hair."[74]

The governor's hairstyle was so newsworthy that reports of a potential change were much cause for concern. The *Austin American-Statesman* began an article on the potential change: "Her stiff, stark white bouffant has stood up against the strongest of political and other winds, but Gov. Ann Richards's gravity-defying hairdo soon may fall to the winds of change."[75] Suggesting the governor might change her hairstyle on a whim implied that she was easily swayed on other issues as well. However, the *Dallas Morning News* approached the story as a potential make-over session for the governor, offering pictures and suggestions by readers.[76] Even late night television host David Letterman got into the act, joking that Richards's hair "reminded him of a café waitress." "Ah, I love it, the Dairy Queen Lady," Richards replied.[77]

With this reply, Richards continued to add a layer of complexity to her beauty queen imagery. Even before her election she espoused the Texas tradition "when there is a mess, a woman has to clean it up."[78] Richards was proud of the fact that she was a homemaker before entering public life and that she was a mother and grandmother *and* governor. Yet the media characterizations of Richards in her traditionally feminine roles attempted to devalue her gubernatorial accomplishments. For example, the *Houston Post* reported that "Texans handed the governor's office to . . . the homemaker-turned-politician."[79] Similarly, the *Austin American-Statesman* reported that the first woman to win the governor's post "in her own right" "might have described herself as a housewife" only fourteen years ago. "Now, at age 57, the white-haired grandmother will become the second woman governor in Texas history."[80] She wasn't described as a leader, but as a housewife and white-haired grandmother, terms that suggest Richards cannot be a serious governor or that she made the decision lightly to enter public life.

Furthermore, the terms metaphorically question her fitness for the job both because of gender and because of age. How could a "white-haired grandmother" possibly be up to the challenges of the Texas governorship? This same theme emerged when Richards's record on necessarily "tough" issues such as crime was discussed. During the campaign "Richards's opponents alluded that she might be soft on crime—like Texas's first woman governor, Miriam 'Ma' Ferguson, who granted pardons liberally."[81] In discussing her reelection possibility, the *Austin American-Statesman* wondered "has the 60-year-old grandmother been tough enough on crime?"[82] Karen Hughes, Texas Republican Party executive director, explained, "She's a tough-talking governor, but she has not been a tough-acting governor."[83] However, the prison system actually doubled in size during Richards's tenure and the crime rate dropped by 25 percent.[84] The criticism is simply an easy one to place on a "white-haired grandmother."

Significantly, Richards choreographed some of this beauty queen imagery. For example, signaling the fact that a woman was in charge of the governor's mansion, she planned "a slumber party" that was "rumored to be at the governor's mansion for about 30 female legislators. Such are the changes sweeping the capital, as Texas's white-male 'cowboy capitalism' yields to the crusading zeal of Richards's 'good-old-girl network.'"[85] A slumber party of "good-old-girls" was most likely not the stereotypical giggly, giddy teenage event. Furthermore, at a media party to celebrate the governor's first year in office, Richards skillfully worked her image. As the *Houston Press* reported: "The door swung open and there was the guv, all pink and white and pearly, surrounded by a pack of adoring youngsters, including granddaughter Lilly."[86] This party "had Ann's own folksy imprint in the form of kids, kids and more kids. They are Richards's natural constituency, as the guv demonstrated to perfection, resplendent in her beehive do, satin blouse and billowy pajama pants."[87] Richards seemed "like a pied piper" not a politician. "Although not a totally uncalculated performance, the Richards's kiddy charisma still charmed the normally cynical-to-the-bone bunch of media hounds."[88] Even though there was the focused discussion of Richards's appearance at such a party, there was also the sense that Richards directed the attention strategically. Her focus was not just her feminine or pretty appearance, but the "calculated" construction of an image, carefully drawing attention not only to the children, but her pink, pearly, and satiny attire.

Such rhetorical adeptness was not lost on Richards the hostess either. The Texas Summit, a meeting between the leaders of the U.S. and Mexico that Richards "engineered," was simultaneously constructed as a "party." The *New York Times* reported that "Ann Richards is wearing the sharp and satisfied smile of a woman who knows her party is going well. . . . The glass-eyed swarm of cameras, the army of reporters bear witness to Richards's coup: She has engineered an unprecedented preinaugural meeting between the two leaders, deftly framing it as the introduction of her 'two good friends.'"[89] Such an event would be chalked up to Richards's party-planning ability rather than her executive skill: "With just five days to plan, the Governor has managed to stamp the occasion with vintage Richards imagery. Den-mother Ann shepherded Clinton and Salinas upstairs to her creamy, informal private living room (soon to be celebrated in *HG*) and left them to deliberate over a plate of homemade chocolate chip cookies."[90] Here was a grandmother who kept her beautiful house in order and was never far from a plate of cookies. But for Richards, the cookies were a negotiation tool. Practicing the art of the hostess was an executive skill.

Often Richards used social style to her advantage. The *Chicago Tribune* reported on Richards's "subtle" style through which "she plied a reluctant committee chairman, for instance, with a bouquet of flowers and a batch of blueberry muffins to persuade him to schedule a hearing on the lottery bill."[91] Similarly, *Time* explained that Richards knew how to "court the legislature." She "wooed the lawmakers, inviting them to breakfasts and lunches at the Governor's Greek-revival mansion. She talked state representative Pete Laney into releasing a lottery bill from his committee on state affairs by plying him with bagels and doughnuts."[92] Hostess Richards knew how to "use the prestige of her office."[93] Legislators coveted an invitation to the governor's mansion for lunch, but Richards didn't get caught up in ceremony. She was "as likely to serve cornbread or coffee herself" as to have someone else do it. When Hillary Clinton responded to questions about her legal career by saying "'I suppose I could have stayed home and baked cookies and had teas,' Richards met with statewide editorial writers in her office. As she personally poured the coffee and served the fresh-baked cookies, the comparison between her and Hillary Clinton was stark: In Richards's hands, cookies were proof of self-assurance."[94]

As a woman executive, Richards was characterized as popular, attractive, well spoken, concerned and compassionate. "Letter writers ask her for advice and sometimes even for recipes. Recovering alcohol and drug abusers thank her for her example."[95] She reminded children of their grandmothers. "Little girls see Richards as a role model, and she always tells them to study hard in math. Sometimes those girls send her copies of their report cards to show that they've listened to what she said."[96] And Richards could not resist an opportunity for mothering. According to *USA Today*, "Running unexpectedly into a prisoner while touring a jail wing . . . Richards just couldn't resist pulling the man into the camera's glare with her and giving him a grandmotherly talking-to."[97]

Richards regularly attends "Lady Longhorn basketball games. She still pays $20 to get her hair washed and set twice a week. And she doesn't mind showing she's a fond grandmother."[98] However, she did not completely fit the beauty queen metaphor. While she certainly played on her status as mother and grandmother, and the press enjoyed discussing her attire and "Dairy Queen" hair, the discussion did not contain Richards. In fact, she often drew attention to it, not content to be the subject of others' gaze and not conforming to the traditional expectations of the beauty queen's focus on appearance and family structure. After all, Richards was divorced.

Richards competently and strategically used the resources of the beauty queen metaphor to assert power in a weak governorship. Her example is instructive in performing executive leadership visibly while calling attention to traditionally feminine attributes in empowering ways. In other words, her ability to be seen carefully directing her political identity construction is the key to her performance.

Engaging Executive Authority as the Unruly Woman

Richards's very public construction of her political identity suggests she knew the value of her "unruliness." While the unruly woman is a metaphor used to contain women executives because of their transgressive behavior, the image of the unruly woman can be an empowering one. Kathleen Rowe explains that the unruly woman is all the extremes, "too fat, too funny, too noisy, too old, too rebellious"; she "unsettles social hierarchies" and "crosses the boundaries of a variety of social practices."[99] In particular she realizes the power of visibility, dominates men, and is a transitional figure. Most often she creates a spectacle of herself in an effort to assert her own power and identity. Thus, the difference between empowerment and containment depends on how the unruly image is appropriated: positively toward abundance and redefinition or negatively toward

loss of control and transgression. It depends upon who is in control of the performance.

Just like the unruly woman, Richards was clearly a "rule-breaker,
joke-maker, and public, bodily spectacle." She realized the importance of "being
seen," for visibility is power. While she is not fat, she is a recovering alcoholic,
noting her penchant for excess, and she has big hair. In an effort to assess Ann
Richards as an unruly persona, the following questions framed this portion of
analysis. How did Richards fashion a spectacle of herself? How did she "affect
the terms on which she is seen"? How did she indicate "new ways of thinking
about visibility as power"?[100] Yet, did the main criticism of Richards—that she
was all image, all style, all charisma and personality, without substance—
contain her as a spectacle rather than allow her to redefine herself as governor of
Texas? The answers to these questions provided evidence as to whether Richards was contained metaphorically, just as other women governors before her, or
whether she was able to make an unruly spectacle of herself and thus make a
difference by "widening the 'behavioral options' for women."[101]

The White Hot Mama: Richards as Spectacle

Richards was not content to allow her governorship to maintain business as
usual, making it clear that things were going to be different in her administration. The *Dallas Morning News* noted that Richards's first one hundred days
broke all the rules as she "stamped her own image on the office of governor."[102]
She "broke [with] tradition" by "aggressively" appointing women and minorities
to state posts, stopping the development of new hazardous waste dumps, enacting one of the "toughest oil spill cleanup laws," and threatening the insurance
board with take-over if Clements's appointees did not resign.[103] In true Richards's style she jumped right into her job.

While her aggressive and threatening tactics marked her as out of bounds
for her gender, this behavior earned her praise. *Texas Monthly* explained that she
had "reformer appeal."[104] According to Bob Squier, a Democratic political consultant quoted in *Texas Monthly*, "Ann Richards is the metaphor for change that
people are asking for."[105] A *Vogue* article called her the "titan" of Texas and
"maverick" without a sense of transgression, only admiration for calling attention to and breaking gender boundaries.[106] She was one of many strong and
powerful Texas women. As Squier asserted, clearly "this is a woman who knows
no limits."[107]

Richards was not contained by gender stereotypes forbidding women to
draw attention to themselves through their speech or laughter, the mark of the
unruly woman. As Rowe explains, "When women make jokes about men, they
invert—momentarily—the social hierarchy."[108] Men were often the targets of
Richards's barbed tongue, from New York Governor Mario Cuomo to the Texas
legislature. For example, after watching the 1993 Super Bowl with Mario

Cuomo, Richards proudly admitted, "I was not gracious at all. I was terrible."[109] According to a male business lobbyist interviewed in *Texas Monthly*, "She can play hardball with the best of 'em."[110] The lobbyist then described a legislative session in which Richards asked the legislators if they were going to "kill" a bill. The legislators said of course they weren't, but Richards told them to get out if they weren't going to help write the bill. If they stayed she would become their enemy. They left.[111] Molly Ivins wrote that Richards "is no pushover. She is . . . 'tougher than a two-dollar steak.' Richards seems to have a way of forcing male challengers to lose their cool."[112]

Governor Richards's most notable act of dominance was announced during her first State of the State address. The *Fort Worth Star Telegram* reported a "heavyweight fight" when the governor demanded that two State Board of Insurance members resign. "Richards backed up the demand with an unprecedented threat to place the board in state conservatoryship."[113] The "verbal fisticuffs" were reported statewide, called a "stinging attack," "a shake-up," and "opening fire."[114]

Richards's most frequent male targets were the "Bubbas" of Texas. The governor explained to the *Dallas Morning News* that "Bubba comes out of his trailer, and he cleans his gun before heading off to the service station on the highway."[115] Significantly, Richards's storytelling allowed her to spoof Bubba without alienating him. According to the *Austin American-Statesman*, Richards's stories, "particularly when spoofing hunting and all things male," set her apart. "A hunter herself, Richards disarms Bubbas with pointed humor about their follies, only thinly veiling a feminist message."[116] Richards made fun of Bubba and considered herself "a sort of quintessential female Bubba."[117] When asked if she was "Bubba in drag," Richards responded "I hope so."[118] Problematically Richards was asserting power over a group while also considering herself a part of that group.

It was not unusual for Richards's humor to be considered transgressive by some. For example, during the 1990 race for governor, Richards's campaign advisors persuaded her to emphasize her grandmotherly side, "after some critics said her 1988 Democratic Convention speech evoked an image of a strident, wisecracking woman."[119] Here Richards the unruly joke-maker was considered too extreme and required to soften her image. The image of grandmother, however, was one that Richards proudly wore privately and publicly. It was not simply for show.

Richards was also praised for her unruly 1988 Democratic Convention Keynote address, providing a balance to the above criticisms. The *Austin American-Statesman* called her "acidly funny and substantive" while the *San Antonio Light* called the address "a study in comic vitriol and flawless timing."[120] Even the *Boston Globe* found it "boffo . . . requir[ing] her to be sassy but not un-ladylike, resolute but not doctrinaire, humorous but not malicious."[121]

There was nothing quiet or passive about Richards as she was known for her spectacle; it became part of her image. She was described as "outspoken" and "the speechmaker."[122] She had a way of mesmerizing a crowd with her "oratorical gifts": "the astringent wit and crowd-pleasing put-down artistry so useful in flaying the Republicans; the coloratura instrument that is her voice; her evocative feel for imagery; the superb timing so integral to her style."[123] These talents have always been among her "arsenal," being recognized even before her 1988 keynote address as "one of the funniest and most in-demand public speakers in the state."[124]

However, Richards had a tendency to come across as brash, and this could backfire if she was seen as devaluing women's traditional roles. According to *Keys to the Governor's Office*, voters think of female Democratic political figures as women first, then Democrats.[125] Thus, it is important to identify with those traditional women's roles, as Richards often did as a grandmother and hostess. However, two examples are problematic. First, when telling a group of Democratic party leaders about a visit she had with the outgoing governor and his wife, according to *USA Today*, Richards told Rita Clements, "What I need to do is go hire some wife."[126] Second, when asked by the *Houston Chronicle* what she hoped her legacy would be as governor, Governor Richards responded, "How about, She changed the economic future of Texas," which "really beats what I feared my tombstone was going to say, and that was, She kept a really clean house."[127] Richards's responses, while noting the progress that she and other women have made in public life, also devalued women's traditional roles and reinforced the dichotomy between the masculine political sphere and the feminine household sphere. While her performance of the unruly woman clearly drew attention to gender roles, it is not clear from these examples that Richards offered in her remarks a metaphoric revision of those roles.

At times, Richards was aware of the unruliness of her humor, commenting that "I can't make jokes because y'all put it in the paper, and then it's not funny anymore."[128] Even though she had an "ability to tell it like it is," according to National Democratic Chairman Paul Kirk, Ed Martin, the state Democratic Party Director called Richards "one of the best good ol' boys we've got in Texas."[129] Sometimes Richards's humor was more harmful than helpful. Molly Ivins explained, "Being a funny woman, it makes people uneasy. . . . I know some older women who think Ann isn't sufficiently a lady. Well, she's not. She's a good ole boy that's a female."[130]

Richards's barbs account for characterizations of her reelection race against George W. Bush as "the Bush-Richards gender battle" and "warfare."[131] Maintaining the Old West theme of her previous election, the *Sacramento Bee* called the race "the shootout between Queen Ann and Prince George."[132] Even though their titles suggested this would not be the down-and-dirty fight of the previous election, the *Sacramento Bee* continued to explain that "the governor has dispensed with courtesy this time around. She is flaying Bush with the razor-edged tongue she previously used on his father."[133]

Not only did Richards draw attention to herself through her speech and laughter. She was also a bodily spectacle, an "identifiable presence"[134] that sometimes came across as excessive, manufactured, or simply a curiosity. Richards called herself "a 'two-headed cow,' a curiosity that corporate leaders allow through the door just so they can see her."[135] Curiosity or not, Richards "represent[ed] everything that is uniquely and stubbornly Texas, from her self-described 'Dairy Whip hairdo,' to the sparkly Lone Star pin that decorate[d] her shoulder."[136] The *Observer* explained that "Campaigning with Richards is like going to the theatre. She looks like an actress, with her dash of silver hair, her leathery complexion that tells all you need to know about her one-time partiality to booze and a painful divorce, and her expertly lipsticked mouth."[137]

One of Richards's most visible features, her hair, was credited with her appeal. Richards's hair came to symbolize "her political personality: solid, serious, stable, and reassuring, because it doesn't change with the times. . . . Her hairstyle—washed, curled, teased, and sprayed—is straight out of the fifties. . . . Her hair makes her a permanent member of the carhop generation, a throwback to small-town values."[138] Her sense of humor didn't hurt either. Thus, Richards's two most spectacle-defining characteristics, her hair and her laughter, endeared her to legislators and the public alike.

The "White Hot Mama" incident was the best example of Richards as bodily spectacle. Several media outlets reported: "Covered in black, including fringed leather gloves, Gov. Ann Richards mounted a pearly white motorcycle outside her Capitol office."[139] Steppenwolf's "Born to be Wild" was playing in the background. All because Richards was heard to say that she would like to ride a Harley on her sixtieth birthday. She even made the cover of *Texas Monthly* in July 1992 wearing white fringed motorcycle leathers pictured on a Harley Davidson with the caption "White Hot Mama." However, a model posed for the picture and then Richards's head was attached via computer. Richards authorized the photo but was in too high demand to find time for the photo shoot.

As a result of her spectacle of speech, laughter, and body, Richards became a "mega-celebrity" who brought "old-fashioned star power" to the Democratic Party.[140] The *Dallas Morning News* called her "one of the hottest properties in town" when discussing her chairing the 1992 Democratic convention.[141] According to Kathleen Rowe, "people become stars because their images play on—and magically resolve—ideological contradictions of their times."[142] The *Houston Chronicle* called Richards "everybody's hip grandmother: a shotgun-toting hunter, a Lone Star motorcycle mama, chair of the Democratic National Convention and a wisecracking chief saleswoman for Texas. . . . With her silver hair, business suits of cobalt blue and sassy homespun charm, Richards . . . is, according to polls, the most popular Texas governor in 30 years."[143] Richards's spectacle had achieved for her a star quality that transcended dichotomies.[144]

But as a celebrity, was she just a "performer"? The *New York Times* suggested that even though Richards controlled her performance, there was something ungenuine about it. "A born performer who deploys her bait-camp-lady drawl with the virtuosity of a Carnegie Hall soloist, Richards has never been shy about role playing to accomplish her ends."[145] John Sharp, the state controller, called Richards a "chameleon."[146] However, the article also suggested that "beneath the bonhomie, Richards's personal and political history have made her fiercely wary and, when need be, as tough as boiled owl."[147] As a spectacle, Richards was showy, but her performance was never just for show; there was always a measured calculation that allowed the unruly woman to maintain control.

The result was a skillfully orchestrated public image that took advantage of gender expectations as well as the realities of the weak office to produce a leader that was boisterous yet observant, demanding and caring, accessible and visible. While she sometimes went too far with her humorous cracks, especially when it came to some traditional roles of women, overall she was a spectacle who endeared herself to the people of Texas in a style all her own. She transformed the weak office by putting people in places where they could make changes, capitalizing on relationships, to move Texas forward economically. She knew that power had to come not by making policy, but by being seen.

The Unruly Woman Redefines Leadership in Texas

Richards was a study in contradictions. She was the governor of a state that required its politicians to be legendary, while maintaining power through a weak office. She appealed to the "Bubbas" just as she appealed to feminists. She was able to bring together so many unthinkable combinations and as a result was a highly successful transitional figure who brought the Texas frontier forward to the new Texas. The result was a reshaping of the terms that defined her and her leadership.

In her first year, Richards became a "chess player" rather "than a linebacker," displaying a "consistent public face," and "operat[ing] within the constraints of political reality."[148] She became an adept student of the workings of Texas politics, making "deals and compromises with other powerful politicians."[149] When she got tough, she picked her targets strategically. She was a rhetorical strategist who knew how to make her audience feel at ease. "She is at home stumping the vastness of the prairies, campaigning in towns so small they don't have a name, or serving hot corn bread to business lobbyists in the governor's mansion. . . . She is tough in a peculiarly Texan way, combining charm and intimidation."[150] The late Governor Connally said of Richards, "She's found the right combination for these times. She functions like an insider but talks like an outsider."[151]

Richards "portray[ed] herself as liberal on social issues and staunchly conservative on fiscal matters."[152] The *Austin American-Statesman* quoted the governor, saying "I think I'm tough. I think I'm a survivor. I think I'm a caring person, I think I'm a human being who's made a lot of mistakes and has had a lot of success. And I'm a mother and grandmother first."[153] Richards skillfully balanced the toughness of the Texas governorship with her image as a grandmother and neither was out of place.

In Richards's administration, the boundaries of leadership were expanded to include "teacher," "consensus builder," and "negotiator."[154] These terms didn't have a weak edge to them with Richards as governor. Managing the state and not necessarily making policy (which was more often what legislators meant by the term leadership) was how the governor approached her job. Her leadership style was not a front to hide the fact that she did not know policy. As the *New York Times* pointed out, "In conversation, she will discuss the intricacies of policy with a dutiful competence that can shade into impatience, but when the talk turns to kicking the Texas bureaucracy into shape, every cell in her body seems to jump alive."[155] According to *Texas Monthly* political writer Paul Burka, "Her view of politics is basically a spoils system. . . . She believes that you put your people in place and change the world that way, not by pushing laws through the Texas Legislature."[156] Leadership occurred through people, not through passing more policy. As a result, Richards's style was more consensual than directive.[157] This explained why Richards's critics got away with comments that she was "AWOL, absent without leadership." Her performance of leadership was not directive but coalition building.

Midway through her term, over 75 percent of those polled believed Richards was a strong, hard working, caring leader who understood the complex issues.[158] Texans thought Richards was an achieving governor, crediting her "political skill, not personality," according to a July 1993 Texas poll.[159] According to an article in *Texas Monthly* "Ann Richards *is* a politician, in the true sense of the word—someone skilled in using the political process."[160]

What these perceptions indicated was that Richards was clearly rhetorically adept. She had so many tensions to manage, and she did so skillfully, without creating or succumbing to existing dichotomies. The result was to broaden the notion of leadership in Texas, at least at this transitional period, revealing the possibility of change. Leadership under Richards became defined as active management through people, motivating attitudes of inclusion and cooperation rather than only the strength and control associated with the Lone Star mystique. Additionally, she developed a sense of power that relied on her status as a spectacle, drawing attention to gender by managing others' gaze instead of being the object of it.

Visibility as Power

Public figures have long understood that public power accrues not only to those who "look" but also to those who are seen. In other words, those who are able to fashion spectacles of themselves may claim not only individual identity, but public power. This is particularly important to women public figures, because women have long been the object of the male gaze, but women rarely disrupt that gaze claiming its power for themselves.[161]

As a governor with "undeniable charisma," it was not uncommon for people to flock to Richards on the street.[162] Wherever she went, people gravitated toward her.[163] Richards used this visibility and charisma to her advantage. As she told the Grand Prairie Chamber of Commerce in 1993, "using the visibility of my office to open doors" is an important way to build the new Texas. While it may require government and citizens alike "to take a whole new approach, welcome a host of new ideas, go out of your way to learn something new, . . . you are going to thank your lucky stars that you live in Texas . . . a state that saw the future coming and got there early and ready to do business."[164]

For Richards, power meant relationship building. She didn't mind if people stopped her at "groceries, restaurants or other public places where she happens to be."[165] Such concern for others earned her the title "a woman of the people," noting her populist concern as well as her focus on including women and minorities in the halls of power.[166] Richards sincerely worked to cultivate this populist concern, which made the criticisms that she lacked substance so much more painful. According to Richards, "I think it is important for people to feel that if I am accessible, then government is accessible."[167] Richards's skill at developing personal relationships scored her some early legislative wins. "She strode the House and Senate floors joshing and har-de-har-har-ing in that highly inflected voice that carries to the far corners of any room, literally scratching and massaging members' backs. She listened, made herself 'accessible'" and left with her lottery and a reduced budget deficit.[168]

Richards's skill at developing relationships also framed her "good ol' gal" image differently. After all, wasn't being a "good ol' gal" relying on your network of relationships? If so, it was no wonder Richards relished the label. It was a badge of power via visibility. Richards's identification with the good ol' boy Texas pioneers began to be redefined as a result. While leading proactively through the power of relationships and the visibility those relationships required with Richards at the table, she infused a sense of accountability that had been missing in Texas government. Instead of being "impatient with the good old boy system," Richards put more people in place making that system work for those for whom it hadn't worked in the past.

Richards's relationships were not one-sided either. She encouraged citizens to participate in democracy, thereby developing relationships in their communities and with their fellow citizens. According to Richards, those people we admire "are the ones who are there when they are needed, who care about what happens to their neighborhood and community . . . who manage to look beyond the tip of their own nose and see the friend in crisis, the stranger in distress, the child who needs attention."[169] As if speaking from personal experience, Richards urged that "[r]eal citizenship, real leadership, real character means love of your countrymen and women . . . for they are your country."[170] As she demonstrated in her example, "[r]eal citizenship is found in participation . . . in family, in community, in the self-government that is so precious to us."[171]

Richards understood that government affected people's lives. As she explained in an article in the *El Paso Times*, "I think that touching people is a way of them knowing that government is something other than a big impersonal bureaucracy—that the person who runs it and is head of it understands that it affects the lives of human beings."[172] If power meant building relationships, then an impersonal bureaucracy wasn't possible in Richards's administration. For Richards, government meant "a personal connection with human beings," a personal connection that mattered.[173] Richards found connections in what some would call an outdated institution: political parties. She argued that political parties still mattered because they provided a "connectedness."[174] This comment linked her leadership style to what Kraemer, Newell, and Prindle argued was the hallmark of traditional Texas politics: relationship building through political parties.[175] As a "good ol' gal" she used the realities of the weak Texas governorship to its fullest, forging a network of relationships through which persuasion took place. She called attention to the way that Texas politics actually worked, yet expanded it to her own design.

Thus the relationships that her visibility forged and the people with whom she interacted were paramount in Richards's administration. This was most clearly demonstrated in her metaphor for change, the "new Texas." Richards's "new Texas" was a diverse Texas where opportunity was available to all. As its architect, she planned and built the new Texas from the frontier Texas that was so dear to her. In that way, the old Texas was not completely dismantled, but re-shaped, just like leadership and power under her administration. The result was a new Texas image and economy that looked forward to the next century with Richards at the drawing board.

Active Ann: Architect of the New Texas

As a governor who changed what leadership meant in Texas, change did not come easily or quickly. After all, she "inherited the flamboyant legacy of Texas political gunfighters."[176] It was her job to guide the state from its "cowboy past" into the era of the new Texas. In doing so, Richards redefined the weak Texas governorship metaphorically, using active terms. As the "architect" of the new Texas, she demonstrated her "proactive" stance.[177] What came through was that Richards as architect was building the new Texas by relying metaphorically on the language of household construction—foundations, doors, and the language of building as well as quilting, cooking, and family metaphors that speak not only to the construction of the structure itself but in making the house a home.

Evidence of Richards's new Texas could be found as early as her primary win. The primary was rough and Richards attempted to bring the Democratic party together saying the time was here "to reach out" to all Texans in preparation for the fall election.[178] Richards's new Texas was one that emphasized inclusion and unity, especially appealing to women and minorities. Inclusion became the marker of the new Texas in media accounts of Richards's election victory. As Richards declared, her election signaled "a state government of inclusion."[179]

Richards's victory marked a period of "sociological change, not just governmental change. . . . It means the doors are open to everyone, and they're not going to be closed again."[180] She saw her governorship as an opportunity to demonstrate to little girls that women can do anything they want to do.[181] Such a sociological change was demonstrated most clearly in the governors' appointments, which reflected "the population of this state in ethnicity and in gender."[182] This change also reflected her view of politics; as she said, "politics is people, not money."[183]

The new Texas also reflected Richards's decision-making style. According to the *Austin American-Statesman*, the governor preferred "to draw on people throughout her organization."[184] Vehicles used to describe her management style were "electioneering from the ground up," "grassroots," "involving people," "consensus," "not bound by tradition," "not afraid to break new ground or old rules." Lobbyist Rusty Kelly called her style "management by walking around."[185] Richards's aides explained, "She wants all factions affected by a decision to have their say before—not after—she makes her call."[186] She believed "that if everyone affected by a decision is involved in the process of making it, they will try much harder to make it work."[187]

The new Texas was evident at Richards's inauguration. There were no fur coats; just "diverse waves of people" joined the celebration.[188] According to Glen Maxey, Richards's Travis County coordinator, "The payoff is for the next four years. . . . People who have been on the outside—poor people, women, children, the dispossessed, those who have been looked down upon by society—finally have an equal place at the table."[189] The new governor's inaugural address captured this sentiment. The new Texas would be a place "where opportunity knows no race or color or gender—a glimpse of the possibilities that can be when the barriers fall and the doors of government swing open."[190] According to one man who attended the inauguration, "Ann is like the first promise of a New Texas: a place for all people, people of color, women and gay people."[191]

Richards used her first State of the State address to unveil her "blueprint" of "achievable goals" for the new Texas.[192] The goals included "improving education, restructuring government and altering Texas's corporate franchise tax."[193] The key to Richards's new Texas was not just that she hoped to make policy decisions regarding education and taxes, but that her vision of leadership involved restructuring government so that the "doors are open" to all. As she claimed in her State of the State address, her administration knows "they are expected to open the doors of their agencies to all Texans—in hiring, in purchasing, in providing extraordinary customer service."[194]

After the address, Senator Judith Zaffirini, a Democrat from Laredo, had this reaction in the *Express News*: "I've heard a lot of speeches before the Legislature, but I've never seen one that got this kind of enthusiastic response. . . . She will help reach a consensus (to solve problems). And in the Legislature, consensus-building is what it's all about."[195] Those outside the legislature quickly felt the arrival of the new Texas.[196] According to Charles Elliott, an East Texas State University political science professor, "It's not business as usual. . . . The old business and oil and gas elite that dominated Texas politics is at least temporarily out of the saddle, or perhaps more accurately, they're having to share power with other people."[197]

Richards's early active accomplishments included insurance and school finance reform.[198] She was "one of the most energetic and productive governors in history," one who had a "vision for the state, a program to carry it out, and the political skills and personal popularity to see it through."[199] She was a productive "negotiator and ambassador," and Tom Smith, the director of Ralph Nader's Public Citizen watchdog group, called her the "best governor we've had in years."[200] As the *Houston Chronicle* noted, "Until Gov. Ann Richards walked into the statehouse, Texas had not had a strong leader since John Connally. In the years between Connally and Richards, this state had suffered through a passel of good ol' boys who talked big and did little."[201] Instead, Richards talked and did much, earning her the titles "Action Annie" and "Ann Schwarzkopf and Desert Storm."[202]

Richards's appointments were probably the best evidence that the new Texas had arrived. The *Dallas Morning News* gave a long list of Richards's appointment firsts during her first one hundred days.[203] It was clear that the governor "named to state boards and commissions a more diverse group of Texans than any other governor."[204] These weren't just diverse appointments for the sake of diversity. The governor believed in the quality of her appointments. According to Richards, "We worked very hard to make sure the appointees are quality appointees. . . . I don't think that we move the cause of minorities or women forward by placing people in positions and having them fail."[205]

Even though many media outlets declared that Richards's new Texas meant the old Texas was going to be dismantled, that was not completely true. After all, "diversity has to work both ways."[206] Richards was in the awkward position of a transitional figure, trying to mold the old Texas frontier into a new Texas of inclusiveness. As a result, her critics were quick to point out anything that resembled the old Texas. For example, even though Richards's appointments clearly approached the diverse make-up of the state, a couple of "old-Texas-style political payoffs . . . mar the picture."[207] The *Houston Chronicle* asserted, Richards had campaigned against "cronyism," but the inside joke was that many of her appointments made the new Texas look like the old Texas.[208] Some of her supporters were even disappointed that Richards was not more aggressive when it came to their interests. For example, Booker T. Morris, a Houston lawyer and Coalition of Black Democrats past president, noted "that

Richards has been unable to persuade the Legislature to adopt the single-member district selection of state judges, which supporters say would dramatically increase the number of blacks and Hispanics in the state judiciary."[209]

Richards's words as well as her actions showed her focus on "contributory democracy." "If you're not a part of it, it will never be a true democracy," said Richards.[210] According to Barbara Jordan, Richards's ethics adviser, because of Richards's appointments, "state boards and commissions have become the 'mosaic' that is Texas."[211] Both Jordan and Richards motivated a different picture of democracy, a more inclusive, less controlling picture. As Richards said after her first year: "It's only been a year, and I feel like we've stitched the pieces, but it isn't a quilt yet. We're getting there though, and that's what gives me hope."[212] Furthermore, Richards strongly claimed, "We're not going to go back to the old days when we had to hope somebody will drop some crumbs from the table. . . . We're going to be sitting at the table."[213] It was up to everyone to work together to make decisions, not just up to Richards as governor. That would be antithetical to her leadership style.

In her own unique style, Richards used narrative to emphasize the diversity of the new Texas. Strategically, her folksy style and rural manner of speech endeared her to audiences and in particular the old pioneer Texas, while the subject of her stories looked to the future. To the Texas Chamber of Commerce, she praised the "firm foundation" of the pioneer Texas. According to the governor, "we come from hardy stock . . . from women and men who began communities with little more than boundaries drawn out on a map. . . . They gave Texas a firm foundation. And the challenge that echoes down to us today is the construction, on that firm foundation, of another hundred years that gives us as much cause for pride as the last hundred."[214]

On that proud foundation relationships were built. As the governor explained during the 1994 Houston Club Centennial Distinguished Speaker Series, "Since Sam Houston and the Allen boys cooperated to move the capital, Texans have recognized that the partnership between government and business and employees can create tremendous advantages."[215] Richards hoped that Texans could "forge the bond" of strong, vital, diverse "communities that welcome the contributions of all our citizens."[216] As the "Governor of *all* Texans" she promised to do all she could to make such an atmosphere possible.[217] She desired to include everyone as "part of the New Texas . . . [only together] can . . . we open the door on a new era in Texas history."[218]

The result was bringing together the new and the old, future and history, sharing rather than competing. As Richards explained early in her term to the Higher Education Appointees, "In Texas, the cowboys may still ride the range . . . but we have more computer chips than cow chips. . . . In Mexico, revolutionaries brandishing guns may still stare out from post cards . . . but the real revolutionaries are wearing business suits. . . . Today, we are looking toward the future and embarking on the greatest adventure in our history."[219] Texas's history is rich, but the focus must be on the future and what we can do together by sharing influence in a way that makes "gender and race . . . of consequence only because they enrich the quality of the decision-making process."[220] The governor believed that "in making contact with those other human beings who share this planet and our lives, we become all we can be."[221]

Sharing power was the only way government could work, not when one side or the other dominated. Referring to a story of the "good ol' boys" who went moose hunting, Richards quipped, "In short, like our friends who are trying to take their hunting prizes home . . . how does this country load the airplane so we all get over the mountain and home safely together? The only way we are going to get that answer is to make certain that everyone who has a piece of the puzzle is at the table when we sit down to put the jigsaw together."[222] For Richards, leadership was in coalition building, not in controlling or bullying.

When Richards finally lost her reelection bid to George W. Bush, she believed she had created a new Texas. Several media outlets concurred. The *Houston Chronicle* claimed, "If there is any promise that Richards has kept unequivocally, that is it [the new Texas]."[223] She also forged relationships. The *Sacramento Bee* reported, "Richards has sought to fulfill her campaign pledge to create a 'new Texas.' . . . Texas was famous for cowboys and wildcatters, with an economic base reliant on oil, gas, cotton and cattle. Now the last frontier is joining the computer age."[224] When asked about her major accomplishment in office Richards replied, "I wanted to change the way Texans saw themselves and outsiders saw Texas. . . . I think we accomplished making Texas and the world think differently about Texas."[225]

Richards did much of what she set out to do, but unfortunately she was not reelected. It was odd that the most popular governor of Texas would not be reelected, but perhaps her role was finished. As a transitional figure, she joined the old Texas with the new Texas of diversity and partnerships. But with her connections to the old Texas, perhaps Texans were reluctant to maintain that foothold and it was time to move on.

After leaving the office of governor, Ann Richards has continued to be a public political figure, teaching, lecturing, appearing on *Larry King Live*, mentoring young women, and most recently campaigning for the Kerry-Edwards presidential ticket in 2004 where she can still get in a good jab at her former rival George W. Bush. At a rally in Boston for the Democratic presidential nominee, Richards was heard to quip at the conclusion of a story, "We're almost four years past our shotgun wedding with this White House, and enough is enough."[226] Her presence is invigorating for the party and she still maintains the same hearty laugh, ability to tell stories, and her spectacle-defining "dairy whip" hairdo. She is a role model for other Democratic political women. A contrast to Richards is Christine Todd Whitman. As the next chapter argues, Whitman negotiated a very different set of rhetorical resources to achieve power from her conservative, East Coast realm.

Notes

1. This chapter examined media reports, opponent rhetoric, and Richards's speeches and public appearances for the time frame beginning with her first campaign for governor in 1990 through her reelection defeat by George W. Bush in 1994. A Lexis Nexis Academic Universe search produced articles and transcripts from national news magazines such as *Newsweek* and *Time*, newspapers such as the *Washington Post*, *New York Times*, and the *New York Daily News*, local Texas newspapers, and television programs from the major broadcast and cable news networks. Additional local and national newspaper articles and Richards's speeches were obtained from Richards's collection of papers at the University of Texas at Austin. The scope of the chapter included the entire campaign, term in office, and reelection campaign, including the significant period preceding Richards's "official" announcement when she was the presumptive candidate after her remarks at the 1988 Democratic National Convention.

2. Elizabeth Fox-Genovese, "Texas Women and the Writing of Women's History," in *Women and Texas History: Selected Essays*, ed. Fane Downs and Nancy Baker Jones (Austin: Texas State Historical Association, 1993), 14.

3. Elizabeth York Enstam, "Where Do We Go From Here?" in *Women and Texas History: Selected Essays*, ed. Fane Downs and Nancy Baker Jones (Austin: Texas State Historical Association, 1993), 179–80.

4. Ann W. Richards, Remarks, Sweet Briar College, October 23, 1993 (Center for American History, University of Texas at Austin), 1. The speech texts analyzed in this chapter came from Governor Richards papers located at the Center for American History, University of Texas at Austin.

5. Ann W. Richards, Remarks, Conference on Women's History, June 3, 1994 (Center for American History, University of Texas at Austin), 1.

6. Richards, Remarks, Conference on Women's History, 1.

7. Ann W. Richards, Remarks, Executive State Agency Heads, April 24, 1991 (Center for American History, University of Texas at Austin), 15.

8. Ann W. Richards, Remarks, Tribute to Sam Houston at Sam Houston State University, March 2, 1993 (Center for American History, University of Texas at Austin), 2.

9. David Maraniss, "The Texas Two-Step in the Race for Governor," *Washington Post*, October 22, 1990, final edition, B1, Lexis Nexis Academic Universe (accessed April 28, 1999).

10. Margaret Wolf Freivogel, "Texas Shootout: Old West Comes Alive in Texas Governor's Race," *St. Louis Post-Dispatch*, September 23, 1990, five star edition, 1B, Lexis Nexis Academic Universe (accessed April 28, 1999).

11. Mike Hailey, "Richards 'Likely' to Run for Governor," *Austin American-Statesman*, September 14, 1987.

12. Billy Porterfield, "Can Ann Richards Ignite Texas Women?" *Austin American-Statesman*, March 19, 1990, 1.

13. Laylan Copelin, "Gender Issue Cutting in on Williams-Richards Political Dance," *Austin American-Statesman*, April 15, 1990.

14. *Texas Monthly*, October 1990, cover.

15. Laylan Copelin, "It's Governor Richards," *Austin American-Statesman*, November 7, 1990.

16. Susan Warren, "Defections by Republican Women Crucial to Richards' Victory," *Houston Chronicle*, November 8, 1990, 1A.

17. Claudia Feldman, "Campaign Widens Gender Gap," *Houston Chronicle*, September 9, 1990, 7G.

18. Roberto Suro, "In Texas Race, Richards Reflects on Negativism," *New York Times*, May 6, 1990, late edition, 24, Lexis Nexis Academic Universe (accessed April 28, 1999).

19. Quoted in Suro, "In Texas," 24.

20. Laylan Copelin, "Richards: 'The Doors are Open,'" *Austin American-Statesman*, November 8, 1990, A1.

21. Karen Potter, "Richards Clinging to Lead in Gubernatorial Dogfight," *Fort Worth Star Telegram*, November 7, 1990; R. G. Ratcliffe, "It's Governor Richards: Overwhelming Support of Women Keys Win," *Houston Chronicle*, November 7, 1990, 2 star edition, 1; Dave McNeely, "Richards's Decision-Making Style Suits Governorship," *Austin American-Statesman*, December 27, 1990.

22. Mike Hailey, "To Tax or Not is the Question," *Houston Post*, September 9, 1990, A1.

23. Mike Hailey, "Williams, Richards Fuss Over Newest Negative Ad," *Houston Post*, September 11, 1990, A13.

24. Ross Ramsey, "Volume of Campaign Ads Increases but Will TV Viewers Turn It Down?" *Dallas Times Herald*, September 17, 1990; Wayne Slater, "Candidates Spar on Final Weekend," *Dallas Morning News*, November 4, 1990, 1A; Wayne Slater, "Richards Pledges 'Sociological' Change," *Dallas Morning News*, November 8, 1990, 1A; "Williams Holds Commanding Lead Over Richards, Poll Shows," *San Antonio Express*, September 16, 1990; Karen Potter and Kaye Northcott, "Slips of the Lip Trip Williams," *Fort Worth Star Telegram*, November 4, 1990, 4.

25. Ross Ramsey, "She Whups Him!" *Times Herald*, November 7, 1990.

26. Clay Robison, "Richards to Take on State's Problems," *Houston Chronicle*, January 16, 1991.

27. "The Titan of Texas," *Vogue*, August 1, 1991, 249.

28. Jeanne Freeman, "She's Tough, Sharp and Pure Texas," *San Diego Union Tribune*, April 17, 1992, D1, Lexis Nexis Academic Universe (accessed April 28, 1999).

29. "The Titan," 248.

30. "The Titan," 248.

31. Karen Potter, "Ann of 100 Days Finds Governor's Work is Never Done," *Fort Worth Star Telegram*, April 22, 1991, 10.

32. Potter, "Ann of 100," 10.

33. Potter, "Richards Clinging."

34. J. Michael Kennedy, "The Cowboy and the Good Ol' Girl," *Los Angeles Times*, October 21, 1990, home edition, 12, Lexis Nexis Academic Universe (accessed April 28, 1999).

35. Richard H. Kraemer, Charldean Newell, and David F. Prindle, *Essentials of Texas Politics*, 6th edition (New York: West Publishing Company, 1995), 4.

36. Sue Tolleson-Rinehart and Jeanie R, Stanley, *Claytie and the Lady: Ann Richards, Gender, and Politics in Texas* (Austin: University of Texas Press, 1994), 36.

37. Beverly Stoeltje, "It Makes a Good Story," *Discovery*, 10, no. 2, 1986, 26.

38. Stoeltje, "It Makes a Good Story," 26.

39. "The Write Stuff," *Texas Monthly*, April 1992, 108.

40. J. Michael Kennedy, "The Cowboy and the Good Ol' Girl," 12.

41. Meg Cullar, "Ann Richards Waco Native Texas Governor," *Discover*, January 1992.

42. "The Titan," 246.

43. "The Titan," 246.

44. Alison Cook, "Lone Star," *New York Times*, February 7, 1993, late edition, 22, Lexis Nexis Academic Universe (accessed April 28, 1999).

45. Stoeltje, "It Makes a Good Story," 28.

46. Ann W. Richards, Remarks, Polk County Chamber of Commerce, March 5, 1992 (Center for American History, University of Texas at Austin), 1.

47. Ann W. Richards, Remarks, Cattle Raisers Association, March 29, 1993 (Center for American History, University of Texas at Austin), 1–2.

48. Richards, Remarks, Cattle Raisers, 2.

49. Harry Ransom, "Spirit of Texas," *Discovery*, 10, no. 2, 1986, 5.

50. Ransom, "Spirit of Texas," 5.

51. Ann W. Richards, Remarks, Joint Session of the Legislature (State of State), *House Journal*, February 6, 1991, 276–78.

52. Richards, Remarks, Joint Session, 1991, 282.

53. Michael Paulson, "Richards Leaves Them Wanting More in N.Y.," *San Antonio Light*, July 19, 1992.

54. Bruce Davidson, "New Governor Pledges Return of Government for the People," *Express News*, January 16, 1991, 1A.

55. R. G. Ratcliffe, and Clay Robison, "Richards, Bullock Pledge a 'New Texas,'" *Houston Chronicle*, January 16, 1991, 5A.

56. Guillermo X. Garcia, "Richards Blazes Her Own Trail to Mansion," *Austin American-Statesman*, November 7, 1990; Warren, "Defections by Republican Women," 14A; Wayne Slater, "Richards Takes Oath as Governor," *Dallas Morning News*, January 16, 1991, 1A.

57. R. G. Ratcliffe, "Campaign '94; Governor; Gender Bias Worrisome Factor," *Houston Chronicle*, September 5, 1994, 2 star edition, A1, Lexis Nexis Academic Universe (accessed April 28, 1999).

58. "Governor's Appointments," Chart, *Dallas Morning News*, April 1991, 21; Potter, "Ann of 100," 10.

59. "Richards Named to *Glamour* List," *Dallas Morning News*, November 5, 1991, 22A.

60. "Richards Named," 22A.

61. "The Titan," 316.

62. David Maraniss, "Richards Seeks to Refocus on Issues; Rough Texas Democratic Campaign Leaves Image Questions," *Washington Post*, April 12, 1990, final edition, A6, Lexis Nexis Academic Universe (accessed April 28, 1999).

63. R. G. Ratcliffe, "Richards and Williams in Dead Heat, Poll Finds," *Houston Chronicle*, October 26, 1990; Ken Herman, "Richards Even with Williams in Gubernatorial Race, Pollster Says," *Houston Post*, October 26, 1990, A13; Kaye Northcott, "Poll Says Governor's Race Even," *Fort Worth Star Telegram*, October 26, 1990, 7.

64. Sam Attlesey, "Richards's 'New Texas' Means Many Things," *Dallas Morning News*, January 20, 1991. Numerous examples substantiate this point further including Sam Attlesey, "Williams Downfall Assessed," *Dallas Morning News*, November 7, 1990, 1A; Arnold Hamilton, "Poll Finds Many Joined Richards Fold Only Recently," *Dallas Morning News*, November 7, 1990; David Maraniss, "Richards Changing Face of Old-Boy Texas Politics; Key Appointees Include Women, Minorities," *Washington Post*, January 13, 1991, final edition, A3, Lexis Nexis Academic Universe (accessed April 28, 1999); R. G. Ratcliffe, "Race Tight in Stretch, Poll Shows," *Houston Chronicle*, November 4, 1990.

65. Wayne Slater, "Richards Makes Mark on Office," *Dallas Morning News*, April 21, 1991, 1A.

66. Laylan Copelin, "A New Texas Tally," *Austin American-Statesman*, July 14, 1991, A1, A14.

67. "Group: Richards No Leader," *San Antonio Express*, June 27, 1991.

68. Carolyn Barta, "Rating Gov. Richards," *Dallas Morning News*, February 17, 1992. Other examples reporting Richards's lack of leadership include the following. According to Tom Craddick, a state Representative and chair of the House Republican Caucus, "I don't think she has exerted any leadership . . . On school finance, we never saw her." Karl Rove, a Republican political consultant explained, "In terms of substance, she is clearly not driving the solution agenda in Texas." See Wayne Slater, "Richards Makes Mark," 1A+.

69. Jan Jarboe, "Ann's Plans," *Texas Monthly*, July 1992, 78.

70. Mary Lenz, "Richards Promises to 'Hit the Ground Running' in Austin," *Houston Post*, November 8, 1990, A1.

71. Guillermo X. Garcia, "Richards's Inaugural to Feature Common Touch," *Austin American-Statesman*, December 17, 1990, A1.

72. Gardner Selby, "Richards Proclaims a 'New Texas.'" *Times Herald*, January 16, 1991, A1.

73. Ken Herman, "30,000 Watch Richards Take Oath of Office," *Houston Post*, January 16, 1991, A9.

74. Karen Potter and Joe Cutbirth, "Richards Vows 'New Texas' as She Takes Office," *Fort Worth Star Telegram*, January 16, 1991, 4. Numerous articles reported on Richards's hairstyle, hairdresser, and trips to the beauty shop including Nancy Kruh, "From Dawn Till Dark, Richards Was on the Go," *Dallas Morning News*, January 16, 1991; Gary Scharrer, "The Richards Style," *El Paso Times*, November 17, 1991.

75. Suzanne Gamboa, "The Buzz on Richards' Big Hair: It Could Go," *Austin American-Statesman*, June 17, 1993, A1.

76. Donnis Baggett, "Splitting Hairs over Guv's Do," *Dallas Morning News*, August 15, 1993.

77. R. G. Ratcliffe, "Texas Governor's Race; Richards Stumps for Bubba's Vote," *Houston Chronicle*, November 4, 1994, 2 star edition, A1, Lexis Nexis Academic Universe (accessed April 28, 1999).

78. Anne Marie Kilday and Terrence Stutz, "Richards Faces Tough Job as Governor, Lawmakers Say," *Dallas Morning News*, November 8, 1990, 23A.

79. Ken Herman, "Shake Hands with Governor Richards," *Houston Post*, November 7, 1990, A1.

80. Garcia, "Richards Blazes."

81. Mike Ward, "Crime Rates Are Down, but Are We Safer?" *Austin American-Statesman*, September 4, 1993, C1.

82. Ward, "Crime Rates are Down," C1.

83. Ward, "Crime Rates are Down," C9.

84. Stuart Eskenazi and Ralph Barrera, "Richards Embraces Future Full of Change in Farewell," *Austin American-Statesman*, December 23, 1994, Lexis Nexis Academic Universe (accessed July 9, 2002).

85. Paul Weingarten, "Richards Takes Texas by Horns," *Chicago Tribune* (Center for American History, University of Texas at Austin).

86. Tim Fleck, "Play It Again, Ann," *Houston Press*, December 26, 1991, 4.

87. Fleck, "Play It Again, Ann," 4.

88. Fleck, "Play It Again, Ann," 4.

89. Cook, "Lone Star," 22.

90. Cook, "Lone Star," 22.

91. Weingarten, "Richards Takes."

92. Richard Woodbury, "Winds of Change Sweep the Lone Star State," *Time*, April 29, 1991, 32.

93. Jarboe, "Ann's Plans," 83.

94. Jarboe, "Ann's Plans," 110.

95. Potter, "Ann of 100," 10.

96. Potter, "Ann of 100," 10.

97. Mark Potok, "Richards in 'Race of Her Life' / Texas Gov Faces Tough Challenge," *USA Today*, October 17, 1994, final edition, 8A, Lexis Nexis Academic Universe (accessed April 28, 1999).

98. Freeman, "She's Tough, Sharp and Pure Texas," D1.

99. Kathleen Rowe, *The Unruly Woman: Gender and the Genres of Laughter* (Austin: University of Texas Press, 1995), 19.

100. Rowe, *The Unruly Woman*, 11.

101. Rowe, *The Unruly Woman*, 11.

102. Slater, "Richards Makes," 1A, 28A.

103. Slater, "Richards Makes," 1A, 28A.

104. Jarboe, "Ann's Plans," 80.

105. Jarboe, "Ann's Plans," 80.

106. "The Titan," 244.

107. Jarboe, "Ann's Plans," 80.

108. Rowe, *The Unruly Woman*, 19.

109. Quoted in Rosalind Jackler, "Capital Gains: Governor Richards was the Center of Attention as the Nation's Governors Convened in Washington D.C.," *Houston Post*, February 7, 1993, A35.

110. Jarboe, "Ann's Plans," 83.

111. Jarboe, "Ann's Plans," 83.

112. Maraniss, "The Texas Two-Step," B1.

113. John Gonzalez, "Get Out, Richards Tells 2 on Insurance Board," *Fort Worth Star Telegram*, February 7, 1991.

114. Laylan Copelin, "Richards Lashes Out in Address," *Austin American-Statesman*, February 7, 1991, A1; R. G. Ratcliffe, "Richards Demands Shake-Up," *Houston Chronicle*, February 7, 1991, 1A; Mary Lenz and Ken Herman, "Richards Tells 2 Members of Insurance Board to Quit," *Houston Post*, February 7, 1991, A1.

115. Wayne Slater, "Richards Helps Women Raise Funds," *Dallas Morning News*, July 15, 1992.

116. Laylan Copelin, "Richards Sharpens Humor at Expense of Men, Hunting," *Austin American-Statesman*, May 8, 1992, A7.

117. David Nyhan, "This Texan is a Straight-Shooter," *Boston Sunday Globe*, October 1, 1989.

118. Wayne Slater, "Richards' Popularity Puts Her in the Limelight Dawn to Dusk," *Dallas Morning News*, July 14, 1992, 6F; Eric Harrison, "Richards Stirs Up Texas Government; Politics: The Democratic Governor's Style, Choice of Appointees Have Taken Austin by Storm, But She Has Critics on Both Sides of Spectrum," *Los Angeles Times*, August 25, 1991, home edition, 4.

119. Karen Potter, "Governor Wows 'em—Again," *Fort Worth Star Telegram*, July 14, 1992, 8.

120. "Witty Richards Easily Wins Fans," *Austin American-Statesman*, July 20, 1988; "Bush-bashing Texans to Preside," *San Antonio Light*, July 12, 1992.

121. Nyhan, "This Texan is a Straight-Shooter."

122. Barta, "Rating Gov. Richards."

123. Cook, "Lone Star," 22.

124. Dave McNeely, "Richards Record Stands a Far Cry from 'Feminist' Labeling," *Austin American-Statesman*, October 8, 1987.

125. *Keys to the Governor's Office* (Brookline, Mass.: Barbara Lee Family Foundation, 2001), 17.

126. Julie Morris, "Texas' Richards to Lead 15,000 to Her Inaugural," *USA Today*, January 14, 1991, final edition, 2A, Lexis Nexis Academic Universe (accessed April 28, 1999).

127. Quoted in R. G. Ratcliffe, "Few Fault Richards on Style, But Substance is Another Thing," *Houston Chronicle*, May 1, 1994, 2 star edition, A1, Lexis Nexis Academic Universe (accessed April 28, 1999).

128. Diana R. Fuentes, "Richards to Reach 100-Day Milestone," *Express News*, April 21, 1991, 18A; "After 100 Days, Governor Enjoying Life at the Top," *San Antonio Light*, April 20, 1991.

129. John C. Henry, "'It's Official' Richards Will Give Keynote," *Austin American-Statesman*, June 28, 1988.

130. Quoted in Julia Prodis, "Texas Governor's Race a Real Ripsnorter," *Los Angeles Times*, October 23, 1994, bulldog edition, A2, Lexis Nexis Academic Universe (accessed April 28, 1999).

131. Ratcliffe, "Campaign '94," 1.

132. Muriel Dobbin, "Richards Takes off Gloves in Texas Fight," *Sacramento Bee*, September 18, 1994, metro edition, A3, Lexis Nexis Academic Universe (accessed April 28, 1999).

133. Dobbin, "Richards Takes off Gloves," A3.

134. Slater, "Richards Makes," 28A.

135. Ratcliffe, "Few Fault," A1.

136. Sue Anne Pressley, "Personal Touch Might Not Be Enough," *Washington Post*, October 4, 1994, final edition, A1, Lexis Nexis Academic Universe (accessed April 28, 1999).

137. Ed Vulliamy, "White Hot Mama Fights a Texan Bush War," *The Observer*, October 2, 1994, 19, Lexis Nexis Academic Universe (accessed April 28, 1999). Even London papers captured her bodily spectacle including Ian Brodie, "Lone Star Governor Struggles to Uproot the Shrub," *The Times*, October 20, 1994, Lexis Nexis Academic Universe (accessed April 28, 1999). Another paper reported that Richards entered a room like a "diva." Rupert Cornwell, "US Mid-term Elections: Bush Boy Has Good Ol' Girl from Texas in His Sights," *The Independent*, October 29, 1994, 9, Lexis Nexis Academic Universe (accessed April 28, 1999).

138. Jarboe, "Ann's Plans," 82.

139. Gardner Selby, "Governor Hogs Spotlight," *Houston Post*, May 16, 1992; Anne Marie Kilday, "Richards Gets Custom-Made Motorcycle," *Dallas Morning News*, May 16, 1992, 31A; Karen Potter, "Governor Accepts Gift for DPS Use," *Fort Worth Star Telegram*, May 16, 1992, 17; Bruce Hight, "High on

the Hog, Richards Promotes Motorcycle Safety," *Austin American-Statesman*, May 16, 1992.

140. Cook, "Lone Star," 22.

141. Slater, "Richards's Popularity Puts Her in the Limelight," 6F.

142. Rowe, *The Unruly Woman*, 59.

143. Ratcliffe, "Few Fault," A1.

144. Numerous sources commented on Richards's star quality that defied easy categorization including Alison Cook, "Lone Star," 22; David Elliot, "Will Richards' 'New Texas' Last 4 More Years?" *Austin American-Statesman*, September 4, 1993, A1+; Curtis Wilkie, "Read Her Lips," *The Boston Globe*, October 25, 1992, 15, Lexis Nexis Academic Universe (accessed April 28, 1999).

145. Cook, "Lone Star," 22.

146. Cook, "Lone Star," 22.

147. Cook, "Lone Star," 22.

148. Roberto Suro, "Texas Governor Proves Adept in Her First Year," *New York Times*, January 19, 1992.

149. Suro, "Texas Governor Proves Adept."

150. Muriel Dobbin, "Texas Leader Blends Charm, Intimidation," *Sacramento Bee*, May 9, 1994, metro edition, A1, Lexis Nexis Academic Universe (accessed April 28, 1999).

151. Quoted in Dobbin, "Texas Leader," A1.

152. "Defining Richards' Place in History: Governor's Mansion is Next Target," *Austin American-Statesman*, January 15, 1990, 2.

153. "Defining Richards's Place," 2.

154. "The Titan," 249.

155. Cook, "Lone Star," 22.

156. Cook, "Lone Star," 22.

157. R. G. Ratcliffe, "Traveling a Bumpy Road Never Musses Richards," *Houston Chronicle*, January 3, 1993, 23A.

158. Wayne Slater, "Richards Still Popular in Poll," *Dallas Morning News*, February 20, 1993, 3A.

159. Wayne Slater, "Richards' Popularity Still High," *Dallas Morning News*, July 24, 1993, 33A.

160. Paul Burka, "Ann of a Hundred Days," *Texas Monthly*, May 1991, 128.

161. Rowe, *The Unruly Woman*, 11.

162. Slater, "Richards Still Popular in Poll," 3A.

163. Debbie Graves, "Richards' 'Star Quality' to Light up Convention," *Austin American-Statesman*, July 12, 1992.

164. Ann W. Richards, Remarks, Grand Prairie Chamber of Commerce Annual Awards Banquet, January 7, 1993 (Center for American History, University of Texas at Austin), 6.

165. Fuentes, "Richards to Reach," 18A.

166. "Jess Jawin," *Texas Jewish Post*, January 23, 1992, 23.

167. Cook, "Lone Star," 22.

168. Cook, "Lone Star," 22.

169. Ann W. Richards, Remarks, Lubbock Eagle Scouts, November 11, 1991 (Center for American History, University of Texas at Austin), 2.

170. Richards, Remarks, Lubbock Eagle Scouts, 2.

171. Richards, Remarks, Lubbock Eagle Scouts, 3.

172. Scharrer, "The Richards Style."

173. Scharrer, "The Richards Style."

174. Bruce Hight, "Richards Talks Across New York," *Austin American-Statesman*, July 13, 1992, A4.

175. Kraemer, Newell, and Prindle, *Essentials of Texas Politics*, 4.

176. Dobbin, "Texas Leader," A1.

177. R. G. Ratcliffe, "Richards Pushes for Whirlwind of Changes," *Houston Chronicle*, February 10, 1991, 1A.

178. Robin Toner, "Bitter Race in Texas Ends with Richards as Democrats' Pick," *New York Times*, April 11, 1990, late edition, A:1, Lexis Nexis Academic Universe (accessed April 28, 1999).

179. Randy Kennedy, "Richards Asks Texas to Unite," *The Daily Texan*, November 8, 1990, 1.

180. Slater, "Richards Pledges," 1A; Richard Smith, "Richards Says She'll 'Hit the Ground Running,'" *Express News*, November 8, 1990.

181. Slater, "Richards Pledges," 23A; Copelin, "Richards: 'The Doors,'" A6; R. G. Ratcliffe and Cindy Rugeley, "Win Hailed By Richards as Inspiring," *Houston Chronicle*, November 8, 1990; Smith, "Richards Says."

182. Copelin, "Richards: 'The Doors,'" A1, A6; Ratcliffe and Rugeley, "Win Hailed."

183. Lenz, "Richards Promises," A1.

184. Laylan Copelin and Dave McNeely, "Governor-elect's Inner Circle Believes in Inclusion, Diversity," *Austin American-Statesman*, December 9, 1990, final edition, A1.

185. Ken Herman, "The First 100 Days," *Houston Post*, April 21, 1991, A1.

186. Copelin and McNeely, "Governor-elect's Inner Circle," A1, A25.

187. McNeely, "Richards' Decision."

188. Potter and Cutbirth, "Richards Vows 'New Texas,'" 4.

189. Potter and Cutbirth, "Richards Vows 'New Texas,'" 4.

190. Ann W. Richards, Inaugural Address, *House Journal*, January 15, 1991, 138.

191. Clifford Pugh and Mary Lenz, "Ann's People Flock to Austin for Celebration," *Houston Post*, January 16, 1991, A12.

192. Wayne Slater, "Richards Says Address Will Offer New Answer to Familiar Themes," *Dallas Morning News*, February 6, 1991, 1A, 12A.

193. Slater, "Richards Says," 1A, 12A.

194. Richards, Remarks, Joint Session 1991, 276.

195. Diana R. Fuentes, "Demos Applaud Governor's View of Texas's Future," *Express News*, February 7, 1991.

196. Others felt the arrival of the new Texas. Max Sherman, LBJ School of Public Affairs Dean, noted: "She has opened the system up. . . . At the highest levels you are seeing ethnic diversity, gender diversity, economic diversity. And my guess is that's going to have a profound impact on what happens in this state." The *Chicago Tribune* explained that "Scarcely more than a month after promising a 'new Texas' in her inaugural address, Gov. Ann Richards is shaping an administration that is markedly different in style and substance from any in state history." See Fuentes, "Richards to Reach," 1A+; Slater, "Richards Makes," 1A+; Weingarten, "Richards Takes."

197. Weingarten, "Richards Takes."

198. Fuentes, "Richards to Reach," 1A.

199. Fuentes, "Richards to Reach," 18A; Burka, "Ann of a Hundred Days," 128.

200. Candace Windel, "Texans Like Richards More and More," *Corpus Christi Caller Times*, May 4, 1992, A1; Copelin, "A New Texas Tally," A1.

201. M. A. Bengtson, "Campaign 94: Richards Deserves Votes," *Houston Chronicle*, November 7, 1994, C17, Lexis Nexis Academic Universe (accessed April 28, 1999).

202. Woodbury, "Winds of Change" 32; Slater, "Richards Makes," 28A.

203. "Governor's Appointments."

204. "Richards Names Diverse Group," *Austin American-Statesman*, April 21, 1991, A16.

205. Quoted in Herman, "The First 100," A25.

206. Burka, "Ann of a Hundred Days," 130.

207. Cook, "Lone Star," 22.

208. Ratcliffe, "Traveling," 23A.

209. Ratcliffe, "Few Fault," A1.

210. Quoted in Kanestra Conley, "La. Women Encouraged to Run for Office," *Baton Rouge Morning Advocate*, September 21, 1991.

211. Barta, "Rating Gov. Richards."

212. Ann W. Richards, "Governor's Report," February 2, 1992.

213. Quoted in Ratcliffe, "Campaign '94," 1.

214. Ann W. Richards, Remarks, Texas Chamber of Commerce, February 10, 1994 (Center for American History, University of Texas at Austin), 8.

215. Ann W. Richards, Remarks, Houston Club Centennial Distinguished Speaker Series, January 27, 1994 (Center for American History, University of Texas at Austin), 3.

216. Richards, Remarks, Houston Club, 6.

217. Ann W. Richards, Remarks, Special Session of the Texas Legislature, July 15, 1991 (Center for American History, University of Texas at Austin), 5.

218. Ann W. Richards, Remarks, Higher Education Appointees, July 17, 1991 (Center for American History, University of Texas at Austin), 4.

219. Richards, Remarks, Higher Education, 6.

220. Ann W. Richards, Remarks, East Texas State University Women's Enrichment Series, November 12, 1991 (Center for American History, University of Texas at Austin), 2.

221. Ann W. Richards, Remarks, Commencement Ceremonies of St. Edwards University, May 9, 1992 (Center for American History, University of Texas at Austin), 2.

222. Ann W. Richards, Remarks, Civil Rights Conference, December 16, 1992 (Center for American History, University of Texas at Austin), 3.

223. Ratcliffe, "Few Fault," A1.

224. Dobbin, "Texas Leader," A1.

225. Quoted in Gregory Curtis, "Ann Richards, Fresh Out of Answers," *Star Tribune*, February 8, 1995, metro edition, 14A, Lexis Nexis Academic Universe (accessed April 28, 1999).

226. Carol Beggy and Mark Shanahan, "Richards Dishes Humor; Kerry Charged with an Error," *The Boston Globe*, July 13, 2004, <www.bostonglobe.com> (accessed August 6, 2004).

Chapter 3

Christine Todd Whitman

Christine Todd Whitman was elected in 1993 as the first woman governor of New Jersey and immediately her popularity soared when she promised at her inauguration a 30 percent tax cut over the next three years. It also won her favor with the national party and demonstrated early her decisive decision-making. A year later, the Republicans tapped her to deliver the response to President Clinton's 1995 State of the Union address, the first governor and first woman to do so. Her presence reinforced moderate Republicanism, an effort to unify the party while also attracting women to the party. She was notably on many "short lists" from vice president to cabinet positions. But during her second term as governor, her star power waned even as her political identity solidified. She was selected as President George W. Bush's Environmental Protection Agency (EPA) administrator, fitting because of her status as steward of New Jersey's "open space," a title she earned during her second term in office.

Whitman was a political persona with many firsts to her credit. As a result, her metaphoric and literal characterization as a pioneer was certainly warranted. She was a pioneer because she traversed new ground as a Republican woman in New Jersey and nationally, bringing visibility to her moderate stance and lending credibility to anyone with whom she associated. She was perceived as an active, independent thinker who was able to forge connections with her New Jersey family. During her second term her pioneer identity lent credibility to her environmental initiatives as her athleticism became part of her public persona.

However, this athletic pioneer was not immune to typical mediated characterizations focusing on gender. Metaphorically, these media frames served to limit the ways in which Whitman's potential as a governor was perceived. Her opponents attempted to contain her in traditional ways, as a puppet and a (beauty) queen. They depicted her as an out-of-touch rich woman who couldn't possibly relate to her public. During her first campaign she was described as elite, aristocratic, and well bred, but as not having much to say. Certainly Whitman comes from a wealthy family, but that is not her defining characteristic

81

nor does it suggest her capability as a leader (though it may suggest her ability to finance a campaign, a significant hurdle for a woman candidate to surmount). Moreover, her appearance was frequently the focus of media attention, via her elegance and grace. While it may be no surprise that women candidates are covered in the media differently than men, metaphorically the implications are far-reaching, potentially undermining a woman candidate's credibility and perceived fit for the office. According to *Framing Gender on the Campaign Trail*, women and men are covered relatively equally in terms of column space. However, female candidates are less likely to have their policy views picked up by the media. Instead the focus is on personal characteristics, giving the impression that male candidates are more fit for office.[1] However, as Whitman performed in the position of governor, what became apparent was that she was actively recast, within the bounds of New Jersey political culture, as strong, spirited, energetic, while also elegant, refined, and patrician. In Whitman these apparent paradoxical constructions were reconciled.

Christine Todd Whitman provides an important case study for those interested in the political identity of public women. This chapter conducts a media analysis of Governor Whitman's campaigns and terms in office to reveal a subtle identity transformation.[2] As a conservative woman in a powerful state position, Whitman had to contend with typical metaphoric characterizations that have plagued women public officials for years. The puppet, pioneer, and (beauty) queen metaphors were often prevalent in media characterizations of Governor Whitman. Yet during her second term the pioneer metaphor finally took hold and her political identity was transformed. Ultimately, Whitman capitalized on the metaphors, confounding their apparent oppositional status, and performed leadership as a conciliator. Her performance is instructive for other conservative women who may find themselves operating within a powerful state apparatus such as the New Jersey governorship. The metaphors served as rhetorical resources for the conservative Governor Whitman.

Regionalism and Political Culture

The New Jersey governor is among the most powerful throughout the country as defined in the state's redesigned constitution of 1947.[3] Such strength of office comes into play when discussing Christine Todd Whitman. According to the *New York Times*, "When it comes to raw power, the Governor of New Jersey has it all. She is the only official elected statewide. . . . [T]he state has no comptroller. . . . No lieutenant governor. . . . No elected attorney general. . . . No judges crowding the ballot."[4] The defining strength of the New Jersey governor is that many "offices are appointed, and appointed by the Governor."[5] The New Jersey governor is expected to be decisive, strong, and stately. Perhaps all of these powers and expectations were what led George Will to describe the New Jersey governor as "an American Caesar."[6]

The modern New Jersey governorship claims many advantages for the governor when it comes to agenda setting and policy decisions. "Broad veto powers, domination of the budget process, use of executive orders, wide-ranging appointment powers, the likelihood of reelection, and the absence of a legislative veto constitute a formidable armaterium [sic] for the chief executive."[7] Most governors have few problems carrying out their policy intentions because of the power, domination, and formidable armory at their disposal. However, that does not mean that the modern governor has an easy time swaying public opinion.

Historically New Jersey has had a problem defining its identity as a state. There is no New Jersey–oriented commercial television station and no statewide newspaper. The state has a diverse population and individual citizens tend to view local matters as more important than state matters, perhaps because of the difficulty of unifying public opinion around any issue and because of the overwhelming suburban make-up of New Jersey.[8] According to Salmore and Salmore, both "change and continuity" characterize New Jersey politics. As a result, "New Jersey [political] parties are dominated by raging moderates" and politics is considered highly volatile.[9] Such a political culture advantages "incumbent and moderate candidates" and voters tend to respond to candidates who are moderate and can make the case that they have the voters' interests in mind.[10] Thus, the New Jersey governor, once elected, has a challenging job ahead when it comes to unifying public opinion in support of policy issues and activating that public to influence the legislature, despite the control inscribed in the position. The challenges of office play out in a variety of ways for a woman political executive. The strength and power of the office and Whitman's gender worked to frame her campaigns.

"Christie's Clueless"

Whitman's opponents relied on metaphors that characterized her as a puppet most clearly during her campaigns or in reference to her campaigns. Several issues were the focus of Whitman as puppet: the bumbling campaign, lack of self-definition, focus, and style, her family wealth, being at the right place at the right time, and receiving help from men including her husband. As a result, her opponents defined Whitman as out-of-touch and inept, being led by men or her party, and not making any decisions on her own to define herself or her agenda. Such metaphors motivate attitudes that contain women as wives, inappropriate for the political realm and indebted to their family role. Women executives as puppets are only in positions of leadership by virtue of someone else pulling the strings. They are passive rather than proactive. Significantly, as this metaphoric cluster has evolved during which time women have been elected as governor "in their own right," the emphasis is on the woman executive's passivity, inability, and lack.

Walter Fisher suggests that human communication can best be understood as narratives whose appeal rests on their plausibility and probability.[11] In a mediated age, audiences are not presented with fully developed stories but instead select fragmented story elements to form cohesive narratives. An image or metaphor can play a defining role in shaping the story that emerges. As Whitman's campaign progressed, the passive construction of her political identity resonated with the overall gendered narrative of how politics works in New Jersey and who should play the game. Whitman's tough decisions did not resonate and were overlooked or were explained as just exceptions to the otherwise clueless image.

A series of missteps enabled Whitman's opponent to frame her as inept at best, unable to make decisions on the running of her campaign, i.e., as a *bumbling idiot*. She committed "embarrassing blunders," "stumbled," and was "off-stride and on the defensive for most of the race."[12] One major misstep was deciding to take a weeklong vacation with her family instead of staying on the campaign. Upon her return Whitman spent "all summer and into the fall defending herself against issues raised by the Florio campaign that were far afield from what the public expected to hear."[13] Whitman wasn't able to maintain pace in the political footrace and her choice to spend time with family was partly to blame.

Thus, Whitman's campaign was "bumbling," her proposals "impractical," and she was a "buffoon."[14] Even a year or two into her first term, *The Record* recounted "her accident-prone campaign" while *The New York Times* recalled "a nightmarishly bumbling election campaign."[15] The bumbling imagery resurfaced in her reelection bid, during which the *National Review* recalled her "inept" performance in which "she bungled . . . [and] backed away."[16] *The Record* explained, "the incumbent's struggle in New Jersey was at least partially of her own campaign's making."[17] Even though by her reelection Whitman had a list of accomplishments to clear her missteps and ineptitude, these images resurfaced.

Coming through from the bumbling campaign is an overall sense of *lacking*, including a lack of credibility on Whitman's part, allowing herself to be defined by her opponents rather than proactively defining the issues. The classic puppet is one who lets others make the decisions and simply reacts to their prodding. This sort of imagery maintains the stereotypical boundaries of women as lacking rationality and allowing others to take the lead.

Throughout the campaign, Whitman was criticized for lacking toughness, an easy criticism to place on a woman. She was not "a serious politician," but a "lightweight."[18] According to *The Record*, Whitman was "'candidate lite,' good taste but less filling, an intriguing, personable antidote to the beleaguered Governor Jim Florio."[19] *The Record* ran this report when Whitman announced her plans to revitalize the New Jersey economy. "Long on potential, she's been short on specifics. Whether her evasiveness is by design or ineptitude is just one reason why her message today is so important."[20] Instead of reporting on her specifics, she was called "elusive."[21] Instead of announcing her message, the media asked: "But what is Whitman fighting for? . . . Since her primary win in June, she has gone into summer hibernation."[22] And finally in an article titled "Christie's Clueless," *The Record* reported on her election. "In a truly ironic twist, New Jersey . . . has elected the first woman politician to whom the recently coined catch phrase applies: She just doesn't get it."[23] Such characterizations contained whatever Whitman did as light, ineffectual, and soft, even when she made the tough decisions. It was an easy depiction to create of the "fairer sex," but it worked to perpetuate stereotypes rather than change them, motivating attitudes that contain women's accomplishments in the political realm.

Whitman's "clueless" image played into her speaking style as well. The media often noted her "measured" and "disciplined" style, suggesting that Whitman cannot think on her feet, or is too vacuous to speak without the most planned remarks.[24] The *New York Times* explained that her style "bore little resemblance to the way most politicians . . . perform."[25] Her speech, suggested the same article, was more of a stream of consciousness series of remarks rather than a rational listing of policy initiatives "with none of the political orator's anecdotes or dramatic gestures. At times, she shifted from one idea to the next without completing her thought."[26] On her response to President Clinton's 1995 State of the Union: "There was a clear contrast between phrases contributed by Washington—the flowery oratory of Capitol Hill—and her own plain-spoken style."[27] Yet her "plain-spoken" style reminded Bob Beckel, former manager of Walter Mondale's 1984 presidential campaign, "of a Girl Scout leader giving a pep talk to the girls at the beginning of the annual cookie drive."[28] Such remarks maintain gender-specific norms in political culture and contain women in mother roles in which they deal most appropriately with children. They also resonate with the "clueless" narrative rather than the fact that Whitman had been singled out for her leadership and accomplishment in New Jersey.

Yet, these puppet characterizations worked most actively during Whitman's campaigns for office. The irony was that even in the face of literal and figurative puppet imagery, Whitman won office, and as her leadership progressed she was framed more complexly, pointing to the necessity of a more complex narrative on the part of the news media when reporting on political figures generally and women political figures specifically. Thus, the puppet imagery did not solely contain Whitman's exercise of leadership, but it did resurface again and again throughout her time in office, affecting the terms through which she would ultimately be seen. Further, the implications of the imagery reinforce New Jersey's political culture highlighting strength, control, and tradition. Political races for New Jersey governor are sporting events, battles or wars pitting competitor against competitor, the weak against the strong. Whitman as a woman was easily cast in the subservient role, motivating traditional gender expectations within political culture. Once in office, the power and prestige associated with the New Jersey governorship as well as the beauty queen and pioneer metaphors complicated the storyline.

The Paradox of the [Beauty] Queen turned Pioneer

Christine Todd Whitman was metaphorically cast in many roles, but more importantly relied on the rhetorical resources of each to perform leadership credibly. Confounding the traditional metaphors somewhat, Whitman benefited from what Karlyn Kohrs Campbell explains is paradox in the modern women's liberation movement in order to confound what Kathleen Hall Jamieson explains as the "double bind."[29] A 2001 study conducted by the Barbara Lee Family Foundation titled *Keys to the Governor's Office* supports Campbell's and Jamieson's arguments, noting that current challenges to women becoming governor include "Leading by Consensus—Decisively" and a leadership style that is "Not Too Tough, Not Too Soft."[30] In order to be successful, women political figures must manage a political identity that confounds dichotomies. Whitman was simultaneously characterized in the media within two competing narratives: the beauty queen and the pioneer. This paradox served to complexify her political identity and provided an opportunity for Whitman to capitalize on the visibility she enjoyed to perform executive leadership as a conciliator, a competent performance for a conservative woman in a powerful state gubernatorial position.

She Looks Good in Royal Blue

Women executives are often characterized metaphorically as beauty queens. As such, their appearance becomes the focus rather than their political issues. Such was the case with Whitman prior to her second term, but for her, appearance became likened to an almost royal sense of style and grace. As a result, Whitman became more of a queen and less of a beauty queen, transforming the typical metaphor somewhat, and suggesting more inherent power by virtue of her family ascension than the typical beauty queen.

With any woman executive, however, there is a focus on appearance. Whitman was no exception, as she bought into the stereotype herself now and then. For example, on her first election night someone commented on Whitman's fresh appearance after such a long campaign. "God bless the tubes and bottles," she said.[31] But more importantly, the media focus is telling. At the 1995 Governor's Association Meeting during which time Whitman gave the Republican response to President Clinton's State of the Union address, her credibility could not have been more highly regarded. However, *The Record* pointed out Whitman's stunning arrival in a "red dress" rather than the credentials that had earned her such a following. "A technician from NBC's 'Today' show sprinted across the hotel floor, hoisting a camera to his shoulder and clicking on a klieg light as he ran. Stepping off the elevator, the woman in the red dress looked up and smiled. Christie Whitman, the governor of the great state of New Jersey, had arrived."[32]

Both Whitman and Rita Edelman, *The Record* columnist, were influenced by the expectations of the woman executive as beauty queen as demonstrated by the following. When discussing Labor Day festivities with the governor, the subject came up of eating at all the banquets the governor attends. "I choose not to eat at the banquets that I do attend. I'd be as big as a house if I did. Besides, I'm always afraid that a piece of spinach would get caught between my teeth just as I get up to speak" said the Governor with her "blue eyes twinkling."[33] As if the "twinkling" eyes were not enough, the "trim" governor admits to a love of chocolate, "especially the dark chocolate that comes in individual little packages. I only take one of those treats. . . . I have to keep myself from overindulging. When I want something sweet to end a meal, I'll have a cappuccino, and I'm satisfied."[34]

At times Whitman left something to be desired in the poise and appearance category. For example, while attending a "swanky affair" in honor of her fifty-second birthday, Whitman discussed expanding Republican control. Yet what made the AP wire was Whitman's dress, one that clearly stood out in the crowd. "The governor bought the sleeveless gown, made of black velvet covered with rainbow-colored sequins, during her recent trade mission to Mexico. The dress took five people 15 days to custom make. . . . Sewn across the chest was a giant gold eagle carrying a snake, a symbol of Mexico."[35]

Though rarely was Whitman quite so flashy. More often she came across as elegant, even aristocratic or noble. In this way the beauty queen became a queen. Even well before her election Whitman's presence during the campaign was metaphorically described using the language of royalty, in contrast to her campaign workers. "The campaign workers, a relaxed group of fresh-faced 20-somethings, many in denim jeans and sweaters, nodded their agreement and sipped their Diet Cokes. Ms. Whitman—formal and aristocratic, wearing a cobalt blue suit—proceeded to the next item on her agenda."[36] Her suit was not just blue, but "cobalt blue," a color noting power and authority. Furthermore, she was called "a blue blood who looks good in blue" and "patrician."[37] During her hosting of *Larry King Live*, Whitman's appearance was described as queen-like. "Christie Whitman wore an elegant but visually uneventful royal blue suit and simple gold necklace a far cry from the flashiness of Larry King's signature suspenders."[38] Her taste and refinement were clear.

During her reelection debate versus Jim McGreevey, Whitman's performance was framed focusing on her royal and elegant appearance rather than the issues. "As for the governor, she did well too. . . . She looked crisp, in a tailored, broad-shouldered turquoise suit. She had an answer, a plausible answer, for every jab from her Democratic opponent."[39] However, despite Whitman's appearance the race was still a close one, in contrast to what was expected a year earlier. "It was going to be a coronation, not a contest. Whichever candidate the Democrats put up against her was going to be a sacrificial lamb."[40] However, something happened to this "noblesse oblige politician."[41] There was a problem in that the race was close, if not exactly even.

Keys to the Governor's Office explains that the most difficult stereotype for women candidates to overcome is the issue of toughness.[42] Certainly the beauty queen metaphor does nothing to counter this stereotype, and it resonates with the narrative of her clueless, symbolic presence. However, "voters think of a Republican woman as a Republican first, woman second."[43] Here the conservative Whitman may have had an advantage and made two decisions especially useful for her credibility. The first had to do with the role of the first lady.

Metaphorically, the beauty queen is all things the traditional woman is allowed to be, including a hostess. However, Whitman hired her own hostess, choosing not to capitalize on the rhetorical power found in social style. Nearly a year into Governor Whitman's first term, Christabel Vartanian became the governor's "head of protocol."[44] According to the *New York Times*, Whitman became governor "equipped with a First Gentleman" who "was not willing to take over traditional First Lady jobs: planning dinners, rescuing guests stranded awkwardly at official cocktail parties, presiding over household staff meetings, charming visiting legislators and business leaders."[45] As Mrs. Vartanian explained, John Whitman "isn't going to organize teas and luncheons."[46] Thus, there was a need to hire "her own First Lady—someone unquestioningly loyal and discreet, with an ambassador's sense of propriety."[47]

Mrs. Vartanian, Governor Whitman's "first lady," was framed as a feminine counterpart to Whitman. Articles pointed out her "tailor-made . . . pink-fitted jacket" and discussed her husband, the "wealthy jewelry wholesaler."[48] As the governor's "first lady" Mrs. Vartanian became the state's official hostess. Traditional gender expectations were reinscribed in a "first lady" as hostess while the governor tended to more important issues of state. Thus Whitman could uphold the masculine expectations of her position a little more easily. Coming from a conservative frame, this move added an extra measure of competence to Whitman as governor in response to the developing narrative highlighting her cluelessness.

Additionally, the beauty queen is also a traditional wife and mother. However, Whitman only brought attention to these roles once. During her reelection bid Whitman ran an advertisement that featured her twenty-year-old daughter proclaiming that Whitman was a "cool mom." Yet, the *Asbury Park Press* criticized the advertisement for being "a diversion from what is really important. Whitman isn't running for PTA president. She is the chief executive of a $17 billion public entity. I think voters would much rather see Whitman making a compelling case for why she deserves four more years in office."[49] While the ad did not make the most compelling case for why Whitman deserved another term, the criticism motivated negative attitudes toward women in traditional gender roles. Perhaps this was why the Republican Whitman chose to distance herself from her family role, downplaying the apparent contradiction in a wife and mother who was also the governor. Strategically this move can add the perception of competence to the conservative/moderate Republican political woman.

Where Whitman's family did come into play was her almost royal sense of ascension to the office. Her politically connected and active family lent her credibility. The *New York Times* quoted Whitman's father, a former New Jersey Assemblyman, saying "Politics really is the family business and she's continuing a job in the family business that she started with dad and Eisenhower when she was just a little kid."[50] Three years later the *New York Times* discussed the political background of Whitman's parents, including her mother, "who attended every Republican convention between 1940 and 1976" and held leadership positions in Republican women's organizations. "During the 1950's, the *Star-Ledger* of Newark ran an article speculating on who might be qualified to run if New Jersey were to elect a female governor. Whitman's mother made the list."[51] Whitman had a "considerable political pedigree," was "steeped in politics," "a child of destiny," and had "politics in her blood,"[52] important since she did not have formal training beyond her role as county freeholder and a state cabinet position. With such a "political pedigree," Whitman "brought a sense of stability to the governor's office."[53] According to former Governor Kean, "It's tremendously helpful to have been brought up the way she has in politics. . . . Her instincts, I find, are better politically than anybody who works for her. Her political instincts are better than the campaign consultants she hires, better than anybody on her staff."[54] Her family connections were not a liability but a boost to her credibility by the time she passed the midway point in her first term.

In Whitman, the traditional beauty queen imagery was transformed somewhat, into a queen with some level of competence to perform her duties. This level of competence may have been aided by simultaneous characterizations of Whitman as a pioneer.

Pioneering the East

The governor as pioneer is a cluster of metaphors noting Whitman's status as the first and connecting her populist rhetoric with her characteristics of strength, athleticism, and activity through which she was given the chance to prove herself a credible executive. This narrative complicated Whitman's beauty queen persona; however it is important to note that this storyline was not consistent during her first term even though it is one on which Whitman attempted to capitalize. In general, praise is given to Whitman as a pioneer governor during her first term for one of two reasons: the 30 percent tax cut announced at her inaugural or her 1994 midterm election campaign successes on behalf of her Republican colleagues (made possible because of her 30 percent tax cut).

As a pioneer, her status as the first most clearly characterized Whitman as New Jersey's chief executive. Hers was a "historic election" as New Jersey's first woman governor.[55] According to James Ahearn writing in *The Record*, "The returns are not just a defeat for Jim Florio but a victory for Christie Whitman. She will be the state's first woman governor. She is also the first candidate to upset a sitting governor in a general election. It was a good day's work for her."[56] While clearly an understatement, Whitman's work had just begun.

Not only was she the first in many ways, but she quickly created more firsts. She named the first African-American and the first woman to judgeships and named the first female Attorney General.[57] In 1995, she was the first woman and first governor to give the formal response to a Presidential State of the Union Address, and in 1996 she was the honorary co-chairperson of the Republican National Convention.[58] Additionally, just moments after she was sworn in she announced that the first stage of her 30 percent tax cut would be retroactive to January 1, seventeen days before her inauguration. She was determined to make her pioneer status count, which is important because, according to *Keys to the Governor's Office*, voters wonder about a female candidate's ability to act decisively.[59]

As a pioneer, the woman executive must possess a strong work ethic that connects with the people. She is practical and hard working. Whitman's populist characteristics eventually worked to her advantage, downplaying her simultaneous characterization as elite and out of touch. Reinforcing her populist pledge to listen to the people, the new governor took calls on a radio call-in show once a month. According to *The Record*, "New Jersey 101.5 is getting another on-air personality who will espouse a populist line of lower taxes and less government regulation."[60] By the time Whitman's reelection campaign was mounting the *New Jersey Lawyer* discussed her "version of populist rhetoric" that consisted of making government more accountable to the people.[61] The *New York Daily News* called her approach "clearer and more practical" than previous governors.[62] The pioneer governor with her populist rhetoric was apparently connecting with the good old-fashioned common sense of the people by the time of her reelection.

As a pioneer, the woman executive is also strong. This characteristic is particularly important for New Jersey political culture. Perhaps the clearest mark of Whitman's stalwart persona is *The Record*'s labeling of her as a "shining Margaret Thatcher clone."[63] Shortly after her election Whitman was at times discussed using active language, even language of battle, fitting for New Jersey political culture. For example, when objecting to a bill proposed by the Florio administration that would affect her tax reduction efforts, the governor "fired a first shot in the budget battle. And she took aim not only at Mr. Florio . . . but at the Republicans who betrayed their anti-tax rhetoric and asked for this increase."[64] According to former Republican governor Tom Kean, people don't "understand how strong she is."[65] She "dominates" the legislature, earning her the title "Superlegislator."[66] Further, the *New York Times* called her "a good soldier" for her 1994 midyear election campaign efforts.[67] Eighteen of the twenty-two candidates for whom she campaigned won. Her midterm campaign popularity also earned her praise as the leader of the "Whitman revolution" and "Whitman Republicanism."[68] As a result, the inevitable questions arose about Whitman's vice-presidential hopes. But she always maintained that her loyalties remained solely as governor of New Jersey.

Possessing great "determination" earned her the reputation of being a "New Jersey powerhouse."[69] She was not "one of the boys," but wasn't afraid to "prove her mettle if necessary."[70] According to Whitman in her biography, "I'll face the toughness thing, or that I don't understand how the game is played. . . . And with all due respect to the men, I do think they feel there has to be some blood on the floor to prove there's a battle. If I can avoid the blood, I will. If there has to be blood, I'm perfectly happy to do it. But I'd just as soon try something else."[71]

Part of Whitman's strength and determination stemmed from her natural athleticism. Thus it was not inappropriate that sports metaphors tended to be used from time to time when discussing Whitman. She was likened to "a quarterback" during her first inaugural address.[72] *The Record* recounted her many athletic excursions including hiking, skiing, biking, rafting, fishing, shooting pool, and calf herding. "Christie Whitman is just about the biggest jock to hold higher office since, oh, Teddy Roosevelt. Any day now, we expect to see her bag a moose. From skeet-shooting to PingPong to tennis to sulky racing to golf to NordicTrak, the governor is so . . . sportif that frankly, the rest of us are getting exhausted watching her."[73] Even suggesting that she could be Meryl Streep's stunt double in *The River Wild*, the article pointed out that "this Whitman-as-jock trait has yet to be incorporated into her public caricature. We still keep hearing about those patrician pearl necklaces. Truth is, her fashion accessory of choice would probably be her bike helmet."[74]

The article was correct. While Whitman's athleticism was no secret, it wasn't until her second term that her political identity regularly included her active pioneering lifestyle. That may have been because four political biographies published in 1996 focused primarily on Whitman's privileged upbringing and her political future as a Republican star. Athletic accounts included mentions of Whitman going fox hunting or her growing up on a farm, or rather estate. With the exception of articles reporting on Whitman's shoulder surgery in February of 1996, the media did not construct the governor as athletic and active until her 1997 reelection campaign. Until that time, the narrative of Whitman as the bumbling, privileged Republican star was the more plausible, and the pioneer imagery was easily chalked up to the exception that proves the rule. But 1997 notes a shift in the narrative. The athletic metaphor took a defining role in shaping that story. In Whitman's case once the athletic pioneer narrative took hold, Whitman's weak characteristics were transformed into positive ones, her political identity was complexified, and her rhetoric depicted in more substantive ways.

As a result, traditional roles for Whitman became transformed into skilled activities rather than gender-defined duties. For example, Whitman loved to cook. Yet, she was not metaphorically contained as a housewife or hostess, but as a chef. The difference was that the chef marks a territory noting skill and expertise. Whereas other governors were hostesses, Whitman was a skilled chef. "The 50th governor of New Jersey is putting the finishing touches to a Labor Day feast. Standing in the second-floor kitchen of Drumthwacket, her official residence on the outskirts of Princeton, Christie Whitman wields a chef's knife with practiced expertise. The garlic cloves on the cutting board before her are quickly reduced to minced bits."[75]

One article in particular recounted her athleticism, mischievousness, and the many complexities of her character. Apparently Whitman would regularly participate in pick-up basketball games with state troopers and had a "mean" streak.[76] This October 1997 article marked a turning point. No longer was Whitman passive, light, or lackluster. The puppet imagery through which she was characterized during her campaigns fell away. With her reelection the governor cultivated her athletic image to initiate the campaign to preserve New Jersey's open spaces. Further, it was just as common to find pictures of the governor engaging in athletic activities as it was engaging in official events, and many times the events were active and official. For example, a photo of the governor from April 19, 2000, canoeing through Mill Creek prior to remarks there was featured on her official web site, along with a discussion of the governor's commitment to the environment, something she often emphasized in her major state addresses.

When Governor Whitman was appointed President Bush's EPA Advisor in 2001, an article titled "Passion for Politics and the Outdoors" noted Whitman's "natural fit" for the position.[77] Ralph Siegel, writing for the Associated Press, writes that Whitman's legacy will be her initiative to preserve one million acres in New Jersey for "farms, parks and refuges."[78] Whitman acknowledged in her final State of the State address that her environmental efforts are personal. "I don't want you to think of this land enclosed in glass with a giant 'Do Not Touch' sign slapped on it," said the governor. "We want people to visit our parks, historic sites, and wildlife areas. We want them to swim, hike, bike and explore our state's natural beauty, not just saving our heritage but savoring it."[79] While her critics were not wholly optimistic on her appointment to the EPA, she is called an "environmental savior" when compared with other potential advisors and because of her balanced approach in New Jersey.[80] As an active pioneer who enjoys New Jersey's natural resources whenever she can, Whitman "clearly has a sense of the importance of conservation and the role of government as steward of the nation's natural riches."[81]

Despite an active lifestyle, pioneer woman governors often become political symbols until they are able to prove themselves, explaining in part the delay in Whitman's pioneer public identity. Such *tokenism* did not escape Whitman, for as early as her election victory the questions were mounting about her ability to carry out her duties as governor. No sooner had *The Record* reported Whitman's victory than the paper also began to question Whitman's "mettle." "As an outsider to Trenton politics, she will have to prove her mettle to legislators who've been around much longer than she has."[82] Yet the paper went on to suggest that Whitman had potential. "[L]awmakers in both parties should understand that if their complaint is that Mrs. Whitman is an outsider and a threat to business as usual, they are unlikely to find much sympathy among the voters, who have made plain that they are looking for constructive change, strong leadership, and an openness to new ideas."[83] However, another writer in *The Record* was not so optimistic. Using sports metaphors that were characteristic of stories about New Jersey political figures, "With the ball on fourth and goal, we have taken the seasoned veteran out of the game and brought in the rookie. Sports jargon aside, there is serious reason to doubt that Whitman is up to the task."[84] This token rhetoric resonates more comfortably with the narrative that had been constructed during her campaign, downplaying her potential toughness as uncharacteristic.

Echoing the token narrative, Whitman's tax-cutting initiatives also were considered strategic and symbolic, rather than substantive. Using sports metaphors again, *The Record* reported after her first inaugural:

> It was as if she sauntered onto the field and tossed a long bomb on the first play of the game. . . . Yes, she scored points. She knew that, as did the crowd. But these are mostly points of symbolism. . . . So why the hoopla? The reason has much to do with the subtle way that symbolism often triumphs over substance in politics. Whitman seems to know this in an instinctive way that belies her lack of State House experience. . . . Christie Whitman knows the value of a good symbol.[85]

Aside from the symbolism, Whitman was clearly characterized as the rookie, suggesting not only her recent entrance into politics, but also skepticism about her abilities on the playing field. For example, when she was chosen to host *Larry King Live*, *The Record* reported that the show's producers chose "New Jersey's rookie Republican governor."[86] And as a rookie, Whitman would be tested. When reporting on Whitman's many stops on "a national tour," *The Record* made clear that "she will be reviewed for her speaking and fund-raising talents, not to mention whether she is in tune with ordinary folk."[87] But even when discussing Whitman's "many talents," the article also reminded readers that "she is a green rookie just the same, with only a state cabinet position and a county freeholder's seat as her previous experience."[88] Further, she is a woman. Jay Severin, a Republican consultant, made it clear that Whitman's gender was what secured her as the respondent to the president's 1995 State of the Union address. "If she were Christopher Whitman and not Christie Whitman, she wouldn't be giving the response to the State of the Union."[89]

As a pioneer woman executive, Whitman was characterized as having a variety of qualities including "the first," her populist connections, strength, athleticism, and even mischievousness indicating independence and a strong will.[90] She was active physically; however, as any pioneer woman, she was an anomaly and had to prove her "mettle" in political battles characterized primarily as sporting contests and secondarily as wars. Whitman held her own, clearly following the rules of the sport. A third component further complicates Whitman's political identity: her star power.

A Rising Star

Whitman walked a fine line between athletic and patrician characterizations in a political culture that required her to be strong and active. She benefited from a star status that was thrust upon her following her successful retroactive tax cut early in her first term. She promised to cut taxes and she did. However, cutting taxes was something that other state political figures did as well, so there must be something more. According to Kathleen Rowe, "people become stars because their images play on—and magically resolve—ideological contradictions of their times."[91] In other words, star power is derived from paradox. However, Whitman did not play on her gender as a contradiction to political culture. In fact, her gender was rarely mentioned. Voters rarely saw Whitman as a mother or wife, as her family was kept out of the spotlight except at key policy defining moments. She was a Republican woman at a time when the party needed to reach out. Calling her a star made it so, and Whitman was fashioned into a spectacle right before her eyes. While some suggested that she was behind the media hype because she had higher political motivations, Whitman herself denied any such calling. Thus she was not the architect of her star persona, but benefited from it. She played within the prescribed boundaries of her conservative frame while also challenging those boundaries, at least when it came to social issues and her party, but her star persona gave her the benefit of the doubt.

The Record suggested that her star appeal was the result of something intangible, the "Tom Kean/Ronald Reagan syndrome."[92] The "syndrome" was explained as the ability to connect on an emotional level with voters. As a woman, Whitman had an extra advantage because women are perceived to be more trustworthy, sincere, and believable than are men.[93] Her popularity affected how "New Jerseyans view[ed] her policies. New Jersey residents seem willing to give her the benefit of the doubt, just as Kean and former President Ronald Reagan were able to deflect criticism of their policies at the height of their popularity."[94]

Whitman was a star because she was "articulate," "terrific," "quick-witted and personable."[95] It also didn't hurt that her party identified her as a rising star.[96] They needed her. She was popular, well-spoken, and a woman, something that created "an extra allure."[97] But she said people were just "curious" about a woman governor.[98] For simply being curious there were a lot of people talking about her. "I'm a Christie Whitman Republican," said one radio caller. George Pataki declared, "What Christie is doing is what we should all be doing." And while campaigning for Connecticut governor, John Rowland stated, "I'm a Whitman Republican, absolutely."[99]

Her presence also affected the state of New Jersey, making it into "a business-friendly, attractive place. In an intangible way, Mrs. Whitman has given us a touch of class."[100] (Yet her notoriety still garnered her the title "Mrs." rather than Governor.) And of course she was "one of the nation's most notable governors" as well as a significant figure nationally, often mentioned as the "perfect" vice-presidential candidate because of "her sex and ideologically moderate Republicanism."[101] According to *Newsweek* magazine, she was "one of the six most influential Republicans" in the country.[102] All because she kept a promise that started out as a last-minute attempt to save her campaign.[103] But more importantly because her party could claim her—she didn't draw attention to her status as a woman, but her party could. While the argument could easily be made that she was being used by her party, Whitman believed that change comes from within. And the political culture of New Jersey demanded a certain deference. Thus her visibility as a conservative woman worked to her advantage when coupled with the simultaneous pioneer and royal metaphors and the decisiveness of her decision-making. The point here is noting how the conservative woman can capitalize on the rhetorical resources at her disposal and perform leadership competently and in the process change the face of the office with her presence.

Even 1996 presidential candidate Bob Dole paid homage to Governor Whitman, promising "to do for America what Christie Whitman has done for New Jersey."[104] The *New York Times* suggested that Whitman and her campaign even "cast an iconic spell over" the party and Dole.[105] In comparison to Dole, Whitman was "young," "fresh," "personable and telegenic," and "caught a rising Republican tide."[106] Apparently he needed a little of that "Christie Whitman magic." In three short years Whitman not only became an icon, but an "idol." Just like Ronald Reagan, "New Jersey Gov. Christie Whitman has become the idol of Republicans everywhere by enacting broad tax cuts."[107] "The world cannot get enough of Christie."[108]

When it became clear that Frank Lautenberg would not seek reelection in 2000 for his New Jersey Senate seat, the *New Jersey Lawyer* declared, "the nomination is Gov. Christie Whitman's if she wants it."[109] She was the most popular Republican in New Jersey, with the possible exception of another governor, Tom Kean. Her mastery of "the bully pulpit" allowed her media attention like no other New Jersey politician. "Hardly a week goes by without her name and face in newspapers or television newscasts. And she has a track record to run on."[110] While it wouldn't be an easy campaign to send this "popular stateswoman to Washington," she "would be a strong and attractive candidate."[111] Here, finally, Whitman was referred to by her title of Governor, noting the credibility associated with her political identity.

The media framed Whitman's political identity relying on contradictory images, eventually lending her an air of credibility as a rising star in a strong state position. She had to battle a tough campaign narrative as well as the negative side of the pioneer metaphor, noting her symbolic, rookie status, but this, combined with her apparent family/royal connection to the office, eventually gave her credibility as a rising Republican star who played by the rules. In particular, her transformation into an athletic pioneer is significant, for as this narrative took hold, it began to rewrite the earlier script. As a woman leader operating from a conservative frame, Whitman also made some astute political decisions when it came to traditional gender roles: hiring her own first lady and keeping her role as mother virtually absent from her role as governor. Thus she was a Republican first, not a woman, and she could use the rhetorical resources of the strength inscribed in the New Jersey governorship to maintain power.

Meeting the Challenges: Whitman Defines Her Governorship

Taking an active part in her political identity formation, Whitman defined her governorship using the language of inclusion and diversity. Her hallmark was reaching out to the people, giving them a voice in government matters. She saw her administration doing work on "an endless continuum toward equality, accomplishment, and achievement."[112] As a pioneer governor she hoped to use her position to create opportunities for achievement, thus making her presence in the office not just symbolic, but meaningful. As she explained, "Being a first isn't any good if you can't use your position to create other 'firsts.'"[113] In particular the governor hoped to bring more women into the process of governing, but not just for the sake of diversity, for the sake of making more thoughtful decisions about the future. And she did. As she often explained, "I'm proud to say that my administration has appointed more women to high-ranking positions than any other in New Jersey history."[114]

Whitman believed she developed a government of inclusion that was a clear change from the way things normally were run in New Jersey. She ran as an "agent of change" with the slogan "Christie Whitman, a change for the better"[115] and relied on the adage "the most effective way to cope with change is to help create it."[116] One media outlet did pick up on her active rhetoric, explaining that Whitman's "response to President Clinton has given her an independent identity as an agent of change and a broader base of support among Americans who want it."[117] She discussed her administration during her first budget address, calling it "a new beginning" and a break from tradition as she gave her budget address during prime time instead of the afternoon.[118] Further, she declared she would "remak[e] government," giving voters a "real voice."[119]

One clear example of Whitman's efforts toward change and inclusion was her invitation to Myra Terry of NOW–New Jersey to become a member of her transition team. "I have a relationship with lots of women who work for Whitman, and the relationship is based on common ground and on common respect," said Terry.[120] Even after the transition was completed, Terry continued to be a valuable Whitman advisor. According to Whitman's chief of staff, "Some critics you listen to and some you don't. . . . Everybody listens to Myra."[121] However, all members of NOW–New Jersey as well as NOW's national leadership were not so optimistic. According to Ruth Mandel, Rutgers' Director of the Center for the American Woman and Politics, some women's rights advocates who work outside the system to make changes are reluctant to work from the inside. "It's going inside and being part of the administration that is so difficult," said Mandel.[122] Former NOW–New Jersey president Linda Bowker agreed. "It's a lot safer to stay on the outside and throw stones than to be on the inside working your tail off. . . . I wanted this job because I felt Whitman's administration would make a difference. I wanted to be a part of that."[123] Bowker was named Whitman's director of the Division on Women and had been instrumental in securing NOW's "recommendation" of Whitman's candidacy. And according to Donna Miller, a member of Northern New Jersey NOW and a member of NOW's state board of directors, "Not every time you talk to somebody are you going to get your way. . . . But to be at the table is a big part of politics. Whitman has always given us an opportunity to be at the table."[124] Even though the New Jersey state government is very hierarchical in nature, Whitman brought in diverse opinions to change the make-up of decision making from within.

In her remarks in a 1998 Los Angeles Town Hall meeting Whitman called listening "a revolutionary new approach. . . . It sounds simplistic, but believe me, it's a radical departure from the way things used to be. For years, when it came to urban revitalization, the prevailing attitude was, 'government knows best.'"[125] Not only did Whitman advocate listening, but also dialogue. In her remarks at the kickoff of the 1999 Urban Summit, Whitman explained: "Today our work begins with a single word: dialogue. *'Dialogue. Noun. An exchange of ideas, especially on a political issue, with a view to reaching an amicable* agreement.' This dictionary definition aptly describes the project and the challenge before us."[126] Explaining her program to "hold conversations" with New Jersey community leaders, Whitman believed it would be revolutionary. "We will *exchange ideas* with the people who know our cities best. . . . We will undoubtedly deal with the *politics* of addressing these critical issues. And we will most assuredly reach an *amicable agreement*—in this case, a plan of action that we all agree will help our cities move dynamically into the new century."[127] Not only listening, but working in partnership with people empowers those same people to make changes and "revitalize from within."[128]

Unifying her diverse public in a way to motivate their participation presented a challenge to Whitman. She created unity metaphorically by redefining the state of New Jersey as a family, which included government as well as its citizens working in partnership. Even as early as the campaign against Florio, Whitman discussed her "faith in the people."[129] She believed "that you have to bring people into the process rather than precipitous decision-making where the governor says, I know what's right for you and here it is and you're going to like it."[130] After Whitman's win over Florio, she embarked on a bus tour to thank her supporters. At one stop she told a group of white, middle-class supporters, "You have given me the opportunity to bring all of you into the process."[131] And when speaking to a mostly African-American audience of affirmative-action officers, Whitman explained, "Government should set an example of inclusiveness for others to follow."[132] The audience erupted with applause. Even her inauguration party in Atlantic City was planned with the "average New Jerseyan" in mind. According to Carl Golden, a Whitman spokesperson, "It's something that's both accessible and affordable."[133]

Partnership, cooperation, community, and working together were frequently a part of Whitman's vocabulary when discussing her administration. Whitman's emphasis on working together became apparent from her first State of the State speech in which she discussed "New Jersey's family," and the "partnership" between citizens and government. "We will go forward together, as one family with many faces, building a future with opportunity."[134] "Many Faces, One Family" became a theme representing Whitman's efforts to unite the diversity of New Jersey. Additionally in her 1995 Budget Address, Whitman brought her message to the people in "the first-ever statewide televised town meeting to get your comments on the budget."[135] In an extra effort to give people a voice in the state budget, Whitman explained that "the budget summary and speech will be on the Internet and in our public libraries by Wednesday. I hope you'll surf the net or scan the shelves and let us know what you think."[136] As she concluded, "we are all partners in this enterprise. As we work together over the next six months, let us go forward in good faith."[137]

In her second inaugural address, Whitman discussed the connections forged during her first term. "These past four years form a tapestry in my mind. A tapestry of faces. Families. Churches. Schools. Forests. Beaches. Wildlife."[138] Extending on the tapestry metaphor, she emphasized the interdependence of politics and the public. "I grew up on a farm. I believe politics and public service are a lot like farming; they only work if everyone pitches in. Our very best ideas won't work—New Jersey won't work—if people don't get involved. To improve the quality of life, everyone has something to give, no matter what their age, where they live, or what they do. I firmly believe that."[139] And Whitman did not exclude herself. "I just as firmly believe that the best leadership is by example."[140] With that Whitman pledged to read at least once a week for Books for the Blind. "As I make this commitment, I recognize that it's not much. But it's more than I am doing today. And I'm doing it not as Governor of New Jersey—but as just one of the Many Faces of our One Family."[141]

A governor of inclusion and diversity did not mean that Whitman was a push-over. Able to see the bigger picture, she stuck to her principles and was ready to fight for them if necessary, especially when it came to the religious right—members of her own party whom she believed were divisive. For example, Pat Buchanan, according to the *New York Times*, "sneered that he would walk away from a convention that would give that nomination to an abortion-rights supporter and 'Rockefeller Republican.'"[142] Whitman's reaction was somewhat amused and defensive. "I don't regret it for an instant. . . . My image of Nelson Rockefeller is as someone with whom people identified. He came through town in an open car, and men ran out of a barbershop with lather still on their faces just to wave at this guy. And he really cared about people and you could see it. . . . I hope I stand for that same connection with people."[143] The governor was sometimes poised as readying for "direct combat with the right."[144] As she often said, "As the party of Lincoln, the Republican Party ought to respect the personal as well as economic liberty of all people, regardless of race, religion, ethnic background or sexual orientation. . . . Intolerance of any group has no place."[145]

According to *Keys to the Governor's Office*, the woman governor must balance collaboration with decisiveness.[146] Whitman did so, and not just with the religious right. The *Asbury Park Press* likened her to the energizer bunny that "keeps on going. She is the Unsinkable Christie."[147] The *New Jersey Lawyer* praised her consistent stance on the issues.[148] The *New York Times* discussed the "steely nature of her character," noting she was not easily "swayed by the windy shifts of polls and party platforms." She did not retreat.[149] Further, she was someone whose "words could become a bond."[150] At reelection time, not only did she take advantage of the "symbols of incumbency," but she also had a strong record on which to run.[151] According to Republican state Chairman Chuck Haytaian, "Christie Whitman, as all incumbents, is running on her record, and the record is well-defined. . . . She said she'd cut taxes, and she cut taxes. She created 180,000 jobs. She said she'd control spending, and she did."[152] In two separate articles in *The Record*, she was declared the "voice of reason."[153] She was credited with restoring "a sense of trust that had been frittered away by previous governors" and with being "tough on crime."[154] She was praised for her diversity efforts, standing "up for her principles within the Republican Party, advocating affirmative action and free choice on abortion. In short, she has been an articulate champion of moderate Republicanism."[155] Interestingly, this praise comes with her reelection campaign when her athletic pioneer image began to solidify. By the time she was appointed President Bush's EPA advisor, articles pointed out that Whitman may have been too decisive, pointing out her "imperial style" in which she handed down decisions by decree instead of consensus.[156]

Whitman defined her governorship relying on themes of inclusiveness and decisiveness. She was equally at home discussing education as she was discussing the budget or crime. And she worked to find a home for her pro-choice position within the Republican Party. Each of these positions presents a challenge to the woman governor, but Whitman was able to confound any dichotomies competently as a conservative within a powerful state structure. As a result, her performance is most aptly described as one of conciliator.

Refining the Performance: Whitman as Conciliator

Whitman defined her governorship in a way that attempted to unify New Jersey as a family, emphasizing cooperation, inclusion, and diversity. Within a conservative frame, Whitman walked a middle ground, trying to keep everyone happy. As a result she engaged leadership as a conciliator. The conciliator is able to unite and bring together, is pleasant, friendly, and agreeable. She possesses goodwill and finds ways to reconcile even the most extreme of dichotomies in a manner that goes unquestioned. In the conciliator, seemingly contradictory aspects are made compatible, noting the importance of paradox as a rhetorical strategy; she is both tough when required (the pioneer), yet elegant in a manner that is poised, serious, measured (the beauty queen). She comes across as practical (the pioneer), knowing when to fight and when not to fight, realizing the power of dialogue and its importance for leadership. She governs by talking with citizens, bringing diverse opinions into the process of governing, inviting consensus, and sticking to her decisions.

Whitman's leadership is instructive in the opportunities the conciliator provides for negotiating the gendered expectations of leadership. According to the *Asbury Park Press*, Whitman "is a conciliator. In crowds and on stage, she is disarming more often than insistent. If some politicians crave conflict, she feeds on consensus."[157] The conciliator is able to manage a moderate public persona and is a credible leader who is gendered feminine—but this does not mean that she emphasizes her status as a woman over that of a Republican. She is a peace-maker and even a nurturer at times. She will stand for what she believes, but will not do so at the expense of party or state unity, reinforcing the hierarchy inherent in the political culture of New Jersey. Yet she is not passive, for she actively works within the system to exercise public power that has been granted to her based on her position as a strong governor, her family status, her political party, and her inclusion of the people at the table of government. Ultimately she is rhetorically sensitive and personable, assertive but not aggressive, well groomed and patrician. While speaking strongly for diversity, she does not believe the solution is to have all women in charge. Thus, she becomes a credible executive who happens to be a woman rather than a woman governor.

Specifically, Whitman's style dictated that she gather as much information as possible and, based on that information, make a decision. Even before she was inaugurated, she had planned a series of town hall meetings, call-in radio and television show appearances, and round table discussions with legislators in order to figure out how to cut New Jersey's budget. According to Whitman, "I am going to cut the state budget . . . the same way I'm going to govern, by consensus and not by decree."[158] Even Democrats were optimistic about their opportunity to participate in the process. Assembly Minority Leader Joseph V. Doria Jr. said, "She wants to work with us. . . . We want to work with her."[159]

Perhaps the most divisive issue facing the Republican Party during Whitman's terms as governor was abortion rights. While the Republican Party supported the right to life in its platform, Whitman was a vocal pioneer of Republicans for Choice. Whitman believed that the Republican platform should invite all voters. Divisive language such as that which supports the right to life and condemns the pro-choice position needs to be eliminated from the party platform. It should be replaced with "something that recognizes that you can be pro-choice and still be a good Republican," said the governor.[160] Yet, she managed to balance the cognitive dissonance. According to Ann Stone, who was the Republicans for Choice national chairwoman, Whitman fought quietly. "Christie spearheaded an attempt to build bridges, and to bring people in the party together."[161] Stone even credited Whitman with Bob Dole's "push for tolerance."[162] Whitman's priority, at least on the abortion issue, was party unity. At the 1996 Republican National Convention, Whitman as co-chair "embraced a compromise that retained the antiabortion platform but recognized the dissenters."[163] Her public role was one of "peace-maker," finding a way to acknowledge all opinions on a divisive issue, rather than one of leader of a convention floor fight.[164] Furthermore, she didn't let the issue define her. "While it's an issue of importance to me, it's not my major issue. It's not the definition of who I am," she says.[165]

In Whitman as conciliator, apparent dichotomies became reconciled. While the *Asbury Park Press* likened Whitman to Margaret Thatcher, calling her "the Iron Lady," the *New York Times* told the story of a little boy who mistook Whitman for Princess Diana. Clearly a study in contradictions, Whitman was able to accomplish what "tough-guy Jim Florio couldn't" and still look "elegant and impeccably groomed."[166] Her presence allowed her to mingle credibility and femininity. As Eugene Kiely put it in *The Bergen Record*, "Christine Todd Whitman is comfortable wielding a velvet hammer."[167] As a conciliator, the woman executive must be strong but not threatening or transgressive. She must be a hard, smart worker who can connect with citizens, making them feel comfortable and confident when sitting at the table. The ability to capitalize on the rhetorical resources of paradox is a hallmark of the conciliator.

Part of Whitman's strength came from her own strong will and part from the "nearly unchallengeable authority" of the New Jersey governorship.[168] Yet many legislators did not realize what they were up against. The *New York Times* explained that "those who have had close contact with New Jersey's Governor know that behind the warm demeanor, beguiling smile and earnest talk of fiscal restraint and social tolerance, is a fearless and sometimes merciless woman, determined to achieve whatever she sets out to do and insistent that she end up looking like a winner."[169] Her "sheer political ability" came from her "masterful" communication skills.[170] She listened, handled questions confidently, and talked to anybody. She even persuaded a consistently Democratic voter to volunteer for her drug policy committee.[171] She was merciless not because she badgered or beat down the opposition, but because she consistently and assertively stuck to her position, even though at times she did so quietly.

All in all, Whitman hoped that her various attributes defined her "not as 'a woman governor' or 'a woman director' or 'a woman employee' but as an effective governor, an able director, a tireless employee," as she told women at the Women in Government Luncheon in 1995. In this way she saw herself as one of many women who "were pioneers. They broke out of the box and reached beyond the expectations of others. They defined themselves by their work." Whitman believed that examples of pioneers such as Elizabeth Cady Stanton, Dorothea Dix, and women currently in public service "stepping out of the box . . . are putting a human face on government. . . . Examples like these not only raise the status of women in government but also raise the quality of public service for all of us in government."[172]

Whitman as conciliator came across as a good mix of attributes, possessing rhetorical sensitivity and a common-sense approach to leadership. In a somewhat odd contrast at the beginning of her first term, *The Record* commented that "Christie Whitman is no Don Quixote. She is not afraid of a fight, but she seems to know what she's doing."[173] Following her reelection victory *The Record* then declared that Whitman "prevailed. She demonstrated leadership and good political skills. She was flexible enough to strike deals when that was needed, and firm enough to dig in her heels when she had to."[174] Former Attorney General Cary Edwards, who ran against Whitman in the 1993 Republican primary, called Whitman's management style a "nice balance" between former governors Kean and Florio.[175] She delegated responsibility when necessary, but rolled up her sleeves too. "I worked with her at the BPU state Board of Public Utilities. . . .

She tends to get involved, but also has the ability to delegate," said Edwards.[176] Balance was also a primary theme in articles discussing Whitman's appointment and potential success as President Bush's EPA administrator.[177]

In achieving this "nice balance," Whitman realized that leadership requires effective communication and a sensitivity to the needs of New Jersey's citizens. As she explained in her 1999 remarks at the Annenberg School for Communication, "Because we live in a political system that depends on the consent of the governed for its success, we must engage the public in effective political communication. Failure to do so risks the failure of our system."[178] Continuing, she explained that "politics without effective communication will never rise to the level of leadership. No elected official will ever be able to lead—to break beyond the mere maintenance of the status quo—if she or he can't convince people that the direction she wants to take makes sense."[179] Whitman believed that as a leader she demonstrated "practical knowledge" and the changes that came about during her administration were simply "common-sense changes to make government smaller and smarter," achieving the goals shared by everyone.[180] When commenting on her EPA appointment, Whitman argued "that a conciliatory approach to business can be effective in attacking environmental problems" insisting "that it is the best method for achieving a cleaner environment and a healthy business atmosphere."[181]

As a result Whitman not only embodied moderate Republicanism but also inhabited a middle ground that worked to unite the diverse population of the state of New Jersey and later opponents and supporters of her EPA appointment. As a conciliator, she united, reconciled, and was hailed for her "new-style" Republican politics that even embraced bipartisanship. In an article that had her popularity "soaring," *The Record* explained that Whitman "burnished her image as a moderate earlier this month with the nomination of James H. Coleman, a registered Democrat, as the first black member of the state Supreme Court. . . . That image has garnered her attention as a new-style Republican" whose credibility came to the aid of Republican candidates nationwide.[182] The *New York Times* described her as "moderate in temperament as well as ideology, she even talks middle-of-the-road" using a "can't-we-all-be-reasonable tone."[183] Whitman explained that she believed in an inclusive Republican party with "lots of room . . . for people who don't agree with me" on social issues.[184] The *New Jersey Lawyer* even conceded that Whitman's "inching to the center seems to make sense."[185]

As a result, feminism even took on a moderate guise when allied with Whitman. The governor was described as a "feminist" by Myra Terry, head of NOW's political action committee, and as possessing "a muted but distinct feminist consciousness" according to Hazel Gluck, longtime Whitman friend and lobbyist.[186] Gluck also described New Jersey's Republican Party "as a natural home for women" because of its support of progressive social issues.[187] Further, Whitman's campaign received a "recommendation" from NOW in her race against Florio, though not a full-fledged endorsement.[188] NOW membership in New Jersey increased, and NOW–New Jersey leadership became active in Whitman's administration.[189]

However, Whitman did not come out and campaign as the feminist candidate or the woman candidate. She did not address "women's issues" directly and was "not a litmus-test feminist."[190] Her stance on welfare denied additional support to women already on welfare who have another child, and she lost ground among suburban women.[191] Perhaps this was why NOW was so divided on Whitman. "While some celebrate their entree to state government, others fear the renowned feminist group has been co-opted by the state's first female governor and her coterie of female appointees."[192] Even Terry "acknowledge[d] she is more soft-spoken these days. But she argues that when you're seated at the table, you don't have to shout."[193] Terry said that Whitman earned the benefit of the doubt. "Once considered a radical Democratic organization, NOW enjoys a respected role in the Whitman administration."[194]

Yet this middle-of-the-road stance as well as her views on abortion may have hurt her in the long run with the Republican Party. Granted, Whitman's star waned somewhat during her second term for three reasons: auto insurance rates, racial profiling problems that received national attention, and borrowing to pay for her tax and budget cutting proposals. However, when she left office and moved into her EPA role, she was still "generally well-liked."[195] Her veto of a ban on late-term abortions and her pro-choice stance made her "radioactive" to right-leaning members of the Republican party[196] even as it secured favor from some Democrats. According to a commentary written in *The Hartford Courant*, "Her reputation as a moderate and an outspoken advocate of abortion rights cost her any chance to be on the Republican national ticket" in 2000.[197] Mike Kelly writing in *The Bergen Record* asserted that Whitman's stance on abortion and her narrow reelection victory in 1997 resulted in conservative Republicans "sabotaging" her national aspirations.[198] Yet her EPA appointment will have nothing to do with abortion or racial profiling. As Kelly concludes, "We will undoubtedly see her hiking forest trails and paddling river canoes, a string of photo ops. After seven years in Trenton, maybe that's not so bad after all."[199] But somehow the EPA appointment seems more of a letdown than a reward for someone who graciously and competently played by the rules.

Christine Todd Whitman is an example of a woman governor who developed a competent, active political identity in spite of a weak start during her first campaign in which the media narrative was more willing to emphasize her "bumbling" campaign rather than the issues. She successfully engaged the challenges of regionalism and the pioneer/beauty queen paradox. When considering the entirety of her terms in office, Whitman's example illustrates the necessity of a tolerance of complexity when it comes to the media narrative itself. She was so many things: puppet, pioneer, token, beauty queen, yet her working from the center pulled together these apparent contradictions in a way that ultimately defined Whitman as credible. The conciliator is an effective metaphor to capture the challenges and successes of Christine Todd Whitman.

Suzanne Fields of the *Times Union* of Albany, New York argued that Whitman's governorship "marks the turning point in American politics. Now women can debate the issues without also drawing attention to their sex. More than any other woman elected to high office, she's neither a Rorschach test nor a 'role model.' She's a big-tent Republican, a pro-choice tax cutter. She understands how the larger issues affect men and women."[200] Whitman's gender was not her defining factor. According to Hazel Gluck, "I think what she is doing is showing everybody that a woman can do this job. This is not a question of gender, it's a question of competence."[201]

As more and more women enter the political realm, they will have the credentials of public office necessary to be considered "worthy" of higher political office. Christine Todd Whitman is one example of a public woman who successfully negotiated a political identity as a credible governor, cracking the glass ceiling that still exists for women in state and national politics. However, she still deferred to the rules as defined by the strong political culture. Negotiating a different sort of political identity is Hillary Rodham Clinton, who moved from first lady and political spouse to Senator. As the next chapter illustrates, the same sorts of gendered metaphors present themselves as Rodham Clinton tapped into the rhetorical resources at her disposal. However, she may not have been so quick to play by the rules.

Notes

1. James Devitt, *Framing Gender on the Campaign Trail: Women's Executive Leadership and the Press* (Women's Leadership Fund, 1999), 5–6.

2. This chapter examined media reports, opponent rhetoric, and Whitman's speeches and public appearances for the time frame beginning with her first campaign for governor in 1993 through her appointment as President George W. Bush's EPA Administrator in 2001. This chapter also includes representative reports as early as Whitman's first Senate run against Bill Bradley in 1990. A Lexis Nexis Academic Universe search produced articles and transcripts from national news magazines such as *Newsweek* and *Time*, newspapers such as the *Washington Post*, *New York Times*, and the *New York Daily News*, local New Jersey newspapers, and television programs from the major broadcast and cable news networks. Whitman's speeches were obtained from <www.state. nj.us/governor> and the governor's office while she was still in office. The scope of the chapter included the entire campaign, two terms in office, and re-election campaign.

3. Barbara G. Salmore and Stephen A. Salmore, *New Jersey Politics and Government: Suburban Politics Comes of Age* (Lincoln: University of Nebraska Press, 1993), 128.

4. Iver Peterson, "On Politics; Think You've Seen Power in Trenton? Just Wait," *New York Times*, October 1, 1995, late edition, 13NJ: 2, Lexis Nexis Academic Universe (accessed August 20, 1999).

5. Peterson, "On Politics," 2.

6. Quoted in Salmore and Salmore, 128.

7. Salmore and Salmore, 131.

8. Salmore and Salmore, 55.

9. Salmore and Salmore, 50, 51, 54.

10. Salmore and Salmore, 77, 78.

11. Walter R. Fisher, "Narration as a Human Communication Paradigm: The Case of Public Moral Argument," *Communication Monographs* 51 (1984): 1–22.

12. Kimberly J. McLarin, "The 1993 Elections: Woman in the News; An Outsider Wins Office: Christine Todd Whitman," *New York Times*, November 3, 1993, late edition, B6, Lexis Nexis Academic Universe (accessed August 29, 1999); Jerry Gray, "The 1993 Elections: Giulliani Ousts Dinkins by a Thin Margin; Whitman is an Upset Winner Over Florio; New Jersey Anger Over Taxes Propels Challenger," *New York Times*, November 3, 1993, late edition, A1, Lexis Nexis Academic Universe (accessed August 20, 1999).

13. Gray, "The 1993 Elections," A1.

14. Paul J. Hendrie, "Campaign's Bottom Line: The Bottom Line; Tax Issue Lifted Whitman and Doomed Florio," *The Record*, November 4, 1993, A20, Lexis Nexis Academic Universe (accessed August 20, 1999).

15. Steve Adubato, Jr., "For Whitman, Not All Tax Increases Are Alike," *The Record*, September 6, 1994, B09, Lexis Nexis Academic Universe (accessed September 14, 1999); Jerry Gray, "Star Over Trenton," *New York Times*, January 28, 1996, late edition, 33, Lexis Nexis Academic Universe (accessed September 15, 1999).

16. Kate O'Beirne, "Nowhere Girl," *National Review*, July 28, 1997, <http://www.state.nj.us/governor/feature.htm> (accessed November 6, 1997). All subsequent references to <www. state.nj.us/governor> were obtained while Governor Whitman was still in office.

17. Thomas Zolper, "Whitman's Star Loses Heat, But Still Glows," *The Record*, November 23, 1997, A01, Lexis Nexis Academic Universe (accessed September 15, 1999).

18. Mike Kelly, "Christie's Odd Tactics," *The Record*, July 11, 1993, O01, Lexis Nexis Academic Universe (accessed August 29, 1999).

19. Mike Kelly, "Christie's Message" *The Record*, September 21, 1993, B01, Lexis Nexis Academic Universe (accessed August 29, 1999).

20. Kelly, "Christie's Message," B01.

21. Kelly, "Christie's Message," B01.

22. Kelly, "Christie's Message," B01.

23. Lisa Baird, "Christie's Clueless," *The Record*, November 19, 1993, C01, Lexis Nexis Academic Universe (accessed August 20, 1999).

24. A year and a half into Whitman's first term, when discussing her likelihood as a vice presidential candidate, her lack of rhetorical style was again noted in B. Drummond Ayres Jr., "Whitman, in California, Fields the Vice Presidency Question," *New York Times*, April 30, 1995, late edition, 37.

25. Jay Romano, "A Day with Christine Whitman," *New York Times*, April 4, 1993, late edition, 13NJ: 1, Lexis Nexis Academic Universe (accessed August 29, 1999).

26. Romano, "A Day with Christine Whitman," 1.

27. "Prime Time: Whitman Responds to Clinton with Brevity," *Asbury Park Press*, July 4, 1996, <http:// www.state.nj.us/governor/primetim.htm> (accessed November 30, 1999).

28. "Prime Time."

29. Karlyn Kohrs Campbell, "The Rhetoric of Women's Liberation: An Oxymoron," *Quarterly Journal of Speech* 59 (1973): 74–86; Kathleen Hall Jamieson, *Beyond the Double Bind: Women and Leadership* (New York, Oxford University Press, 1995).

30. *Keys to the Governor's Office* (Brookline, Mass.: Barbara Lee Family Foundation, 2001).

31. David Gibson, "Whitman Stops Bus in Morris to Thank Supporters," *The Record*, November 4, 1993, A21, Lexis Nexis Academic Universe (accessed August 20, 1999).

32. Thomas J. Fitzgerald, "Whitman Steals Show at Governors Meeting," *The Record*, January 31, 1995, A01, Lexis Nexis Academic Universe (accessed September 14, 1999).

33. Rita Edelman, "Chef of State; Governor Whitman Takes to the Grill for Labor Day," *The Record*, August 27, 1997, F01, Lexis Nexis Academic Universe (accessed September 15, 1999).

34. Edelman, "Chef of State," F01.

35. Wendy Ruderman, "Republicans Turn Out to Raise Money, Profiles at 'Governor's Gala,'" *The Associated Press*, September 26, 1998, Lexis Nexis Academic Universe (accessed October 11, 1999).

36. Romano, "A Day with Christine Whitman," 1.

37. Suzanne Fields, "Christy Whitman Just Happens to be a Woman," *The Times Union*, January 30, 1995, three star edition, A7, Lexis Nexis Academic Universe (accessed September 14, 1999); Fitzgerald, "Whitman Steals," A01; "Christine Whitman for Governor," *New York Times*, October 27, 1997, 22, Lexis Nexis Academic Universe (accessed September 15, 1999).

38. Virginia Rohan, "Governor Never Forgot She's a Politician," *The Record*, July 7, 1995, A06, Lexis Nexis Academic Universe (accessed September 14, 1999).

39. James Ahearn, "Whitman's Reelection is No Longer a Sure Thing," *The Record*, October 22, 1997, L09, Lexis Nexis Academic Universe (accessed September 15, 1999).

40. Ahearn, "Whitman's Reelection," L09.

41. Ahearn, "Whitman's Reelection," L09.

42. *Keys to the Governor's Office*, 29.

43. *Keys to the Governor's Office*, 17.

44. Barbara Stewart, "In Person; Mrs. Whitman's First Lady," *New York Times*, November 12, 1995, late edition, 13NJ: 4, Lexis Nexis Academic Universe (accessed August 20, 1999).

45. Stewart, "In Person," 4.

46. Brett Pulley, "The 1997 Elections: Profile—Born with Politics in Her Veins; Behind Whitman's Earnest Talk, a Fierce Spirit Lies," *New York Times*, October 29, 1997, late edition, B1, Lexis Nexis Academic Universe (accessed August 20, 1999).

47. Stewart, "In Person," 4.

48. Stewart, "In Person," 4; Pulley, "The 1997," B1.

49. Steve Adubato, Jr., "'Cool Mom' Whitman Getting Nervous About How Close Polls Show the Race," *Asbury Park Press*, October 20, 1997, A11, Lexis Nexis Academic Universe (accessed September 15, 1999).

50. Jerry Gray, "Whitman Pursues 'Family Business,'" *New York Times*, June 9, 1993, late edition, B4, Lexis Nexis Academic Universe (accessed August 20, 1999).

51. Lisa Belkin, "Keeping to the Center Lane," *New York Times*, May 5, 1996, late edition, 50, Lexis Nexis Academic Universe (accessed August 20, 1999).

52. "Christine Todd Whitman," AP Candidate Bios, *Associated Press Political Service*, Lexis Nexis Academic Universe (accessed August 29, 1999); Pulley, "The 1997," B1; Lawrence Arnold, "Whitman Tries to Balance Personal, Political Lives" *Asbury Park Press*, October 26, 1997, A12, Lexis Nexis Academic Universe (accessed September 15, 1999).

53. Arnold, "Whitman Tries," 12.

54. Quoted in Arnold, "Whitman Tries," 12.

55. Dustan McNichol, "Warm Welcome Expected at Icy Inauguration, Safety Fears Cancel Parade, But Whitman Show Will Go On," *The Record*, January 18, 1994, A01, Lexis Nexis Academic Universe (accessed September 14, 1999); Gray, "The 1993 Elections."

56. James Ahearn, "A New Leader, A New Era," *The Record*, November 7. 1993, O02, Lexis Nexis Academic Universe (accessed August 20, 1999); Steve

Adubato, Jr., "Good Luck Christie," *The Record*, November 9, 1993, B15, Lexis Nexis Academic Universe (accessed August 20, 1999).

57. "Whitman's Big Hurdles are Still Ahead of Her," *The Record*, January 8, 1995, A24, Lexis Nexis Academic Universe (accessed September 14, 1999).

58. "Biography of Governor Christine Todd Whitman," <http://www.state.nj.us/governor/bio.html> (accessed July 29, 1999).

59. *Keys to the Governor's Office*, 24.

60. Bill Sanderson, "Look Out Howard Stern! Whitman Show's Coming," *The Record*, March 6, 1994, A25, Lexis Nexis Academic Universe (accessed September 14, 1999).

61. David P, Rebovich, "McGreevey and Whitman Woo 'Working' Jerseyans," *New Jersey Lawyer*, June 23, 1997, 3, Lexis Nexis Academic Universe (accessed September 15, 1999).

62. "Christie Whitman for New Jersey," editorial, *New York Daily News*, October 27, 1997, 36, Lexis Nexis Academic Universe (accessed September 15, 1999).

63. "Rollins Scandal Clouds Whitman's Victory," *The Record*, November 28, 1993, O03, Lexis Nexis Academic Universe (accessed August 20, 1999).

64. "Revise the Tank Cleanup," *The Record*, December 27, 1993, A14, Lexis Nexis Academic Universe (accessed August 20, 1999).

65. James Ahearn, "Things May Change, But for Now Whitman Is Doing Quite Well," *The Record*, June 8, 1994, B11, Lexis Nexis Academic Universe (accessed September 14, 1999).

66. James Ahearn, "In Trenton, it's Quite Clear Who's in Control," *The Record*, May 10, 1995, N07, Lexis Nexis Academic Universe (accessed September 14, 1999).

67. Belkin, "Keeping to the Center Lane," 50.

68. Iver Peterson, "The 1994 Campaign: Whitman; Move Over, Rockefeller, G.O.P.'s Got a New Idol," *New York Times*, October 4, 1994, late edition, B5, Lexis Nexis Academic Universe (accessed August 20, 1999).

69 Belkin, "Keeping to the Center Lane," 50; Rich Bond, "Why GOP Should Still Embrace Foes of Abortion Bans," *The Record*, February 16, 1998, A21, Lexis Nexis Academic Universe (accessed October 11, 1999).

70. "Christine Todd Whitman."

71. "Christine Todd Whitman."

72. Mike Kelly, "The Politics of Symbols," *The Record*, January 23, 1994, O01, Lexis Nexis Academic Universe (accessed September 14, 1999).

73. Kathleen O'Brien, "The Governor Exercises More than Authority, Behind the Pearls Lies a Player," *The Record*, November 26, 1994, A08, Lexis Nexis Academic Universe (accessed September 14, 1999).

74. O'Brien, "The Governor Exercises," A08.

75. Edelman, "Chef of State," F01.

76. Pulley, "The 1997," B1.

77. David M. Halbfinger, "Passion for Politics and the Outdoors," *New York Times*, December 23, 2000, late edition, A15, Lexis Nexis Academic Universe (accessed June 26, 2002).

78. Ralph Siegel, "Land Makes for a Governor's Best Legacy as Whitman Touts Open Space," *The Associated Press State & Local Wire*, January 20, 2001, Lexis Nexis Academic Universe (accessed June 26, 2002).

79. Quoted in John P. McAlpin, "Whitman Offers Modest Proposals in Her Farewell Address," *The Associated Press State and Local Wire*, January 9, 2001, Lexis Nexis Academic Universe (accessed August 24, 2002).

80. "A Symbol at EPA; Whitman's Pro-choice but is She Pro Environment?" editorial, *Pittsburgh Post Gazette*, December 27, 2000, A14, Lexis Nexis Academic Universe (accessed June 26, 2002).

81. "A Symbol at EPA," A14.

82. "A Grumpy Greeting for a Trenton Outsider," *The Record*, November 5, 1993, B18, Lexis Nexis Academic Universe (accessed August 20, 1999).

83. "A Grumpy Greeting," B18.

84. Walter Fields, "It's Very Doubtful Whitman is Up to Task," *The Record*, November 8, 1993, A17, Lexis Nexis Academic Universe (accessed August 20, 1999).

85. Kelly, "The Politics of Symbols," O01.

86. Kelly Richmond, "Whitman at Center Stage in Washington, Trenton Picked from Many Governors for CNN's Political Talk Show," *The Record*, January 29, 1994, A03, Lexis Nexis Academic Universe (accessed September 14, 1999).

87. Mike Kelly, "Go West Young Guv," *The Record*, August 30, 1994, D01, Lexis Nexis Academic Universe (accessed September 14, 1999).

88. Kelly, "Go West Young Guv," D01.

89. "Christine Whitman Seen as Vice Presidential Material," *Chicago Tribune*, January 25, 1995, evening update edition, 2, Lexis Nexis Academic Universe (accessed August 20, 1999).

90. Whitman's athleticism sometimes turned into mischievousness, For example, the *New York Times* reported her frequent efforts to "ditch" her security detail in Pulley, "The 1997," B1. Whitman's active and independent nature has been with her since childhood according to Brett Pulley, "Woman in the News: Christine Todd Whitman; Just in Time, a Listener," *New York Times*, November 5, 1997, late edition, B7, Lexis Nexis Academic Universe (accessed August 20, 1999).

91. Kathleen Rowe, *The Unruly Woman: Gender and the Genres of Laughter* (Austin: University of Texas Press, 1995), 59.

92. Steve Adubato Jr., "Whitman Sailing Right Along, No Doubt about It," *The Record*, October 11, 1994, C11, Lexis Nexis Academic Universe (accessed September 14, 1999).

93. Romano, "A Day with Christine Whitman," 1.

94. Eugene Kiely, "Whitman's Popularity Soaring; Poll: Job-Approval Rating 68%," *The Record*, October 24, 1994, A01, Lexis Nexis Academic Universe (accessed September 14, 1999).

95. Richmond, "Whitman at Center Stage," A03.

96. Kelly, "Go West Young Guv," D01.

97. Fitzgerald, "Whitman Steals," A01; Peterson, "The 1994," B5.

98. Adubato Jr., "For Whitman," B09.

99. Quoted in Peterson, "The 1994," B5.

100. "Whitman's Big," A24.

101. "Whitman's Big," A24; Ayres Jr., "Whitman, in California," 37.

102. Jerry Gray, "For Whitman, A Political Star Adding Luster," *New York Times*, January 9, 1995, late edition, B1, Lexis Nexis Academic Universe (accessed August 19, 1999).

103. Belkin, "Keeping to the Center Lane," 50.

104. Pulley, "The 1997," B1.

105. R. W. Apple Jr., "He's No Christie Whitman; 15% Hasn't Been Dole's Solution," *New York Times*, September 8, 1996, late edition, 1, Lexis Nexis Academic Universe (accessed September 15, 1999).

106. Apple Jr., "He's No Christie," 1.

107. Lars-Erik Nelson, "Whitman Stars in the GOP's Fiscal Follies," editorial, *New York Daily News*, March 26, 1997, 33, Lexis Nexis Academic Universe (accessed September 15, 1999).

108. James Ahearn, "Christie the Unsinkable; Like the Energizer Bunny, She Keeps Going Full Speed Ahead," *Asbury Park Press*, May 21, 1997, A15, Lexis Nexis Academic Universe (accessed September 15, 1999).

109. David P. Rebovich, "Sen. Christie Whitman? No Foregone Conclusion," *New Jersey Lawyer*, March 1, 1999, 3, Lexis Nexis Academic Universe (accessed October 14, 1999).

110. Rebovich, "Sen. Christie," 3.

111. Rebovich, "Sen. Christie," 3.

112. Christine Todd Whitman, "Breaking the Glass Ceiling," WESG Awards Luncheon, Washington, D.C., January 31, 1995 (Governor's Office, Trenton, N.J.), 1. Speech texts 1994–2001 were obtained directly from the Governor's Office or from the Governor's Website while the Governor was still in office <www.state.nj.us/governor>.

113. Whitman, "Breaking the Glass Ceiling," 1.

114. Christine Todd Whitman, Remarks, American Legion Girls State, Rider University, June 28, 1996 (Governor's Office, Trenton, N.J.), 2; Christine Todd Whitman, Remarks, American Legion Girls State, Rider University, July 2, 1998, 2, <http://www.state.nj.us/governor/girls98.htm> (accessed November 30, 1999); Christine Todd Whitman, Remarks, National Council of Women of the United States, March 8, 1994 (Governor's Office, Trenton, N.J.), 6; Christine Todd Whitman, "Unique Voices/Unique Service: Women Serving in the NJ

Legislature," Trenton, N.J., September 12, 1995 (Governor's Office, Trenton, N.J.), 2.

115. Eugene Kiely, "Real Change is Whitman's Big Challenge; Will She Deliver on Promises?" *The Record*, November 7, 1993, A01, Lexis Nexis Academic Universe (accessed August 20, 1999).

116. Christine Todd Whitman, Remarks, The 1999 CEO Summit, Waldorf–Astoria Hotel, September 28, 1999, <http://www.state.nj.us/governor/ ceosum.htm> (accessed November 29, 1999).

117. David P. Rebovich, "As America Assesses Whitman, Does New Jersey Win or Lose?" *New Jersey Lawyer*, February 6, 1995, 3, Lexis Nexis Academic Universe (accessed September 14, 1999).

118. Christine Todd Whitman, Remarks, Budget Address, March 15, 1994, Trenton, N.J. (Governor's Office, Trenton, N.J.), 1.

119. Christine Todd Whitman, Budget Address, 1994, 3; Christine Todd Whitman, Remarks, Joint Session of the New Jersey Legislature Regarding the Fiscal Year 1998 State Budget, February 10, 1998, <http://www.state.nj.us/ governor/budget98.htm> (accessed July 29, 1999).

120. Michelle Ruess, "NOW Battles Division Within; An Opened Door Has Brought a Chill," *The Record*, October 25, 1994, A01, Lexis Nexis Academic Universe (accessed September 14, 1999).

121. Ruess, "NOW Battles," A01.

122. Ruess, "NOW Battles," A01.

123. Ruess, "NOW Battles," A01.

124. Ruess, "NOW Battles," A01.

125. Christine Todd Whitman, Remarks, Town Hall, Los Angeles, Calif., September 10, 1998, <http://www.state.nj.us/governor/town.htm> (accessed November 30, 1999).

126. Christine Todd Whitman, Remarks, Urban Summit Kickoff, Trenton, N.J., September 14, 1999, <http://www.state.nj.us/governor/urbsum.htm> (accessed November 30, 1999).

127. Whitman, Remarks, Urban Summit.

128. Whitman, Remarks, Urban Summit.

129. Romano, "A Day with Christine Whitman," 1.

130. Romano, "A Day with Christine Whitman," 1.

131. Gibson, "Whitman Stops Bus in Morris," A21.

132. "White New Jersey Governor Strongly Supports Affirmative Action Programs," *Jet* (December 25, 1995–January 1, 1996), 30, Lexis Nexis Academic Universe (accessed August 20, 1999).

133. "Whitman Planning Party Average Jerseyan Can Afford," *The Record*, November 22, 1993, A03, Lexis Nexis Academic Universe (accessed August 20, 1999).

134. Christine Todd Whitman, Remarks, The First State of the State Speech, January 10, 1995 (Governor's Office, Trenton, N.J.), 10.

135. Christine Todd Whitman, Remarks, Budget Address, January 23, 1995 (Governor's Office, Trenton, N.J.), 1.

136. Whitman, Remarks, Budget Address, 1995, 1.

137. Whitman, Remarks, Budget Address, 1995, 11.

138. Christine Todd Whitman, Remarks, Second Inaugural Address, Newark, N.J., January 20, 1998, <http://www.state.nj.us/governor/ inAugust98.htm> (accessed November 30, 1999).

139. Whitman, Remarks, Second Inaugural.

140. Whitman, Remarks, Second Inaugural.

141. Whitman, Remarks, Second Inaugural.

142. Belkin, "Keeping to the Center Lane," 50.

143. Quoted in Belkin, "Keeping to the Center Lane," 50.

144. Belkin, "Keeping to the Center Lane," 50.

145. Quoted in Belkin, "Keeping to the Center Lane," 50.

146. *Keys to the Governor's Office*, 26.

147. Ahearn, "Christie the Unsinkable," 15.

148. David P. Rebovich, "Report Card on Whitman; School's Still Out On Impact of Policies in First Two Years," *New Jersey Lawyer*, January 8, 1996, 3, Lexis Nexis Academic Universe (accessed September 15, 1999).

149. Pulley, "The 1997," B1.

150. Pulley, "Woman in the News," B7.

151. Tom Kean, "Whitman Gets Rolling," *The Record*, April 20, 1997, O01, Lexis Nexis Academic Universe (accessed September 15, 1999).

152. Quoted in Thomas J. Fitzgerald, "She's Ready for the Democrats," *The Record*, June 4, 1997, A01, Lexis Nexis Academic Universe (accessed September 15, 1999).

153. Thomas Zolper, "Gubernatorial Rivals Stress Law and Order: After 4 Years, Whitman Has Tougher Image," *The Record*, October 5, 1997, A01, Lexis Nexis Academic Universe (accessed September 15, 1999); "Whitman for Governor," *The Record*, October 26, 1997, O02, Lexis Nexis Academic Universe (accessed September 15, 1999).

154. "Whitman for Governor," O02.

155. "Whitman for Governor," O02.

156. Halbfinger, "Passion for Politics," A15.

157. Arnold, "Whitman Tries," 12.

158. Quoted in Michelle Ruess, "Cutting Spending by Consensus; Whitman: I'll Ask Public's Advice," *The Record*, December 9, 1993, A03, Lexis Nexis Academic Universe (accessed August 20, 1999).

159. Quoted in Ruess, "Cutting Spending," A03.

160. Quoted in Belkin, "Keeping to the Center Lane," 50.

161. Quoted in Arnold, "Whitman Tries," 12.

162. Quoted in Arnold, "Whitman Tries," 12.

163. Thomas Martello, "Whitman Tried by Abortion Issue; Walks Tricky Line within GOP," *The Record*, February 9, 1998, A03, Lexis Nexis Academic Universe (accessed October 11, 1999).

164. Martello, "Whitman Tried," A03.

165. Quoted in Belkin, "Keeping to the Center Lane," 50.

166. James Ahearn, "Velvet Gloves, Iron Will," *Asbury Park Press*, July 12, 1995, A13, Lexis Nexis Academic Universe (accessed September 14, 1999).

167. Eugene Kiely, "Both Born to Run; Whitman Accustomed to Being at Wheel," *The Record*, October 26, 1997, A01, Lexis Nexis Academic Universe (accessed June 27, 2002).

168. Peterson, "On Politics," 2.

169. Pulley, "The 1997," B1.

170. Pulley, "The 1997," B1.

171. Pulley, "The 1997," B1.

172. Christine Todd Whitman, Remarks, Women in Government Luncheon, Masonic Temple, February 23, 1995 (Governor's Office, Trenton, N.J.), 3.

173. James Ahearn, "It Only Looks Quixotic," *The Record*, February 13, 1994, O02, Lexis Nexis Academic Universe (accessed September 14, 1999).

174. James Ahearn, "Whitman's Hard Won Victory," *The Record*, June 15, 1997, O02, Lexis Nexis Academic Universe (accessed September 15, 1999).

175. Kiely, "Real Change," A01.

176. Kiely, "Real Change," A01.

177. "A Symbol at EPA," A14; Alison Vekshin, "Whitman is Confirmed Unanimously; Heads to EPA Post Today; Defrancesco to Take Oath," *The Record*, January 31, 2001, A1, Lexis Nexis Academic Universe (accessed June 26, 2002); Halbfinger, "Passion For Politics," A15; Siegel, "Land Makes for a Governor's Best Legacy."

178. Christine Todd Whitman, Remarks, Annenberg School for Communication, University of Pennsylvania, Philadelphia, September 29, 1999, <http://www.state.nj.us/governor/annen.htm> (accessed November 22, 1999).

179. Whitman, Remarks, Annenberg School.

180. Christine Todd Whitman, Remarks, General Assembly of the American Legion Jersey Boys State, Lawrenceville, N.J., June 22, 1995 (Governor's Office, Trenton, N.J.), 2; Christine Todd Whitman, Remarks, Budget Address, January 29, 1996 (Governor's Office, Trenton, N.J.), 5, 6, 13.

181. "A Symbol at EPA," A14.

182. Kiely, "Whitman's Popularity Soaring," A01.

183. Belkin, "Keeping to the Center Lane," 50.

184. Quoted in Belkin, "Keeping to the Center Lane," 50.

185. David P. Rebovich, "Picking Next Election: Don't Bet the House!" *New Jersey Lawyer*, November 23, 1998, 3, Lexis Nexis Academic Universe (accessed October 11, 1999).

186. "Whitman Gets Nod from NOW," *United Press International*, August 9, 1993, Lexis Nexis Academic Universe (accessed August 29, 1999); Iver Peterson, "Whitman's Right-Hand Woman in Trenton; Hazel F, Gluck, Lobbyist, Friend and Political Pro, Has No Office but Plenty of Power," *New York Times*, January 7, 1994, late edition, B1, Lexis Nexis Academic Universe (accessed August 20, 1999).

187. Peterson, "Whitman's Right-Hand," 1.

188. "Whitman Gets Nod."

189. Ruess, "NOW Battles," A01.

190. Fields, "Christy Whitman Just," A7.

191. Steve Adubato, Jr., "Whitman Facing Gender Gap Over Her School Funding Plan," *Asbury Park Press*, June 10, 1996, A11, Lexis Nexis Academic Universe (accessed September 15, 1999).

192. Ruess, "NOW Battles," A01.

193. Ruess, "NOW Battles," A01.

194. Ruess, "NOW Battles," A01.

195. Charles Stile, "Whitman Ending Era of Peaks and Valleys; A Look Back at Her Years as Governor," *The Record*, December 25, 2000, A1, Lexis Nexis Academic Universe (accessed July 1, 2002).

196. Herb Jackson, "Whitman Parlayed Skill and Luck into Success, Ascendancy to EPA Only Appears Planned," *The Record*, December 21, 2000, A18, Lexis Nexis Academic Universe (accessed August 24, 2002).

197. "The Administration Takes Shape," *The Hartford Courant*, December 24, 2000, C2, Lexis Nexis Academic Universe (accessed August 24, 2002).

198. Mike Kelly, "Christie's New Gig," *The Record*, December 24, 2000, 01, Lexis Nexis Academic Universe (accessed August 24, 2002).

199. Kelly, "Christie's New Gig," 01.

200. Fields, "Christy Whitman Just," A7.

201. Quoted in Howard Altschiller, "Gluck Urges Women Lawyers to Get Involved and Go After Power," *New Jersey Lawyer*, January 30, 1995, 5, Lexis Nexis Academic Universe (accessed September 14, 1999).

Chapter 4

Hillary Rodham Clinton

Connie Chung: Mrs. Gingrich, what has Newt told you about President Clinton?
Kathleen Gingrich: Nothing, and I can't tell you what he said about Hillary.
Chung: You can't?
Gingrich: I can't.
Chung: Why don't you just whisper it to me, just between you and me.
Gingrich: "She's a bitch." About the only thing he ever said about her. I think they had some meeting, you know, and she takes over.[1]

When Kathleen Gingrich, mother of Speaker of the House Newt Gingrich, called the first lady of the United States a "bitch," her comment was treated as an aberration of public discourse and a sign of her political naïveté. Connie Chung was lambasted by the public and professional colleagues alike for compromising journalistic ethics by "tricking" Mrs. Gingrich into an embarrassing disclosure.[2] The morning after the interview Newt Gingrich lamented, "I think it is unprofessional and frankly pretty despicable to go to a mother, who is not a politician, not in public life, and say 'whisper to me' and then share it with the country."[3] Others viewed the incident as merely a sign of Mrs. Gingrich's lack of sophistication. Emory linguist Lee Pederson concluded, "I can't imagine Rose Kennedy saying anything like that publicly."[4] Whether or not Kathleen Gingrich's revelation was an unwitting disclosure or a deliberate jab at the first lady, it revealed the challenge Hillary Rodham Clinton had been battling since her entree onto the political stage—how does a woman in a public position of power cultivate an image of competence and leadership without being dismissed as a "bitch"?

The first lady may have found an answer to that question during the infamous Clinton scandal in which the president admitted to having an "improper relationship" with White House intern Monica Lewinsky. Although the Lewinsky scandal triggered impeachment charges for her husband, Rodham Clinton seemed to rise above the fray through her stoic support of the president and commitment to her family. Words such as "grace" and "dignity" were used in connection with the first lady, standing in marked contrast to epithets such as "shrill" and "bossy," terms more likely to be used to describe her early in the Clinton presidency. What triggered this symbolic transformation? In part, it can be attributed to Rodham Clinton's careful and measured attempts to change the story that defined her. *New York Times* columnist Maureen Dowd remarked that Rodham Clinton "came in as Eleanor Roosevelt and left as Madonna."[5]

Like former Texas governor Ann Richards, Hillary Rodham Clinton was cast as an "unruly woman" by the press and public alike.[6] Rodham Clinton, however, failed to benefit from the more empowering aspects of that metaphoric cluster, contained instead by the "bitch" image connoted explicitly in Gingrich's interview and implicitly in a host of other sources. This case study explores the rhetorical dynamics of a political spouse who evolved into a candidate in her own right. Rodham Clinton's strategic appeal to tradition and use of the "Madonna" metaphor to contradict the "bitch" image enabled her to resuscitate her credibility, promote a feminist agenda, and accomplish pragmatic political goals. In order to understand the rhetorical strategies she employed, the transition from "bitch" to "Madonna" must first be examined.

Hillary Rodham Clinton as "Bitch"

As part of the metaphoric cluster that casts political figures as "unruly women," "bitch" is more than a term tossed idly into conversation and forgotten. In Rodham Clinton's case, it became the underlying subtext of the controversies surrounding her role in Bill Clinton's presidency from 1992 to 1994. At the outset of the 1992 presidential campaign, and even during the early stages of the health-care reform campaign, many people supported Rodham Clinton's activist role in the administration.[7] Although evidence can be found during this period of media coverage that criticizes and/or degrades the first lady, ample favorable or supportive coverage is present in the mainstream press as well. Early in the campaign, a *Time* profile of Rodham Clinton characterized her as "interesting," noting her personal commitment to her family as well as her professional accomplishments.[8] The *Economist* hailed her as an "intelligent, successful person by anybody's standards (twice voted one of America's 100 most influential lawyers)."[9] After the election, *Time* dubbed the Clintons "The Dynamic Duo," crediting Rodham Clinton with a large share in the couple's political success.[10] A *U.S. News & World Report* poll taken in January 1993 indicated that 63 percent of those responding had a "favorable" opinion of Rodham Clinton, while only 23 percent reported an "unfavorable" opinion.[11] A *New York Times* editorial characterized Rodham Clinton's role in policymaking as "a logical evolution of earlier developments in a society where women are seen as partners and co-workers, not simply homemakers."[12]

However, following the failure of the Clintons' health-care reform efforts and the Republican rout in the 1994 elections, the positive images of an activist and productive first lady were subsumed almost entirely by the dominant story of a bossy and strident wife who "takes over." Although Rodham Clinton had been an effective stump speaker, winning over individual audiences during both the presidential and health-care reform campaigns, by late 1994 she was unable to convince the broader American public that she was competent but not threatening, assertive but not pushy. When Kathleen Gingrich identified Rodham Clinton as a "bitch" in 1995, she simply titled a narrative that was being written into public memory during the preceding three years. Walter Fisher suggests that human communication can best be understood as narratives whose appeal rests on their plausibility and verisimilitude.[13] In a mediated age, audiences are not presented with fully-developed stories but instead select fragmented story elements to form cohesive narratives. An image or metaphor can play a defining role in shaping the story that emerges. In the case of Rodham Clinton, several rhetorical episodes became defining components of the story that eventually would cast the first lady as "bitch." Once the "bitch" narrative took hold, Rodham Clinton's positive characteristics were transmuted into negative ones, her political identity was caricatured and oversimplified, and her substantive rhetoric was dismissed, ignored, or forgotten.

"Buy One, Get One Free"

The first episode pivotal to the "bitch" narrative occurred during the 1992 presidential campaign when candidate Bill Clinton proudly proclaimed that by electing him, voters could "buy one, get one free."[14] Rodham Clinton echoed her husband's sentiments, stating, "If you elect Bill, you get me."[15] The Clintons' decision to promote Rodham Clinton's professional accomplishments and involvement in political affairs was rooted in the perception that Americans were ready to accept a first couple with an egalitarian marriage relationship and a first lady with career experience that justified legitimate participation in the administration's work. Rodham Clinton was quoted as saying, "The idea that I would check my brain at the White House door is something that just doesn't make sense to me."[16] Moreover, the Clintons' tenure in Arkansas supplied them with evidence that as long as Rodham Clinton made gestures toward tradition (for example, by taking Bill's last name as her own), Arkansas voters would be receptive to an expanded role for her in politics. Rodham Clinton had been successful heading an educational initiative in the state of Arkansas in 1983.[17]

While the Clintons were banking on the assumption that most baby-boom generation voters viewed politics and gender relations as they did, Republicans recognized Clinton's "buy one, get one free" statement as a golden opportunity to paint Rodham Clinton as a radical feminist and play on cultural fears about powerful women.[18] Even democratic societies historically have had strong pro-

They elect him;
She controls him.

hibitions against the public use of power by women. These norms stem, in large part, from the traditional separation of public and private spheres and the affiliation of men with the public sphere and women with the private sphere. Arlene Saxonhouse notes that the separation of spheres was a defining component of ancient Greek democracy, and that women who transgressed "those established borders appear as perversions of good women, as either domineering dowagers or scheming concubines."[19] The public/private dichotomy was articulated in nineteenth-century America through the concept of "true womanhood" and the cult of domesticity. Karlyn Kohrs Campbell explains:

> As the cult of domesticity was codified in the United States in the early part of the [nineteenth] century, two distinct subcultures emerged. Man's place was the world outside the home, the public realm of politics and finance; man's nature was thought to be lustful, amoral, competitive, and ambitious. Woman's place was home, a haven from amoral capitalism and dirty politics, where "the heart was," where the spiritual and emotional needs of husband and children were met by a "ministering angel." Woman's nature was pure, pious, domestic, and submissive. She was to remain entirely in the private sphere of the home, eschewing any appearance of individuality, leadership, or aggressiveness.[20]

The cult of true womanhood reinforced the notion that it was unnatural for women to possess and exercise public power. Even after women in the United States achieved legal access to political and professional realms, cultural norms of femininity persisted, curtailing women's political agency. Writing in 1992, Dorothy Cantor and Toni Bernay observed that "politics and political behavior are seen as masculine endeavors" and that "in our society women who are aggressive and autonomous have been seen as deviant and have been considered unacceptable and undesirable as women."[21]

Given Americans' historical resistance to women in public positions of power, the Bush campaign saw "considerable political value in portraying Hillary Clinton as an ambitious and proud careerist in contrast to Barbara [Bush] as a loyal and self-deprecating helpmate."[22] Margaret Carlson noted that the "foundations of the anti-Hillary campaign were carefully poured and were part of a larger effort to solidify Bush's conservative base," suggesting that "the controversy swirling around Hillary Clinton . . . reflects a profound ambivalence toward the changing role of women in American society over the past few decades."[23] Republicans deemed Clinton and Clinton candidates for a "co-presidency," a derisive label meant to suggest potential for improper influence.

Cookies and Tea

In the spring of campaign '92, at an event staged by Clinton staffers outside of a Chicago restaurant, an offhand comment made by Rodham Clinton became the second episode crucial to the development of the "bitch" narrative. When asked about a potential conflict of interest between her duties as a lawyer and her husband's role as governor of Arkansas, her reply detailed careful attempts to balance private and professional responsibilities. At the end of the explanation she quipped, "You know I suppose I could have stayed home and baked cookies and had teas but what I decided to do was fulfill my profession which I entered before my husband was in public life."[24] Journalists immediately identified that comment as the "sound bite of the day,"[25] and later it was recognized as "one of [Rodham Clinton's] most serious gaffes in primary season."[26] Since the quotation was presented out of context in virtually all the mainstream broadcast and print reports immediately following the event, it quickly came to be understood as a statement "reeking with contempt for women who do not work outside the home."[27] Critics of the Clintons pointed to the sound bite as an admission of Rodham Clinton's anti-family, radical feminist agenda. *U.S. News & World Report* stated that, following the "cookies and tea" remark, some Americans viewed Rodham Clinton as "the overbearing yuppie wife from hell, a sentiment that led GOP media guru Roger Ailes to quip that 'Hillary Clinton in an apron is like Michael Dukakis in a tank.'"[28] Although Rodham Clinton hastily contextualized the statement, claiming that her work as an advocate "has been aimed in part to assure that women can make the choices that they should make—whether it's full-time career, full-time motherhood, some combination, depending upon what stage of life they are at," her "cookies and tea" remark fit neatly within the "bitch" narrative that slowly was being spun into public memory.[29]

"Taking Over"

Despite the controversy surrounding the Clintons during the 1992 campaign, Bill Clinton won the election and quickly appointed Rodham Clinton to head his Task Force on Health-Care Reform. The rhetorical theme that emerged in the subsequent two years was of a pushy first lady who "takes over," in meetings *and* presidential administrations.

Rodham Clinton's appointment garnered some criticism from those who questioned the propriety and even constitutionality of giving an official administration post to a presidential spouse. A *New York Times* editorial observed, "It makes no difference if the spouse is knowledgeable and uses power skillfully, as Mrs. Clinton usually does. However used, in a democracy, political power must not be bestowed with the marriage vows."[30] Some suggested that because Rodham Clinton was unelected, she would not be properly accountable for her actions, yet Houchin Winfield rightly noted that "[o]bjections to Mrs. Clinton's unelected power conveniently ignore the fact that many men have held such positions, from Alexander Hamilton in George Washington's administration to John Sununu and James Baker in more recent White Houses."[31] Katha Pollitt reminded her readers that the Clintons advised the electorate well in advance of the election that Rodham Clinton would play an active role in the administration, "so if people couldn't live with that, they could choose to vote for George and Barbara."[32]

The controversy over Rodham Clinton's role in health-care reform did not turn on accountability but rather on gender, power, and publicity. Pierre Saint-Amand contended that Rodham Clinton's "threat stems from the degree to which she has appeared as a model of women's political power, of their success in social and professional spheres traditionally reserved for men, of women's dramatic exit from domestic confinement."[33] The problem with Rodham Clinton's political power was that she exercised it publicly. Although she opened herself up to public scrutiny during the health-care reform campaign, preserving the machinations of democratic governance, Rodham Clinton violated the long tradition of first ladies employing their power only in private. It was the public use of power that made people uncomfortable. The discomfort was captured in and magnified by the "bitch" narrative within which Rodham Clinton's health-care reform efforts were located.

Criticisms of the first lady quickly became laced with sexual undertones and misogynistic themes. Michael Barone of *U.S. News & World Report* charged that Rodham Clinton's appointment to head the health-care reform task force was Bill Clinton's "payback to the woman who stood by him when Gennifer Flowers accused him of adultery."[34] Connie Bruck of *The New Yorker* echoed Barone, stating "To the questions about Hillary's role—essentially, the degree and scope of her influence and authority—there is a nagging subtext: the nature of the ties that bind the Clintons. It seems plain that his indebtedness to her must only increase with each new allegation of sexual impropriety."[35]

The sexualization of Rodham Clinton's authority was portrayed vividly on the February 1993 cover of *Spy* magazine, where Rodham Clinton was pictured as a dominatrix in studded black leather and fishnet stockings, wielding a riding crop.[36] The framing of Rodham Clinton's appointment in these terms suggests that the origins of women's political power lie not in their talents or professional qualifications, but rather in the ability to capitalize upon a sexual contract. The coding of women's power as primarily sexual is rooted in the traditional dichotomy between public and private spheres, where women "exercised power only covertly in their homes through emotional and sexual influence." Carolyn Johnston explains that covert sexual power relies on "persuasion, manipulation, giving and withholding sex," is generally used "to get one's way," and only works "when it is unseen and undetected."[37] While masculine political power is valorized as the instrument of justice, order, and the common good, feminine sexual power is trivialized, condemned, and/or feared. The sexual power of political women, particularly first ladies, often is characterized as "influence," where influence is coded as "hysterical persuasion" and "condemns the woman to illegitimacy" insofar as it functions as "a sort of ventriloquism, a cover-up, a dissimulation of the enunciator who is revealed only in the utterance of the other, the one vested with authority of discourse and action."[38]

The sexualization of women's power renders it illegitimate in one of two ways. Either sexual power is viewed as a weak substitute for political power, a desperate grasp for influence, or it is characterized as an unnatural deviation from a woman's proper role, a threatening intrusion into the male realm. When women's political power is sexualized, it is an attempt to remind women of the public/private dichotomy and confine them to their traditional place within that dichotomy.

Although most criticisms of Rodham Clinton avoided the crassness of the *Spy* cover, those images, like Kathleen Gingrich's later accusation, gave presence to the "bitch" narrative that had become the defining subtext of Rodham Clinton's initial years as first lady. The theme that emerged during the health-care reform campaign was of a bossy first lady "taking over" not only the health-care reform campaign but also the Clinton administration. When characteristics that previously were considered positive attributes were read alongside negative ones, they worked against Rodham Clinton by bolstering the "bitch" narrative. Robert L. Ivie has demonstrated the ways in which significant terms in a narrative cluster to form "vocabularies of motives" that influence conduct.[39] In Rodham Clinton's case, terms that gained presence in public dialogue clustered around "bitch," shaping popular opinion and molding her political identity. Initially, Rodham Clinton was touted for being a "superior administrator, watching over many details and keeping her schedule punctual," a quality which served as a useful counterbalance to the President's "loosey goosey" approach (as one aide put it).[40] Over time, however, this professionalism was viewed as contributing to Rodham Clinton's reputation as a "hard edged careerist."[41] News reports characterized Rodham Clinton's approach as "bold"[42] and "aggressive,"[43] terms that clustered with other, sexist descriptions and functioned to feed the image of Rodham Clinton as "bitch." Typical of these accounts was Michael Barone's characterization of the health-care reform campaign as "bossy social engineering." As Barone saw it, Bill Clinton unwisely "ceded" the health-care campaign to his wife, carrying "the boomer liberal faith of feminism too far" and making himself look weak.[44] That type of media commentary echoed Richard Nixon's admonition that "[i]f the wife comes through as being too strong and too intelligent it makes the husband look like a wimp."[45]

Other types of coverage bolstered the "bitch" narrative as well. When Jonathan Alter of *Newsweek* commended Rodham Clinton during the health-care reform campaign for strategically speaking out against the health insurance industry, his essay was laced with images of a threatening, confrontational, and out-of-control first lady. The headline on Alter's essay read "Go Ahead, Bust Some Chops," and in the article Alter noted that "Hillary was smart to rip their [health insurance professionals] heads off." Even though the text of the essay was largely complimentary of Rodham Clinton, its headline, photo art, and key outtakes fit within the "bitch" narrative. The photo, labeled with the caption "Blasting health insurers," featured the first lady behind a podium, speaking forcefully and gesturing as if she was pounding the podium as she spoke. The article noted that the address earned Rodham Clinton "the new nickname 'Shrillary,'" and reported that "her attack" "shatter[ed]" the "silly tradition . . . requiring First Ladies to speak only in soothing platitudes."[46] Alter was speaking metaphorically when he described the ripping off of heads; however, anecdotes of Rodham Clinton's so-called violent streak surfaced in media accounts during this period as well. A story that garnered wide circulation described Rodham Clinton hurling a lamp at her husband during a row at the White House.[47]

Some critics took the "bitch" narrative to its terrifying conclusion, suggesting that Rodham Clinton was compromising America's heroic masculinity. In an essay critiquing Bill Clinton's foreign policy, Barbara Amiel made Rodham Clinton her scapegoat, charging her with the downfall of America and concluding: "The First Lady has emasculated America. I guess that is what radical feminists always wanted to do, but when the Bobbitt syndrome hits the only superpower left in the world, it's not only the Mr. Bobbitts who are in pain. We all are."[48]

Similarly, Noemie Emery dubbed Clinton Democrats "the Androgyny party," and yearned for the party of "Lyndon Johnson, who between civil-rights bills went out and shot things." Invoking "bitch" imagery, if not the word itself, Emery characterized Rodham Clinton as follows: "She orders. . . . She demands. . . . She wants to be feared. . . . Her hunger for power is open and palpable."[49]

The tone of media coverage during the health-care reform campaign begs the question, did Rodham Clinton's own discourse contribute to the "bitch" persona? Were those who covered and criticized her in the press simply reflecting the mood of her own rhetoric? The majority of Rodham Clinton's health-care reform speeches followed a standard format in which the first lady articulated the key components of the Clinton reform plan, highlighting issues such as universal coverage and access to health care for all Americans, primary and preventative health care, choice for patients and physicians in terms of health plans and treatments, cost control, and preservation of quality in medical research and medical care.[50] Rodham Clinton also typically outlined the financing options for the proposed reforms, rejecting the single payer (publicly funded) and individual mandate (privately funded) proposals and advocating a system whereby both individuals and employers contribute to the funding of health care. Campbell argues that during the health-care reform campaign the first lady failed to "feminize her advocacy" in the way that other successful politicians have done, adopting instead the persona of "expert and advocate," and delivering policy speeches rather than personalized narratives. Campbell concludes that Rodham Clinton's rhetorical style was at least partly to blame for her unpopularity as an advocate, especially because "the role she chose [was] so unambiguously public and ha[d]

involved extensive speech-making on a major public policy issue—public performances in a role that is gender-coded masculine—the gender norms calling
for a feminine rhetorical style take on new intensity and urgency, and performing femininity discursively becomes more salient."[51]

Not only were the majority of Rodham Clinton's health-care reform
speeches structured like traditional public policy addresses, her rhetorical stance
as a policy advocate also was a striking departure from the personal and ceremonial tone typically adopted by previous U.S. first ladies. In addition, we have
found that embedded in Rodham Clinton's rhetoric were literalized metaphors
connoting a rhetoric of confrontation and control that fed the "bitch" narrative.
Rodham Clinton attempted to balance confrontation and control metaphors with
messages of partnership and repair, yet because those attempts lacked fidelity to
the "bitch" narrative, they were either forgotten or deemed inauthentic.

At the outset of the health-care reform campaign, the first lady attempted to
position herself as facilitator rather than leader, orchestrating a number of "conversations on health" designed to provide a forum where regular citizens could
air their complaints about the current health-care system and suggestions for
reform. Although the *Economist* covered this move in a brief article entitled
"Listen with Hillary," it also noted that the "conversations" were mainly a political ploy designed to "create a sense of participation" and a "perception of
open government."[52] The suggestion that Rodham Clinton could act as a neutral
facilitator was not credible, even in the spring of 1993. Rodham Clinton stuck
with the "conversation" theme once she began to stump for the Clinton reform
package, characterizing the health-care debate as a "national discussion" and
insisting that the Clinton plan was the "result of literally thousands, and tens of
thousands, of conversations."[53] She told the audience at the Institute of Medicine's annual meeting that when she initially conceptualized her role in
health-care reform, "it was with the idea that I would do much less talking than
listening."[54] Despite this approach, however, most Americans viewed her as the
leader of a reform campaign rather than as the facilitator of a national discussion, an impression that was validated, in part, by the implicit metaphors in
Rodham Clinton's health-care reform rhetoric.

Examination of the metaphors embedded in the first lady's speeches during
the 1993–94 health-care reform campaign reveals a rhetoric of confrontation and
control that contradicted Rodham Clinton's explicit "conversation" message and
fed the "bitch" narrative governing media accounts during this period. First, war
and combat metaphors dominated Rodham Clinton's health-care reform rhetoric. Without identifying a specific foe, she contended that the U.S. health-care
system was under "attack" and that there was "a disturbing assault on the doc-
tor/patient relationship."[55] She commended the American Hospital Association
for "sound[ing] the alarm about what is happening on the front lines of health
care," and derided those who, in the past, "have marched to the edge of health
care reform only to cower in fear and shrink away."[56] She repeatedly characterized the American health-care situation as a "crisis,"[57] castigating the "forces

arrayed against the changes that we seek."[58] The war imagery was made explicit in a speech to the American Legion when Rodham Clinton thanked Legion members for their efforts in "fighting external threats," then characterized the U.S. health care system as an "internal threat."[59] By declaring war on opponents of health-care reform, Rodham Clinton not only undermined her explicit intention to launch a national "conversation" on health care, she also established herself as de facto general in the health care revolution. Such imagery fostered fears that Rodham Clinton was stepping outside the boundaries of her proper role as first lady, acting as a leader rather than a facilitator and achieving a dangerous amount of political agency.

Rodham Clinton's implicit rhetoric of confrontation was compounded by a rhetoric of control which also emerged during the health-care reform campaign. Control was an overt theme in her health-care reform speeches because cost control was a major plank in the Clinton reform policy. Covertly, however, the threat of female control in the public realm of politics emerged with the suggestion that the first lady, rather than the president or his cabinet, was steering the reform campaign. Just as she attempted to position herself as a facilitator rather than leader early in 1993, Rodham Clinton explicitly emphasized her status as someone who spoke on behalf of the president rather than someone who shared his authority, referring to the Clinton reform plan as "the president's proposal."[60] At the same time, however, Rodham Clinton accepted the role of official chairperson of the President's Task Force on Health-Care Reform. Since the Clintons ran on a "buy one, get one free" ticket, the image of an historic "co-presidency" was still vivid in many Americans' minds. When Rodham Clinton encouraged the American Hospital Association to "let us move forward together in trying to fashion a health care system that represents the best about what each of you believe and do every day," it suggested that AHA members would be moving forward most directly with her, not the president.[61] The fear of a woman "taking over" the business of governance seemed to gain credence during a ceremony in the East Room of the White House, when the first lady took the liberty of correcting Vice President Al Gore. The exchange took place as follows:

> Gore: And one doctor said that in adding up the amount of time that he spent on paperwork, he could have seen an extra 500 patients per week—I believe it was per week—per year, I'm sorry. (Laughter). I don't want to get carried away with this. No, I don't think it was per year. I think it was more than one per day.
> Rodham Clinton: It was one and a half per day.
> Gore: In any event, it was a lot (Laughter and applause).[62]

Although the exchange was marked by a jovial tone, the image it presents is of a vice president out of touch with the details of the administration's key domestic policy, and a first lady in control of the operation. This picture was reinforced at another White House event when Tipper Gore lauded "Hillary Clinton and her leadership on this whole issue." After noting Rodham Clinton's contributions to the health-care reform efforts, Gore joked, "And now, of course, the President did a great job in presenting—we don't want to forget him."[63]

The rhetoric of confrontation and control may have been an implicit component of Rodham Clinton's health-care reform rhetoric, but because it achieved fidelity with the "bitch" narrative it was absorbed into the larger story. When the health-care reform period is examined *in toto*, competing images of Rodham Clinton can be found. Some reports present a professional and competent first lady aiding her husband's political efforts. Others offer a brash and threatening political operator. A few offer a messy blend of both. What is striking rhetorically about this period, however, is the way in which the "bitch" narrative gained prominence and colored even the flattering portraits of Rodham Clinton's talents. Evidence that the "bitch" persona did, indeed, resonate with most Americans lies in Rodham Clinton's own behavior. Following the defeat of health-care reform and the 1994 elections, Rodham Clinton gauged public opinion, noted significant opposition, and recast herself in an effort to escape the "bitch" narrative. The move toward tradition enabled her to regain some popularity as first lady and even positioned her to run a successful campaign for the U.S. Senate in the 2000 election. The next section of this study examines the ways in which the resuscitation of Rodham Clinton's political identity occurred only after she began to conform more explicitly to norms of femininity.

Hillary Rodham Clinton as "Madonna"

The Madonna metaphor falls within the larger hostess/beauty queen metaphoric cluster which has encapsulated so many political spouses. Madonna allows for an emphasis on tradition and "womanly" power; however, just as the social style of the hostess/beauty queen holds promise for women's political agency, the Madonna metaphor has more room for radicalism within its imagistic grasp than one might realize at first glance. Although Rodham Clinton first enacted a traditionally feminine version of Madonna as she responded to the decimation of her image in 1994, in both domestic and international rhetoric the first lady employed paradox as a rhetorical strategy to make her Madonna persona complex and heterogeneous, and to blur the lines between femininity and feminism. This new political identity enabled Rodham Clinton to promote her own political agenda, respond to the Clinton sex scandals, and position herself as a credible candidate for the U.S. Senate. For Rodham Clinton, "Madonna" became a well from which she could draw rhetorical resources. The Madonna metaphor is rich, in part, because of its long history in U.S. culture.

Madonna in the American Imagination

The appeal of the Madonna image lies in its elasticity as a metaphor. Madonna originated in the Biblical story of Mary, the mother of Jesus, and is woven into American myth and culture. John Gatta's study of the Madonna theme in American literature highlights varying manifestations of the Madonna trope, from the paradigmatic mother seen in the work of Harriett Beecher Stowe to the early-twentieth-century Madonna exemplified in Harold Frederic's writings where Madonna was associated with a mystique of covert sexuality. Henry Adams's work rounded out the Madonna persona by giving it both a morally redemptive capacity reminiscent of the nineteenth-century cult of true womanhood, as well as a sexual dimension; Adams describes the Madonna as a "self-subsistent monarch who owns and rules the place. . . . She reigns in defiance of patriarchal authority, whether exercised on a divine or ecclesiastical plane." [64]

Of course, any discussion of "Madonna" in American culture could not stop at the literary version. Much more familiar to contemporary audiences is the pop icon, the material girl lauded for individuality and image savvy but vilified for cagey consumerism. What the pop star brings to the metaphor is heterogeneity—the ability to embody the "both/and." Critics examining pop icon Madonna have produced diverse, sometimes contradictory, readings of her public persona. Some view her as a sign of heterogeneity, encompassing oppositional discourses in a way that is liberatory for women. Postmodern feminists contend that through parodic performance Madonna begins to deconstruct the notion of gender. Others critique what they see as an excessive emphasis on wealth and pleasure in Madonna's discourse, claiming that the commodification of her image blunts any liberatory potential that it might otherwise have.[65] E. Dierdre Pribram explains that "feminists' ambivalence toward Madonna derives from arguments of whether she works to destroy stereotypes or only confirms traditional roles and representations of women. These contentions are fueled by the difficulties surrounding the Madonna persona, the difficulties of *fixing* her as one set of meanings or another."[66] Such critique has been leveled similarly at Rodham Clinton, with some feminists arguing that her turn toward femininity in 1995 was a betrayal of her liberal feminist sensibilities and others applauding her for resisting familiar stereotypes and easy categorizations. In fact, in 1996 a political cartoon explicitly conflated the public personae of Madonna and Rodham Clinton, portraying the first lady as Evita, a figure then being depicted in film by Madonna. In the cartoon, a silhouetted first lady is standing on the White House balcony, singing "Don't cry for me, Arkansas," while a voice from within the White House urges her to "Come to bed, Hillary." The cartoon, reprinted in the December 23, 1996 issue of *Newsweek* magazine in its "Perspectives" section, invokes both the Whitewater scandal and the song from the film, *Evita*, entitled "Don't Cry for Me Argentina." The song was a popular single for pop artist Madonna.

The Madonna metaphor historically has encompassed a variety of female identities, from sexless saint to empowered mother to heterogeneous individual. As such, it can be employed for conservative, liberal, and radical political ends. Because Madonna represents this continuum of female identities, it serves as a useful analog for Rodham Clinton's own political transformation. Initially, Rodham Clinton seemed to be stifled by the hyper-feminized dimensions of the ancient archetype. As she rounded out her image on the international stage, however, the first lady began to develop a robust political identity that tapped into the heterogeneity and diversity of the Madonna trope.

It is important to note at this point the difficulty in making any generalized claims about how Rodham Clinton was "viewed" or "received" by the "public." Taken as a sign of U.S. womanhood, First Lady Hillary Rodham Clinton was polysemous and contradictory. Just as audience responses to pop icon Madonna varied, so too did public reactions to Rodham Clinton. Additionally, assigning rhetorical intentionality to Rodham Clinton or her handlers is problematic because this research examines public texts only, and because often those public texts are mediated by news organizations. Shawn Parry-Giles argues forcefully that television news organizations "typecast" First Lady Hillary Rodham Clinton, relying on crude stereotypes of women and feminism to inform their stories; thus her own rhetorical strategies are often erased by the simpler and more familiar news narrative.[67] What this chapter examines, however, is rhetorical evidence that Rodham Clinton was cognizant of some of those crude stereotypes, and in fact used them strategically both to recoup her image and expand her political identity.

Mother Superior

Attempts in 1995 to become a more conventionally feminine first lady were designed to trigger a more positive affective response from those who were put off by her political persona during the preceding three years. Specifically, Rodham Clinton employed motherhood as an archetypal image. Michael Osborn has demonstrated the rhetorical force of archetypal metaphors in discourse, and Lynn M. Stearney explains that motherhood is one such archetype.[68] According to Stearney, motherhood functions as an archetype because it "transcends particular situations and constructs similarities in meaning which both reflect and capture assumptions and thus is persuasive."[69] To become a feminine mother, Rodham Clinton first altered her physical appearance. In 1995, bold-colored business suits gave way to pastel outfits. The short, simple hairstyle Rodham Clinton chose during the health-care reform campaign was replaced first by a Jacqueline Kennedy–style bouffant, and then by a more simple bob that softly framed her face. Cosmetic changes signaled more significant revisions in the first lady's political duties. Immediately following the defeat of the health-care reform bill, Rodham Clinton shifted her energies from domestic politics to international travel and diplomacy. Trips abroad gave her a venue to promote the welfare of women and children worldwide, and also fell more closely within the purview of traditionally acceptable action for a United States first lady. Rodham Clinton also traveled abroad with daughter Chelsea, a significant move since, prior to 1995, the Clintons were careful to keep their daughter out of the public eye. Although Rodham Clinton undoubtedly wanted to spend more time with her daughter before Chelsea left for college and likely viewed the trips abroad as educational opportunities, the many photographs of mother and daughter also bolstered the new, feminine, maternal image she was working to cultivate.

Perhaps the most visible manifestation of the Madonna trope in this phase of Rodham Clinton's political life was her book, *It Takes a Village and Other Lessons Children Teach Us*, published in 1996.[70] The book combines personal experiences from Rodham Clinton's life with expert testimony about child rearing and welfare, and descriptions of successful private and governmental programs for children. It is underscored by themes of civic responsibility that likely emerge from Rodham Clinton's Methodism as well as her liberalism. The book's promotion and distribution in the public sphere served to promote Rodham Clinton's maternal and feminine image. The dust jacket on the book portrays an exuberant first lady, surrounded by children who are laughing and smiling. The inside, back cover describes Rodham Clinton as follows: "Hillary Rodham Clinton is America's First Lady. A longtime child advocate, she lives in the White House with the President and their daughter, Chelsea. This is her first book." That narrative frames Rodham Clinton as a stay-at-home-mom whose life has been consumed with caring for her own child and the needs of other children. The last line makes her sound like a novice writer, rather than as a professional who cut her literary teeth writing legal briefs, articles, and opening statements.

The ad campaign for the book featured a photograph that portrayed Rodham Clinton in soft tones, with a bouffant version of the Jackie Kennedy hairstyle; her blond hair shimmered and framed a radiant smile. The photograph looks as if it was taken through diffusion filters, a technique used by Hollywood film makers to glamorize their subjects. Rodham Clinton invoked the title of the book in numerous speeches to underscore the maternal tone of this phase of her political life, a tone exemplified in her speech to the 1996 Democratic National Convention, in which she stated her intention to "talk about what matters most in our lives and in our nation—children and families."[71] Rodham Clinton exuded maternal character when she invited her DNC audience, figuratively, into her private sphere, stating, "I wish we could be sitting around a kitchen table, just us, talking about our hopes and fears, about our children's futures. For Bill and me, family has been the center of our lives."[72] Denise M. Bostdorff's analysis of Rodham Clinton's 1996 campaign discourse confirms that the first lady

> took great pains to cast herself as a traditional wife and mother.
> When asked by Barbara Walters about her future plans, the first lady
> admitted: "I want to continue to work, especially on behalf of chil-

dren," while the president made his fleeting remarks about how she should have an unofficial role in welfare reform. Beyond these comments, Rodham Clinton made brief references to "jobs" she had held and the difficulty of being a working parent, but did little to emphasize her professional or personal independence. The first lady did not need to make special efforts to appeal to professional women and others who desired a more independent first lady—they were already in her camp—so much as she needed to reassure the majority of voters that she would not overstep her bounds in the future.[73]

Rodham Clinton's Madonna persona traded upon images of pristine femininity, maternal character, and purity associated with the Virgin Mother. Many critics viewed this new identity as evidence that Rodham Clinton had been goaded into a powerless, traditionally feminine stance. If not an outright rejection of feminism, this phase also could represent an enactment of what Bonnie Dow has termed "maternal feminism."[74] As Dow explains, maternal feminism is rooted in the "difference" or "cultural" feminism of the 1980s, popularized by the work of Sarah Ruddick and Carol Gilligan, who argue respectively for the existence of "maternal thinking" and the virtue of women's moral reasoning, governed by "a standard of relationship, an ethic of nurturance, responsibility, and care."[75] Maternal feminists seek to highlight, rather than occlude, the differences between women and men, celebrating femininity and locating power in maternal sensibilities. Rodham Clinton's move to embrace the role of national Madonna could be seen as consistent with her rhetoric, which touted the strength of women and the virtue of women's communities. Maternal feminism, however, is not just an innocuous appreciation of the feminine. Maternal feminism has a tendency to reify women's role as mothers, negating many of the other subject positions women occupy. Moreover, as Dow points out, the suggestion that *women* have a unique capacity for maternal thinking places the burden of social transformation entirely on women's shoulders, while "men's position remains curiously static, as if they cannot change (which would seem to admit the permanence of patriarchy) or there is no need to demand that they do so (which is patently unfair)."[76] If Rodham Clinton's Madonna phase represents a political articulation of maternal feminism, it may restrict women as it underscores traditional gender roles and reinscribes the dichotomy between feminine and masculine. What makes this period so rhetorically significant, however, is the way in which Rodham Clinton managed to placate her critics and at the same time promote a feminist message. Rodham Clinton's international rhetoric illustrates the ways in which her Madonna image promoted feminist politics by making a radical feminist message more palatable to the first lady's audiences.

Women's Rights on the International Stage

In 1995, Rodham Clinton increased her visibility in international quarters, traveling the globe and giving speeches on behalf of women's rights. During the health-care reform campaign she addressed domestic audiences comprised of policy-makers in traditionally male-dominated groups such as physicians' groups, labor unions, and Congress. After the failure of health-care reform, she increased her international visibility and spoke to audiences comprised mostly of women who often did not fulfill official policy-making roles.

The central theme in Rodham Clinton's international, ceremonial rhetoric was empowerment and access for women and girls. She articulated this theme in different cultural contexts, including her much-publicized speech at the United Nations Fourth World Conference on Women, held in Beijing, China on September 5, 1995. There, the first lady spoke out against practices such as dowry deaths, ritualized rape as a weapon of war, domestic violence, genital mutilation, lack of family planning options, and forced abortion and sterilization, calling each a "violation of human rights."[77]

Initially, there was controversy over the first lady's participation in the conference; however, Rodham Clinton was praised following the speech.[78] CNN's William Schneider of *Inside Politics* named the address the political play of the week, noting:

> A lot of people didn't want First Lady Hillary Rodham Clinton to go to China this week to address the United Nations Conference on Women. They said her visit would hand China a propaganda victory. Or show U.S. indifference toward Chinese human rights violations. Or endanger the recent warming in U.S.-Chinese relations. They were wrong. The first lady gave a tough, hard hitting speech. She got a rousing reception when she criticized violations of women's rights all over the world . . . .[79]

The toughness of the China address was emphasized in media accounts. A *New York Times* report opened with the lead, "Speaking more forcefully on human rights than any American dignitary has on Chinese soil, Hillary Rodham Clinton catalogued a devastating litany of abuse that has afflicted women around the world today and criticized China for seeking to limit free and open discussion of women's issues here."[80] A headline in the *Daily Telegraph* stated, "Hard-Hitting Hillary Savages Beijing; Mrs. Clinton strikes blow for women worldwide."[81]

Although Rodham Clinton was presented in media accounts as aggressive and forceful, the impact of those stories was significantly different than that of similar stories published during the health-care reform campaign. The tough first lady presented in 1995 was celebrated rather than criticized, admired rather than feared. There are several possible explanations for the shift in meaning. First, place most likely was a factor. Rodham Clinton could get away with more on the international stage than she could at home, perhaps because she was attacking "others" rather than "us." On the international stage Rodham Clinton acted as a missionary for two U.S. ideals: democracy and capitalism. That represented a radical shift from her focus in 1992–94, when she was seen to be taking over domestic politics and making a push for socialized medicine.

Second, Rodham Clinton's persona undoubtedly affected the interpretation of her rhetoric. Although the rhetorical themes in her health-care reform speeches and her Madonna phase speeches were similar (social responsibility, equality, human rights), the narrative that framed those themes caused them to be read differently. When she was labeled "co-president" her rhetoric was viewed as meddlesome and pushy, but when she was viewed as Madonna her toughness was easier to swallow because it could be interpreted as maternal strength.

The imagery Rodham Clinton employed during this period also contributed to the Madonna persona. Although her speech in China was touted for its toughness, the majority of Rodham Clinton's international rhetoric was not viewed as particularly forceful, even though a strong women's rights message was included in every speech. An analysis of the discourse reveals a striking departure from the imagery used during the health-care reform campaign. While her health care speeches were infused with war metaphors and calls to battle, the Madonna discourse exhibited more traditionally feminine images. In a speech at the Radio Free Europe headquarters, Rodham Clinton told audience members that democracy "requires constant nurturing," and urged that future challenges could best be met if the West "expand[ed] its democratic family."[82] In Kazakhstan, she claimed that "democracy is nurtured and sustained by what we in America call the 'habits of the heart,' in the way people live their lives and in the lessons they teach their children as they tuck them into bed at night."[83] She expressed the desire to "weave all people into the work of building this democracy" as she spoke in Capetown, South Africa.[84]

Feminine imagery supported what some would call a more feminized approach to both discourse and policy than was seen during health-care reform. As Campbell has noted, Rodham Clinton's health-care reform speeches focused on specific policy initiatives and did not contain indicators of a feminine style of speaking, a choice Campbell says contributed to Rodham Clinton's loss of credibility as an advocate.[85] During the Madonna phase, the first lady's speeches did not advocate specific policy initiatives, but instead focused on broader themes such as empowerment, access, and unity. Since these speeches displayed Rodham Clinton's ceremonial presence and cast her as an ambassador to the world, they helped her fulfill the role of U.S. first lady in a way that was both recognizable to the American people and widely accepted.

Although Rodham Clinton worked to feminize her public voice, the rhetorical strategy that her Madonna-phase rhetoric employs, more than feminine style, is oxymoron. Campbell argues that the concept of woman speaker, itself, is oxymoronic and that "the oxymoron figuratively captures the dynamic of women's rhetoric"[86] The utility of embracing oxymoron as a tactic is illustrated by Kenneth Burke's notion of perspective by incongruity, in which paradox and oxymoron become sources of new perspectives.[87] In Rodham Clinton's international discourse, she merged femininity and feminism. Media accounts during this period focused on the first lady's new-found femininity, evidenced by her pastel attire, soft hairstyle, ceremonial presence, and tendency to emphasize her role as mother. Yet, this feminine exterior was rounded out with rhetorical themes that were explicitly and forcefully feminist. Rodham Clinton touted the need for empowerment for women worldwide and spoke out harshly against violations of women's human rights. Because both her feminine and feminist strategies achieved resonance in media coverage, the first lady was perceived, paradoxically, as both tough and soft.[88] This apparent incongruity created space for a new perspective in which femininity and feminism are no longer cast as antithetical.

A second oxymoron evident in Rodham Clinton's Madonna discourse was the challenge she posed to the logic of separate spheres. The notion of diverse realms of influence—public, private, intimate, and technical—is inherent to much political theory and has become normalized as an accurate conception of social life. In her speech to the Rajiv Gandhi Foundation, however, Rodham Clinton noted that the "new world" in which we exist at the turn of the new century is a "world in which many old divisions have diminished or disappeared."[89] Her rhetoric was aimed at disrupting one influential division: the clean separation between public and private spheres, where public sphere issues are thought of as political and private sphere concerns are conceived of as personal. She noted that while governments historically have engaged in "realpolitik," they should begin to recognize that "'real-life politik' may be just as intimately connected with whether or not democracies survive and flourish."[90] She explicitly challenged the distinction between spheres in her speech to the World Economic Forum, saying:

> I think it is probably more appropriate to refer to this gathering as the World Economic, Political and Social Forum, because certainly in the discussions that I have been privileged to hear about and to hear directly, it has struck me that there is a very strong awareness of how interdependent the economic, political and social spheres of life happen to be.[91]

In Australia, she explained that "kitchen table issues" recently had taken on increased political importance, further politicizing the private sphere.[92]

Rodham Clinton's international rhetoric is striking in terms of how she inhabited the Madonna persona and created an empowered, paradoxical political actor—one that was palatable both to the American public and to international audiences. Madonna became a fitting response to "bitch." By initially carrying out the traditional, ceremonial duties tied to the first lady's role as ambassador to the world, Rodham Clinton generated space within which she could articulate a feminist message. That message explicitly called for empowerment and access to be granted to women and girls worldwide. Implicitly, it enacted a paradoxical fusion of femininity and feminism and challenged the logic of separate spheres. The promise of the paradoxical Madonna persona was not fully realized, however, because in 1998, like so many times before in the Clintons' political career, the story switched from politics to sex.

Defending Hearth, Home, and Poll Numbers

On January 20, 1998, the most salacious story of the Clinton presidency broke in the news. The president was accused of having a sexual relationship with Monica Lewinsky, a twenty-four-year-old former White House intern. Moreover, tapes secretly recorded by Lewinsky's friend and former White House staffer, Linda Tripp, suggested that Clinton and his friend, Vernon Jordan, might have encouraged Lewinsky to lie about their relationship under oath to lawyers in the Paula Jones sexual harassment case. Although Rodham Clinton had remained fairly quiet with regard to the Paula Jones lawsuit, she would emerge forcefully to defend her husband after the Lewinsky scandal broke, drawing on strategies that had served the Clintons well in the 1992 presidential campaign, when they dealt with allegations that Clinton had engaged in a twelve-year extramarital affair with Gennifer Flowers while he was governor of Arkansas. The Madonna persona proved to be a strategically sound, politically effective defense strategy that bolstered not only President Clinton's credibility with the electorate but also Rodham Clinton's image. The version of Madonna that proved useful in the context of the scandal, however, was the less paradoxical, more traditionally feminine Mother Superior. As such, the scandal effectively shut down the component of Rodham Clinton's Madonna image that held the most promise for women's agency.

Soon after the Lewinsky story broke, Rodham Clinton stalwartly stood for (and by) her husband. She kept all regularly scheduled appearances and supported President Clinton on NBC's *Today* show, broadcast on January 27, the morning of the president's State of the Union address. Rodham Clinton's *Today* interview was the first extended discussion of the scandal offered by the White House since the story broke. Although in the preceding week, the president had denied having a sexual relationship with Lewinsky or asking her to lie under oath, he had not made himself available to reporters for questions. The fact that Rodham Clinton was designated as the White House spokesperson in this particular scandal was significant and her rhetorical strategies reveal why she chose to step up to the front line.

Rodham Clinton's demeanor during the *Today* interview was that of a wife protecting her husband and family, calmly dismissing the legitimacy of the charges, and appearing eager to move on to the topic of child care, which she originally had been scheduled to discuss on the broadcast.[93] The Madonna persona assumed by Rodham Clinton during the broadcast was useful due to its flexibility. Those who chose not to believe the president's accusers would relate to the purity of Madonna, insisting that someone as morally upstanding as the first lady would never condone such behavior from her husband; consequently, the charges must be a manufactured lie. Thus, if she supported him, so could voters who considered themselves to be people of conviction. Conversely, those who were inclined to believe the charges but still approved of President Clinton's governance could identify with the merciful side of Madonna. Rodham Clinton's forgiveness, like the blessing of the Virgin Mary, absolved the president of his guilt and made it possible for the electorate to forgive him.

Rodham Clinton's appearance on *Today* served her image-making needs as well by allowing her to affiliate herself with patriotism and family values. The first lady became a loyal and/or forgiving wife as well as a loyal American, saying, "I'm not only here because I love and believe my husband. I'm also here because I love and believe in my country." Although in domestic policy contexts the Madonna persona purported to soften Rodham Clinton and make her less threatening, Lewinsky scandal stories were peppered with war metaphors to describe the first lady's defense of her husband. *Newsweek* announced, "Hillary Clinton Goes to War."[94] *The New York Times* stated that "Hillary Clinton has again rushed to her husband's defense—in battle mode."[95] Tom Brokaw of *NBC Nightly News* declared, "Well, Hillary Clinton is leading the charge in her husband's defense."[96] Ted Koppel, during the *Nightline* broadcast following the *Today* interview and the State of the Union address, titled his story, "the first family in full battle regalia."[97] Rather than feeding a re-vamped "bitch" narrative, however, the war metaphors underscored maternal images gleaned from the realm of nature. How many times have Americans seen images of a fiercely protective mother bear as a formidable opponent to those threatening her young? Insofar as the charges of Bill Clinton's infidelities can be seen as a threat to Rodham Clinton's marriage and the well-being of her daughter Chelsea, maternal defenses could be interpreted as an appropriate response. In an ABC News interview, author and Washington insider Sally Quinn asked how Lewinsky's charges could "do anything but devastate [Chelsea]?"[98] Former White House press secretary Dee Dee Myers told NBC News, "I think people would certainly rather see [the first lady] err on the side of being a little bit naive and saving her marriage than going out and questioning his integrity in front of the country."[99] Indeed, according to Rodham Clinton's testimony on *Today*, she was most interested in protecting sacred unions—the union of her marriage, her family, and even of America itself.

Rodham Clinton's appearance on *Today* and strong defense of her husband was credited as a major contributor to the soaring public approval ratings President Clinton earned in the days and weeks following the initial Lewinsky stories. The strategy they employed in 1998 was strikingly similar to their 1992 reaction to the Gennifer Flowers scandal. Appearing on *60 Minutes*, Rodham Clinton expressed her love for and belief in her husband and noted the long history of personal attacks Bill Clinton had received from political opponents. Her performance was credited with securing the presidency for her husband, and excerpts from that *60 Minutes* interview were replayed widely in 1998, underscoring Rodham Clinton's defense of her husband and the consistency of her message. Although some were surprised by Rodham Clinton's unwavering support for the president in 1998, they should not have been. The Clintons historically have fielded allegations using similar tactics and have not only survived, but have thrived in American politics.

Not all commentators interpreted Rodham Clinton's response to the Lewinsky scandal as appropriate or convincing. *Time* columnist Barbara Ehrenreich labeled Rodham Clinton's appearance on the *Today* show "the sorriest performance," and admonished, "Someone needs to tell this woman that the first time a wife stands up for an allegedly adulterous husband, everyone thinks she's a saint. The second or third time, though, she begins to look disturbingly complicit."[100] One male respondent featured on *CNN Worldview* commented on Rodham Clinton's claim that Bill Clinton was innocent by saying, "Oh, I don't believe it. I think she's just covering it up."[101] Yet, the Madonna metaphor even provided a rationale for Rodham Clinton's commitment to a less than perfect marriage, one that was picked up in media coverage. *Newsweek* reporters Matthew Cooper and Karen Breslau speculated that the Clintons' marriage has lasted and will continue to last because "they see themselves in almost Messianic terms, as great leaders who have a mission to fulfill."[102] Rodham Clinton's Methodism frequently was cited as a force compelling her to make personal sacrifices and remain committed to her marriage. The selfless Madonna who fiercely protects home and country may be a more palatable figure to the majority of Americans than the independent feminist who abandons an unfaithful spouse.

Although the empowered mother Madonna persona helped Rodham Clinton fulfill the immediate political goal of rehabilitating her own and her husband's image, she was forced to retreat temporarily from the more oxymoronic persona that promoted women's agency. The tactic was primed for revival and emerged in the seemingly innocuous "Save America's Treasures" tour that would launch the first lady into a U.S. Senate campaign.

Return to Oxymoron: "Honor the Past, Imagine the Future"

Not surprisingly, the first lady did not simply rest high atop her positive poll numbers. She instead embarked upon an endeavor that would retain the public favor her more traditional stance had garnered, while still accomplishing her own political goals. During the summer of 1998, the impending turn of the millennium prompted the White House to launch the "Save America's Treasures" tour. The explicit purpose of the campaign, according to the first lady's web site, was to "preserve those aspects of our shared heritage . . . which define our nation and transcend the generations."[103] Rodham Clinton kicked off the campaign on July 13th, 1998, with a four-day tour of the Northeast United States, where she visited sites in need of preservation, raised funds, and delivered speeches. Reporters repeatedly observed that Rodham Clinton's latest public campaign was a "traditional first lady–like endeavor," that put this first lady in the company of predecessors such as Lady Bird Johnson and Jacqueline Kennedy who similarly had been interested in preservation.[104] The first lady also played up the mainstream appeal of her new project, saying, "No one is going to stand up against The Star-Spangled Banner and its need for preservation."[105]

Although Save America's Treasures was presented as an innocuous and rather bland endeavor, it cloaked an assertive push for women's empowerment. The theme of the campaign was "Honor the past, imagine the future," and that could describe Rodham Clinton's political identity during this period. With Save America's Treasures the first lady was returning to the Madonna of the international stage—someone who conformed explicitly to tradition and simultaneously envisioned new possibilities for women. The tour emphasized women's contributions to U.S. history, visiting the homes of labor organizer Kate Mullany and abolitionist Harriet Tubman, meeting with Native American clan mothers, commending the work of woman suffrage proponents and abolitionists Maryann and Thomas M'Clintock, and culminating with an address to commemorate the 150th anniversary of the first woman's rights convention at Seneca Falls, New York. In her speeches, Rodham Clinton recognized little-known as well as famous individuals, praising women such as Hannah Lord Montague, the inventor of the detachable collar. She stated:

> I can just imagine what was going through Mrs. Montague's mind, can't those of you who have ever ironed a shirt, men and women. It was a lot harder in those days because you couldn't just plug in the iron, you had to heat it up and you had to keep heating it up. And I can just imagine Mrs. Montague standing there ironing those shirts because she had to wash her husband's entire shirt just to get the collar clean because lots of men's shirts don't get as dirty as their collars do, even today, and she thought there's got to be a better way. So she became an inventor, and a manufacturer, again when not many women were doing that. And others saw a business opportunity to go forward with that, and that's how we created this great industry that stood on the banks of the river that brought so many people here.[106]

That example recognizes the mundane yet significant nature of the work women historically have done, begins to collapse private and public spheres by examining how housework launched a local manufacturing boom, and connects the historical efforts of an ordinary woman to the contemporary success of a town.

In addition to acknowledging women's contributions to society, Rodham Clinton's Save America's Treasures speeches used historical commemoration as a vehicle for advancing arguments in favor of women's rights and women's empowerment. That message was presented most forcefully in her Seneca Falls speech when she asserted:

> If we are to finish the work begun here—then no American should ever again face discrimination on the basis of gender, race, or sexual orientation anywhere in our country. If we are to finish the work begun here then $0.76 in a woman's paycheck for every dollar in a man's is still not enough. Equal pay for equal work can once and for all be achieved.[107]

That refrain continued with the first lady calling for universal health care, improved education, preservation of Social Security, wariness of media-driven consumerism, protection against domestic violence, and an end to voter apathy among women. She linked the current need for improved child care with the history of women's struggle to balance multiple roles, noting that suffrage leader and mother Elizabeth Cady Stanton had implored her friend Susan B. Anthony to "Come here and I will do what I can to help you with your address, if you will hold the baby and make the pudding."

Rodham Clinton also used the tour as a chance to respond indirectly to the insults and charges that had been hurled at her during the preceding six years, telling her Seneca Falls audience that "woman suffragists understood that the Declaration of Sentiments would create no small amount of misconception, or misrepresentation and ridicule; they were called mannish women, old maids, fanatics, attacked personally by those who disagreed with them. One paper said, 'These rights for women would bring a monstrous injury to all mankind.' If it sounds familiar, it's the same thing that's always said when women keep going for true equality and justice."

In addition to making an implicit rebuttal to the criticisms leveled against her, Rodham Clinton used the Save America's Treasures tour to position herself where she wanted to be politically. Her interest in women's rights made woman suffrage a natural choice as the central focus of her speeches, but it surely was no accident that most of the sites on her 4-day tour were located in New York State. The first lady used the positive press she was guaranteed to get on the tour as a way of bolstering her credibility with New York voters, priming her for the Senate bid she would make one year later. A *Newsweek* article about the Treasures campaign published in July of 1998 opened with the following anecdote: "Hillary Clinton was looking out the window, and into the future. Cruising in a limousine over Manhattan's 59th Street bridge one evening, another black-tie political event behind her, the first lady gazed out over the water and mused to an old friend, I'd love to have an apartment in New York someday."[108]

Just over two years later, Clinton had a house in Chappaqua, a seat in the U.S. Senate, and a place in history as the first first lady to seek and win elective office. In the next section of this case study, we explore the ways in which gender norms influenced the public persona of *each* candidate in the 2000 U.S. Senate race in New York. Not only did Rodham Clinton's status as a woman drop to the background of her high-profile campaign, but both of her opponents (New York Mayor Rudolph Giuliani and Congress member Rick Lazio) struggled with how their masculinity was portrayed in mainstream media.

From Spouse to Senator

When Candidate "Hillary" waved to cheering crowds as she announced her intention to represent the state of New York in the U.S. Senate, many critics were left shaking their heads, wondering, "how did she do it?" How did a controversial and often reviled first lady recover from the abysmal public failure of the health-care reform campaign, the shadow cast by relentless Congressional investigations, and the humiliation of a philandering husband? The answer lies not in shady, back-room political dealmaking but instead in public, rhetorical maneuvering. What is striking about Rodham Clinton's hard-fought Senate race was not just that she won, but that she went from being viewed primarily as a woman to being judged predominantly as a candidate. Analysis of media coverage before and after the 2000 campaign reveals a clear pattern.[109] During her tenure as first lady, Rodham Clinton either was reviled or lauded for the challenges she posed to traditional femininity. She was seen as an icon of feminism, a threat to femininity (or masculinity), an embodiment of the complex roles facing modern women, an everyday baby-boomer struggling with marital problems and empty-nest syndrome. But the controversy and commentary that swirled around Rodham Clinton before she began a public bid for the Senate hinged on her status as a woman and wife of the president. Gender was the fulcrum on which Rodham Clinton's political identity and corresponding public opinions about her turned.[110] Once she began the transition from spouse of the president to candidate for the U.S. Senate, the subject of news critiques switched from issues of person to issues of place. The question was not that Hillary Rodham Clinton should not be running for office because she is a woman. The charge was that she should not be running for the U.S. Senate in *New York* because she is not a *New Yorker*. Candidate Rodham Clinton was tagged a "carpetbagger."[111]

The 2000 Senate campaign in New York had a high national profile not only because the first lady was a candidate, but also because her presumptive opponent was outspoken New York City mayor, Rudolph Giuliani. The race was a tight and colorful one, but midway through the campaign season Giuliani was forced to drop out, ostensibly due to his recently-diagnosed prostate cancer, but also because reports of marital infidelity could jeopardize his candidacy. Following Giuliani's departure, Congressman Rick Lazio became the Republican candidate.

Early in the campaign, the issue of place framed news stories about Rodham Clinton's candidacy. There was, after all, much imagery to work with for editors and writers who mined the New York landscape, songs about the Big Apple, and popular stereotypes about the city in order to spice up their news coverage. A

Newsweek article that addressed how a Rodham Clinton Senate bid might interfere with Gore's presidential campaign was titled "The Potholes of New York."[112] A *Time* cover story invoked a classic Frank Sinatra refrain when it hypothesized, "If She Can Make It There . . ." and a sidebar to the story listing reasons not to run urged her to "Fuhgeddaboutit!"[113] The focus on place naturally begged the question, "Why New York?" Why not represent a state in which Rodham Clinton had actually lived? Early in the campaign *Newsweek* writers Evan Thomas and Debra Rosenberg suggested that the carpetbagger charge "would probably not stick in a state with a traditionally cosmopolitan view of its senators."[114] Republican voter Janette Pfeiff, quoted in a *Washington Post* story, underscored the *Newsweek* hypothesis, saying, "I think most of us would prefer someone from New York as a senator. But that doesn't mean we won't support her. The economy is the overwhelming issue. That comes first."[115] Nevertheless, both of Rodham Clinton's opponents made the carpetbagger charge the focus of their campaign against her. A fundraising letter sent by Giuliani stated: "Love me or hate me, I don't think there is anyone in our state who would ever accuse me of not having the interests of the people of New York absolute first and foremost in my mind. To me, New York is not a political 'stepping stone.' New York is my life."[116]

The carpetbagger theme resonated with the press. The *New York Daily News* headline framing the story about the Giuliani fundraising letter read "She's Carpetbagger, Sez Rudy in Fund Drive." The *New York Times* reported that "Giuliani has taken to mocking Clinton repeatedly in recent weeks for seeking public office in a state where she has never resided. To that end, Giuliani has planned a campaign trip later this month to Arkansas, where Clinton has lived most of her adult life."[117] That same edition of the *Times* stated the primary critique leveled against candidate Rodham Clinton was "running for the Senate from a state in which she has never lived."[118] Calvin Butts III, pastor of the Abyssinia Baptist Church, summed it up when he said, simply, "Someone from New York would be better."[119]

The issue of place served as the backdrop for Rodham Clinton's first major campaign gaffe—a June 1999 photo op of the candidate in a New York Yankees baseball cap. She donned it while hosting the 1998 world championship Yankees at a White House event. *Washington Post* writer Frank Ahrens mused about the "curious timing" of the Yankees' visit to the White House, which came "eight months after they won the World Series but only days after Hillary Rodham Clinton announced she was forming an exploratory committee to run for a New York seat in the U.S. Senate."[120] When Katie Couric grilled Rodham Clinton about the cap on the *Today* show, she feebly responded that although she was a Cubs fan, she "needed an American League team . . . so as a young girl, I became very interested and enamored of the Yankees."[121] The move dogged the candidate three months later when it was heavily analyzed on the September 13, 1999 edition of *Nightline*. Ardent Clinton supporter Ed Koch called it "ridiculous" and admonished, "You don't become a Yankee fan by putting on a

Yankee cap when you've been supporting other teams over the years." *New York Post* reporter Jack Neufeld, labeled by *Nightline* as a "Bobby Kennedy Democrat," lambasted Rodham Clinton, saying, "I've seen her on television at Cubs games. That's OK, to be a Cubs fan. But to say, put on the hat and then say I've always been a Yankees fan and now when I come to New York I'm going to root for the Yankees, it was bogus."[122]

The Yankee cap incident was to the 2000 campaign what Rodham Clinton's "cookies and tea" sound bite was to her husband's 1992 campaign. It invoked larger questions about Rodham Clinton's character and qualifications. What is significant is that while "cookies and tea" set off alarm bells about Rodham Clinton's womanhood, femininity, and her ability to act constructively as the nation's "first lady," the Yankee cap story raised concerns not tied to Rodham Clinton's gender. Critics cited it as an example of Rodham Clinton's willingness to pander to New York voters—to do or say anything to get elected. The photo invoked other, more substantive stories that called Rodham Clinton's authenticity into question. The most prominent example was the case of the president's August 11, 1999 offer of clemency to twelve Puerto Rican nationalists who had been accused of weapons possession and sedition in connection with terrorist acts that had killed six people in the 1970s and 1980s. Critics contended that the presidential pardon was a political act designed to curry favor for Al Gore and Hillary Rodham Clinton with Latino voters in New York. Candidate Rodham Clinton first seemed to support the president, but later joined with the majority of members of Congress in condemning the president's pardon, citing concerns from law enforcement officials that the pardon sent a signal that the U.S. is soft on terrorism. Rodham Clinton's denouncement of the pardon drew fire from New York Latino leaders, and she shifted positions again. A *New York Daily News* lead read, "Hillary Rodham Clinton conceded yesterday that she failed to consult adequately with Hispanic leaders before opposing clemency for FALN militants, and she promised such a breakdown 'will never happen again.'"[123] In assessing the issue of candidate Rodham Clinton's authenticity, *Nightline* anchor Chris Bury asked:

> Is the real problem here one of pandering? In other words, Jack Neufeld pointed out in the opening piece that there seems to be a combination of factors going back to the Yankees cap and her vacation in New York and now her flip flop on the clemency issue. Is that the real problem for Mrs. Clinton, the perception that she seems to be almost craven in appealing to certain groups of voters in New York?[124]

"Craven" is no laudatory term and candidate Rodham Clinton could not have enjoyed the characterization. But a change was afoot in the mainstream media with respect to Hillary Rodham Clinton. No longer were critiques peppered with images of a henpecked husband or a fanatical feminist. Instead candidate Rodham Clinton became like any other candidate—someone whose au-

thenticity was called into question because of her character, not her chromo-
somes.

The issue of gender still resonated in the campaign in other, more subtle
ways. What set candidate Rodham Clinton apart from other Senate hopefuls was
her unique status as the spouse of the president. Although her tie to the president
gave critics pause during the clemency debacle, the media took pains to separate
the two and present candidate Clinton as an independent woman. The March 1,
1999 *Time* cover story about the prospects of a Rodham Clinton Senate bid was
titled "A Race of Her Own." That same week, *Newsweek*'s cover ran the banner
"Her Turn" over a photo of a smiling Rodham Clinton, looking out on a seemingly bright future. The subhead read, "Senate or world stage? Either way,
Hillary's ready for her own run at history." Both substantive and symbolic acts
fed the media narrative of Rodham Clinton the independent candidate. When she
called Jerusalem the "eternal and indivisible" capital of Israel (adapting, some
said, to New York's Jewish voters), the White House distanced itself from her
stance. An ABCNEWS.com story announced in a headline that Rodham Clinton
"Speaks for Herself."[125] Much was made of her move from the White House to a
private residence in Chappaqua. An ABCNEWS.com story entitled "Moving
Day" contained the subheads "Lonely Move" and "Breaking Away," and
claimed that the "symbolism of this transition cannot be overstated."[126] Commenting on ABC's *This Week* with Sam Donaldson and Cokie Roberts, Senator
Robert Toricelli brushed aside the suggestion that the move was confirmation of
further strain in the Clinton marriage, saying, "I don't think anyone in this fool-
ish debate about the president's residence can expect the president of the United
States to move out of the White House because Hillary Clinton is now running
in New York." Toricelli concluded, however, that the move was a signal that
Rodham Clinton had become "a full-time candidate."[127]

As a full-time candidate, Rodham Clinton constructed a political persona
that fit within the media frames shaping coverage of her candidacy—narratives
that presented her as an independent woman struggling to prove her own authenticity to New York voters. She addressed the carpetbagger charge head-on in the
official announcement of her candidacy, saying: "Now, I know some people are
asking why I'm doing this here and now, and that's a fair question. Here's my
answer and why I hope you'll put me to work for you. I may be new to the
neighborhood, but I'm not new to your concerns."[128]

That statement reflected more rhetorical savvy than Rodham Clinton had
shown in the past. Her tendency toward lengthy and complex responses to reporters' questions was understandable given her legal training, but it was a trait
that landed her in PR hot water more than once. The "cookies and tea" comment
is the most infamous example of reporters excavating a juicy sound bite from
one of Rodham Clinton's dull statements, and circulating it regardless of the fact
that the small sentence misrepresented the content of the statement as a whole.
In her announcement speech, Rodham Clinton provided reporters with her own
sound bite, one that effectively answered the carpetbagger charge. She then

turned to the issues during the remainder of her speech. Analysts agreed that Rodham Clinton had the upper hand over the Republican opposition when it came to New Yorkers' stands on the issues.[129]

Republicans clearly thought that the carpetbagger charge was their best strategy in countering Rodham Clinton.[130] In response to her announcement speech, Giuliani was quoted saying "I think it's nice to see that she's finding her way around New York."[131] When Giuliani dropped out of the race, his successor Rick Lazio picked up the theme. During the September 13, 2000 debate with Rodham Clinton, Lazio's opening response to Tim Russert's question about health-care reform asserted, "A New Yorker would never had made that proposal."[132] A campaign bumper sticker on the Lazio bus read "From New York, for New York," and lines from his stump speeches included claims that New York taxpayers were "'subsidizing Arkansas,' that he [was] 'the only candidate in the race who has paid New York state income taxes,' and that 'no one from Little Rock, Arkansas, or Washington, D.C., or Hollywood, California is going to tell us as New Yorkers who should represent us.'"[133] The *Washington Post* dismissed the carpetbagger charge in March of 2000, however, stating that "even polls that show Giuliani ahead, such as one by the Marist College Institute of Public Opinion, also show Clinton's 'carpetbagger' status no longer a concern of a majority of voters, following her several months of extensive travel around the state."[134] The *Washington Post* hypothesized that the carpetbagger label was even less convincing once Giuliani dropped out, claiming that "western New Yorkers don't all see Lazio as one of their own; the western part of that state is about as close to Hillary's hometown of Chicago—500 miles—as it is to Lazio's eastern Long Island."[135] Election results confirmed the *Post*'s predictions. A Voter News Service poll found that "one of every two voters said Rodham Clinton's lack of New York roots was of little or no concern," and that Rodham Clinton "won slightly more than a third of the voters who said they were somewhat concerned with the carpetbagger factor" and even won "over 13% of those who were very concerned by it."[136] That led *New York Post* editors to conclude that the "Carpetbag Tag Didn't Halt Hil Steamroll" in their November 8, 2000 edition.

In addition to responding to the "carpetbagger" charge that framed so much of the coverage of Rodham Clinton's 2000 Senate bid, the candidate had to address her unique status as the spouse of the president. This status had garnered her plenty of negative press during the preceding eight years, so it is not surprising that she followed the mainstream media's lead and separated herself from her husband. The most notable example that this was a calculated campaign strategy was Rodham Clinton's choice not to have the president speak when she formally announced her candidacy. Instead, the president of the United States played the role of a traditional political spouse. In an interview with the Associated Press, candidate Rodham Clinton cultivated that image. Responding to the question, "What's the president's role in your campaign," Rodham Clinton said, "He has been incredibly supportive, has given me lots of good advice, listened to me practice my speech, he's just been there for me." Later in the interview, she explained her decision not to have the president speak at the announcement, saying, "We just believed that it was my responsibility to present myself to the people of New York. I have sat on many stages on the edge of my chair watching my husband deliver a speech. He thought it was his turn to do the same."[137] The strategy to cast the president as a supportive spouse was a deft rhetorical move on two counts. First, it dissipated the cloud of suspicion that perpetually hovers over the Clinton marriage, suggesting that the couple had moved past the strain of the Lewinsky affair and reaffirmed a legitimate personal partnership (as opposed to a contrived public one). Second, it cast Clinton as a credible candidate—one with the requisite supportive spouse. In case anyone missed the symbolic significance of the president's silence, Rodham Clinton made another public assertion of her independence. When campaign banners with the candidate's name were unveiled, they read, simply, "Hillary For U.S. Senate." No Rodham to remind voters of the controversial first lady. No Clinton to remind voters of uncomfortable presidential scandals. Just Hillary—an independent woman getting a fresh start in a new town.

Once she had separated herself from the president and answered the carpetbagger charge, Rodham Clinton was free to construct her own political persona. What is interesting about media accounts of candidate Rodham Clinton following the February 7 announcement speech is that although her political agenda as a candidate matched almost exactly the one she promoted as first lady, her public persona changed significantly. As a Senate candidate, Rodham Clinton was able to employ strategies that had benefited other women candidates. Jamieson recounts one of Dianne Fienstein's early campaign slogans, "Tough and Caring," stating:

> Those—including many male reporters—who couldn't conceive of the terms as cohabitants transmuted it to "Tough BUT Caring." Yet the [campaign] ad, showing Feinstein with children in one shot, with police in another, standing for abortion rights and for the death penalty, invited audiences to suspend their assumptions about women and judge this woman on her positions.[138]

In her announcement speech, Rodham Clinton presented herself as a "woman leader," something that used to be so scarce in American politics Campbell termed it "oxymoronic," but something that U.S. voters are increasingly coming to recognize. Rodham Clinton's version of the woman leader was a "fighter" who was concerned about (what are typically but erroneously labeled) "women's issues." After dispensing with the carpetbagger charge in her announcement speech, Rodham Clinton ticked off five issues significant to her campaign: public school education, supporting small businesses, breast-cancer research, media and gun violence, and child care. Four of these five issues fall clearly within the category of "women's" political issues. As Rodham Clinton laid them out, she eschewed the policy tone that characterized her speeches during the health-care reform campaign, and adopted a more personal, narrative mode. She began each paragraph with phrases like, "When I ate lunch with teachers at a school in Queens," and "when I sat on porches in backyards from Elmira to New Rochelle." This technique introduced the "feminine style" that Campbell said was missing from the health-care reform speeches, insofar as it employed concrete language, personal tone, anecdotal evidence, and because it invited audience identification. The examples also functioned as tacit support for her claim that she had talked to New Yorkers and understood their concerns, thus the carpetbagger charge was moot.

After introducing five key campaign issues through personal narratives, Rodham Clinton switched the tone of her speech, calling herself a "fighter" and taking on a more stereotypically masculine rhetorical approach. She said, "To fulfill that basic bargain for New York I'll have to fight. Well, I've had some experience with that too." In the next segment of the speech, Rodham Clinton demonstrated self-awareness and even humor, two qualities that critics often charge she lacks. She stated that her three major battles were for education reform in Arkansas, women's rights awareness in China, and health-care reform in the U.S. Rodham Clinton noted, "I won the first two battles and, as you may recall, I lost the last one. But instead of giving up, I learned to take a different approach." She continued by promising to "fight" on behalf of New York in a whole host of issues that included paying down the national debt, working for targeted tax cuts, promoting hate crime legislation, supporting gun control, helping the homeless, strengthening the national defense, and expanding the Family and Medical Leave Act. In this part of her speech Rodham Clinton echoed the Feinstein strategy of intercutting images of typically "male" political issues (like crime and defense) with typically "female" political issues (like education and health care). The virtue of this strategy is twofold. It expands the candidate's leadership persona, making the candidate more appealing to diverse communities of voters. As more candidates adopt this strategy, it also begins to expand the definition of leadership, so that leaders are not measured against a narrow set of stereotypically masculine traits. Moreover, as more women candidates succeed with these types of rhetorical appeals, the double bind between femininity and competence is confounded. In Rodham Clinton's case, the complex political persona she cultivated during the campaign seemed to resonate with the media in ways that benefited her candidacy. A *Washington Post* article lauded Rodham Clinton for projecting a "kaleidoscope of images," saying:

> One moment on Friday she was the maternal first lady, singing with Ithaca preschoolers ("I'm a little teapot, short and stout. Here is my handle, here is my spout") as she mimicked the handle and spout with her arms. Another moment she transformed into the partisan pol, caustically warning that Republicans George W. Bush and Giuliani would slash education and "do a U-turn back to the days [of] exploding deficits." Then she turned philosophical, lecturing at Cornell

against excessive materialism and saying that "earning a living is not living a life."

The article commended Rodham Clinton for showing "discipline" as a campaigner and honing her political skills.[139] News accounts prior to the 2000 campaign also described Rodham Clinton's complex persona, but they typically sought to call the first lady's authenticity into question and support the thesis that she was politically manipulative. This story represents a shift in which Rodham Clinton goes from being chameleonlike (and, by implication insincere and self-serving) to being multifaceted, and therefore better suited to the task of leadership.

Analysis of media accounts, assessment of Rodham Clinton's own rhetorical strategies during the 2000 campaign, and the outcome of the election itself suggest that candidate Rodham Clinton was successful in establishing herself as a credible public leader. We have argued that place, rather than gender, became the most salient media frame for stories about candidate Rodham Clinton. There were tacit gender stereotypes that seemed to shape Rodham Clinton's campaign strategies (in her use of feminine style, her first-name moniker, and Bill Clinton's "supportive spouse" persona). Ironically, however, gender did play a role in media coverage of her two opponents.

Giuliani's challenge early in the campaign was being perceived as too mean to represent New York as a whole. Rodham Clinton played upon his image by lambasting his policy of, as one reporter for ABCNEWS.com put it, "kicking homeless people out of shelters if they refuse to work, and putting them in jail if they sleep on the street."[140] Giuliani's demeanor during a press conference about a police shooting of an unarmed black man fed this reputation, and press accounts played up the imagery. An *L.A. Times* lead read, "When Rudolph W. Giuliani met the press one morning last week to discuss the latest police shooting of an unarmed black man here, the mayor sprayed the room with invective as if he were some sort of automatic weapon himself."[141] Following that incident, Giuliani lost his lead in the polls, with ABCNEWS.com reporting, "A new poll finds that New York City Mayor Rudolph Giuliani's handling of a police shooting has substantially hurt his Senate campaign as his once-solid lead has dissolved into a dead heat with his rival, first lady Hillary Rodham Clinton."[142] A *New York Magazine* cover story summed up the general media consensus that although both candidates in the Senate race were displaying behavior that was tough and aggressive, it reflected positively only on Rodham Clinton. Referring to the mayor's conduct after the police shooting, the article stated:

> For the first time, after months of fragile caution, Hillary Clinton tore into the mayor, who, as is his custom, tore back. The mayor's actions in the past week reinforced for New Yorkers just how well we know him—in maintaining his barrage on Dorismond's [the shooting victim's] character, Giuliani was not making elaborate political calculations beyond the understanding of others; he was just being himself.

> By contrast, Mrs. Clinton's verbal grenades showed a side of her
> we've never seen, more aggressive and direct than she's ever been
> since she started coming to the state last July. It underscored, her
> immense fame notwithstanding, how little we know about her—as a
> candidate, to be sure, and simply as a person in her own right.[143]

That lead-in to the magazine's interview with Clinton cast Giuliani's aggressiveness in a negative light, portraying him as predictable, one-dimensional, and hyper-masculine. Rodham Clinton, conversely, came across as more authentic because of her toughness, and more "direct," a quality that curries favor with American voters. Toughness was no longer a liability for candidate Rodham Clinton (as it often was for the first lady), but it somehow called Giuliani's competence into question. That was new in American politics—for a male candidate to think twice about projecting an assertive image while his female opponent was lauded for being similarly aggressive. That was a sign that the glass ceiling imposed by the double bind may finally be cracking.

If Giuliani was too masculine for the job of U.S. senator, then Rick Lazio may not have been masculine enough. One descriptor that emerged consistently in media accounts of Lazio was "boyish." A *Washington Post* profile described him as follows: "The 42-year-old New York Republican Senate candidate, perpetually grinning and ingratiating himself, resembles nothing so much as an overage Boy Scout."[144] The *New York Daily News* concurred with the following anecdote:

> When Lazio arrived at Shea Stadium last week for Game 3 of the
> World Series, he was flanked by Gov. Pataki and Mayor Giuliani,
> giving the distinct impression that he was being propped up by the
> more substantial guys. It was an unfortunate reminder that Lazio, the
> un-Hillary, has little going for him but boyish charm. Like Bush, he's
> one of Campaign 2000's likable lightweights.[145]

During the first debate with Rodham Clinton, Lazio attempted to shed his boyish image and interject drama into the campaign—two things that should have played well in the media—by crossing over to Rodham Clinton and trying to get her to sign a pledge to eschew soft money contributions for the duration of the campaign. That move backfired on Lazio with the media and voters alike. Columnist Maureen Dowd castigated Lazio for "acting like a bully at the pulpit" and observed that "many of the women who had liked the glowing Long Island congressman recoiled from his glowering performance in Buffalo."[146] Post-election polling supports Dowd's assessment. The *New York Times* quoted a Rodham Clinton pollster who argued that "Mrs. Clinton benefited most famously during the first of three debates when Mr. Lazio strode over to her side of the stage, waved a paper in her face and demanded she sign it to disavow the use of soft money in her campaign." The *Times* continued with a quotation from pollster Celinda Like who claimed that "you cannot be in a woman candidate's face. Women feel like guys are always in their face like that."[147] Voter Marilyn Schurig agreed, telling a *New York Times* reporter that "He shoved this thing in her face and I got very offended."[148]

Ironically, Lazio used feminist logic to defend his conduct during the debate, contending, "The idea that somehow that there's a double standard because you're a man or a woman, and you can't make a point forcefully if you're a man, and the person you're making the point with is a woman, I just think that's sexist."[149] Sexist or not, media coverage of Giuliani and Lazio during campaign 2000 may point to slow, and very slight, reversal in the challenges facing candidates for public office. Whereas women used to have the most trouble negotiating the line between "too tough" and "not tough enough," in this case the male candidates fared worse than the female one on the toughness tightrope.

As noted in previous chapters, women can more easily inhabit the role of representative than the role of chief executive, so it may come as no surprise that Hillary Rodham Clinton's gender was not the focus of media coverage of her during her 2000 Senate campaign. That does not mean, however, that eighty years after the passage of woman suffrage America finally has worked through its anxieties about gender and leadership. The last case study in this book examines two unique elements of women's political personae that collided when Elizabeth Dole made a bid for the Republican presidential nomination. Her short but significant campaign brought together the dynamics of a political spouse vying for a chance to lead the free world—and running into what is perhaps the last glass ceiling in American politics.

Notes

1. Transcript reprinted in "Gingrich Cries Foul over Mom's Whisper," *Sacramento Bee*, January 5, 1995, A1, Lexis Nexis Academic Universe (accessed February 2, 1996); also see Roger Simon, "Just Answer in a Whisper: Can Connie be Trusted?" *Baltimore Sun*, January 6, 1995, final edition, 2A, Lexis Nexis Academic Universe (accessed February 2, 1996).

2. See, for example, Deborah Hurley, "The Whisper Heard 'Round the World," *The Quill* 83 (1995): 13, Expanded Academic ASAP (accessed February 2, 1996); Reuven Frank, "Celebrity Journalism on Television," *The New Leader*, January 30, 1995, Lexis Nexis Academic Universe (accessed February 2, 1996).

3. Karen DeWitt, "The 104th Congress; The Speaker's Mother; Quick Indignation After CBS Interview," *New York Times*, January 5, 1995, late edition, A23, Lexis Nexis Academic Universe (accessed February 2, 1996).

4. Maureen Downey, "It Rhymes with Gingrich: Remark by Mother of the House Speaker Sparks Debate on Use of 'Bitch' to Describe Women with Power," *Atlanta Journal and Constitution*, January 5, 1995, D1, Lexis Nexis Academic Universe (accessed February 2, 1996).

5. Quoted in Howard Fineman, "A Crisis at Home," *Newsweek*, December 21, 1998, 27.

6. For discussions of the ways in which norms of femininity impacted Rodham Clinton see Karlyn Kohrs Campbell, "Shadowboxing with Stereotypes: The Press, the Public, and the Candidates' Wives," Research paper R–9 (President and Fellows of Harvard College, 1993): 1–19; Karlyn Kohrs Campbell, "The Rhetorical Presidency: A Two-Person Career," in *Beyond the Rhetorical Presidency*, ed. Martin J. Medhurst (College Station: Texas A&M University Press, 1996), 179–95; Karlyn Kohrs Campbell, "The Discursive Performance of Femininity: Hating Hillary," *Rhetoric & Public Affairs* 1 (1998): 1–19; Kathleen Hall Jamieson, *Beyond the Double Bind: Women and Leadership* (New York: Oxford University Press, 1995), Ch. 2; Janette Kenner Muir and Lisa M. Benitez, "Redefining the Role of the First Lady: The Rhetorical Style of Hillary Rodham Clinton," in *The Clinton Presidency: Images, Issues, and Communication Strategies*, ed. Robert E. Denton, Jr. and Rachel L. Holloway (Westport, Conn.: Praeger, 1996), 139–58; Patricia A. Sullivan and Lynn H. Turner, *From the Margins to the Center: Contemporary Women and Political Communication* (Westport, Conn.: Praeger, 1996), Ch. 4; and Betty Houchin Winfield, "'Madame President': Understanding a New Kind of First Lady," *Media Studies Journal* 8 (1994): 59–71.

7. Gallup Poll results from February 1993 stated that 67% of respondents "favored Hillary Clinton's role as First Lady" and 59% "approved of her participation" in health-care reform. See Leslie McAneny, "New First Lady Making Headway—on Her Own Terms," *The Gallup Poll Monthly*, February 1993, 2, Expanded Academic ASAP (accessed February 2, 1996). Similarly, a poll conducted by *U.S. News & World Report* in May 1993 reported that 51% of those responding perceived Hillary Clinton to have the "right amount" of power. See Kenneth T. Walsh, "America's First (Working) Couple," *U.S. News & World Report*, May 10, 1993, 32, Expanded Academic ASAP (accessed February 2, 1996). In early 1994, Rodham Clinton's favorability ratings continued to be positive. The April 1994 Gallup Poll listed the first lady's favorability rating at 56%. Polls, of course, can be a problematic measure of audience sentiment. *Time* reports a thirteen point differential in the favorability rating when Americans were polled on their feelings about "Hillary Rodham Clinton" versus "Hillary Clinton" (the lower rating matched "Rodham Clinton"). See "What's in a Name?" *Time*, April 5, 1993, 15, Expanded Academic ASAP (accessed February 2, 1996). Nevertheless, both an analysis of media coverage and Rodham Clinton's own actions suggest that although her "new" role received mixed reviews initially, support for her direct, public involvement in the administration plummeted in late 1994.

8. Margaret Carlson, "Hillary Clinton: Partner as Much as Wife," *Time*, January 27, 1992, 19, Expanded Academic ASAP (accessed October 29, 1995).

9. "The Merry Wives of Washington," *The Economist*, August 8, 1992, 26.

10. Margaret Carlson, "The Dynamic Duo," *Time*, January 4, 1993, 38–41.

11. Kenneth T. Walsh, "Now, the First Chief Advocate," *U.S. News & World Report*, January 25, 1993, 46.

12. Karl Meyer, "The President's Other Running Mate," *New York Times*, January 27, 1993, A22.

13. Walter R. Fisher, "Narration as a Human Communication Paradigm: The Case of Public Moral Argument," *Communication Monographs* 51 (1984): 1–22.

14. Scott Steele, "A Man of Hope (Ark.)," *Maclean's*, November 16, 1992, 42.

15. Deirdre McMurdy, "The Political Wife: Hillary Clinton Redefines Her Role," *Maclean's*, July 20, 1992, 34.

16. Steele "A Man of Hope," 42.

17. Matthew Cooper, "The Hillary Factor," *U.S. News & World Report*, April 27, 1992, 37. David Brock credits Rodham Clinton's successful efforts for educational reform in Arkansas with Bill Clinton's political success at the state and national level. See David Brock, *The Seduction of Hillary Rodham* (New York: Free Press, 1996), 179.

18. Winfield, "'Madame President,'" 64.

19. Arlene W. Saxonhouse, "Introduction—Public and Private: The Paradigm's Power," in *Stereotypes of Women in Power: Historical Perspectives and Revisionist Views*, ed. Barbara Garlick, Suzanne Dixon, and Pauline Allen (New York: Greenwood Press, 1992), 4–5.

20. Karlyn Kohrs Campbell, *Man Cannot Speak for Her*, vol. 1 (New York: Greenwood Press, 1989), 10. For additional discussion of the cult of true womanhood in the United States, see Carolyn Johnston, *Sexual Power: Feminism and the Family in America* (Tuscaloosa: University of Alabama Press, 1992).

21. Dorothy W. Cantor and Toni Bernay, *Women in Power: The Secrets of Leadership* (Boston: Houghton Mifflin, 1992), 7.

22. Kenneth T. Walsh, "Barbara Bush's Subtle and Significant Campaign Role," *U.S. News & World Report*, April 27, 1992, 36.

23. Margaret Carlson, "All Eyes on Hillary," *Time*, December 14, 1992, 28, Expanded Academic ASAP (accessed February 2, 1996).

24. The full answer, according to Jamieson, *Beyond the Double Bind*, 26–27 is as follows: "I thought number one it [Jerry Brown's attack on Rodham Clinton during the preceding night's debate] was pathetic and desperate, and also thought it was interesting because this is the sort of thing that happens to the sort of women who have their own careers and their own lives. And I think it's a shame but I guess it's something that we're going to have to live with. Those of us who have tried and have a career, tried to have an independent life and to make a difference and certainly like myself who has children but other issues, uh you know I've done the best I can to lead my life but I suppose it'll be subject to attack but it's not true and I don't know what else to say except it's sad to me." Rodham Clinton then was asked about the possibility of avoiding the appearance of conflicts of interest and she continued, saying, "I wish that were true. You

know I suppose I could have stayed home and baked cookies and had teas but what I decided to do was fulfill my profession which I entered before my husband was in public life. And I've tried very, very hard to be as careful as possible and that's all I can tell you." Jamieson's recounting of the episode is particularly useful because she works from a time-coded transcript obtained from a network source whose anonymity she protects. Jamieson's account is the most complete published record of Rodham Clinton's statements available and she notes the ways in which subsequent revisions in the popular press failed to convey the context and tone of the quotation. See Jamieson, *Beyond the Double Bind*, 218, note 12.

25. Jamieson, *Beyond the Double Bind*, 27.

26. Patricia A. Sullivan and Carole Levin, "Women and Political Communication: From the Margins to the Center," in *Political Rhetoric, Power, and Renaissance Women*, ed. Carole Levin and Patricia A. Sullivan (New York: State University of New York Press, 1995), 277.

27. Michael Barone, "Entering the Combat Zone," *U.S. News & World Report*, March 30, 1992, 39, Expanded Academic ASAP (accessed October 29, 1995).

28. Cooper, "The Hillary Factor."

29. Jamieson, *Beyond the Double Bind*, 27.

30. "Hillary Rodham Clinton's Job," editorial, *New York Times*, January 27, 1993, A22.

31. Winfield, "'Madame President,'" 68.

32. Katha Pollitt, "The Male Media's Hillary Problem; First-Lady Bashing," *The Nation*, May 17, 1993, 657, Expanded Academic ASAP (accessed October 27, 1995).

33. Pierre Saint-Amand, "Terrorizing Marie Antoinette," *Critical Inquiry* 20 (1994): 384.

34. Michael Barone, "Bad News for Boomer Liberals," *U.S. News & World Report*, August 29, 1994, 32, Expanded Academic ASAP (accessed October 27, 1995).

35. Connie Bruck, "Hillary the Pol," *The New Yorker*, May 30, 1994, 90.

36. *Spy*, February 1993, cover.

37. Johnston, *Sexual Power*, ix.

38. Saint-Amand, "Terrorizing Marie Antoinette," 385.

39. Robert L. Ivie, "Presidential Motives for War," *Quarterly Journal of Speech* 60 (1974): 337–45. Also see Robert L. Ivie, "Cold War Motives and the Rhetorical Metaphor: A Framework of Criticism," in *Cold War Rhetoric: Strategy, Metaphor, and Ideology*, ed. Martin J. Medhurst, Robert L. Ivie, Philip Wander, and Robert L. Scott (East Lansing: Michigan State University Press, 1990), 71–79.

40. Walsh, "America's First," 32.

41. Neil A. Lewis, "Back to College for an Image Makeover," *New York Times*, national edition, May 30, 1992, L9.

42. Walsh, "Now, the First," 46.

43. Robert Pear, "First Lady Sets Aggressive Tone for Debate on Health-Care Plan," *New York Times*, May 27 1993, A1.

44. Barone, "Bad News."

45. Steele, "A Man of Hope," 43.

46. Jonathan Alter, "Go Ahead, Bust Some Chops," *Newsweek*, November 15, 1993, 34.

47. Walsh, "America's First."

48. Barbara Amiel, "The Trouble with Bill and Hillary," *Maclean's*, April 11, 1994, 13.

49. Noemie Emery, "The Androgyny Party," *Commentary* 95 (1993): 49, Expanded Academic ASAP (accessed February 2, 1996).

50. The speech texts analyzed in this chapter came from a variety of sources. The first lady's official web site contained the complete text of selected speeches from 1993 to 2000. We obtained them while President Clinton was still in office at <http://www.whitehouse.gov/WH/EOP/First_Lady/html>. We also obtained speech texts by mail from the office of the White House Press Secretary. The July 1993 speech to the American Medical Association, entitled "Health Care: We Can Make a Difference," can be found in *Vital Speeches of the Day* 59 (July 15, 1993): 580–85.

51. Campbell, "The Discursive Performance," 5, 11, 14. See also Jane Blankenship and Deborah Robson, "A 'Feminine Style' in Women's Political Discourse: An Exploratory Essay," *Communication Quarterly* 43 (1995): 353–66; Bonnie J. Dow and Mari Boor Tonn, "'Feminine Style' and Political Judgment in the Rhetoric of Ann Richards," *Quarterly Journal of Speech* 79 (1993): 286–302; and Kathleen Hall Jamieson, "The 'Effeminate' Style" in *Eloquence in an Electronic Age: The Transformation of Political Speechmaking* (New York: Oxford University Press, 1988), 67–89.

52. "Listen with Hillary," *The Economist*, March 20, 1993, 26.

53. Hillary Rodham Clinton, Address at Marshall University, Huntington, W.Va., November 4, 1993 (Office of the Press Secretary, The White House), 2.

54. Hillary Rodham Clinton, Address to the Institute of Medicine Annual Meeting, Washington, D.C., October 19, 1993 (Office of the Press Secretary, The White House), 2

55. H. R. Clinton, "Health Care," 581, 583.

56. Hillary Rodham Clinton, Address to the American Hospital Association, Orlando, Fla., August 9, 1993 (Office of the Press Secretary, The White House), 2, 12.

57. Hillary Rodham Clinton, Address to the American Legion's Annual Conference, Sheraton Washington Hotel, Washington, D.C., February 15, 1994 (Office of the Press Secretary, The White House), 4; Hillary Rodham Clinton, Address to the Health Care Forum, Denver, Colo., March 14, 1994 (Office of the Press Secretary, The White House), 2; Hillary Rodham Clinton, Address to the United Auto Workers, Sheraton Washington Hotel, Washington, D.C.,

March 22, 1994 (Office of the Press Secretary, The White House), 3.

58. Hillary Rodham Clinton, Address to the National Institutes of Health, February 17, 1994 (Office of the Press Secretary, The White House), 10.

59. H. R. Clinton, Address to the American Legion, 11.

60. See, for example, Hillary Rodham Clinton, "Health Care," 582; Townhall Meeting in Minneapolis, Minn., September 17, 1993, 2.

61. H. R. Clinton, Address to the AHA, 2.

62. William J. Clinton, Hillary Rodham Clinton, Al Gore, Tipper Gore, and C. Everett Koop, Address to Physicians and Supporters, East Room of the White House, Washington, D.C., September 20, 1993 (Office of the Press Secretary, The White House), 3.

63. William J. Clinton, Al Gore, Hillary Rodham Clinton, and Tipper Gore, Address at a Health Care Rally, South Lawn of The White House, Washington, D.C., September 23, 1993 (Office of the Press Secretary, The White House), 1.

64. John Gatta, *American Madonna: Image of the Divine Woman in Literary Culture* (New York: Oxford University Press, 1997), 54, 80, 97–98.

65. For different perspectives on pop icon Madonna, see Cathy [Ramona Liera] Schwichtenberg, ed. *The Madonna Connection: Representational Politics, Subcultural Identities, and Cultural Theory* (Boulder, Colo.: Westview Press, 1993). Also see John Fiske, "British Cultural Studies and Television," in *Channels of Discourse Reassembled: Television and Contemporary Criticism*, 2d ed., ed. Robert C. Allen (Chapel Hill: University of North Carolina Press, 1992), 304–05; D. Lynn O'Brien Hallstein, "Feminist Assessment of Emancipatory Potential and Madonna's Contradictory Gender Practices," *Quarterly Journal of Speech* 82 (1996): 125–41; and Pamela Robertson, *Guilty Pleasures: Feminist Camp from Mae West to Madonna* (Durham, N.C.: Duke University Press, 1996), 113–38.

66. E. Dierdre Pribram, "Seduction, Control, & the Search for Authenticity: Madonna's Truth or Dare," in *The Madonna Connection: Representational Politics, Subcultural Identities, and Cultural Theory*, ed. Cathy [Ramona Liera] Schwichtenberg (Boulder, Colo.: Westview, 1993), 196–97.

67. Shawn J. Parry-Giles, "Mediating Hillary Rodham Clinton: Television News Practices and Image-Making in the Postmodern Age," *Critical Studies in Media Communication* 17 (2000): 205–26.

68. Michael Osborn, "Archetypal Metaphor in Rhetoric: The Light-Dark Family," *Quarterly Journal of Speech* 53 (1967): 115–26; and Lynn M. Stearney, "Feminism, Ecofeminism, and the Maternal Archetype: Motherhood as a Feminine Universal," *Communication Quarterly* 42 (1994): 145–59.

69. Stearney, "Feminism, Ecofeminism and the Maternal Archetype," 146.

70. Hillary Rodham Clinton, *It Takes a Village and Other Lessons Children Teach Us* (New York: Simon & Schuster, 1996).

71. Hillary Rodham Clinton, Address at the Democratic National Convention, Chicago, Ill., August 27, 1996 (Office of the Press Secretary, The White House).

72. H. R. Clinton, Address at the DNC.

73. Denise M. Bostdorff, "Hillary Rodham Clinton and Elizabeth Dole as Running 'Mates' in the 1996 Campaign: Parallels in the Rhetorical Constraints of First Ladies and Vice Presidents," in *The 1996 Presidential Campaign: A Communication Perspective*, ed. Robert E. Denton, Jr. (Westport, Conn.: Praeger, 1998), 216.

74. Bonnie Dow, *Prime-Time Feminism: Television, Media Culture, and the Women's Movement Since 1970* (Philadelphia: University of Pennsylvania Press, 1996), 164–202.

75. Dow, *Prime-Time Feminism*, 166–67. See Sarah Ruddick, "Maternal Thinking," *Feminist Studies* 6 (1980): 342–67; and Carol Gilligan, *In a Different Voice: Psychological Theory and Women's Development* (Cambridge, Mass.: Harvard University Press, 1982).

76. Dow, *Prime-Time Feminism*, 196–97.

77. Hillary Rodham Clinton, Address to the United Nations Fourth World Conference on Women, Beijing, China, September 5, 1995, *WIN News*, August 1995, Expanded Academic Index (accessed February 6, 1996).

78. Rodham Clinton was slated to skip the conference until China released Chinese-American human rights activist Harry Wu. See Bob Edwards, "Critics Question Treatment of Women Within U.N.," *National Public Radio*, September 4, 1995, Lexis Nexis Academic Universe (accessed February 6, 1996).

79. William Schneider, "First Lady's Unwavering Words Win Her Play of Week," *CNN*, September 8, 1995, Lexis Nexis Academic Universe (accessed February 20, 1996).

80. Patrick Tyler, "Hillary Clinton, in China, Details Abuse of Women," *New York Times*, September 6, 1995, A1, Lexis Nexis Academic Universe (accessed February 20, 1996).

81. Graham Hutchings, "Hard-Hitting Hillary Savages Beijing; Mrs. Clinton Strikes Blow for Women Worldwide," *The Daily Telegraph,* September 6, 1995, Lexis Nexis Academic Universe (accessed February 6, 1996).

82. Hillary Rodham Clinton, Address at Radio Free Europe, Prague, The Czech Republic, July 4, 1996 (Office of the Press Secretary, The White House), 3–4.

83. Hillary Rodham Clinton, Address to the Central Asian Conference on Women in Politics, Almaty, Kazakhstan, November 12, 1997 (Office of the Press Secretary, The White House).

84. Hillary Rodham Clinton, Address at the University of Capetown, Capetown, South Africa, March 20, 1997 (Office of the Press Secretary, The White House).

85. K. K. Campbell, "The Discursive Performance of Femininity," 1–19.

86. Karlyn Kohrs Campbell, "'The Rhetoric of Women's Liberation: An Oxymoron' Revisited," *Communication Studies* 50 (1999): 142. See also Karlyn Kohrs Campbell, "The Rhetoric of Women's Liberation: An Oxymoron," *Quarterly Journal of Speech* 59 (1973): 74–86.

87. Kenneth Burke, *Attitudes Toward History*, 3d ed. (Berkeley: University of California Press, 1984), 309.

88. There is a precedent for a woman's physical appearance affecting the way the media interpret her feminism. Susan J. Douglas argues that in the 1960s, the media accepted a far more radical feminist message from Gloria Steinem than from Betty Friedan, in large part because Steinem fit the norms of physical attractiveness, whereas Friedan was portrayed as dowdy. See Susan J. Douglas, *Where the Girls Are: Growing Up Female with the Mass Media* (New York: Random House, 1994), 230–31.

89. Hillary Rodham Clinton, Address to the Rajiv Gandhi Foundation, New Delhi, India, March 29, 1995 (Office of the Press Secretary, The White House).

90. Hillary Rodham Clinton, Address for International Women's Day, The State Department, Washington, D.C., March 12, 1997 (Office of the Press Secretary, The White House), 3. For another example of her use of the term "real-life politik," see Hillary Rodham Clinton, Address to the Women's Leadership Forum, April 18, 1997 (Office of the Press Secretary, The White House), 4.

91. Hillary Rodham Clinton, Address to the Annual Meeting of the World Economic Forum, Davos, Switzerland, February 2, 1998 (Office of the Press Secretary, The White House), 1.

92. Hillary Rodham Clinton, Remarks by the First Lady to the Women of Australia, Sydney, Australia, November 21, 1996 (Office of the Press Secretary, The White House), 3.

93. All references to the *Today* show interview are taken from a personal video recording of the broadcast. "Interview with Hillary Rodham Clinton," *Today*, NBC, January 27, 1998.

94. Matthew Cooper, "Hillary Clinton Goes to War," *Newsweek*, February 2, 1998, 24.

95. "More on the Presidential Crisis," *New York Times*, January 25, 1998, 1, Lexis Nexis Academic Universe (accessed February 9, 1998).

96. "Hillary Clinton Leading Defense of Her Husband, Denying All Charges against Him," *NBC Nightly News*, January 27, 1998, Lexis Nexis Academic Universe (accessed February 9, 1998).

97. "The First Family in Full Battle Regalia," *Nightline*, January 27, 1998, Lexis Nexis Academic Universe (accessed February 9, 1998).

98. Michelle Norris and Lisa McRee, "Hillary Clinton Plays Hardball," *Good Morning America*, January 26, 1998, Lexis Nexis Academic Universe (accessed February 9, 1998).

99. "Hillary Clinton Stands by Husband," *MSNBC*, <msncb.com> (accessed February 10, 1998).

100. Barbara Ehrenreich, "The Week Feminists Got Laryngitis," *Time*, February 9, 1998, 68, Lexis Nexis Academic Universe (accessed February 9, 1998).

101. Jeanne Meserve and Eileen O'Conner, "First Lady Responds to Allegations Claiming Right-Wing Conspiracy," *CNN Worldview*, January 27, 1998,

Lexis Nexis Academic Universe (accessed February 9, 1998).

102. Matthew Cooper and Karen Breslau, "For Better and for Worse," *Newsweek*, February 9, 1999, 41.

103. The First Lady's Treasures Tour, <http://www.whitehouse.gov/WH/EOP/First_Lady/html/treasures/index.html> (accessed November 21, 1999).

104. Patricia Leigh Brown, "Hillary Clinton Inaugurates Preservation Campaign," *New York Times*, July 14, 1998, A12, Lexis Nexis Academic Universe (accessed November 21, 1999). The phrase "First lady–like" was repeated in Kathy Kiely, "Hil Fiery in Rights Talk," *New York Daily News*, July 17, 1998, 30, Lexis Nexis Academic Universe (accessed November 21, 1999).

105. Brown, "Hillary Clinton Inaugurates Preservation Campaign."

106. Hillary Rodham Clinton, Address at the Kate Mullany House, Troy, N.Y., July 15, 1998 (Office of the Press Secretary, The White House), 3.

107. Hillary Rodham Clinton, Address at the 150th Anniversary of the First Woman's Rights Convention, Seneca Falls, N.Y., July 16, 1998 (Office of the Press Secretary, The White House), 4.

108. Karen Breslau, "Hillary's Next Life," *Newsweek*, July 20, 1998, Lexis Nexis Academic Universe (accessed November 21, 1999).

109. A Lexis Nexis Academic Universe search produced articles and transcripts from national news magazines such as *Newsweek* and *Time*, newspapers such as the *Washington Post*, *New York Times*, and the *New York Daily News*, and television programs from the major broadcast and cable news networks. We examined articles that appeared from July 1998 through November 2000. The scope of the study included the entire campaign, including the significant period preceding Rodham Clinton's "official" announcement when she was the presumptive candidate.

110. For examination of how media reports drew on gender stereotypes and, in turn, affected public perceptions of Rodham Clinton see Parry-Giles, "Mediating Hillary Rodham Clinton."

111. Place was not the sole media frame for stories about Rodham Clinton's candidacy. Questions about her competence and experience emerged, as did echoes of scandal narratives in stories about how Rodham Clinton's campaign was funded. But place was the dominant and, we would argue, most important narrative underscoring coverage of the 2000 Senate campaign in New York.

112. Howard Fineman, "The Potholes of New York," *Newsweek*, May 31, 1999, 31.

113. Romesh Ratnesar, "A Race of Her Own," *Time*, March 1, 1999, 28–40.

114. Evan Thomas and Debra Rosenberg, "Hillary's Day in The Sun," *Newsweek*, March 1, 1999, 29.

115. Michael Grunwald, "Hope, Thy Name is Hillary, in One Hurting N.Y. Mill Town," *Washington Post*, March 3, 1999, <washingtonpost.com> (accessed March 4, 1999).

116. Michael R. Blood, "She's Carpetbagger, Sez Rudy in Fund Drive,"

New York Daily News, June 4, 1999, <www.nydailynews.com> (accessed February 9, 2000).

117. David M. Herszenhorn, "On Eve of Four-Day Tour, Hillary Clinton Makes It Official," *New York Times*, July 7, 1999, <nytimes.com> (accessed July 9, 1999).

118. "New York U.S. Senate," *New York Times*, July 7, 1999, <nytimes.com> (accessed July 9, 1999).

119. Ratu Kamlani, "In Case She Wants Some Free Advice . . .," *Time*, March 1, 1999, 38–39.

120. Frank Ahrens, "Infield Chatter; Hillary Clinton Toasts the 'Home' Team," *Washington Post*, June 11, 1999, Lexis Nexis Academic Universe (accessed December 29, 2000).

121. Quoted in Ahrens, "Infield Chatter."

122. "A Viable Candidate?" *Nightline,* September 13, 1999, <abcnews.go.com> (accessed September 15, 1999).

123. Joel Siegel, "Hillary Rues Slip in Advice on Clemency," *New York Daily News*, September 11, 1999, Lexis Nexis Academic Universe (accessed December 29, 2000). For examples of how the clemency story played out in the media, see Lynne Duke and William Claiborne, "12 Puerto Ricans Accept Clemency," *Washington Post*, September 8, 1999, Lexis Nexis Academic Universe (accessed December 29, 2000); Maureen Dowd, "The 'I Love Hillary' Show," *Denver Post*, September 9, 1999, Lexis Nexis Academic Universe (accessed December 29, 2000); William Safire, "Clemency Episode Just More Clinton Deceit," *Houston Chronicle*, September 14, 1999, Lexis Nexis Academic Universe (accessed December 29, 2000); and Debra Rosenberg and Michael Isikoff, "Forgive Us Our Revolution," *Newsweek*, September 20, 1999, 30.

124. "A Viable Candidate?" *Nightline.*

125. Ann Compton, "She Speaks for Herself," *abcnews.com*, July 9, 1999, <abcnews.go.com> (accessed November 17, 1999).

126. Ann Compton, "Moving Day," *abcnews.com*, January 4, 2000, <abcnews.go.com> (accessed January 4, 2000).

127. "Hillary Clinton In or Out?" *This Week*, November 28, 1999, <abcnews.go.com> (accessed December 2, 1999).

128. Hillary Rodham Clinton, "Hillary's Announcement Speech Purchase College (SUNY)," February 7, 2000, <hillary2000.org> (accessed December 28, 2000). Also available from the February 7, 2000 issue of *New York Times*, <nytimes.com> (accessed February 8, 2000).

129. The *Los Angeles Times* reported that "independent observers and Clinton's own advisors believe her best chance is to sharpen the issue debate with the mayor. That's the one terrain where Clinton may have an advantage. 'It's a very good environment for her in that way,' says Lee Miringoff, who directs the nonpartisan Marist College Poll." Ronald Brownstein, "Hillary Clinton Needs to Be a Woman of Substance in a Race Big on Style," *Los Angeles Times*, March 27, 2000, <latimes.com> (accessed March 27, 2000).

130. Republicans' choice to emphasize the issue of place over the issue of gender is a significant one since, during the 1992 presidential campaign, gender (and specifically Hillary Clinton's political activism) was seen by Republicans as Bill Clinton's Achilles heel. Kenneth T. Walsh reported that the Bush campaign saw "considerable political value in portraying Hillary Clinton as an ambitious and proud careerist in contrast to Barbara [Bush] as a loyal and self-deprecating helpmate." See Walsh, "Barbara Bush's Subtle," 36.

131. "Hillary Makes it Official," *abcnews.com*, February 7, 2000, <abcnews.go.com> (accessed February 7, 2000).

132. "The First Debate: Clinton vs. Lazio," *MSNBC*, September 13, 2000.

133. Dana Milbank, "Meet the Man Who Isn't Hillary; Rick Lazio, the Other New York Senate Candidate," *Washington Post*, October 7, 2000, Lexis Nexis Academic Universe (accessed December 28, 2000).

134. John F. Harris and Lynne Duke, "First Lady Gets a N.Y. Makeover," *Washington Post*, March 13, 2000, A1, <washingtonpost.com> (accessed March 13, 2000).

135. Milbank, "Meet the Man Who Isn't Hillary."

136. Bob Port and Frank Lombardi, "Carpetbag Tag Didn't Halt Hil Steamroll," *New York Daily News*, November 8, 2000, Lexis Nexis Academic Universe (accessed December 28, 2000).

137. "Hillary Clinton Q & A," *abcnews.com*, February 8, 2000, <abcnews.go.com> (accessed February 9, 2000).

138. Jamieson, *Beyond the Double Bind*, 130–31.

139. Harris and Duke, "First Lady Gets a N.Y. Makeover," A1.

140. Eileen Murphy, "Hillary Slams Giuliani Homeless Sweeps," *abcnews.com*, December 1, 1999, <abcnews.go.com> (accessed December 2, 1999).

141. Brownstein, "Hillary Clinton Needs to Be a Woman of Substance."

142. "Senate Race Dead Even," *abcnews.com*, March 29, 2000, <abcnews.go.com> (accessed March 29, 2000).

143. Michael Tomasky, "Hillary's Turn," *New York Magazine*, March 30, 2000, <nymag.com> (accessed March 30, 2000).

144. Milbank, "Meet the Man Who Isn't Hillary."

145. E.R. Shipp, "Hillary and Rick: Safe, Bland and Dull," *New York Daily News*, October 29, 2000, Lexis Nexis Academic Universe (accessed December 28, 2000).

146. Maureen Dowd, "A Man and a Woman," *New York Times*, September 20, 2000, <nytimes.com> (accessed October 10, 2000).

147. Elisabeth Bumiller, "The Election: It Took a Woman; How Gender Helped Elect Hillary Clinton," *New York Times*, November 12, 2000, Lexis Nexis Academic Universe (accessed December 28, 2000).

148. Joyce Purnick, "Gender Chasm for Hillary Clinton; Candidate Drew 60% of Women's Votes," *Milwaukee Journal Sentinel*, November 12, 2000, Lexis Nexis Academic Universe (accessed December 28, 2000).

149. Dowd, "A Man and a Woman."

Chapter 5

Elizabeth Dole

During the 1996 presidential campaign the spouses of candidates Bill Clinton and Bob Dole received much attention in the press. Perhaps more than any other set of presidential spouses, Hillary Rodham Clinton and Elizabeth Dole were compared to (and against) one another. A *Washington Post* article published in the spring of the campaign began with the following lead:

> After watching Elizabeth Dole deliver a stump speech, Victoria Schulz, a 19-year-old college student, takes a breath and casts her vote: "I'm sure Hillary would be very intelligent to talk to, but I'd rather hang out with Elizabeth Dole." "I'm anxious to see her in her ball gown," says Janet Klein, a gray-haired woman. Diane Gilbert, cradling her baby, says: "I look at her and I see class and taste."[1]

Encapsulating the hostess/beauty queen persona, the lead played up Dole's social and physical appeal. The potential bonus of her professional experience in government was addressed as well, a full four paragraphs later in the article. The *Post*'s discussion of Dole's accomplishments at Harvard Law School, her role in various presidential administrations, and her post at the head of the American Red Cross followed a lengthy discussion of whether or not Elizabeth Dole was "Cinderella" to Hillary Rodham Clinton's "Lady Macbeth."

Elizabeth Dole is an important figure in U.S. politics because of the way she marks the transitions women are making in American public leadership. The "pioneer" metaphor certainly would resonate with Dole's experience as one of only 24 women in her class of 550 at Harvard Law School. She was the first woman to hold cabinet posts in two different presidential administrations, and she was the first Republican woman to run, what was called at the time, a "credible" presidential campaign.[2] She is only the third U.S. Senator to have been married to a Senator from a different state.[3] Dole has made many transitions in her political career: from political appointee to political spouse; from spouse to presidential candidate; from failed presidential candidate to member of the U.S. Senate. This chapter assesses Dole's political identity as it was presented in national media, considering both news frames as well as Dole's own rhetorical strategies.[4] In the first two of Dole's three nationally-prominent campaigns, a distinct narrative is drawn: In 1996, acting as a political surrogate for husband Bob Dole's presidential campaign, Elizabeth Dole was cast as a hostess/beauty queen. That image lingered over her 2000 bid for the Republican presidential nomination, combining with the narrative of Dole as a pioneer—her candidacy was commended for its symbolic value but dismissed in terms of political viability. When Dole campaigned for the U.S. Senate, a single news narrative failed to emerge. Instead, the media portrayed a more complex candidate who appealed to voters as a potential partner in governance, rather than as a leader. The Dole case serves as another example of the notion that the U.S. electorate accepts women in representative positions more easily than in executive leadership.

The Good Wife

Although Dole had been active in government for nearly thirty years before the 1996 presidential campaign, it was that campaign that thrust her into the national spotlight. Consequently, she gained prominence nationally as the spouse of presidential candidate Bob Dole, rather than as an active politico in her own right. The Dole campaign's choice to downplay Elizabeth's professional accomplishments was understandable for two reasons. First, no presidential candidate wants to look like a Washington insider. Bob Dole was so concerned about avoiding that appearance that he retired from the U.S. Senate and campaigned as a "regular citizen." Touting his wife's professional accomplishments would only remind voters that the Doles had existed inside the beltway for decades. More important, however, was the Doles' decision to position Elizabeth in opposition to Hillary. A *Time* magazine article reported that the "Dole camp, having studied the pathology of Hillary's troubles early last year, is eager to argue that this is a marriage, not a political partnership. Dole has called Elizabeth his 'secret weapon,' his 'Southern strategy,' all the while making it clear that he is old-fashioned about the East Wing, that Elizabeth won't be sitting in on Cabinet meetings and serving as the unofficial Minister of Health Care."[5] The political identity being forged in public memory was that of a loyal and supportive wife, an attractive and likeable complement to her husband's serious demeanor, who had the ability to humanize him for the electorate.

The image that both Doles worked to create in 1996 resonated in media accounts. One report heralded the complementary nature of the relationship, stating that "on the campaign trail Elizabeth Dole is the splashy color to this GOP presidential hopeful's grayness. Bob Dole is the dark suit standing on the podium before the fixed microphone. She's the sunny yellow dress with the body mike that frees her to roam the aisles."[6] The narrative emerging across the media was that Dole was a complementary spouse because, despite her impressive resume, she didn't overshadow her spouse as did her Democratic counterpart, Hillary Clinton. A *Time* cover story characterized Dole as supportive: "Yes, time and again, Elizabeth Dole has put her own career on hold to help her husband's. She has modified her more moderate views on issues like affirmative action to complement her husband's more conservative ones."[7] Similarly, the *New York Times* stated that "throughout the campaign, she has remained the dutiful and dependable surrogate, never staking out her own positions, always taking what her husband says and pitching it to her audiences."[8] In an article titled, "The Woman Behind That Unwavering Smile," *Newsweek* reassured voters that "Politically, she is his [Bob Dole's] closest adviser, but far from a controlling influence."[9] Voters were assured of Dole's submission to her husband pictorially as well. One striking example is a photo in the July 1, 1996 issue of *Time* magazine. The photo accompanied a cover story comparing Hillary and Elizabeth as prospective first ladies. The largest photo in the layout was a black and white shot of Bob and Elizabeth Dole in Bob Dole's office. Bob Dole is in the background of the shot, sitting at a table eating pizza with the family dog begging for scraps at his feet. Elizabeth is in the foreground of the photo, smiling, on her knees and gesturing toward the table. The caption suggests that Elizabeth is "lament[ing] that Leader [the dog] is more interested in Bob's take-out pizza than in her," but the not-so-subtle subtext of the photo is that Mrs. Dole is an appropriately cheerful and submissive political wife.[10] *Newsweek* published a posed photo, also of the Doles with Leader, that portrayed Bob Dole gazing out and Elizabeth Dole holding the dog, smiling broadly, and gazing up at her husband.[11]

Dole's physical appearance also was the subject of media commentary. The fact that physical characteristics were described by reporters as they set the scenes for their stories is not unique—even male politicians are subjected to physical scrutiny in this televisual era. What is striking is the nature of the media descriptions. They followed the hostess/beauty queen script, analyzing in close detail Dole's fashion choices and sometimes drawing attention to her sexual appeal. The following excerpt from a *New York Times* essay is representative of such characterizations:

> At 60, Elizabeth Dole is still a beautiful woman, thinner than she was a decade ago, with smooth skin flushed prettily in the [Kentucky] heat. Up close you can see she has freckles. She is wearing stockings and three-inch pumps with her slim, confining black skirt, as if a Washington career woman air-dropped into the land of baseball caps and beer t-shirts should be impervious to the climate.[12]

Time magazine underscored the prominence of Dole's physical appearance, stating, "She smiles a lot, as if to encourage her husband by example, and wears suits with such obsessively matched accessories that voters may be forgiven if they forget that this is the woman who is responsible for those little lights at the center of the rear window of our cars that tell tailgating drivers to hit the brakes."[13] A *USA Today* report on Dole's appearance at a fundraiser attended by "Republican women bused in from the suburbs" began as follows: "The women in the audience are hungry for glamour, for showmanship, for a brush with power. Elizabeth Dole does not disappoint. Sheathed in electric blue silk, her lipstick and fingernails flaming red, she creates excitement just by being there."[14]

Although the vast majority of Dole's media coverage during the 1996 campaign took an overtly complimentary tone, reporters simultaneously were cognizant of the strategic nature of her campaign efforts. Susan Baer of the *Baltimore Sun* reported that "In this Age of Hillary, when political spouses nearly pledge that they will not be co-anything, Dole, who is on leave from her job as president of the Red Cross, has been selling herself as her husband's 'supportive helpmate.' She plays up her candy-coated May Queen side and plays down her brilliant career."[15] Regardless of the strategic nature of Dole's supportive discourse, it appealed to the party faithful and voters alike. John Rowland, Connecticut's Republican governor during the 1996 campaign, stated that Dole "pumps up the faithful. . . . Everybody she does talk to becomes an ambassador. It's hard not to be impacted by her delivery. You become a believer."[16] Following her address to the 1996 Republican National Convention, the *New York Times* credited Dole with "swaying more undecided voters toward her husband than his own acceptance speech."[17]

Despite the dividends of Dole's hostess/beauty queen persona, there were drawbacks as well. Women hailed for their physical attractiveness and/or their social skills often are castigated for their obsessive perfectionism. Consider, for example, critiques of hostess/media mogul Martha Stewart. Repeated criticisms of Dole's perfectionism emerged in the press, with some reporters sounding more like jealous rivals than detached observers. One *Time* article called Dole a "slave" to preparation and described her as "ordering up dozens of position papers and memos from staff and driving campaign aids crazy with requests for clippings and briefings and updates. . . . Elizabeth never gets a word or pause or chuckle out of place, but she can no more ad lib than levitate."[18] This perfectionist bent dated back to her days at Harvard Law School, where one *Newsweek* report described her as "Always fretting" because she "found it terrifying that the final exams counted for your entire grade."[19] A *Houston Chronicle* report began with a lead describing Dole as an "overeager flight attendant,"[20] and *Time* magazine asserted that her "syrupy charm and perfect manners do exactly what charm and manners are meant to do: persuade people to like her but not let them get too close."[21]

As if to counter her impressive resume and perfectionist standards, the press underscored her status as a cheerful spouse by invoking her childhood nickname, "Liddy," despite requests from Dole that press use "Elizabeth" in stories about her. The trend was especially noticeable in headlines, where copyeditors no doubt would cite their need to conserve space; however, because the headline frames the narrative of a news story, using the nickname there was particularly significant. For example, a *Time* cover story was titled "Hillary vs. Liddy" and a companion profile of Dole in the same issue announced that "Liddy Makes Perfect"; A *Newsweek* article asked, "The Relentless Mrs. Dole: Is Liddy—devout and astute—another Hillary"; The *Boston Herald* warned, "Convention '96; Look Out, Hillary; Liddy, not Bob, Steals the Show." [22] These headlines also reveal the prominence of other components of the campaign '96 news narrative: the competition between spouses and Dole's "relentless" perfectionism.

Several reporters overtly mocked Dole's request that her adult name be used. *Time*'s Richard Stengel warned, "heaven forbid, don't call her Liddy—that's only for those who knew her when she was in pigtails. Lesley Stahl got the Look that chills when she made that fatal error on *60 Minutes*."[23] Marianne Means, whose column appeared in the *Denver Post*, touted the "power of the Elizabeth Factor" in Bob Dole's campaign, adding, "(During Dole's previous presidential bids, we called this the Liddy Factor, but this year she decreed the nickname insufficiently dignified and therefore inoperative)."[24] The issue of naming is a critical one for women. A society's linguistic norms lend insight into the relationship between gender and power in that society. Elizabeth Dole's struggle to control her own name echoes battles women have fought for gender-inclusive language and parallel professional titles.

The persona of Dole presented in the press during the 1996 campaign was contradictory; however, even the conflicting elements fit within the hostess/beauty queen persona. Although the majority of media reports were complimentary of her skill as a campaigner, her experience in politics, and her personal appeal, those same reports often belittled Dole by castigating her attention to detail, mocking her Southern accent, criticizing her for being too attractive or too polite, or calling her "Liddy." An examination of Dole's own rhetoric reveals the ways in which she adopted the public image constructed for her in the press, making the best of the strategic advantage it offered Bob Dole's presidential campaign.

The best-known speech of the 1996 campaign was Elizabeth Dole's address to the Republican National Convention. The speech was notable because, prior to the 1990s, spouses of presidential candidates rarely addressed the convention, and it was one of the few speeches covered by the major television networks.[25] The speech catapulted Dole to national prominence and echoed the rhetorical strategies she used throughout the campaign.[26] She wove together carefully scripted, seamlessly memorized vignettes about Bob Dole's character, walking comfortably among the audience as she made intimate contact with those in the convention hall, as well as with viewers at home.

Press coverage of the speech was overwhelmingly favorable. The *Seattle Times* led its coverage with a quotation from voters Daphne and Chico Fernandez who, according to the *Times*, "haven't been impressed with most of what they've heard from the Republican National Convention," but who "liked Elizabeth Dole." The *Times* article quoted Mrs. Fernandez who said "She's really good. If Bob Dole is elected, she'll make a great first lady." According to the *Times*, Mr. Fernandez went a step farther to assert, "maybe Elizabeth Dole should be running for president. . . . She does make Hillary Clinton look like a lightweight."[27] The *Houston Chronicle* quoted voters who dubbed Dole's speech "an inspiration to modern women" and "absolutely superb."[28] *USA Today* reported that the speech bolstered Dole's poll ratings, giving her a 58% favorable rating, a 7 point increase from her August rating and one that pushed her 11 points ahead of Hillary Rodham Clinton in the same poll.[29] Seasoned political reporters who often couch their reports with the vocabulary of "balance" and "objectivity" found themselves gushing over Dole's speech. An essay by media critic Tom Shales quoted news anchors as follows:

> "It was not so much a performance of Oprah as it was 'My Fair Liddy,'" said Dan Rather on CBS. "An impressive piece of stage-craft," ventured Peter Jennings on ABC. Dole "electrified" the crowd, said Tom Brokaw on NBC. CBS consultant Kevin Phillips called Mrs. Dole's solo "enormously powerful" and said, "Now Bob Dole has a woman on his ticket."[30]

The success of Dole's 1996 speech can be attributed, at least in part, to the fact that she highlighted her own femininity and normalized traditional gender roles, inhabiting the hostess/beauty queen persona constructed for her by the press. At the beginning of the speech, Dole declared her intent to "break with tradition" and step down from the "imposing podium" for "two reasons. I'm going to be speaking to friends and secondly I am going to be speaking about the man I love. It's just a lot more comfortable for me to do that down here with you."[31] Although the speaker's choice to roam the convention hall was treated as a radical break from tradition, it was not a new strategy for Dole. Whenever possible while speaking on the stump during the 1996 campaign, Dole walked around making personal contact with audience members. Rhetorically, however, it was a sly move that adapted well to the goal of reaching television audiences. Kathleen Hall Jamieson contends that the advent of televised political campaigns changed the rhetorical demands placed on candidates. Television requires candidates to come across as warm, genuine, and caring; thus women and men both benefit from a more personal, intimate, and in her words "effeminate" style of communication.[32] The media quickly feminized Dole's speech tactics as well, invoking the Oprah Winfrey talk show as an analog.

Just moments into the speech, a live image of Bob Dole appeared on the convention hall video screens. Like royalty, he nodded and waved to the adoring crowd. The *Washington Post* reported that

> Cheers interrupted Dole when her husband's image—live from a nearby hotel suite—popped up on the giant video screens behind her. It was another break with GOP tradition, as the man who would be nominated later in the evening made an early, if electronic, entry into

the hall. Acting surprised by the appearance, his wife said, tongue apparently in cheek, "now what do I do? Is he going to speak or am I?"[33]

Bob Dole's brief appearance in his wife's address seemed to confirm his promise that she wouldn't involve herself inappropriately in affairs of state, as First Lady Hillary Rodham Clinton supposedly had. His image was projected onto giant video screens in the convention hall after she had descended from the podium, her position of authority, to join audience members on their level. Bob Dole literally loomed over his wife. Elizabeth Dole inhabited the persona of hostess/beauty queen both in the nonverbal and verbal elements in the speech. Dole's telegenic smile, feminine attire, and decision to move around the room as she spoke invoked the aura of a beauty queen parading onstage. As the perfect hostess, Dole introduced her "guests" at the convention to her husband, who she referred to as "my own personal Rock of Gibralter." Although the speech was designed, ostensibly, to reveal Bob Dole's more personal, intimate side, it also served to underscore his heroic masculinity—historically an important characteristic for candidates seeking the nation's highest office.[34] Dole's first vignette cast her husband as the war hero who beat medical odds to "[will] himself to walk" after a period of paralysis. Although Dole acknowledged the doctors and nurses who cared for him after his injury on the battlefield, the suggestion was that her husband's sheer masculine strength and determination enabled him to recover from his injuries. Dole's recounting of her husband's political victories made him sound similarly heroic. She stated:

> I will certainly not forget his last day as majority leader of the United States Senate. I was seated up in the balcony, you know, and I was watching as Senator after Senator, Democrat and Republican, stood and paid tribute to my husband on the Senate floor. They talked about his countless legislative achievements. How he had led the United States Senate to successfully pass the largest tax cut in the history of the United States of America. They talked about how he saved Social Security.

At the conclusion of her speech, Dole entreated the audience to "please indulge a very proud wife this one final story. . . ." Accepting the role of supporter and cheerleader, Dole encouraged the audience to view her husband as an archetype of the U.S. presidency—strong, independent, and able to care for those he governs. By casting her husband in that role, she implicitly confirmed the political persona the media had created for her during the 1996 presidential campaign.

Although many in the media sought to turn campaign '96 into a national referendum on femininity vs. feminism, examination of Dole's rhetorical choices underscores the reality that many women know: those two terms do not exist in opposition to one another. A woman can be a successful professional and a supportive spouse. She can be brilliant and attractive. She can be strong and soft. The paradox confronting Elizabeth Dole was not the usual disjunction between competence and femininity. Dole emerged from the 1996 campaign as the model political wife *and* a sentimental favorite for the presidential nomination. An anecdote reported by the *Washington Post* likened Dole to that other archetypal political wife, Barbara Bush, stating, "at one campaign stop, Elizabeth [was] accidentally introduced as 'Barbara Dole.' 'That's good' Elizabeth [said], chuckling."[35] At the same time, however, stories of Elizabeth being the more electable Dole peppered campaign reports. A *New York Times* story promised that "[a]t least one Dole has a political future beyond the 1996 election, and at this point it may not necessarily be the candidate."[36] Similarly, the *Washington Post* reported that

> [a]fter she addressed a crowd of 1,100 recently at the nonpartisan Women's Economic Forum in Detroit, the club's executive director, Gerry Barron said: "Most of the comments I heard were, 'she should be running.'" Mari Will, her close friend and political strategist, was even more succinct: "She is a leading contender to be the next Republican nominee."[37]

A London *Times* headline summed up the sentiment: "Elizabeth leaves [the GOP] wondering if they've chosen the right Dole."[38] The *Houston Chronicle* confirmed the British supposition, claiming that "along the campaign trail, there's talk among some supporters that perhaps the wrong Dole is at the top of the ticket."[39] Was it true that the popularity Dole garnered by inhabiting the hostess/beauty queen persona could bolster her viability as a candidate? The answer came sooner than many thought it would. Less than four years after her husband lost his bid for the presidency, Elizabeth Dole threw her own hat into the ring, vying for the Republican presidential nomination.

A Woman First

The 2000 campaign was a logical next step for Dole, an experienced Washington insider who was well-received within the Republican party but who also appealed to non-Republican voters, particularly moderate female swing voters. Republicans were looking for a way to win back some of the women's vote that Bill Clinton had owned in the last two presidential elections. Dole's popularity in 1996 gave her name recognition and even a certain star quality that others in the party lacked. Consequently, Elizabeth Dole resigned her post as president of the American Red Cross on January 5, 1999 to pursue U.S. presidential aspirations. But the favorable image she cultivated in 1996 was inextricably linked to her hostess/beauty queen persona. She could not abandon that image; however, it worked against her as a presidential contender. By October 20 of the same year she was out of the race, ostensible prey to the George W. Bush money-making machine. Due to the complexity of the U.S. political landscape, there are many factors that could have contributed to the failure of Dole's campaign. Fundraising played a major role, as did George W. Bush's popularity within the GOP and tactical errors made by the Dole campaign. Of interest to scholars of politics, the media, and communication, however, are the symbolic and narrative elements that placed Dole in a position of weakness as a candidate. In addition to highlighting Dole's gender, the press reinscribed the political image they created for her during the 1996 campaign: Dole as hostess/beauty queen. The story of Dole as a "pioneer" also got more ink in 1999 than it did three years earlier; however, Dole failed to benefit from the more positive aspects of that metaphor. As the "pioneering woman candidate," Dole was simultaneously lauded in press reports for her efforts and dismissed as nothing more than a symbolic step forward for women.

Analysis of media coverage reveals that Dole was viewed, first and foremost, as the woman candidate for president. A *New York Times* story about a Dole foreign policy speech delivered at the U.S. Naval Academy dubbed her "a Republican Presidential contender and the only woman in the race," and asserted that the speech "allowed [Dole] to show that a woman can talk tough on military matters."[40] *Newsweek*'s coverage of a Dole speech at a refugee camp in Macedonia asserted that as of April 1999 Dole "hadn't expanded the rationale of her candidacy beyond her gender and bureaucratic resume."[41] Dole was labeled not only as a "woman candidate," but also as a women's candidate—someone whom women could support but who did not appeal particularly to men. A *Washington Post* lead combined these two themes as follows:

> The uniqueness of Elizabeth Dole's presidential candidacy is instantly obvious wherever she campaigns. The audiences are overwhelmingly female: younger women, older women, women with babies, women with husbands, women who are Republican Party veterans and women who have never participated in the political process before.[42]

The *New York Times* ran a similar lead in a story the following week, saying, "She has said time and again that she is not running as a woman but instead is a woman running. Still, one of the most notable things about Elizabeth Dole's quest for the Republican Presidential nomination is the large number of women, especially young women not much involved in politics, who turn out whenever she makes a campaign stop."[43] Dole attempted to counter that image in an interview with CBS anchor Bob Schieffer, saying, "as you see the crowds, there are a lot of men involved as well, and certainly a lot of young people. The college students are just extremely supportive, men and women."[44]

Dole's political identity as the "woman candidate" was underscored by a much-publicized account of her husband's intent to donate funds to rival John McCain's campaign. Candidate Dole responded to the *New York Times* by saying that Bob apologized and assuring reporters that "I joked with him about it. I told him I loved him. I told him he was in the woodshed." The "woodshed" quotation was great copy—too good for most media outlets to ignore, so headlines like the *New York Times*'s "Elizabeth Dole Exiles Mate to Woodshed" abounded for weeks.[45] *U.S. News & World Report* added insult to injury by reporting that Bob Dole said "his wife might need help sorting out the issues and he would be willing to 'direct her' if asked."[46] That article had the troubling headline, "Psst, Bob Dole Beats His Wife," suggesting that some headline editors are willing to satirize the tragic issue of gendered violence if it makes clever copy.

All campaigns have unfortunate sound bites with which to contend, but this story was particularly problematic for a presidential candidate because it called into question the loyalty and supportiveness of her spouse and seemed to suggest that a man could not perform the requisite duties of first spouse. Even the sitting Commander in Chief, Bill Clinton, had been able to silently support his spouse in her campaign for a U.S. Senate seat. The "woodshed" quotation functioned almost as enthymematic proof that a woman candidate was ill-suited for the U.S. presidency. Even after Dole turned a corner in fundraising, raising over $2.7 million in three months, the *New York Times* placed Dole in a position of weakness. The headline for the corresponding story about Dole's success at getting women to contribute to her campaign read as follows: "Women to the Rescue of Elizabeth Dole."[47]

A study conducted by Caroline Heldman, Susan J. Carroll, and Stephanie Olson supports the claim that Dole's candidacy was covered differently by the mainstream press than were the candidacies of her male competitors. The authors suggest that Dole did not receive as much coverage as her male competitors, a striking fact considering that for most of the race she ran second only to George W. Bush and her favorability ratings consistently topped those of prospective Democratic opponent Al Gore. Furthermore, the study concludes that the media covered Dole as a presumptive loser in the campaign; they were more likely to report on her personality traits and personal appearance than on the traits and appearances of her opponents, and the media framed her candidacy within a "first woman" narrative, "suggesting, implicitly, if not explicitly, that she was a novelty in the race rather than a strong contender with a good chance of winning."[48]

Attention to Dole's physical appearance was as prominent in 1999 as it had been three years earlier. A *Newsweek* article on the topic of political fundraising began with a lead that introduced Dole, but had nothing to do with the main topic of the essay. It read, "It's 9 a.m. and Elizabeth Dole is, as usual, immaculately coifed and tailored as she readies herself for an interview in her suite in Manhattan's Grand Hyatt."[49] For his column about a Dole speech in Manhattan, the *Washington Post*'s Richard Cohen chose to lead with a clothing metaphor:

> This is a black town—and I'm not talking African American. I'm
> talking women's clothing—dresses, pants, suits and other things for
> which I do not know the right terms. This is not, definitely, a tur-
> quoise town, which is the color Elizabeth Dole wore last week when

she addressed a mostly female audience here. I thought she did about everything wrong. I came away impressed anyway.

Cohen's dismissive "other things for which I do not know the right terms" foreshadowed the tone of his column, in which he reported on how the "female audience" was impressed by Dole and found her experiences to resonate with their lives, even though he found her speech to be "Wrong . . . all wrong." [50] Although Cohen admitted (almost grudgingly) that Dole articulated positions better than the other contenders for the GOP nomination, his approach in the column reminded readers of Dole's status as a woman candidate (hence, the clothing metaphor instead of, say, the war metaphors that dominated coverage of John McCain), and suggested that she appealed primarily to women voters.

Although the aura of the hostess/beauty queen hung over Dole's 2000 campaign, she failed to benefit from the more flattering aspects of that persona and continued to suffer from its negative associations. The following lead from a *U.S. News & World Report* cover story illustrates the ways in which the media trivialized Dole by mocking her perfectionism and invoking her childhood nickname:

> Look at the scrapbooks first, because that's where you'll find the early cues. "Elizabeth's work is excellent," wrote her second-grade teacher on a 1944 report card pasted in one of 20 scrapbooks carefully kept by her mother. "She tries so hard to do everything just exactly right—and she succeeds." Now listen to the 97-year-old mother, Mary Handford: One day, "Liddy" was sent home from school because she forgot a book, and she sobbed the entire five-block walk to the house. "She thought her life had been ruined."
>   Elizabeth Hanford Dole has spend a lifetime buffing her image, trying to do everything "just exactly right," and making sure she's never caught with that unreturned book.[51]

Later, that same article characterized Dole's perfectionism as follows: "Dole loyalists say she only expects of others the same perfection she demands of herself. Few pols today are as compulsively prepared. Dole practices her speeches repeatedly, often in front of a TelePrompTer, rehearsing every smile, every inflection, every joke."[52] The same press corps that ribbed George W. Bush for his shortcomings as a speaker cast Dole's public speaking prowess as a sign of "compulsive" preparation. *Newsweek* characterized Dole as the girl who gets it all, stating that "In the past, her tightly wound efficiency has earned her everything she's wanted: a diploma from Harvard Law School, two cabinet stints, the presidency of the Red Cross."[53] This line sends the message that a successful woman must be "tightly wound," whereas her male counterparts would be seen as driven.

Articles also reflected the media's continued pique over the fact that Dole still insisted on being called by her adult name, rather than by her childhood nickname. A *U.S. News & World Report* essay recounted an anecdote that had been circulated during the 1996 campaign: "Once, during a 1996 interview, CBS-TV newswoman Lesley Stahl inadvertently called her by her hated childhood nickname, Liddy. 'Elizabeth, Lesley,' Dole corrected her frostily."[54] Given the number of times journalists chose to use the "Liddy" moniker during the 1996 campaign, it is unlikely that Stahl's choice was "inadvertent." Interestingly, the report cited this story as an example of Dole's temper, as if a grown woman's insistence that her adult name be used in a professional context is evidence of a bad temper.

Dole's attempts to counteract the hostess/beauty queen image that largely was left over from her husband's 1996 campaign produced a paradox she was unable to escape. On one hand, she attempted to neutralize the gender factor by emphasizing her personal character (in contrast to the scandal-ridden Democrats) and her political experience (in contrast to the relative political newcomer, George W. Bush). On the other hand, she called attention to her gender by embracing the "pioneer" persona as potentially the first female U.S. president.

The strategy of emphasizing character and experience over gender was introduced even before Dole announced her candidacy, by Earl Cox, the national campaign manager for "Draft Elizabeth Dole 2000," an organization based in Dole's home town of Salisbury, North Carolina. Cox was interviewed on CNN by Miles O'Brien. When O'Brien asked the question, "Why do you think the time is right now for a female president?" Cox answered as follows:

> I don't think gender is going even to be a question. As I've traveled across the United States, the question that has come forth more often than not has been a person's character. Is the next person going into the presidential election going to have to carry a brigade of people behind her to put out fires? No. In this case, Elizabeth Dole has been researched for 25 years, and we fully expect that we will have a squeaky clean candidate, with no baggage, coming into this presidential election.[55]

Dole articulated her message of character and experience during a speech delivered early in her candidacy. She asserted that "At a time when the Presidency has been tarnished, when words have been devalued and institutions have squandered respect, our confidence in leaders is shaken. But we can rebuild it." She also referred to "my 30-plus years in public life."[56] Later in the campaign she stated, "I think you do have to run on your record. You've got to let people know what it is you've done and what prepares you for a position such as this, so your experience is a very major part of it."[57] Covering Dole's address at the U.S. Naval Academy, Alison Mitchell of the *New York Times* reported that "Time and time again tonight she sought to show that she does have international experience. She spoke of visiting the borders of Rwanda and Bosnia as the president of the American Red Cross and of meeting with Solidarity leaders in Poland as Labor Secretary. And she mentioned her role as a negotiator with China as Transportation Secretary."[58] After a strong showing in the Iowa straw poll, held in August of 1999, Dole told NBC's Tim Russert that "with six months to the caucuses, I have an opportunity to demonstrate during that period of time that the candidate with the most experience is more qualified than the candidates with the most money. And I hope the pundits will take my candidacy seriously now."[59]

Elizabeth Dole had a good reason for trying to downplay her gender. Republican pollster and political strategist Christine Matthews explained that "having a woman run for an executive office—for president, for governor, for mayor—is always tougher than running for legislative office. Voters have a bit more difficulty envisioning a woman as a chief executive."[60] Former Democratic Congresswoman Patricia Schroeder, who briefly made a run at the top office herself, agreed, noting that "we tend to say in the same sentence, 'President of the United States, commander in chief, and leader of the free world.' And so I think that what [Christine Matthews] was talking about in executive abilities, that really becomes a very major issue when you look at any presidential candidate, because people want to know, do they have the stuff to stand up?"[61]

Even so, Dole invoked the pioneer persona when it seemed strategically advantageous, urging supporters to "Be a part of history." That approach prompted *Washington Post* reporter Dan Balz to assert that "the history-making aspect of her campaign was her strongest appeal."[62] Dole incorporated pioneer imagery into her stump speeches, telling the Greater Manchester Chamber of Commerce, "like the pilgrims and pioneers who founded this nation, as a free people, we must insist that our government reflects our values . . . ."[63] The pioneer image resonated with many of Dole's supporters. Recounting an interview with women who were big contributors to the Dole campaign, *National Journal* correspondent Paul Starobin stated:

> I kick off the discussion by noting that some GOPers say that the country isn't ready for a woman President. Nobody is surprised to hear such a comment. "Many of us in this room have had to face the experience of being first," says Linda Morrison Combs, who has a doctorate in educational administration and held various posts in the Reagan and Bush Administrations.[64]

Some, however, bought into the symbolic significance of the pioneer persona but cast doubt on Dole's chances in 1999. Marie Wilson, president of the White House Project, an organization that attempts to create a political climate that would accept a woman as president, was quoted by the *Washington Post*, saying that

> The most important part of [Dole's decision to seek the nomination] is that it 'opens the door' in the next decade for a lot of women to walk through so that by 2008 it becomes "very normal" to have women running for the presidency. Dole's exploratory step "allows people in this country to start seeing women through different eyes and different ears."[65]

That same *Washington Post* article, written in January of 1999, deemed Dole's campaign for the presidency to be futile even before it started, concluding that "whatever [Dole] decides, she'll end up on the short list of vice presidential candidates. That job is proving to be a great launching pad for the White House. And, as [Republican strategist Steve Hoffman] points out, 'number two is still a nice address.'"[66] Voters, also, had an easier time envisioning Dole as vice president, rather than Commander in Chief. The *Washington Post* quoted citizen Jane Wiggins who said "'I would like to see George W. Bush as president and Elizabeth Dole as vice president.'" The article continued, "Given how impressed she was with Dole, why not a Dole–Bush ticket, Wiggins was asked? 'It seems that George W. Bush has the momentum,' she replied."[67] Similarly, an article in the *National Journal* asked, "And what about Liddy Dole for President? 'I'm not sure the country is ready for a woman,' says Oconee County supervisor Harrison Orr. The consensus here [at a family picnic] seems to be that Dole would make a great Vice President on a ticket headed by Bush."[68]

When Dole withdrew from the race in October of 1999, the *Washington Post* collapsed pioneer and beauty queen images into this single, maudlin lead: "In the end, symbolism was all that was left of Elizabeth Dole's bid for the presidency. With her eyes glistening and her face a mask of chipper resolve, she spoke the words that must be heartbreaking for any candidate: 'It would be futile to continue . . . .'"[69] Republican frontrunner George W. Bush reacted to Dole's departure from the race by underscoring the pioneer image, stating that "Dole has been a friend, a trailblazer, and an inspiration to many women."[70] Ultimately, the media punished Dole for resisting the narrative frame they had created. The *Washington Post* article quoted above concluded: "Running on gender was not her style. She was ambivalent about barreling through walls and not inclined to boast about making history. As a result, she robbed herself of a defining image."[71]

Elizabeth Dole's image had been defined for her by the media in two presidential campaigns. When she was acting as a political spouse, the hostess/beauty queen persona paid off strategically, even as it reinforced sexist stereotypes. The strategic benefits her husband's campaign garnered from Dole's political image turned into liabilities that hampered her own presidential bid. Nevertheless, in the speech announcing the end of her campaign for the Republican presidential nomination, Dole promised, "While I may not be a candidate for the presidency in 2000, I'm a long way from twilight."[72]

Senator Dole

In February, 2002, Elizabeth Dole officially kicked off her third nationally prominent political campaign, vying for the Senate seat vacated by conservative Jesse Helms, who had occupied the office representing the state of North Carolina for the preceding thirty years. From day one, this campaign differed from her presidential bid two years earlier. By almost every measure, Dole was the favorite. She led in the polls, had the most fundraising potential, and got support from Republican party leaders as well as from President Bush, who hosted numerous fundraisers for Dole throughout the campaign. Dole also received key endorsements from organizations such as the U.S. Chamber of Commerce.[73] National Public Radio reported that Dole's "name recognition and fund-raising ability are considered so strong that several prominent Republicans got out of the race when she got in."[74] Some conservatives questioned whether or not Dole was too moderate to represent their interests as Helms had, but even they acknowledged Dole's momentum as a candidate. Phyllis Schlafly was quoted in the *New York Times* saying, "She's an able woman but certainly doesn't come out of the conservative movement. . . . It's obvious that she has been anointed and it looks like we're headed to a coronation."[75]

As the media highlighted the unique features of Dole's 2002 campaign— her status as a political-spouse-turned-candidate seeking to represent a state in which she had not lived for thirty years—comparisons to former rival Hillary Rodham Clinton were inevitable. During Rodham Clinton's bid for the U.S. Senate in New York, the "carpetbagger" charge was the most significant challenge faced by her campaign. A report aired on the *Today* show quoted Dole opponent Erskine Bowles saying, "On issue after issue that is vital to the future of our state, that [*sic*] Mrs. Dole is out of step with the citizens of North Carolina." NBC's Lisa Meyers followed that quote by asking, "There are the inevitable comparisons to another high-voltage wife of a prominent politician who decided to run for office herself, Hillary Clinton. Do you think you all have anything in common?"[76] Later in the campaign, the comparison lingered. A July 1 issue of *USA Today* noted that "That seeming contradiction [between "modern career woman" and "dutiful political wife"]—one half power couple, but also a political spouse—prompts comparisons with Hillary Clinton, the former first lady elected to the Senate from New York in 2000."[77]

The carpetbagger label became a key feature of the narrative surrounding Dole's 2002 campaign. For example, in the first question posed to Dole by CNN anchor Wolf Blitzer, in an interview conducted shortly after she announced her candidacy, Blitzer stated, "I'm sure the criticism you've heard from people in North Carolina, including Erskine Bowles and others, is you've been out of touch, out of that state for so long, what gives you the right to come back and try to become the senator for North Carolina?"[78] One of Dole's opponents in the Republican primary, Jim Snyder, echoed the carpetbagger charge, saying, "I've got a huge mountain to climb, I know . . . I can't compete with Mrs. Dole's 35 years in Washington. But I don't think she can compete with my 56 years in Lexington."[79] News reports consistently identified the carpetbagger charge as one of Dole's biggest hurdles. *USA Today* stated: "Democrats note that she lives in Washington's famed Watergate condominium and has never voted in North Carolina. Dole says government work required that she live in Washington. She frequently mentions that the North Carolina Press Association named her 'North Carolinian of the Year' in 1993."[80]

Dole's standard response to the carpetbagger question was typified by this quotation, taken from the Blitzer interview. Dole stated, "It's amazing to hear that, because, you know, my roots are deep in North Carolina. Obviously, if you serve in the president's cabinet or you're president of the Red Cross, you can't do it from Salisbury, North Carolina, which is where I grew up, my family home I'm living in, have a business in Salisbury, served on the Duke board, where I went to school for 11 years. And I've campaigned for the people, Wolf, up and down the state for years. So this is my home."[81]

Aside from the carpetbagger theme, it is difficult to discern a dominant metaphor shaping Dole's news coverage. Elements of the pioneer and hostess/beauty queen personae can be found in some articles; however, they often are contained within broader descriptions of Dole as a credible candidate and experienced leader. For example one *USA Today* article made reference to Dole's physical appearance, but mitigated its potential to invoke the beauty queen personae by placing the focus on Dole's political experience. The article stated, "Campaigning through the hot countryside recently in a long-sleeved purple suit and gold necklace, Dole said her experience and contacts inside the Bush administration would help her get things done for North Carolina."[82]

The media continued to refer to Dole's perfectionist bent, sometimes in ways that retained the negative connotations seen during her presidential campaign. For example, in an interview with Dole, NBC's Lisa Meyers asked, "A North Carolina girl who blazed trails and now, at age 68, has come home seeking one more triumph, a seat in the United States Senate. A lot of people wonder what drives you to do this. You're already one of the most admired women in America, do you really need another accomplishment?"[83] That query underscored Dole's "pioneer" status, but also suggested that her continued involvement in the public sphere was an indicator of her relentless perfectionism. Men who pursue political office after achieving success in the private, military, or governmental spheres are rarely (if ever) asked why they continue to accomplish things with their life. The perfectionist moniker also was used as proof that the carpetbagger charges had merit. The *Washington Post* reported that "She has been called 'scripted,' a characterization that would feed the conceit that Dole is more of a rehearsed celebrity than a cozy and authentic purebred." The article quoted Dole's deputy communications director who responded, "Is she prepared, yes, but the word 'scripted' drives us nuts around here."[84]

Most references to Dole's perfectionism, however, changed in tone during the 2002 campaign. A *USA Today* profile contextualized Dole's perfectionism by pointing out the challenges women leaders face, noting that "Friends say Dole is a deeply driven perfectionist. What appears to some as contrived flawlessness, they say, is her determination to be the best-prepared person in any meeting. Climbing to power in male-dominated Washington, 'there wasn't a lot of room for error,' says former aide and longtime friend Mari Maseng Will, wife of syndicated columnist George Will."[85] A *Washington Post* report on Dole's victory in the general election described Dole as "hard driving and highly organized," pairing a positive attribute (organizational skills) with the perfectionist characteristic, connoting competence rather than obsessiveness.[86]

The pioneer imagery that dominated Dole's 2000 campaign surfaced occasionally during 2002, as in one *Christian Science Monitor* article, which noted that, "Dole would become the first woman senator from North Carolina."[87] A subheading in a *USA Today* article read "Part pioneer, part spouse." The subsequent narrative described Dole as "both a modern career woman and a throwback to another era."[88] But the pioneer references were few and far between in 2002 news reports. Instead, journalists frequently chose not to draw attention to gender issues, or to place Dole in a position of power rather than weakness. A *New York Times* article comparing the Dole and Rodham Clinton Senate campaigns downplayed gender as a campaign issue, arguing that "For her to be successful, Mrs. Dole has much the same imperative as Mrs. Clinton: to convince voters that there is more to her than celebrity and that she will work to earn the support of voters."[89] This is notably different from the refrain played over and over during the 2000 campaign, that Dole needed to convince voters that a woman could perform the duties of the presidency. Also, in a reversal of roles, the *New York Times* described a number of prominent men campaigning for Dole: "Prominent Republicans from Washington are going all out for Mrs. Dole, who does not face strong Republican competition. Vice President Dick Cheney is scheduled to be at a lunch for her here on Friday, and President Bush is planning to come next month. Her husband has started six days of campaigning for her. 'He's going to be a good surrogate,' Mrs. Dole said in a telephone interview. 'The role reversal is going very smoothly.'"[90] This anecdote provided a change of pace from familiar stories of wives putting their careers on hold to campaign for their political spouses.

Another difference between coverage of Dole's bid for the Senate and her presidential campaign was the supposed role of Bob Dole. During the 2000 campaign, he was cast as the experienced politician available to "direct" his wife. In 2002, the narrative was reversed. A *New York Times* article highlighted Bob Dole's sense of humor and emphasized that he would take on the role of supportive spouse. The article, which appeared after a much-publicized incident of anthrax spores being detected in Senator Tom Daschle's official congressional mail, began with the following lead:

> This is his day job now, stumping for his wife, who is campaigning to join the club he left. "Will you have any role in her office?" a man calls out from a group gathered around Bob Dole on the steps of the little brick courthouse here. "Opening mail," Mr. Dole shoots back. "I'm on antibiotics and I won't get anthrax."

Later, the article notes that "Mr. Dole reassures voters he would not meddle if his wife beat Erskine B. Bowles, the Democrat, to reach the Senate, and she is ahead in the polls. 'I won't be telling her how to vote," he says, but adds that he would be available to advise her on issues dear to him—disability, agriculture, foreign policy. 'I'll be glad to be a dollar-a-year consultant,' he says. 'Or I'll stay home. Whatever she wants.'"[91]

Even the metaphors reporters used to frame their stories took on a different tone in the 2002 race. During the 2000 presidential campaign, a memorable article featured the use of an extended clothing metaphor. In 2002, *USA Today* employed the following sports metaphor:

> When the legendary Dean Smith was basketball coach up the road at the University of North Carolina, fans knew what to expect when his team got the lead. He'd go to his trademark 'four corners' slow-down offense to salt away the victory. Elizabeth Dole doesn't call it four corners. She graduated from Duke, in Durham, N.C. But she is pursuing her own run-out-the-clock strategy as she sits on a huge lead in her quest for the U.S. Senate, a critical race in the GOP's bid to retake control of the chamber.[92]

Despite these changes in media coverage, a few articles from the 2002 campaign repeated the gendered condescension that populated the media in 2000. A *Washington Post* article addressing the carpetbagger charge invoked Dole's childhood nickname in a headline that used wordplay to feminize Dole, stating, "Liddy Dole in North Carolina, Hoping Her Roots Show." [93] In that article, *Post* reporter Mark Leibovich played on stereotypes of women and southerners. Consider the following excerpts:

> The state seems to love her back, at least those in this downhome sampling of 800 who skipped the high scnool football game and a fish fry to watch Dole in a sweltering tobacco warehouse. They are tobacco workers, farmers, and retirees, offering their highest political praise. "She reminds me of Uncle Jesse," says Tom Roberts, a 68-year-old hay farmer . . . Likewise: "She's a pretty lady," says W.C. Williford, 80, a retired tobacco salesman. . . . It's easy to recognize Dole in this Bubba swarm: She is the one who is poised and glamorous in a loud pink suit and burgundy lipstick. . . . Dole speaks in a loud rolling voice that sounds earnest enough, if somewhat syrupy. . . Dole is a promiscuous thanker, saying 27 "thank yewws" in one five-minute sprint of well-wishing, to go with five "thank yeww VERY MUCHs," four "bless yewws" and two "bless y'r hearts."

In an odd juxtaposition of identities, the *Christian Science Monitor* addressed Dole's North Carolina roots: "Even as the adviser to five presidents and as the former Red Cross chief, Ms. Dole made regular trips back to the textile town of Salisbury, where as a girl she was given her nickname, Liddy."[94] Although Dole's professional posts and hometown ties were relevant to a story about her Senate bid, the unnecessary inclusion of Dole's childhood name served to undercut her credibility and remind the reading audience of the hostess/beauty queen persona that hung over the 1996 and 2000 presidential campaigns. Similarly, a *USA Today* article invoked the nickname in conjunction with references to Dole's failed campaigns: "Though she flopped as a presidential candidate in 2000—just as her husband, Bob Dole, did in 1988 and 1996—Liddy Dole is a hit in her state of birth."[95]

Yet references to "Liddy" Dole occurred less frequently in the press during 2002 than in past campaigns, and were most likely to appear in boisterous publications such as the *New York Post*, which ran the headline: "Politics as Usual: Prez Boosts Liddy,"[96] or small, regional papers like the *News-Herald*, which titled one of its stories, "Bob Dole visits for Liddy.[97]

The portrait that emerged in media coverage of Dole during the 2002 campaign was of a strong candidate who had moved beyond her status as a spouse and was using her considerable political experience to wage a tough campaign for the U.S. Senate. Analysis of Dole's campaign rhetoric demonstrates the ways in which Dole's message was well-suited to the immediate rhetorical situation. Traditional Republican themes such as national security, local control of education, increased defense spending, and protection of Social Security dominated her speeches. Dole also devoted time to issues of particular concern to North Carolinians, such as help for the ailing tobacco and textile industries. Dole couched this discussion of her conservative platform in a rhetoric of coalition-building and teamwork, a strategy that differed sharply from her attempt in 2000 to stress her individual expertise and leadership capacity. By employing a rhetoric of coalition-building and teamwork, Dole responded to the tendency of voters to accept women more readily when they pursue representative posts and place themselves on the same level as voters, rather than when they seek executive office and position themselves in power over voters.

Highlighting her coalition-building skills was relevant to the political climate in North Carolina, since, as noted by the *Christian Science Monitor*, "Dole will have to walk the fine line between the modern sensibilities of the cities and the languidity and churchliness of the rural regions. It's a coalition that Helms himself could barely hold together."[98] Dole made explicit reference to her coalition-building skills in an interview with CNN's Mark Shields and Robert Novak, stating, "But coalition-building, working across the aisle, this is kind of my style, because I like results. I want to go into a job and find, here are the six or eight key things that cry out for change right now. Get the best possible team around you, go for it, get it done. And I think my record shows that I can do that."[99] She echoed the theme of coalition-building in a speech following her victory in the Republican primary election, thanking "Students for Dole, Women for Dole, Farmers for Dole, yes, even Democrats for Dole!—these and many other groups have energized this campaign."[100]

The image of Dole as a coalition builder was complemented by references to Dole as a team player. In her remarks following her victory in the primary election, Dole focused on her campaign "team" rather than accepting credit for the victory herself, saying, "The Dole Team has had a terrific win across the state."[101] She concluded a speech to the group "Women for Dole" by saying, "I look forward to working for and with all North Carolinians—and with the Women for Dole team—to get the job done."[102] One of Dole's campaign ads addressing North Carolina's economic slowdown began with Dole stating, "I worked beside some wonderful folks recently in a textile mill."[103] The message posted on her campaign web site following her victory in the general election emphasized governance as a team effort as well, stating, "I look forward to working with you to achieve these worthy goals."[104]

Crediting Dole's victory to her rhetorical strategies during the 2002 campaign would be naïve; however, it is useful to note how the tone of Dole's discourse shifted in each of three campaigns. In 1996, Dole embraced the hostess/beauty queen persona because of the strategic advantage it offered to her husband's presidential campaign. In 2000, Dole worked against that persona, trying instead to portray herself as an experienced and credible leader. In 2002, Dole achieved a balance that voters were more likely to accept, mitigating the hostess/beauty queen image with a picture of a competent public servant who would work with her constituents.

Analysis of post-election media coverage is interesting because it demonstrates the prominence of the carpetbagger theme and the resilience of the pioneer image in the 2002 campaign narrative. It also points to the ways in which the media recognized Dole's pioneering victory as symbolic for women, yet gave credit for the win to the president. The *New York Times* led its November 6, 2002 story as follows: "Elizabeth Dole swept to victory tonight in North Carolina, in the most expensive Senate race in the country, her universal name recognition overcoming complaints that she had not lived in the state for four decades."[105] The *Washington Post* framed Dole's victory with the pioneer narrative, leading its post-election report with the statement, "In the most expensive Senate race of the year, Elizabeth Dole (R) dispelled doubts about her abilities as a campaigner and will become the first female senator from North Carolina."[106] MSNBC's coverage stated, "Republican former Cabinet Secretary Elizabeth Dole easily won the U.S. Senate seat that retiring conservative icon Jesse Helms of North Carolina had held for 30 years, defeating Clinton White House official Erskine Bowles in the year's most expensive senatorial race. 'We will never forget this night,' said the 66-year-old Dole, who became the first woman U.S. senator elected from North Carolina."[107]

News reports undercut Dole's victory by attributing it primarily to former political rival President George W. Bush. A *Newsweek* report credited the president for getting Dole into the race and the ease with which she sailed through the Republican primary, stating:

> Team Bush set about moving the chess pieces around the 2002 campaign board, clearing primary fields here, wooing reluctant entrants there. In North Carolina, *Newsweek* has learned, [chair of the GOP Senatorial Campaign committee Bill Frist] began recruiting Elizabeth

Dole (still living in Washington at the time) in the summer of 2001—barely a year after she dropped her own challenge to Bush for the GOP presidential nomination and long before the incumbent senator, Jesse Helms, announced his retirement. The White House made it clear, early and often, that Dole was its choice, avoiding what could have been a more divisive primary.[108]

The *New York Times* asserted that "Elizabeth Dole's victorious Senate campaign was as much about President Bush as it was about Mrs. Dole. . . ."[109] The fact that Republicans controlled the House of Representatives, the Senate, and the Presidency after the 2002 elections was significant, and media consensus was that Bush's choice to risk his political reputation by campaigning aggressively for Republican candidates paid off big for the Republican party.[110] In that respect, the media did not treat Dole differently than male candidates who benefited from Bush's support. However, in Dole's case, the narrative functioned to undercut some of the autonomy and credibility Dole gained in the press during her Senate campaign.

No definitive portrait was drawn of Dole in the press during the 2002 campaign. Instead, media coverage formed a collage of various images—some leftover from previous campaigns and some new to the Senate race. Analysis of Dole's political identity(ies) suggests that women candidates benefit when news coverage accommodates some level of complexity, presenting several coequal images rather than one stereotypical persona. In 2002, Elizabeth Dole was attractive without being a mere beauty queen, pioneering without being strictly symbolic, a North Carolina native with an impressive Washington resume, and a team player who was also a credible political candidate. In the concluding chapter of this book, we reflect on the importance of complexity in political news coverage, the utility of paradox, and the subtle but significant role of metaphor in shaping political identity.

Notes

1. Laura Blumenfeld, "And One of Them Shall Be First: Elizabeth Dole and Hillary Clinton Offer Conflicting Visions," *Washington Post*, national weekly edition, April 8–14, 1996, 6.

2. *Newsweek* dubbed Dole "the country's first viable female candidate" and the *Washington Post* called her "the first serious female candidate for president." See Julia Reed, "Running Against Hurricane 'W,' Scrambling for Dollars," *Newsweek*, July 12, 1999, Lexis Nexis Academic Universe (accessed January 7, 2001), and Dan Balz, "Hoping to be 'Part of History,'" *Washington Post*, July 15, 1999, Lexis Nexis Academic Universe (accessed October 29, 1999). Two Democratic women, however, have made significant bids for the U.S. presi-

dency: Shirley Chisholm and Patricia Schroeder. Women also have represented third parties in presidential contests.

3. "North Carolina," *Washington Post*, November 7, 2002. Lexis Nexis Academic Universe (accessed November 14, 2002).

4. The authors conducted a Lexis Nexis Academic Universe survey of national news coverage of Dole during the 1996, 2000, and 2002 campaigns. Dole's discourse was obtained from a variety of sources: a personal video tape of her address to the 1996 Republican National Convention, excerpts of speeches contained in news stories, transcripts of news interviews, and copies of speeches posted on the official web site for her U.S. Senate campaign. Specific references are provided in conjunction with each source citation.

5. Nancy Gibbs and Michael Duffy, "Just Heartbeats Away," *Time*, July 1, 1996, 25.

6. "Dole Has a Campaigner As Skilled As Clinton—Mrs. Dole," *Dow Jones News Retrieval* (accessed May 29, 1996).

7. Richard Stengel, "Liddy Makes Perfect," *Time*, July 1, 1996, 30.

8. Elisabeth Bumiller, "Running Against Hillary," *New York Times*, October 13, 1996, late edition, Lexis Nexis Academic Universe (accessed September 4, 2000).

9. John Sedgwick, "The Woman Behind That Unwavering Smile," *Newsweek*, August 19, 1996, 36.

10. *Time*, July 1, 1996, 30–31.

11. "Dole's Bold Gamble," *Newsweek*, August 19, 1996, 3.

12. Bumiller, "Running Against Hillary."

13. Gibbs and Duffy, "Just Heartbeats Away," 28.

14. Jill Lawrence, "On the Road, Spouses Making Strides," *USA Today*, September 25, 1996, 4A.

15. Susan Baer, "Elizabeth Dole is Turning Heads: Politicians Wonder Whether She Can Turn Votes," *Times-Picayune*, October 10, 1996, Lexis Nexis Academic Universe (accessed September 4, 2000).

16. Baer, "Elizabeth Dole is Turning Heads."

17. Bumiller, "Running Against Hillary."

18. Gibbs and Duffy, "Just Heartbeats Away," 28.

19. Sedgwick, "The Woman Behind," 36.

20. Clifford Pugh, "'96 Campaign: Elizabeth Dole: Asset and Ally," *Houston Chronicle*, October 29, 1996, Lexis Nexis Academic Universe (accessed September 4, 2000).

21. Stengel, "Liddy Makes Perfect," 32.

22. See, for example, the headline "Hillary vs. Liddy" on the cover of *Time*, July 1, 1996; Weston Kosova and Michael Isikoff, "The Relentless Mrs. Dole: Is Liddy—Devout and Astute—another Hillary," *Newsweek*, February 5, 1996, 30; Andrew Miga, "Convention '96; Look Out, Hillary; Liddy, not Bob, Steals the Show," *Boston Herald*, August 15, 1996, Lexis Nexis Academic Universe (accessed September 4, 2000); "Liddy's Walk," editorial, *Houston Chronicle*, Au-

gust 16, 1996, Lexis Nexis Academic Universe (accessed September 4, 2000); Francis L. Loewenheim, "Why not a (Hillary) Clinton vs. (Liddy) Dole Debate?" *Houston Chronicle*, September 1, 1996, Lexis Nexis Academic Universe (accessed September 4, 2000).

23. Stengel, "Liddy Makes Perfect," 33.

24. Marianne Means, "The Elizabeth Factor," *Denver Post*, October 10, 1996, Lexis Nexis Academic Universe (accessed September 4, 2000).

25. The broadcast networks reduced their prime-time coverage of the 1996 convention, carrying only one hour per night. News anchors argued that the convention was not newsworthy insofar as it was an "infomercial" for the Republican party. Ted Koppel, of ABC News's *Nightline*, left the convention deeming it not newsworthy. The business executives at the networks had their own reasons for not assigning more air time to the convention. Ratings for the event have declined 33% since 1988. See Ellen Debenport, "Careful Packaging is Turning Viewers Off," *St. Petersburg Times*, August 15, 1996, Lexis Nexis Academic Universe (accessed September 4, 2000).

26. *New York Times* reporter Elizabeth Kolbert stated that Dole's address to the 1996 Republican National Convention was "almost word for word the one she has been delivering around the country." See Elizabeth Kolbert, "The Republicans: The Tribute: A Wife Takes a Star Turn," *New York Times*, August 15, 1996, Lexis Nexis Academic Universe (accessed September 4, 2000).

27. Eric Pryne, "Convention Doesn't Impress; Elizabeth Dole Does, Viewers Say," *Seattle Times*, August 15, 1996, Lexis Nexis Academic Universe (accessed September 4, 2000).

28. "Liddy's Walk," editorial.

29. Judi Hasson, "Elizabeth Dole Soars in Poll," *USA Today*, August 20, 1996, Lexis Nexis Academic Universe (accessed September 4, 2000).

30. Tom Shales, "Mrs. Dole's Political Oprah," *Washington Post*, August 15, 1996, Lexis Nexis Academic Universe (accessed September 4, 2000).

31. Elizabeth Dole, "This is a Defining Moment in Our Nation's History: Speech to the 1996 Republican National Convention." Transcript reprinted by the *New York Times*, August 15, 1996, A24. Also available online at *Gifts of Speech*, <http://gos.sbc.edu/d/dole.html> (accessed November 4, 2002), although that version does not include the unplanned remarks she made when Bob Dole appeared on screen or when she had technical difficulties with her microphone.

32. Kathleen Hall Jamieson, "The 'Effeminate' Style," in *Eloquence in an Electronic Age: The Transformation of Political Speechmaking* (New York: Oxford University Press, 1988), 67–89.

33. Marc Fisher, "'Speaking About the Man I Love,' Elizabeth Dole Takes Talk-Show Theatrics To Convention Floor," *Washington Post*, August 15, 1996, Lexis Nexis Academic Universe (accessed September 4, 2000).

34. See, for example, Michael Kimmel, *Manhood in America: A Cultural History* (New York: Free Press, 1996), 36–38; Murray Edelman, *Constructing*

the Political Spectacle (Chicago: University of Chicago Press, 1988), 61; and Suzanne M. Daughton, "Women's Issues, Women's Place: Gender-Related Problems in Presidential Campaigns," *Communication Quarterly* 42 (1994), 106–19.

35. Blumenfeld, "And One of Them Shall Be First," 7.

36. Bumiller, "Running Against Hillary."

37. Kevin Merida and Susan Schmidt, "The Candidate's Wife And Partner in Climb; Ascendant or Not Tuesday, Elizabeth Dole Rung Up a Win," *Washington Post*, November 2, 1996, Lexis Nexis Academic Universe (accessed September 4, 2000).

38. Martin Fletcher, "Elizabeth Leaves Them Wondering if They've Chosen the Right Dole," *The Times*, August 16, 1996, Lexis Nexis Academic Universe (accessed September 4, 2000).

39. Pugh, "'96 Campaign."

40. Alison Mitchell, "Elizabeth Dole Questions Clinton's Policies on Iraq and Serbia," *New York Times*, April 15, 1999, Lexis Nexis Academic Universe (accessed October 29, 1999).

41. Howard Fineman, "The Kosovo Primary," *Newsweek*, April 26, 1999, 32, Lexis Nexis Academic Universe (accessed January 7, 2001).

42. Balz, "Hoping to be 'Part of History.'"

43. B. Drummond Ayres Jr., "Women to the Rescue of Elizabeth Dole," *New York Times*, July 22, 1999, Lexis Nexis Academic Universe (accessed October 29, 1999).

44. Bob Schieffer, "Elizabeth Dole Discusses Straw Poll Results in Iowa and Her Presidential Campaign," *Face the Nation*, August 15, 1999, Lexis Nexis Academic Universe (accessed December 30, 2000).

45. "Elizabeth Dole Exiles Mate to Woodshed," *New York Times*, May 19, 1999, Lexis Nexis Academic Universe (accessed October 29, 1999).

46. Kenneth T. Walsh and Gloria Borger, "Psst, Bob Dole Beats his Wife," *U.S. News & World Report*, May 31, 1999, Lexis Nexis Academic Universe (accessed January 7, 2001).

47. Ayres Jr., "Women to the Rescue."

48. Caroline Heldman, Susan J. Carroll, and Stephanie Olson, "Gender Differences in Print Media Coverage of Presidential Candidates: Elizabeth Dole's Bid for the Republican Nomination," paper presented at the Annual Meeting of the American Political Science Association, Washington, D.C., August 31–September 3, 2000, <www.rci.rutgers.edu/~cawp/> (accessed December 31, 2000). This paper was featured on the web site for the Center for American Women in Politics.

49. Reed, "Running Against Hurricane 'W'."

50. Richard Cohen, "A Dole Moment in Manhattan," *Washington Post*, May 11, 1999, Lexis Nexis Academic Universe (accessed September 15, 1999).

51. Lynn Rosellini, "The Woman Who Could Beat Him," *U.S. News & World Report*, March 15, 1999, <usnews.com> (accessed July 18, 2001).

52. Rosellini, "The Woman Who Could Beat Him."

53. Reed, "Running Against Hurricane 'W'."

54. Rosellini, "The Woman Who Could Beat Him."

55. Miles O'Brien, "Campaign 2000: Is the Time Right for Madame President?" *CNN Sunday Morning*, January 10, 1999, Lexis Nexis Academic Universe (accessed December 30, 2000).

56. Richard L. Berke, "Eye on 2000: Elizabeth Dole Talks of Race for President," *New York Times*, February 9, 1999, Lexis Nexis Academic Universe (accessed October 29, 1999).

57. Quoted in Balz, "Hoping to be 'Part of History.'"

58. Mitchell, "Elizabeth Dole."

59. Tim Russert, "Elizabeth Dole Discusses the Straw Poll Results from Iowa and Her Presidential Campaign," *Meet the Press*, August 15, 1999, Lexis Nexis Academic Universe (accessed December 30, 2000).

60. O'Brien, "Campaign 2000."

61. O'Brien, "Campaign 2000."

62. Balz, "Hoping to be 'Part of History.'"

63. Speech excerpts broadcast on "All Things Considered," *National Public Radio*, March 10, 1999, Lexis Nexis Academic Universe (accessed December 30, 2000).

64. Paul Starobin, "McCain's Men, Dole's Women." *National Journal* (September 4, 1999): 2510. Lexis Nexis Academic Universe (accessed January 7, 2001).

65. Judy Mann, "For Elizabeth Dole, Time Will Tell," *Washington Post*, January 8, 1999, Lexis Nexis Academic Universe (accessed October 29, 1999).

66. Mann, "For Elizabeth Dole, Time Will Tell."

67. Balz, "Hoping to be 'Part of History.'"

68. Starobin, "McCain's Men, Dole's Women."

69. Robin Givhan, "One Small Step for Womankind; Elizabeth Dole's Candidacy Became Merely the Symbol She Avoided," *Washington Post*, October 21, 1999, Lexis Nexis Academic Universe (accessed October 29, 1999).

70. "Dole Drops Out," *abcnews.com*, October 20, 1999, <abcnews.com> (accessed October 20, 1999).

71. Givhan, "One Small Step for Womankind."

72. "Dole Drops Out."

73. See Scott Mooneyham, "Elizabeth Dole Kicks Off Campaign," *Associated Press*, February 23, 2002, Lexis Nexis Academic Universe (accessed August 16, 2002); David Sanger, "Bush Campaigns for Mrs. Dole in North Carolina Race," *New York Times*, February 28, 2002, Lexis Nexis Academic Universe (accessed August 16, 2002); "Dole Receives Business Group Endorsement," *Associated Press State & Local Wire*, March 20, 2002, Lexis Nexis Academic Universe (accessed August 16, 2002); Dana Damico, "Critics Say Big Money Favors Dole, Bowles," *Reidsville Review*, April 17, 2002, Lexis Nexis Academic Universe (accessed August 16, 2002); "NC: Both Party Polls Show

Dole Out Front Against Bowles," *The Bulletin's Frontrunner*, April 18, 2002, Lexis Nexis Academic Universe (accessed August 16, 2002).

74. "Elizabeth Dole Launches Run for U.S. Senate Seat Being Vacated by Jesse Helms," *Morning Edition*, February 25, 2002, Lexis Nexis Academic Universe (accessed August 16, 2002).

75. Richard L. Berke, "Echoes Aside, Dole Insists She Is No Clinton," *New York Times*, April 8, 2002, Lexis Nexis Academic Universe (accessed August 16, 2002).

76. "Elizabeth Dole's Race for the Senate Seat of North Carolina and Her Battles to Get There," *Today*, September 26, 2002, Lexis Nexis Academic Universe (accessed October 1, 2002).

77. William M. Welch, "'Rock Star' Dole Protects Lead in Key Senate Race," *USA Today*, July 1, 2002, Lexis Nexis Academic Universe (accessed August 16, 2002).

78. "Interview with Elizabeth Dole." *CNN Wolf Blitzer Reports*, February 28, 2002, Lexis Nexis Academic Universe (accessed August 16, 2002).

79. Eric Dyer, "Snyder Begins Race for Helms' Seat with Jab at Dole," *News & Record*, March 1, 2002, Lexis Nexis Academic Universe (accessed August 16, 2002).

80. Welch, "'Rock Star'."

81. "Interview with Elizabeth Dole," *CNN Wolf Blitzer Reports*. Dole gave similar answers in other interviews. See "Elizabeth Dole's Race."

82. Welch, "'Rock Star'."

83. "Elizabeth Dole's Race."

84. Mark Leibovich, "Liddy Dole in North Carolina, Hoping Her Roots Show," *Washington Post*, October 7, 2002, <washingtonpost.com> (accessed October 7, 2002).

85. Welch, "'Rock Star'."

86. "North Carolina."

87. Patrik Jonsson, "In Senate Bid, Dole Takes Shot at a New Glass Ceiling," *Christian Science Monitor*, February 22, 2002, Lexis Nexis Academic Universe (accessed August 16, 2002).

88. Welch, "'Rock Star'."

89. Berke, "Echoes Aside."

90. David E. Rosenbaum, "Many Questions Arise in Race for Helms Seat," *New York Times*, June 28, 2002, Lexis Nexis Academic Universe (accessed August 16, 2002).

91. Katharine Q. Seelye, "After Pepsi and Viagra, Dole Is Pushing Dole," *New York Times*, October 1, 2002, <www.newyorktimes.com> (accessed October 1, 2002).

92. Welch, "'Rock Star'." The basketball imagery was repeated in David S. Broder, "In N.C. Endorsement Race, It's Dean Vs. Coach K.," *Washington Post*, September 29, 2002, Lexis Nexis Academic Universe (accessed November 14, 2002).

93. Leibovich, "Liddy Dole."

94. Jonsson, "In Senate Bid."

95. Welch, "'Rock Star'."

96. Deborah Orin, "Politics as Usual: Prez Boosts Liddy," *New York Post*, February 28, 2002, Lexis Nexis Academic Universe (accessed August 16, 2002).

97. Sharon McBrayer, "Bob Dole Visits for Liddy," *News-Herald*, June 29, 2002, Lexis Nexis Academic Universe (accessed August 16, 2002).

98. Jonsson, "In Senate Bid."

99. "Interview with Elizabeth Dole," *CNN Evans, Novak, Hunt & Shields*, August 10, 2002, Lexis Nexis Academic Universe (accessed August 16, 2002).

100. Elizabeth Dole, "Elizabeth Dole Primary Remarks," September 10, 2002, Salisbury, N.C., <www.elizabethdole.org> (accessed October 29, 2002).

101. Dole, "Elizabeth Dole Primary Remarks."

102. Elizabeth Dole, "Remarks at the Women for Dole Press Conference," September 23, 2002, Greensboro, N.C., <www.elizabethdole.org> (accessed October 29, 2002).

103. "Elizabeth Dole: Mill," campaign ad, <http://www.elizabethdole.org/multimedia.asp> (accessed December 1, 2002).

104. Elizabeth Dole, "Dear Friends," <www.elizabethdole.org> (accessed November 5, 2002).

105. Kat Zernike, "The 2002 Elections: North Carolina; Elizabeth Dole Easily Defeats Clinton Aide in Senate Bid," *New York Times*, November 6, 2002, Lexis Nexis Academic Universe (accessed November 14, 2002).

106. "North Carolina."

107. "Elizabeth Dole Wins N.C. Seat," *msncb.com*, November 5, 2002, <msnbc.com> (accessed November 5, 2002).

108. Howard Fineman, "How Bush Did It," *Newsweek*, November 18, 2002, Lexis Nexis Academic Universe (accessed November 29, 2002).

109. "The 2002 Elections: South; North Carolina," *New York Times*, November 7, 2002, Lexis Nexis Academic Universe (accessed November 14, 2002).

110. For example, *The Boston Globe* reported that "in race after race, Bush's campaign blitz across nearly two dozen states in the final six weeks before the election appeared to have worked. 'George Bush's travels swung the election, period,' a senior Democratic strategist said." Anne E. Kornblut, "Elections 2002: The National Battle GOP Victories; Bush's Outreach Bears Fruit," *Boston Globe*, November 6, 2002, Lexis Nexis Academic Universe (accessed November 14, 2002). Also see Fineman, "How Bush Did It"; Adam Nagourney, "The Republicans Win Their Bet," *New York Times*, November 10, 2002, Lexis Nexis Academic Universe (accessed November 29, 2002); and Mark Steyn, "I Was Wrong Again! Hurrah!" *Spectator*, November 9, 2002, Lexis Nexis Academic Universe (accessed November 29, 2002).

Conclusion

Cracking the Governing Codes

At the outset of this book, we promised an examination of "the codes that govern us and how public women use them." Our study addressed three interrelated themes: gender, metaphor, and political identity. The conclusions yielded by this discussion are of interest both to political practitioners and to scholars of rhetoric, language, and politics. The crux of our argument is that metaphors act as constraints *and* rhetorical resources for political leaders. The four case studies detailed in this book illustrate the myriad ways in which that dynamic can play out in the U.S. political sphere.

Gender

In many ways, our case studies confirm the old adage that "the more things change, the more they stay the same." No one can deny the empirical gains women have made in the political sphere: their numbers in elective office are increasing, their fundraising clout is expanding, and issues of import to them are central themes of political debates and major party platforms. According to McGlen and O'Connor, when women run against non-incumbent candidates, they win political office just as often as men do.[1] Yet in a time labeled by the popular media as the era of "sexual correctness" and heralded by some scholars as the "postfeminist" age, media images of political women continue to stereotype and trivialize them. Take, for example, the lead for a December 12, 2002 *Washington Post* story about the historic election of two sisters to the U.S. Congress:

> Linda Sanchez has a new haircut. Her big sister doesn't approve.
> "She thinks it's too spiky," Linda explains.
> "Who cut it for you? Donna?" asks Loretta Sanchez, referring to the hairdresser they both use.
> Linda nods. "I told her I wanted something young and a little bit edgy."

189

> Linda is younger and, yes, a little bit edgy. Loretta is older and, yes, a
> little bit bossy. Together they're making history as the first sisters
> ever to serve together in Congress.[2]

That lead invokes stereotypes about women's preoccupation with physical appearance (as though hairstyles are at the top of the agenda for these two incom-
ing members of Congress) and women leaders as transgressive ("edgy") and
bossy. The article goes on to detail a hot debate between the sisters about what
type of pet to procure for the Capitol Hill apartment they will share, as well as
each woman's orientation toward cooking:

> Loretta looks around the rowhouse. "Maybe we'll buy a little kitty for
> this place," she says, primarily to annoy her sister.
> "A little dog," says Linda.
> "Kitty," coos Loretta.
> "No no no," answers Linda.
> Truth is, they probably won't get a cat or dog. Nor will they cook in
> the kitchen, which—given their schedules and habits—they are
> unlikely to use.
> "I haven't cooked in about six years," admits Loretta.
> "We grew up in a family of seven, and you learn to cook Mexican
> food by watching, not by recipes," says Linda. "So whenever I cook,
> it's got to be for nine people because I don't know how to make any-
> thing smaller."[3]

Similarly, an August 8, 2002 *New York Times* article about Jennifer Granholm's
victory in the Democratic primary for the Michigan gubernatorial nomination
placed Granholm in a position of weakness (despite her victorious status) and
highlighted a stereotypically feminine achievement over her political qualifications. The lead read as follows:

> At the morning-after unity breakfast, the giants of the Michigan De-
> mocratic Party were quiet—or absent. James J. Blanchard, the only
> Democratic governor in 40 years, hugged the winner and slipped
> away. Representative David E. Bonior, who has spent much of his 26
> years in Congress in the House leadership, clasped a coffee mug off
> to the side, clapping politely.
>   Glowing at the center table was Jenni the giant-slayer, a former
> beauty queen turned Phi Beta Kappa lawyer who ran for office the
> first time only four years ago. On Tuesday, Jennifer N. Granholm, the
> state attorney general, won a bitter three-way primary with 48 percent
> of the vote, beating Mr. Blanchard and Mr. Bonior by 20 points.[4]

It's not just women candidates who suffer from stereotyping in the media.
The female electorate is trivialized as well. An ABCNEWS.com article that ran
during the 2000 presidential primaries featured the headline "Bush Charms the
Ladies." The story covered an appearance by George W. Bush at a convention

of the National Federation of Republican Women, an organization that boasts 100,000 members. Using romance metaphors to explain Bush's appeal to this particular audience, author Jonathan Dube said that Bush "courted" his female audience and that "it didn't take long for him to win their hearts, judging by the glowing smiles and thunderous applause that swept across the Convention Center auditorium."[5] The not-so-subtle implication was that women vote for emotional and sentimental reasons, a charge that was underscored by the article's subhead: "Republican Women Fall for George W." By using language that invoked images of star-struck teenage girls, Dube turned a story about a serious political event into a fluff piece about one candidate's personal attractiveness, dismissing the importance of women's political organizations. Interestingly, Dube posted a story on ABCNEWS.com just three days later, covering Elizabeth Dole's speech at that same convention. Casting Dole in a position of weakness, Dube's subhead read that "Liddy Wins Their Support, But Not Necessarily Their Vote." According to Dube's account, the audience was almost as giddy about Dole as they were about Bush. The article stated that "women flocked to Dole as they might a movie star, pleading for autographs and posing with her for photos."[6] Although it is reasonable for Dube to report on Dole's popularity with the group, the verb "pleading" positions the National Federation of Republican Women as a group of overly emotional fans rather than as a serious and influential political organization.

When journalists resist gender stereotyping to provide more equitable coverage, the news itself often reveals political contexts that remain gendered in a surprisingly old-fashioned way. A 2002 *Washington Post* profile of Kendel Ehrlich, spouse of former Congressman and Maryland Governor-elect Robert J. Ehrlich Jr., reported that in 1994 an orientation for new congressional wives featured a handout on "The 14 Points of Accessorizing."[7] The sexism confronted by the women profiled in this book was, at times, similarly explicit—from charges that Hillary Rodham Clinton's intelligence would make her husband look weak to characterizations of Christine Todd Whitman's rhetoric as "a Girl Scout leader giving a pep talk to the girls at the beginning of the annual cookie drive."[8]

This book examined different types of political campaigns—those waged by Democrats and Republicans, campaigns by candidates as well as spouses, bids for gubernatorial and senatorial offices. One finding that was consistent throughout our case studies is the notion that women can be perceived more easily as representatives than as leaders in executive office. Interestingly, however, the most debilitating metaphors were advanced about Ann Richards and Christine Todd Whitman as candidates. It seems that women aspiring to executive positions are the most vulnerable during the candidacy phase, but once elected are given an opportunity to engage leadership more freely. Conversely, the case studies of Hillary Rodham Clinton and Elizabeth Dole indicate that women running for representative positions are framed more positively during their campaigns than are their gubernatorial counterparts. Rodham Clinton even obtained limited strategic benefit from the gendered stereotyping of her male opponents: Guiliani as too masculine and Lazio as too boyish. Media coverage of Dole's 2002 Senate campaign, while still sprinkled with metaphors of the beauty queen, emphasized her competence and ability to do the job and relied less on the good wife and woman first images of the 1996 and 2000 presidential campaigns.

When the issue of gendered stereotyping arises in relation to women's political agency, emphasis usually is placed on strategies for avoiding such stereotyping. Although that quite obviously is the ultimate goal, an important insight suggested by our case studies is that gender stereotypes sometimes can be manipulated by political women for strategic advantage. The utility of this approach can be envisioned on a continuum. On one end are those strategies that afford strategic benefits but ultimately undermine women's agency. On the other end are strategies that appear to conform to traditional notions of gender, but function to challenge them from within.

First, Bob Dole's 1996 presidential campaign benefited from Elizabeth Dole's willingness to act as a supportive and traditional wife; however, that move reinscribed stereotypes about women and power and ultimately inhibited Dole's own political agency in her subsequent bid for the presidency. So, although Dole's choice helped her achieve a political goal she shared with her husband, it also reinforced the double bind between femininity and competence.

Christine Todd Whitman's very presence demonstrated that women executives can be perceived as credible, as long as they remain within specific gender-defined boundaries. In Whitman's case, coming from a conservative Republican standpoint within the powerful New Jersey political culture, she was able to capitalize on the gendered nature of the conciliator. Because she was the peace-maker and deferred to her party or her state at appropriate times, she was deemed competent. Whitman was also allowed to be strong, confident, and pro-active, as demanded by the political culture, corresponding with the athletic pioneer persona of her second term in office. Whitman's performance of leadership did not capitalize on feminine stereotypes such as the hostess or a mother figure, yet she demonstrated the hierarchical relationship between the political culture as masculine and her leadership as feminine.

Ann Richards moved farther down the continuum, accepting the "unruly woman" label but demonstrating that, within a liberal framework, that persona can be empowering. As the unruly woman, Richards capitalized on the rhetoric of visibility and reframed what power and control meant within Texas political culture. Richards's visibility, paired with her strategy of forging relationships, legitimized the act of relationship building, redefined what it meant to enact power as a good ol' girl, and brought accountability and inclusiveness to a weak Texas government. Yet Richards's performance of executive authority was not without one significant problem. Although she aligned herself with Texas's past and used that past as foundational for her vision of a new Texas, she did not significantly revise the sexism and stereotypes associated with that past, even sometimes relying on those very stereotypes herself. Thus, when engaging executive authority it is important not simply to stress inclusion, but also to think about what the rhetoric of inclusion entails. Does it truly offer a revision of political culture, or does it offer a contradictory position that potentially could work to undermine any advances that the woman executive makes. Ultimately Richards does offer one explanation for how to resolve the woman/leader problematic within our liberal democracy. Her governorship is instructive to this end, taking into account not only her successes but also her shortcomings. Her advances have made it possible to see women leaders as credible and powerful, while also seeing them as mothers and grandmothers. In particular, by demonstrating the power of the feminine, Richards' leadership confounded the femininity-competence double bind. As Richards herself believed, when little girls see her in a position of leadership, they too realize they can do anything they set their mind to.

Hillary Rodham Clinton's experiences demonstrate that the "unruly woman" persona is not equally liberating for all political women. Rodham Clinton's status as a political spouse made her transgressions as an unruly woman more problematic for the mainstream media and some voters than they were when coming from an independent, pioneering, governor-grandmother like Ann Richards. Yet, although Rodham Clinton, perhaps more than any other woman profiled in this book, suffered under the weight of sexist stereotyping, she also was the most successful at co-opting those stereotypes *both* for strategic political advantage and for the symbolic purpose of challenging the double bind. Rodham Clinton's retreat to tradition during the 1995–1998 "Madonna" phase gave Rodham Clinton a quick boost in the polls, but it also led the media to report on her strong feminist rhetoric and even cast it in a positive light. As she became more "first ladylike" during the "Save America's Treasures" campaign, she also launched a successful bid for the U.S. Senate. By the end of Bill Clinton's two terms in office, Hillary Rodham Clinton exemplified the both/and, becoming both first lady and senator-elect.

We conclude, then, that it is possible for political women to manage their public personae in ways that afford them political advantages and challenge age-old stereotypes. This remains, however, a tall order in American politics. To truly appreciate how this task can be accomplished, one must revisit what our study reveals about metaphor and U.S. political processes.

Metaphor

Although metaphors have long been recognized as foundational to language, their influence on politics has been examined in a less substantive way. As previously noted, our focus on metaphor is not meant to discount the influence of sociological and economic forces at work in the political system; however, the role of metaphor is of special interest to scholars and practitioners who have a rhetorical sensibility. Critics understand the role that explicit metaphors serve as framing devices in news stories, citing, for example, the characterization of politics in terms of sports, war, and/or romance.[9] But metaphor shapes our political understanding in a much more subtle and profound way. Metaphors such as "pioneer" and "Madonna" are deeply rooted in American culture. Their existence within news narratives does not always need to be explicitly recognized because they germinate at the level of the implicit, perhaps even of the subconscious. One task that should be undertaken by critics of political media is to uncover and make explicit the metaphoric clusters that form our political understanding. Christine Todd Whitman's athletic persona took so long to emerge in the media, in part, because early narratives that formed around her first gubernatorial campaign clustered around Whitman as "clueless" and "inept." Similarly, it is the clustering effect that, for example, causes many people to think "bitch" when they hear a political woman being described as aggressive, strident, or strong. When Elizabeth Dole was quoted saying that husband Bob would be exiled to the "woodshed" for his intentions to contribute to rival John McCain's campaign, it was the clustering effect that prompted a media narrative in which Bob Dole's contribution to a political rival was seen as an act of his independence from Elizabeth—then his assertion of independence was translated into a sign of her dependence on him (he would be available to "direct her" in political matters)—and finally her dependence on him was used to insinuate (however satirically) an abusive relationship in the headline "Psst, Bob Dole Beats His Wife."

Numerous studies point out the stereotypes that affect women public office holders, and argue that women should capitalize on those stereotypes in order to become elected and then work to revise the stereotypes once elected.[10] This book suggests it's not that simple. When running for the governor's office, the gendered nature of the campaign affects women candidates regardless, and neither Richards nor Whitman were given the opportunity to define themselves effectively during their campaign. They were always perceived to be on the defensive, at best countering and responding to their opponents. Neither was able to capitalize on issues related to gender, and Whitman was specifically criticized for engaging in family-oriented activity (a family vacation) during the campaign, putting her at a severe disadvantage. Instead, what saved Whitman's election was her promise of a tax cut, in other words, an economic issue gendered masculine according to Kahn and Gordon.[11] Additionally, leading in a gendered manner, as Whitman did, can be easily co-opted, leaving little room to revise the stereotypes later. Further, the case of Elizabeth Dole in 2000 reinforces the argument that women running for executive positions are damaged by playing into traditional stereotypes. The 1996 image of Dole as the dutiful spouse resurfaced in 2000 to frame her as too weak for a presidential bid.

Whitman, however, gained credibility during her 1990 Senate race against Bill Bradley because she "hammered" and "pressed" him, and Richards was a part of one of the most negative campaigns in Texas history, noted as an exam-

ple of the "Kamikaze Campaign" by Maria Braden.[12] Reinforcing the stereotypes in the first place does nothing to unsettle the gendered metaphors already
so instantiated in our political culture. Instead, this study suggests that calling
attention to gender does more to bridge the symbolic gap between perceptions of
women and political leadership. Richards, through her visibility, demanded that
she be taken seriously as a woman and grandmother and governor, refiguring
leadership in Texas in the process.

In addition to suggesting the ways in which metaphor shapes political understanding, this study reveals how the metaphors that surface in media coverage of political woman can serve both as lock and key for these women. Ann
Richards, Christine Todd Whitman, Hillary Rodham Clinton, and Elizabeth
Dole each explored her unique metaphorical landscape for the rhetorical strategies necessary to accomplish her political goals. Sometimes in constraining and
sometimes in empowering ways, each woman managed to employ metaphor
creatively, often capitalizing on its inventional potential to complicate the containment logic and confound the double bind that historically has challenged
women's political agency. Whether it be Rodham Clinton's transformation from
"bitch" to Madonna or Richards's demonstration of how truly appealing an "unruly woman" can become, the women in this study took the familiar saying "if
you can't beat 'em, join 'em" and did one better—if you can't beat 'em, make it
seem like you're joining them, then change them. This is very different from a
simple manipulation of sexist stereotypes for short-term pragmatic gain. Instead,
it is a strategy that recognizes the elasticity of metaphor. A candidate who is
fully aware of the pitfalls of appealing to tradition can design an appeal that invokes tradition even as it challenges it, a strategy that rings familiar even as it
produces something totally new. Metaphor is a particularly useful resource for
leaders who are required to work for change from within the political system.

Political Identity

The case studies examined in this book illustrate the ways in which women
leaders have constructed distinct political styles. One would expect that a
woman politician's political style would be markedly different from a man's
because of the cultural forces discussed in this book: the double bind, containment logic, and the gendering of political power. What is perhaps surprising is
the notion that when cultivating a political style, place is almost as important a
consideration as gender. Even a cursory look at Ann Richards's tenure as the
governor of Texas reveals the central role that place played in her political style
and public persona. The *mythos* of Texas, the language of the frontier, and the
swagger of the good ol' girl shaped not only Richards's political style but also
the media coverage of her campaigns. When constructing a public persona, politicians should examine carefully the narrative and metaphoric elements of their
geographic and cultural location. That will lead them to make linguistic choices

with which their audience is likely to resonate. The media, too, must be able to recognize a candidate's political style. If a political style complements the narratives invoked by the locale, it will fit more neatly into existing media frames, thus the candidate is more likely to get coverage that reflects the political style s/he is trying to create.

When considering the rhetoric of place, the actual, geographic location of the campaign is a good starting point, but it is not the only dimension of place. Christine Todd Whitman's position as a moderate Republican woman located her in a specific symbolic place. Responding to the constraints of her location, Whitman performed the political style of a conciliator. This was a comparatively weak metaphoric choice. Richards's unruly woman persona provided her more room to maneuver and more avenues for creativity. Whitman's choice, however, was responsive to her positioning within the Republican party and thus can be instructive for a woman executive asserting power from a conservative frame in our political culture. As Whitman demonstrates, the conservative woman may want to stay away from the unruly woman metaphor because it will likely frame her as transgressive, especially by fellow conservatives. The pioneer and the beauty queen can be strong choices for the conservative woman. However, in Whitman's case, she did not highlight her motherly or hostess side. This too was appropriate because she was already framed in such a weak manner as a conciliator. Even though she earned and wielded considerable power as a woman, she did so within the boundaries of New Jersey's political culture, always deferring to the accepted hierarchy of the office or the party. Despite this deferential stance, Whitman's importance as a leader within the party was recognized by former Massachusetts Governor Jane Swift, who credited Whitman with being her role model because of Whitman's ability to balance "leadership and humanness."[13]

The Senate campaigns of Hillary Rodham Clinton and Elizabeth Dole illustrate a final way that place influences candidates' political style. If a candidate is perceived to be disconnected from her/his constituency because of issues of place, location can challenge a candidate, putting her on the defensive. Both Rodham Clinton and Dole were tagged as "carpetbaggers" early in their Senate campaigns—Rodham Clinton because she had never lived in New York, and Dole because she had resided in Washington for more than thirty years. It was the pressure of locale that prompted Rodham Clinton to make cosmetic changes to her persona—donning the black pantsuits to which she jokingly referred in her acceptance speech. Place triggered an early campaign gaffe, when Rodham Clinton was photographed wearing a Yankees' cap despite her much publicized allegiance to the Chicago Cubs. She recovered from that early mistake, and her speeches demonstrated that Rodham Clinton could negotiate the geographical gap between her and her prospective constituency by demonstrating their close proximity on the issues. The promise issued in her speech accepting the Democratic nomination that "I may be new to the neighborhood, but I'm not new to your concerns" encapsulated Rodham Clinton's rhetorical response to the carpetbagger charge. She structured her political identity around the notion of authenticity. Rodham Clinton's critics would charge that she failed to prove an authentic connection to New York and sought the Senate seat merely as a stepping stone to a potential presidential bid, yet examination of Rodham Clinton's public persona during the 2000 Senate race illustrates the powerful influence of place on a political persona.

Similar insights can be gleaned from examining the way that Elizabeth Dole responded to the challenge that she was more connected to Washington than to the state of North Carolina. Dole had the advantage of having lived in the state, so she was able to address the question more directly than could Rodham Clinton. Throughout the campaign Dole repeated the mantra that she grew up in North Carolina, was a Duke graduate, and owned a home and a business in the state. She also used the carpetbagger charge as an opportunity to remind voters of her professional resume, stating that "if you serve in the president's cabinet or you're president of the Red Cross, you can't do it from Salisbury, North Carolina." The place issue had a more substantive effect on Dole's political identity, transforming, for example, her stance on gun control and causing her to turn her attention to issues of regional importance like bolstering the tobacco and textile industries.

In addition to being fundamentally connected to place, political style is shaped by the rhetoric of visibility. Ann Richards capitalized on the power of being seen. Her case is instructive for women hoping to achieve political office, for power accrues to those who are seen, who touch, who demonstrate through their behavior and their language that they are accessible. But simple prominence is not sufficient for the rhetorical construction of political power. Dole was tapped as a potential presidential candidate because of her "star power"; however, during that presidential run she was criticized for being too scripted, too stylized. Similar criticisms were levied against Whitman. Thus, it may be the case that the woman leader must be able to manage her public presence in a way that is not only visible but also comfortable, prominent but also active. Politicians of both genders and all political affiliations can employ rhetorics of visibility—although the means by which they attain visibility will differ depending on their specific situation.

An underlying insight suggested by our case studies is that political power is situated within particular contexts—contexts that produce a host of rhetorical strategies that may be of use to others. Men as well as women can control their political identity more effectively if they respond to the constraints of place and mine their geographic and ideological locations for useful metaphors and narratives. When women politicians undertake this task, however, they have to remember that the same rhetorical choices are often evaluated differently by voters because of gendered stereotypes about power and leadership. The common denominator in each of the successful political campaigns examined in this book is that when our women candidates succeeded, they were able to garner media coverage that reflected the complexity of their political identities, rather than confining them within very narrow but recognizable narrative frames. The key to these successes is paradox. The woman leader must find a way to capitalize on the rhetorical resources of paradox within the context of her political culture. Richards's "good ol' girl" was, in itself, a paradoxical persona, and she played up the oxymoronic elements of her identity as part of her rhetoric of visibility. Richards's "White Hot Mama" photograph combined the oppositional images of a white-haired grandmother-governor in leather pants astride a Harley Davidson motorcycle. This cosmetic example of paradox mirrored a more important political move made by Richards when she used appeals to Texas tradition to support her move toward an inclusive "New Texas." Whitman capitalized on her moderate status by enacting executive power, paradoxically, through the strategy of conciliation. During her second term as New Jersey's governor, she enacted the "both/and" approach by balancing her aristocratic image with an environmentalist political agenda. Rodham Clinton's "Save America's Treasures" Tour allowed her to engage in a traditional first lady–like activity that also, paradoxically, gave her an opportunity to push for women's empowerment. Elizabeth Dole was most successful when she embraced both the traditional and progressive sides of her identity. During the 1996 campaign, Dole played up her status as a traditional spouse and was contained within that narrow image. In the 2000 campaign, she attempted to move to the opposite end of the spectrum, casting herself as a strong conservative with an impressive Washington resume. When campaigning in North Carolina, however, Dole cultivated a more complex political identity that heralded her feminine appeal and portrayed her as a down-home Southern woman, but also foregrounded her political clout and professional experience. The media responded to Dole's paradoxical political identity by creating a number of different narratives, tolerating more complexity in 2002 than in previous campaigns.

The strategy of paradox, along with the successes experienced by grandmothers-turned-governors and spouses-turned-senators provide a hopeful view of women's political agency. We endorse hope for the future, but simultaneously acknowledge certain political realities of the present. Women didn't make many advances in the 2002 election. In fact, their numbers in Congress remained the same while picking up one gubernatorial seat. Women representatives and executives still have much ground to cover, financially as well as personally. It may be that qualified women choose not to run for statewide office because of the strain it places on women who are still the primary caregivers in the family. After all, as recently as 1992, the "Year of the Woman," women were still found to delay their entrance into public life until their children were grown, if they chose to have a family at all.[14] According to Susan Carroll, the political opportunity structure disadvantages women candidates.[15] Ann Richards acknowledged one of these elements, the difficulty of raising funds, which was also the reason that Christine Todd Whitman gave when dropping out of the Senate race in 1999. It was Elizabeth Dole's downfall in her 2000 presidential bid. Yet, when running for the Senate, Rodham Clinton and Dole each raised significant amounts of money and had the backing of the major party players. Fortunately, more and more organizations are making themselves available to women hoping to run for political office, such as "Emily's List" (a Democratic donors' network), the Women's Campaign Fund (a bipartisan fund supporting pro-choice and pro-ERA women candidates), WISH (supporting pro-choice Republican women), and the "Susan B. Anthony List" (an organization promoting pro-life women candidates), making it easier to raise the necessary funds. And with conservative as well as liberal women becoming more visible in public life, there are more role models who demonstrate that women can run and successfully win public office. With instructive cases such as former governors Ann Richards and Christine Todd Whitman as well as Elizabeth Dole and Hillary Rodham Clinton, women may have more role models to encourage them to run for political office. While winning office won't guarantee political change for women, not running for office certainly won't change anything.

We hope that our case studies can serve as resources for those with political and public aspirations, illustrating the complexities of image formation. We acknowledge that ours is an incomplete portrait of women's political identity— omitting important questions by examining women who share the same race and economic status. The fact that our cases cannot stand for all women does not mean that they cannot be instructive to candidates who do not share these individuals' race, economic status, or even gender. Ellen Goodman writes "The year of what? In 2002, there isn't A Woman's Story to stretch across the political map. But there are a lot of women's stories, including some cautionary tales."[16] Here are only four women's stories and each is different. We look forward to reading many more.

Notes

1. Nancy E. McGlen and Karen O'Connor, *Women, Politics, and American Society*, 2d ed. (Upper Saddle River, N.J.: Prentice Hall, 1998), 80.

2. Roxanne Roberts, "House Mates: Loretta and Linda Sanchez are Congress's First Sister Act, They Work Well Together, The Question Is, Can They Live Together?" *Washington Post*, December 12, 2002, <www.washingtonpost.com> (accessed December 12, 2002).

3. Roberts, "House Mates."

4. Jodi Wilgoren, "A Nominee with Vigor Gives Michigan Democrats Hope," *New York Times*, August 8, 2002, <www.nytimes.com> (accessed August 8, 2002).

5. Jonathan Dube, "Bush Charms the Ladies," *abcnews.com*, October 15, 1999, <abcnews.com> (accessed October 19, 1999).

6. Jonathan Dube, "Republican Women Rally Behind Dole," *abcnews.com*, October 18, 1999, <abcnews.com> (accessed October 19, 1999).

7. April Witt, "Next Md. First Lady No Junior Partner," *Washington Post*, November 9, 2002, <www.washingtonpost.com> (accessed November 9, 2002).

8. See Ch. 4, page 123 and Ch. 3, page 85.

9. See Kathleen Hall Jamieson, "The Subversive Effects of a Focus on Strategy in News Coverage of Presidential Campaigns," in *1-800-president: The Report of the Twentieth Century Fund Task Force on Television and the campaign of 1992* (New York: Twentieth Century Fund Press, 1993), 37; and Dan F. Hahn, "The Marriage Metaphor in Politics," *Political Communication: Rhetoric, Government, and Citizens*, 2d ed., (State College, Penn.: Strata Publishing, 2003), 163–88.

10. For example, "candidates are best advised to play on their 'own' turf" in Shanto Iyengar, Nicholas A. Valentino, Stephen Ansolabehere, and Adam F. Simon, "Running as a Woman: Gender Stereotyping in Women's Campaigns," in *Women, Media, and Politics*, ed. Pippa Norris, (New York: Oxford University Press, 1997), 77–98. They cite numerous studies as evidence.

11. Kim Fridkin Kahn and Ann Gordon, "How Women Campaign for the U.S. Senate: Substance and Strategy," in *Women, Media, and Politics*, ed. Pippa Norris (New York: Oxford University Press, 1997), 63.

12. Maria Braden, *Women Politicians and the Media* (Lexington: University Press of Kentucky, 1996), 141–43.

13. Mary Leonard, "Role Models Are Few For Swift in New Office," *The Boston Globe*, February 18, 2001, A1, Lexis Nexis Academic Universe (accessed June 26, 2002).

14. McGlen and O'Connor, 82–84.

15. Carroll writes a book length study on what she terms the "political opportunity structure" that disadvantages women candidates. Included in this political opportunity structure are the "single-member, plurality election system," the lack of recruiting of women candidates, the lack of financial resources, and women's lack of elective experience. Susan J. Carroll, *Women as Candidates in American Politics* (Bloomington: Indiana University Press, 1994).

16. Ellen Goodman, "Post-gender Politics and Cautionary Tales; Women Candidates are in a Double Bind, But Some Manage to Wriggle Free," editorial, *Pittsburgh Post Gazette*, November 13, 2002, A17, Lexis Nexis Academic Universe (accessed December 12, 2002).

Bibliography

"The Administration Takes Shape." *The Hartford Courant*, December 24, 2000, C2. Lexis Nexis Academic Universe (accessed August 24, 2002).

Adubato, Steve Jr. "'Cool Mom' Whitman Getting Nervous About How Close Polls Show the Race." *Asbury Park Press*, October 20, 1997, A11. Lexis Nexis Academic Universe (accessed September 15, 1999).

———. "For Whitman, Not All Tax Increases Are Alike." *The Record*, September 6, 1994, B09. Lexis Nexis Academic Universe (accessed September 14, 1999).

———. "Good Luck Christie." *The Record*, November 9, 1993, B15. Lexis Nexis Academic Universe (accessed August 20, 1999).

———. "Grim Expectations." *The Record*, June 15, 1993, B11. Lexis Nexis Academic Universe (accessed August 29, 1999).

———. "Talking Democracy." *The Record*, December 7, 1993, B11. Lexis Nexis Academic Universe (accessed August 20, 1999).

———. "Whitman Facing Gender Gap Over Her School Funding Plan." *Asbury Park Press*, June 10, 1996, A11. Lexis Nexis Academic Universe (accessed September 15, 1999).

———. "Whitman Sailing Right Along, No Doubt about It." *The Record*, October 11, 1994, C11. Lexis Nexis Academic Universe (accessed September 14, 1999).

———. "A Winning Demeanor." *The Record*, January 11, 1994, C11. Lexis Nexis Academic Universe (accessed September 14, 1999).

"AEC Gets a Female Boss." *Senior Scholastic*, March 5, 1973, 17.

"After 100 Days, Governor Enjoying Life at the Top." *San Antonio Light*, April 20, 1991.

Ahearn, James. "Christie the Unsinkable; Like the Energizer Bunny, She Keeps Going Full Speed Ahead." *Asbury Park Press*, May 21, 1997, A15. Lexis Nexis Academic Universe (accessed September 15, 1999).

———. "It Only Looks Quixotic." *The Record*, February 13, 1994, O02. Lexis Nexis Academic Universe (accessed September 14, 1999).

———. "A New Leader, A New Era." *The Record*, November 7, 1993, O02. Lexis Nexis Academic Universe (accessed August 20, 1999).

————. "Things May Change, But for Now Whitman Is Doing Quite Well." *The Record*, June 8, 1994, B11. Lexis Nexis Academic Universe (accessed September 14, 1999).

————. "In Trenton, it's Quite Clear Who's in Control." *The Record*, May 10, 1995, N07. Lexis Nexis Academic Universe (accessed September 14, 1999).

————. "Velvet Gloves, Iron Will." *Asbury Park Press*, July 12, 1995, A13. Lexis Nexis Academic Universe (accessed September 14, 1999).

————. "Whitman's Hard Won Victory." *The Record*, June 15, 1997, O02. Lexis Nexis Academic Universe (accessed September 15, 1999).

————. "Whitman's Reelection is No Longer a Sure Thing." *The Record*, October 22, 1997, L09. Lexis Nexis Academic Universe (accessed September 15, 1999).

Ahrens, Frank. "Infield Chatter; Hillary Clinton Toasts the 'Home' Team." *Washington Post*, June 11, 1999. Lexis Nexis Academic Universe (accessed December 29, 2000).

Alexander, Shana. "On the Lookout for Lurleen." *Life* (July 22, 1966): 19.

"All Things Considered." *National Public Radio*, March 10, 1999. Lexis Nexis Academic Universe (accessed December 30, 2000).

Alter, Jonathan. "Go Ahead, Bust Some Chops." *Newsweek* (November 15, 1993): 34.

————. "How He Could Recover." *Newsweek* (November 21, 1994). Lexis Nexis Academic Universe (accessed July 17, 2002).

Altschiller, Howard. "Gluck Urges Women Lawyers to Get Involved and Go After Power." *New Jersey Lawyer*, January 30, 1995, 5. Lexis Nexis Academic Universe (accessed September 14, 1999).

Amiel, Barbara. "The Trouble with Bill and Hillary." *Maclean's* (April 11, 1994): 13.

Anderson, Karrin Vasby. "From Spouses to Candidates: Hillary Rodham Clinton, Elizabeth Dole, and the Gendered Office of U.S. President." *Rhetoric & Public Affairs* 5 (2002): 105–32.

————. "'Rhymes with Rich,' 'Bitch' as a Tool of Containment in Contemporary American Politics." *Rhetoric & Public Affairs* 2 (1999): 599–623.

Apple, R. W. Jr. "He's No Christie Whitman; 15% Hasn't Been Dole's Solution." *New York Times*, September 8, 1996, late edition, 1. Lexis Nexis Academic Universe (accessed September 15, 1999).

Arnold, Lawrence. "Whitman Tries to Balance Personal, Political Lives." *Asbury Park Press*, October 26, 1997, A12. Lexis Nexis Academic Universe (accessed September 15, 1999).

Attlesey, Sam. "Richards' 'New Texas' Means Many Things." *Dallas Morning News*, January 20, 1991.

————. "Williams Downfall Assessed." *Dallas Morning News*, November 7, 1990, 1A.

Ayres, Jr., B. Drummond. "Whitman, in California, Fields the Vice Presidency Question." *New York Times*, April 30, 1995, late edition, 37. Lexis Nexis Academic Universe (accessed October 29, 1999).

———. "Women to the Rescue of Elizabeth Dole." *New York Times*, July 22, 1999. Lexis Nexis Academic Universe (accessed October 29, 1999).

Back, Melinda. "The Voice of the Victims." *Newsweek* (January 23, 1995): 48.

Baer, Susan. "Elizabeth Dole is Turning Heads: Politicians Wonder Whether She Can Turn Votes." *Times-Picayune*, October 10, 1996. Lexis Nexis Academic Universe (accessed September 4, 2000).

Baggett, Donnis. "Splitting Hairs over Guv's Do." *Dallas Morning News*, August 15, 1993.

Baird, Lisa. "Christie's Clueless." *The Record*, November 19, 1993, C01. Lexis Nexis Academic Universe (accessed August 20, 1999).

Balz, Dan. "Hoping to be 'Part of History.'" *Washington Post*, July 15, 1999. Lexis Nexis Academic Universe (accessed October 29, 1999).

Barone, Michael. "Bad News for Boomer Liberals." *U.S. News & World Report* (August 29, 1994): 32. Expanded Academic ASAP (accessed October 27, 1995).

———. "Entering the Combat Zone." *U.S. News & World Report* (March 30, 1992): 39. Expanded Academic ASAP (accessed October 29, 1995).

Barta, Carolyn. "Rating Gov. Richards." *Dallas Morning News*, February 17, 1992.

Beasley, Maureen. *Eleanor Roosevelt and the Media: A Public Quest for Self-Fulfillment*. Urbana: University of Illinois Press, 1987.

Beggy, Carol and Mark Shanahan. "Richards Dishes Humor; Kerry Charged with an Error." *The Boston Globe*, July 13, 2004. <www.bostonglobe.com> (accessed August 6, 2004).

Belkin, Lisa. "Keeping to the Center Lane." *New York Times*, May 5, 1996, late edition, 50. Lexis Nexis Academic Universe (accessed August 20, 1999).

Bengtson, M. A. "Campaign 94: Richards Deserves Votes." *Houston Chronicle*, November 7, 1994, C17. Lexis Nexis Academic Universe (accessed April 28, 1999).

Bentley, Max. "'I'll Be Governor, Not Jim,' Says Ma Ferguson." *Collier's* (September 27, 1924): 12.

Berke, Richard L. "Echoes Aside, Dole Insists She Is No Clinton." *New York Times*, April 8, 2002. Lexis Nexis Academic Universe (accessed August 16, 2002).

———. "Eye on 2000: Elizabeth Dole Talks of Race for President." *New York Times*, February 9, 1999. Lexis Nexis Academic Universe (accessed October 29, 1999).

"Biography of Governor Christine Todd Whitman." <http://www.state.nj.us/governor/bio.html> (accessed July 29, 1999).

Blankenship, Jane and Deborah Robson. "A 'Feminine Style' in Women's Political Discourse: An Exploratory Essay." *Communication Quarterly* 43 (1995): 353–66.

Blood, Michael R. "She's Carpetbagger, Sez Rudy in Fund Drive." *New York Daily News*, June 4, 1999. <www.nydailynews.com> (accessed February 9, 2000).

Blumenfeld, Laura. "And One of Them Shall Be First: Elizabeth Dole and Hillary Clinton Offer Conflicting Visions." *Washington Post*, April 8–14, 1996, national weekly edition, 6.

Bond, Rich. "Why GOP Should Still Embrace Foes Of Abortion Bans." *The Record*, February 16, 1998, A21. Lexis Nexis Academic Universe (accessed October 11, 1999).

Bostdorff, Denise M. "Hillary Rodham Clinton and Elizabeth Dole as Running 'Mates' in the 1996 Campaign: Parallels in the Rhetorical Constraints of First Ladies and Vice Presidents." Pp. 199–228 in *The 1996 Campaign: A Communication Perspective*, edited by Robert E. Denton. Westport, Conn.: Praeger, 1998.

Braden, Maria. *Women Politicians and the Media*. Lexington: University Press of Kentucky, 1996.

Bradley, Patricia Hayes. "The Folk-Linguistics of Women's Speech: An Empirical Examination." *Communication Monographs* 48 (1981): 73–90.

Breslau, Karen. "Hillary's Next Life." *Newsweek* (July 20, 1998). Lexis Nexis Academic Universe (accessed November 21, 1999).

Bridges, A. and H. Hartman. "Pedagogy by the Oppressed." *Review of Radical Political Economics* 6 (Winter 1975): 75–79.

Brock, David. *The Seduction of Hillary Rodham*. New York: Free Press, 1996.

Broder, David S. "In N.C. Endorsement Race, it's Dean Vs. Coach K." *Washington Post*, September 29, 2002. Lexis Nexis Academic Universe (accessed November 14, 2002).

Brodie, Ian. "Lone Star Governor Struggles to Uproot the Shrub." *The Times*, October 20, 1994. Lexis Nexis Academic Universe (accessed April 28, 1999).

Brotman, Barbara. "Courting Votes." *Chicago Tribune*, November 3, 1999, 2.

———. "1995: One Step Forward, One Back; The Year of Any Woman Brought Out the Best in Us—and the Worst." *Chicago Tribune*, December 31, 1995, C1. Lexis Nexis Academic Universe (accessed February 2, 1996).

Brown, Patricia Leigh. "Hillary Clinton Inaugurates Preservation Campaign." *New York Times*, July 14, 1998, A12. Lexis Nexis Academic Universe (accessed November 21, 1999).

Brownstein, Ronald. "Hillary Clinton Needs to Be a Woman of Substance in a Race Big on Style." *Los Angeles Times*, March 27, 2000. <www.latimes.com> (March 27, 2000).

Bruck, Connie. "Hillary the Pol." *The New Yorker* (May 30, 1994): 90.

Bumiller, Elisabeth. "The Election: It Took a Woman; How Gender Helped Elect Hillary Clinton." *New York Times*, November 12, 2000. Lexis Nexis Academic Universe (accessed December 28, 2000).

———. "Running Against Hillary." *New York Times*, October 13, 1996, late edition. Lexis Nexis Academic Universe (accessed September 4, 2000).

Burka, Paul. "Ann of a Hundred Days." *Texas Monthly* (May 1991): 126–30.

Burke, Kenneth. *Attitudes Toward History*. 3d ed. Berkeley: University of California Press, 1984.

———. *Language as Symbolic Action: Essays on Life, Literature, and Method*. Berkeley and Los Angeles: University of California Press, 1968.

Burnham, Alexander. "Governor Grasso's Troubles." *The Progressive* (January 1978): 36.

———. "The Testing of Ella Grasso." *The Progressive* (April 1976): 34.

Bush, Barbara. *A Memoir*. New York: St. Martin's, 1994.

"Bush-bashing Texans to Preside." *San Antonio Light*, July 12, 1992.

Bynum, Chris. "Defining the B-Word; Hillary Clinton Isn't the Only Woman in Authority Who Is Dogged by a Particular Label. The Question Is, What Does it Mean?" *Times-Picayune*, January 17, 1995, F1. Lexis Nexis Academic Universe (accessed February 2, 1996).

Campbell, David. *Writing Security: United States Foreign Policy and the Politics of Identity*. Minneapolis: University of Minnesota Press, 1992.

Campbell, Karlyn Kohrs. "The Discursive Performance of Femininity: Hating Hillary." *Rhetoric & Public Affairs* 1 (1998): 1–19.

———. *Man Cannot Speak for Her*. vol. 1. New York: Greenwood Press, 1989.

———. "The Rhetoric of Women's Liberation: An Oxymoron." *Quarterly Journal of Speech* 59 (1973): 74–86.

———. "'The Rhetoric of Women's Liberation: An Oxymoron' Revisited." *Communication Studies* 50 (1999): 138–42.

———. "The Rhetorical Presidency: A Two-Person Career." Pp. 179–95 in *Beyond the Rhetorical Presidency*, edited by Martin J. Medhurst. College Station: Texas A & M University Press, 1996.

———. "Shadowboxing with Stereotypes: The Press, the Public, and the Candidates' Wives." Research paper R–9. President and Fellows of Harvard College, 1993.

———. "The Sound of Women's Voices." *Quarterly Journal of Speech* 75 (1989): 212–20.

———, editor. *Women Public Speakers in the United States: A Bio-Critical Sourcebook*, 2 vols. Westport, Conn.: Greenwood Press, 1994.

Cantor, Dorothy W. and Toni Bernay. *Women in Power: The Secrets of Leadership*. Boston: Houghton Mifflin, 1992.

Carlson, Margaret. "All Eyes on Hillary." *Time* (September 14, 1992). Expanded Academic ASAP (accessed October 27, 1995).

———. "The Dynamic Duo." *Time* (January 4, 1993): 38–41.

———. "Hillary Clinton: Partner as Much as Wife." *Time* (January 27, 1992): 19. Expanded Academic ASAP (accessed October 29, 1995).

———. "Muzzle the *B* Word." *Time* (January 16, 1995): 36.

Caroli, Betty Boyd. *First Ladies.* Expanded edition. New York: Oxford University Press, 1995.

Carroll, Susan J. *Women as Candidates in American Politics.* Bloomington: Indiana University Press, 1994.

"Christie Whitman for New Jersey." Editorial. *New York Daily News,* October 27, 1997, 36. Lexis Nexis Academic Universe (accessed September 15, 1999).

"Christine Todd Whitman." AP Candidate Bios. *The Associated Press Political Service.* Lexis Nexis Academic Universe (accessed August 29, 1999).

"Christine Whitman for Governor." *New York Times,* October 27, 1997, A22. Lexis Nexis Academic Universe (accessed September 15, 1999).

"Christine Whitman Seen as Vice Presidential Material." *Chicago Tribune,* January 25, 1995, evening update edition, 2. Lexis Nexis Academic Universe (accessed August 20, 1999).

Chu, Daniel with William J. Cook. "Governors: Whistling Dixy." *Newsweek* (October 4, 1976): 47.

Clinton, Hillary Rodham. Address to the American Hospital Association. Orlando, Fla., August 9, 1993. Office of the Press Secretary, The White House.

———. Address to the American Legion's Annual Conference. Sheraton Washington Hotel. Washington, D.C., February 15, 1994. Office of the Press Secretary, The White House.

———. Address to the Annual Meeting of the World Economic Forum. Davos, Switzerland, February 2, 1998. Office of the Press Secretary, The White House.

———. Address to the Central Asian Conference on Women in Politics. Almaty, Kazakhstan, November 12, 1997. Office of the Press Secretary, The White House.

———. Address at the Democratic National Convention. Chicago, Ill., August 27, 1996. Office of the Press Secretary, The White House.

———. Address to the Health Care Forum. Denver, Colo., March 14, 1994. Office of the Press Secretary, The White House.

———. Address to the Institute of Medicine Annual Meeting. Washington, D.C., October 19, 1993. Office of the Press Secretary, The White House.

———. Address for International Women's Day. The State Department. Washington, D.C., March 12, 1997. Office of the Press Secretary, The White House.

———. Address at the Kate Mullany House. Troy, N.Y., July 15, 1998. Office of the Press Secretary, The White House.

———. Address at Marshall University. Huntington, W.Va., November 4, 1993. Office of the Press Secretary, The White House.

———. Address to the National Institutes of Health. February 17, 1994. Office of the Press Secretary, The White House.

———. Address at the 150th Anniversary of the First Woman's Rights Convention. Seneca Falls, N.Y., July 16, 1998. Office of the Press Secretary, The White House.

———. Address at Radio Free Europe. Prague, The Czech Republic, July 4, 1996. Office of the Press Secretary, The White House.

———. Address to the Rajiv Gandhi Foundation. New Delhi, India, March 29, 1995. Office of the Press Secretary, The White House.

———. Address to the United Auto Workers. Sheraton Washington Hotel. Washington, D.C., March 22, 1994. Office of the Press Secretary, The White House.

———. Address to the United Nations Fourth World Conference on Women. Beijing, China, September 5, 1995. *WIN News*, August 1995. Expanded Academic Index (accessed February 6, 1996).

———. Address at the University of Capetown. Capetown, South Africa, March 20, 1997. Office of the Press Secretary, The White House.

———. Address to the Women's Leadership Forum. April 18, 1997. Office of the Press Secretary, The White House.

———. "Health Care: We Can Make a Difference." *Vital Speeches of the Day* 59 (July 15, 1993): 580–85.

———. "Hillary's Announcement Speech Purchase College (SUNY)." February 7, 2000. <hillary2000.org> (accessed December 28, 2000). Also available from the *New York Times*, February 7, 2000, <nytimes.com> (accessed February 8, 2000).

———. *It Takes a Village and Other Lessons Children Teach Us*. New York: Simon & Schuster, 1996.

———. Remarks by the First Lady to the Women of Australia. Sydney, Australia, November 21, 1996. Office of the Press Secretary, The White House.

———. Townhall Meeting in Minneapolis, Minn., September 17, 1993.

Clinton, William J., Hillary Rodham Clinton, Al Gore, Tipper Gore, and C. Everett Koop. Address to Physicians and Supporters. East Room of the White House. Washington, D.C., September 20, 1993. Office of the Press Secretary, The White House.

Clinton, William J., Al Gore, Hillary Rodham Clinton, and Tipper Gore. Address at a Health Care Rally. South Lawn of the White House. Washington, D.C., September 23, 1993. Office of the Press Secretary, The White House.

Cohen, Richard. "A Dole Moment in Manhattan." *Washington Post*, May 11, 1999. Lexis Nexis Academic Universe (accessed September 15, 1999).

Compton, Ann. "Moving Day." *abcnews.com*, January 4, 2000. <abcnews.go.com> (accessed January 4, 2000).

———. "She Speaks for Herself." *abcnews.com*, July 9, 1999. <abcnews.go.com> (accessed November 17, 1999).

Conley, Kanestra. "La. Women Encouraged to Run for Office." *Baton Rouge Morning Advocate*, September 21, 1991.

"Connecticut's Favorite Daughter: Ella T. Grasso, 1919–1981." *Time* (February 16, 1981): 20.

Cook, Alison. "Lone Star." *New York Times*, February 7, 1993, late edition, 22. Lexis Nexis Academic Universe (accessed April 28, 1999).

Cooper, Matthew. "Hillary Clinton Goes to War." *Newsweek* (February 2, 1998): 24.

———. "The Hillary Factor." *U.S. News & World Report* (April 27, 1992): 37.

Cooper, Matthew and Karen Breslau. "For Better and for Worse." *Newsweek* (February 9, 1999): 41.

Copelin, Laylan. "Gender Issue Cutting in on Williams–Richards Political Dance." *Austin American-Statesman*, April 15, 1990.

———. "It's Governor Richards." *Austin American-Statesman*, November 7, 1990.

———. "A New Texas Tally." *Austin American-Statesman*, July 14, 1991, A1+.

———. "Richards: 'The Doors are Open.'" *Austin American-Statesman*, November 8, 1990, A1+.

———. "Richards Lashes Out in Address." *Austin American-Statesman*, February 7, 1991, A1.

———. "Richards Sharpens Humor at Expense of Men, Hunting." *Austin American-Statesman*, May 8, 1992, A1+.

Copelin, Laylan and Dave McNeely. "Governor-elect's Inner Circle Believes in Inclusion, Diversity." *Austin American-Statesman*, December 9, 1990, final edition, A1+.

Cornwell, Rupert. "US Mid-term Elections: Bush Boy Has Good Ol' Girl from Texas in His Sights." *The Independent*, October 29, 1994, 9. Lexis Nexis Academic Universe (accessed April 28, 1999).

Costrich, Norma, Joan Feinstein, Louise Kidder, Jeanne Marecek, and Linda Pascale. "When Stereotypes Hurt: Three Studies of Penalties for Sex-Role Reversals." *Journal of Experimental Social Psychology* 11 (1975): 520–30.

Cullar, Meg. "Ann Richards Waco Native Texas Governor." *Discover* (January 1992).

Curtis, Gregory. "Ann Richards, Fresh Out of Answers." *Star Tribune*, February 8, 1995, 14A. Lexis Nexis Academic Universe (accessed April 28, 1999).

"Cynthia Jeanne Shaheen." AP Candidate Bios. *The Associated Press Political Service*. November 7, 1996. Lexis Nexis Academic Universe (accessed October 20, 1998).

Damico, Dana. "Critics Say Big Money Favors Dole, Bowles." *Reidsville Review* (April 17, 2002). Lexis Nexis Academic Universe (accessed August 16, 2002).

Daughton, Suzanne. "Women's Issues, Women's Place: Gender–Related Problems in Presidential Campaigns." *Communication Quarterly* 42 (1994): 106–19.

Davidson, Bruce. "New Governor Pledges Return of Government for the People." *Express News*, January 16, 1991, 1A.

Debenport, Ellen. "Careful Packaging is Turning Viewers Off." *St. Petersburg Times*, August 15, 1996. Lexis Nexis Academic Universe (accessed September 4, 2000).

"Defeat for Dixy Lee Ray." *Time* (September 29, 1980): 25.

"Defining Richards' Place in History: Governor's Mansion is Next Target." *Austin American-Statesman*, January 15, 1990, 2.

Devitt, James. *Framing Gender on the Campaign Trail: Women's Executive Leadership and the Press*. Women's Leadership Fund, 1999. <http://www.appcpenn.org/political/archive/wlfstudy.pdf>.

DeWitt, Karen. "The 104th Congress; The Speaker's Mother; Quick Indignation After CBS Interview." *New York Times*, January 5, 1995, late edition, A23. Lexis Nexis Academic Universe (accessed February 2, 1996).

"Dixy Lee Ray, Former Head of U.S. Atomic Agency, Dies." *Los Angeles Times*, January 3, 1994, A3.

"Dixy Rocks the Northwest." *Time* (December 12, 1977): 31.

Doan, Michael and Michael Bosc. "Kay Orr and Helen Boosalis: Woman Power on the Prairie." *U.S. News & World Report* (May 26, 1986): 8.

Dobbin, Muriel. "Richards Takes off Gloves in Texas Fight." *Sacramento Bee*, September 18, 1994, metro edition, A3. Lexis Nexis Academic Universe (accessed April 28, 1999).

———. "Texas Leader Blends Charm, Intimidation." *Sacramento Bee*, May 9, 1994, A1. Lexis Nexis Academic Universe (accessed April 28, 1999).

Dole, Elizabeth. "Dear Friends." <www.elizabethdole.org> (accessed November 5, 2002).

———. "Elizabeth Dole Primary Remarks." September 10, 2002. Salisbury, N.C. <www.elizabethdole.org> (accessed October 29, 2002).

———. "Remarks at the Women for Dole Press Conference." September 23, 2002. Greensboro, N.C. <www.elizabethdole.org> (accessed October 29, 2002).

———. "This is a Defining Moment in Our Nation's History: Speech to the 1996 Republican National Convention." Transcript reprinted by the *New York Times*, August 15, 1996. Also available *Gifts of Speech*. <http://gos.sbc.edu/d/dole.html> (accessed November 4, 2002).

"Dole Drops Out." *abcnews.com*, October 20, 1999. <abcnews.com> (accessed October 20, 1999).

"Dole Has a Campaigner As Skilled As Clinton—Mrs. Dole." *Dow Jones News Retrieval* (accessed May 29, 1996).

"Dole Receives Business Group Endorsement." *Associated Press State & Local Wire*, March 20, 2002. Lexis Nexis Academic Universe (accessed August 16, 2002).

"Dole's Bold Gamble." *Newsweek* (August 19, 1996): 3.

Donlan, Barbara. "'B' Word Still Hangs in the Air Like a Bad Vapor." *Boston Herald*, January 22, 1995, second edition, 49. Lexis Nexis Academic Universe (accessed February 2, 1996).

Douglas, Susan J. *Where the Girls Are: Growing Up Female with the Mass Media*. New York: Random House, 1994.

Dow, Bonnie J. *Prime-Time Feminism: Television, Media Culture, and the Women's Movement Since 1970*. Philadelphia: University of Pennsylvania Press, 1996.

Dow, Bonnie J. and Mari Boor Tonn. "'Feminine Style' and Political Judgment in the Rhetoric of Ann Richards." *The Quarterly Journal of Speech* 79 (1993): 286–302.

Dowd, Maureen. "The Alpha-Beta Macarena." *New York Times*, November 3, 1999. Lexis Nexis Academic Universe (accessed August 1, 2002).

———. "The 'I Love Hillary' Show." *Denver Post*, September 9, 1999. Lexis Nexis Academic Universe (accessed December 29, 2000).

———. "A Man and a Woman." *New York Times*, September 20, 2000. <www.nytimes.com> (accessed October 10, 2000).

Downey, Maureen. "It Rhymes with Gingrich: Remark by Mother of the House Speaker Sparks Debate on Use of 'Bitch' to Describe Women with Power." *Atlanta Journal and Constitution*, January 5, 1995, D1. Lexis Nexis Academic Universe (accessed February 2, 1996).

Dube, Jonathan. "Bush Charms the Ladies." *abcnews.com*, October 15, 1999. <abcnews.com> (accessed October 19, 1999).

———. "Republican Women Rally Behind Dole." *abcnews.com*, October 18, 1999. <abcnews.com> (accessed October 19, 1999).

Duke, Lynne and William Claiborne. "12 Puerto Ricans Accept Clemency." *Washington Post*, September 8, 1999. Lexis Nexis Academic Universe (accessed December 29, 2000).

Dyer, Eric. "Snyder Begins Race for Helms' Seat with Jab at Dole." *News & Record*, March 1, 2002. Lexis Nexis Academic Universe (accessed August 16, 2002).

Edelman, Murray. *Constructing the Political Spectacle*. Chicago: University of Chicago Press, 1988.

Edelman, Rita. "Chef of State; Governor Whitman Takes to the Grill for Labor Day." *The Record*, August 27, 1997, F01. Lexis Nexis Academic Universe (accessed September 14, 1999).

Edwards, Bob. "Critics Question Treatment of Women Within U.N." *National Public Radio*, September 4, 1995. Lexis Nexis Academic Universe (accessed February 6, 1996).

Ehrenreich, Barbara. "The Week Feminists Got Laryngitis." *Time* (February 9, 1998): 68. Lexis Nexis Academic Universe (accessed February 9, 1998).

"Elizabeth Dole Exiles Mate to Woodshed." *New York Times*, May 19, 1999. Lexis Nexis Academic Universe (accessed October 29, 1999).

"Elizabeth Dole Launches Run for U.S. Senate Seat Being Vacated by Jesse Helms." *Morning Edition*, February 25, 2002. Lexis Nexis Academic Universe (accessed August 16, 2002).

"Elizabeth Dole: Mill." campaign ad. <http://www.elizabethdole.org/multimedia.asp> (accessed December 1, 2002).

"Elizabeth Dole Wins N.C. Seat." *msnbc.com*, November 5, 2002. <msnbc.com> (accessed November 5, 2002).

"Elizabeth Dole's Race for the Senate Seat of North Carolina and Her Battles to Get There." *Today*, September 26, 2002. Lexis Nexis Academic Universe (accessed October 1, 2002).

Elliott, David. "Will Richards' 'New Texas' Last 4 More Years?" *Austin American-Statesman*, September 4, 1993, A1+.

Elshtain, Jean Bethke. *Real Politics at the Center of Everyday Life*. Baltimore, Md.: Johns Hopkins University Press, 1997.

Emery, Noemie. "The Androgyny Party." *Commentary* 95 (1993): 49. Expanded Academic ASAP (accessed February 2, 1996).

Enstam, Elizabeth York. "Where Do We Go From Here?" Pp. 177–82 in *Women and Texas History: Selected Essays*, edited by Fane Downs and Nancy Baker Jones. Austin: Texas State Historical Association, 1993.

Eskenazi, Stuart and Ralph Barrera. "Richards Embraces Future Full of Change in Farewell." *Austin American-Statesman*, December 23, 1994. Lexis Nexis Academic Universe (accessed July 9, 2002).

Feldman, Claudia. "Campaign Widens Gender Gap." *Houston Chronicle*, September 9, 1990, 7G.

Field, Robert M. "Will 'Ma' Ferguson Be Impeached?" *The Outlook* (December 9, 1925): 554.

Fields, Suzanne. "Christy Whitman Just Happens to be a Woman." *The Times Union*, January 30, 1995, three star edition, A7. Lexis Nexis Academic Universe (accessed September 14, 1999).

Fields, Walter. "It's Very Doubtful Whitman is Up to Task." *The Record*, November 8, 1993, A17. Lexis Nexis Academic Universe (accessed August 20, 1999).

Fineman, Howard. "A Crisis at Home." *Newsweek* (December 21, 1998): 22+. Lexis Nexis Academic Universe (accessed August 20, 1999).

———. "How Bush Did It." *Newsweek* (November 18, 2002). Lexis Nexis Academic Universe (accessed November 29, 2002).

———. "The Kosovo Primary." *Newsweek* (April 26, 1999): 32. Lexis Nexis Academic Universe (accessed January 7, 2001).

———. "The Potholes of New York." *Newsweek* (May 31, 1999): 31.

"The First Debate: Clinton vs. Lazio." *MSNBC*, September 13, 2000.

"The First Family in Full Battle Regalia." *Nightline*, January 27, 1998. Lexis Nexis Academic Universe (accessed February 9, 1998).

The First Lady's Treasures Tour. <http://www.whitehouse.gov/WH/EOP/First_Lady/ html/treasures/index.html> (accessed November 21, 1999).

Fisher, Marc. "'Speaking About the Man I Love,' Elizabeth Dole Takes Talk-Show Theatrics To Convention Floor." *Washington Post*, August 15, 1996. Lexis Nexis Academic Universe (accessed September 4, 2000).

Fisher, Walter R. "Narration as a Human Communication Paradigm: The Case of Public Moral Argument." *Communication Monographs* 51 (1984): 1–22.

Fiske, John. "British Cultural Studies and Television." Pp. 284–326 in *Channels of Discourse Reassembled: Television and Contemporary Criticism*. 2d ed. edited by Robert C. Allen. Chapel Hill: University of North Carolina Press, 1992.

Fitzgerald, Thomas J. "She's Ready for the Democrats." *The Record*, June 4, 1997, A01. Lexis Nexis Academic Universe (accessed September 15, 1999).

———. "Whitman Steals Show at Governors Meeting." *The Record*, January 31, 1995, A01. Lexis Nexis Academic Universe (accessed September 14, 1999).

Fleck, Tim. "Play It Again, Ann." *Houston Press*, December 26, 1991, 4.

Fletcher, Martin. "Elizabeth Leaves Them Wondering if They've Chosen the Right Dole." *The Times*, August 16, 1996. Lexis Nexis Academic Universe (accessed September 4, 2000).

Foote, Jennifer. "Arizona's 'Rosie' New Boss." *Newsweek* (February 22, 1988): 27.

Fox-Genovese, Elizabeth. "Texas Women and the Writing of Women's History." Pp. 3–14 in *Women and Texas History: Selected Essays*, edited by Fane Downs and Nancy Baker Jones. Austin: Texas State Historical Association, 1993.

Frady, Marshall. "Governor and Mister Wallace." *The Atlantic Monthly* (August 1967): 35–37.

Frank, Reuven. "Celebrity Journalism on Television." *The New Leader*, January 30, 1995. Lexis Nexis Academic Universe (accessed February 2, 1996).

Freeman, Jeanne. "She's Tough, Sharp and Pure Texas." *San Diego Union Tribune*, April 17, 1992, D1. Lexis Nexis Academic Universe (accessed April 28, 1999).

Freivogel, Margaret Wolf. "Texas Shootout: Old West Comes Alive in Texas Governor's Race." *St. Louis Post-Dispatch*, September 23, 1990, five star edition, 1B. Lexis Nexis Academic Universe (accessed April 28, 1999).

Friedman, H. S., T. I. Mertz, and M. R. DiMatteo. "Perceived Bias in the Facial Expressions of Television News Broadcasters." *Journal of Communication* 30 (1980): 103–11.

Fuentes, Diana R. "Demos Applaud Governor's View of Texas' Future." *Express News*, February 7, 1991.

———. "Richards to Reach 100-Day Milestone." *Express News*, April 21, 1991, 1A+.

Gamboa, Suzanne. "The Buzz on Richards' Big Hair: It Could Go." *Austin American-Statesman*, June 17, 1993, A1.

Garcia, Guillermo X. "Richards Blazes Her Own Trail to Mansion." *Austin American-Statesman*, November 7, 1990.

———. "Richards' Inaugural to Feature Common Touch." *Austin American-Statesman*, December 17, 1990, A1.

Gatta, John. *American Madonna: Image of the Divine Woman in Literary Culture*. New York: Oxford University Press, 1997.

"Gender Gap in Government," <http://www.gendergap.com/governme.htm #STATE%20GOVERNMENT> (accessed July 21, 2004).

Gibbs, Nancy and Michael Duffy. "Just Heartbeats Away." *Time* (July 1, 1996): 25.

Gibson, David. "Whitman Stops Bus in Morris to Thank Supporters." *The Record*, November 4, 1993, A21. Lexis Nexis Academic Universe (accessed August 20, 1999).

Gilligan, Carol. *In a Different Voice: Psychological Theory and Women's Development*. Cambridge, Mass.: Harvard University Press, 1982.

"Gingrich Cries Foul Over Mom's Whisper." *Sacramento Bee*, January 5, 1995, A1. Lexis Nexis Academic Universe (accessed February 2, 1996).

Givhan, Robin. "One Small Step for Womankind; Elizabeth Dole's Candidacy Became Merely the Symbol She Avoided." *Washington Post*, October 21, 1999. Lexis Nexis Academic Universe (accessed October 29, 1999).

Gonzalez, John. "Get Out, Richards Tells 2 on Insurance Board." *Fort Worth Star Telegram*, February 7, 1991.

Goodman, Ellen. "Post-gender Politics and Cautionary Tales; Women Candidates are in a Double Bind. But Some Manage to Wriggle Free." Editorial. *Pittsburgh Post Gazette*, November 13, 2002, A17. Lexis Nexis Academic Universe (accessed December 12, 2002).

"The Governor-Elect Moves to Take Charge." *The Record*, November 4, 1993, B06. Lexis Nexis Academic Universe (accessed August 20, 1999).

"The Governor Lady Finds that in the East as in the West Americans Are 'Mine Own People.'" *Good Housekeeping* (July 1928): 67.

"Governor's Appointments." Chart. *Dallas Morning News*, April 1991, 21.

"Grasso: Piedmont Spoken Here." *Time* (November 18, 1974): 10.

Graves, Debbie. "Richards' 'Star Quality' to Light Up Convention." *Austin American-Statesman*, July 12, 1992.

Gray, Jerry. "For Whitman, A Political Star Adding Luster." *New York Times*, January 9, 1995, late edition, B1. Lexis Nexis Academic Universe (accessed August 19, 1999).

———. "The 1993 Elections: Giulliani Ousts Dinkins by a Thin Margin; Whitman is an Upset Winner over Florio; New Jersey Anger Over Taxes Propels Challenger." *New York Times*, November 3, 1993, late edition, A1. Lexis Nexis Academic Universe (accessed August 20, 1999).

———. "Star Over Trenton." *New York Times*, January 28, 1996, late edition, 33. Lexis Nexis Academic Universe (accessed September 15, 1999).

————. "Whitman Pursues 'Family Business.'" *New York Times*, June 9, 1993, late edition, B4. Lexis Nexis Academic Universe (accessed August 20, 1999).

Greer, Germaine. "Abolish Her: The Feminist Case Against First Ladies." *New Republic* (June 26, 1995): 20. Expanded Academic ASAP (accessed October 27, 1995).

Gross, Beverly. "Bitch." *Salmagundi* (Summer 1994): 146. Expanded Academic ASAP (accessed February 2, 1996).

"Group: Richards No Leader." *San Antonio Express*, June 27, 1991.

"A Grumpy Greeting for a Trenton Outsider." *The Record*, November 5, 1993, B18. Lexis Nexis Academic Universe (accessed August 20, 1999).

Grunwald, Michael. "Hope, Thy Name is Hillary, in One Hurting N.Y. Mill Town." *Washington Post*, March 3, 1999. <washingtonpost.com> (accessed March 4, 1999).

Gruson, Lindsey. "A Familiar Role for Acting Governor." *New York Times*, February 7, 1988, late city final edition, 26.

Hacker, K. L. *Candidate Images in Presidential Elections.* Westport, Conn.: Praeger, 1995.

Hahn, Dan F. "The Marriage Metaphor in Politics." *Political Communication: Rhetoric, Government, and Citizens.* 2d ed. State College, Penn.: Strata Publishing, 2003.

Hailey, Mike. "Richards 'Likely' to Run for Governor." *Austin American-Statesman* September 14, 1987.

————. "To Tax or Not is the Question." *Houston Post*, September 9, 1990, A1.

————. "Williams, Richards Fuss Over Newest Negative Ad." *Houston Post*, September 11, 1990, A13.

Halbfinger, David M. "Passion For Politics and the Outdoors." *New York Times*, December 23, 2000, late edition, A15. Lexis Nexis Academic Universe (accessed June 26, 2002).

Hallstein, D. Lynn O'Brien. "Feminist Assessment of Emancipatory Potential and Madonna's Contradictory Gender Practices." *Quarterly Journal of Speech* 82 (1996): 125–41.

Hamilton, Arnold. "Poll Finds Many Joined Richards Fold Only Recently." *Dallas Morning News*, November 7, 1990.

Hariman, Robert. *Political Style: The Artistry of Power.* Chicago: University of Chicago Press, 1995.

Harris, John F. and Lynne Duke. "First Lady Gets a N.Y. Makeover." *Washington Post*, March 13, 2000, A1. <washingtonpost.com> (accessed March 13, 2000).

Harrison, Eric. "Richards Stirs Up Texas Government; Politics: The Democratic Governor's Style, Choice of Appointees Have Taken Austin by Storm, But She Has Critics on Both Sides of Spectrum." *Los Angeles Times*, August 25, 1991, home edition, 4.

Harrison, T. M., T. D. Stephen, W. Husson, and B. J. Fehr. "Image Versus Issues in the 1984 Presidential Election." *Human Communication Research* 18 (1991): 209–27.

Hasson, Judi. "Elizabeth Dole Soars in Poll." *USA Today*, August 20, 1996. Lexis Nexis Academic Universe (accessed September 4, 2000).

Heilman, Madeline E. and Melanie H. Stopeck. "Attractiveness and Corporate Success: Different Causal Attributes for Males and Females." *Journal of Applied Psychology* 70 (1985): 379–88.

Heldman, Caroline, Susan J. Carroll, and Stephanie Olson. "Gender Differences in Print Media Coverage of Presidential Candidates: Elizabeth Dole's Bid for the Republican Nomination." Paper presented at the annual Meeting of the American Political Science Association, Washington, D.C., August 31–September 3, 2000. <www.rci.rutgers.edu/~cawp/> (accessed December 31, 2000).

Hellweg, S. A. "An Examination of Voter Conceptualization of the Ideal Political Candidate." *Southern Speech Communication Journal* 44 (1979): 373–85.

Hendrie, Paul J. "Campaign's Bottom Line: The Bottom Line; Tax Issue Lifted Whitman and Doomed Florio." *The Record*, November 4, 1993, A20. Lexis Nexis Academic Universe (accessed August 20, 1999).

Henry, John C. "'It's Official' Richards Will Give Keynote." *Austin American-Statesman*, June 28, 1988.

Herman, Ken. "The First 100 Days." *Houston Post*, April 21, 1991, A1+.

———. "Richards Even with Williams in Gubernatorial Race, Pollster Says." *Houston Post*, October 26, 1990, A13.

———. "Shake Hands with Governor Richards." *Houston Post*, November 7, 1990, A1.

———. "30,000 Watch Richards Take Oath of Office." *Houston Post*, January 16, 1991, A1.

Herszenhorn, David M. "On Eve of Four-Day Tour, Hillary Clinton Makes It Official." *New York Times*, July 7, 1999. <nytimes.com> (accessed July 9, 1999).

Hight, Bruce. "High on the Hog, Richards Promotes Motorcycle Safety." *Austin American-Statesman*, May 16, 1992.

———. "Richards Talks Across New York." *Austin American-Statesman*, July 13, 1992, A1+.

"Hillary Clinton In or Out?" *This Week*, November 28, 1999. <abcnews.go.com> (accessed December 2, 1999).

"Hillary Clinton Leading Defense of Her Husband, Denying All Charges against Him." *NBC Nightly News*, January 27, 1998. Lexis Nexis Academic Universe (accessed February 9, 1998).

"Hillary Clinton Q & A." *abcnews.com*, February 8, 2000. <abcnews.go.com> (accessed February 9, 2000).

"Hillary Clinton Stands By Husband." *MSNBC*, <msnbc.com> (accessed February 10, 1998).

"Hillary Makes it Official." *abcnews.com*, February 7, 2000. <abcnews.go.com> (accessed February 7, 2000).

"Hillary Rodham Clinton's Job." Editorial. *New York Times*, January 27, 1993, A22. (accessed September 15, 1999).

Hinck, Edward A. and Shelly S. Hinck. "Politeness Strategies in the 1992 Vice Presidential and Presidential Debates." *Argumentation & Advocacy* 38 (2002): 234–50.

Hollihan, Thomas A. "Nurturing Political Images." Pp. 55–72 in *Uncivil Wars: Political Campaigns in a Media Age.* Boston, Mass.: Bedford/St. Martin's, 2001.

Hurley, Deborah. "The Whisper Heard 'Round the World.'" *The Quill* 83 (1995): 13. Expanded Academic ASAP (accessed February 2, 1996).

Husson, W., T. Stephen, T. M. Harrison, and B. J. Fehr. "An Interpersonal Communication Perspective on Images of Political Candidates." *Human Communication Research* 14 (1988): 397–421.

Hutchings, Graham. "Hard-Hitting Hillary Savages Beijing; Mrs. Clinton Strikes Blow for Women Worldwide." *The Daily Telegraph*, September 6, 1995. Lexis Nexis Academic Universe (accessed February 6, 1996).

Iker, Sam. "Changes in Dixyland." *Time* (November 5, 1973): 98.

"In the First Big Test of the Negro Vote." *U.S. News & World Report* (May 16, 1966): 39.

"Interview with Elizabeth Dole." *CNN Evans, Novak, Hunt, & Shields*, August 10, 2002. Lexis Nexis Academic Universe (accessed August 16, 2002).

"Interview with Elizabeth Dole." *CNN Wolf Blitzer Reports*, February 28, 2002. Lexis Nexis Academic Universe (accessed August 16, 2002).

"Interview with Hillary Rodham Clinton." *Today*, NBC. January 27, 1998.

"Is Pa or Ma Governor of Texas?" *The Literary Digest* (April 11, 1925): 15.

Ivie, Robert L. "Cold War Motives and the Rhetorical Metaphor: A Framework of Criticism." Pp. 71–79 in *Cold War Rhetoric: Strategy, Metaphor, and Ideology*, edited by Martin J. Medhurst, Robert L. Ivie, Philip Wander, and Robert L. Scott. New York: Greenwood Press, 1990.

———. Editorial Statements. *Quarterly Journal of Speech* 79 (1993) – 81 (1995).

———. "Metaphor and the Rhetorical Invention of Cold War 'Idealists.'" *Communication Monographs* 54 (1987): 165–82.

———. "Presidential Motives for War." *The Quarterly Journal of Speech* 60 (1974): 337–45.

Ivins, Molly. "A Texas Treasure." *Ms* (October 1988): 26.

Iyengar, Shanto, Nicholas A. Valentino, Stephen Ansolabehere, and Adam F. Simon. "Running as a Woman: Gender Stereotyping in Women's Campaigns." Pp. 77–98 in *Women, Media, and Politics*, edited by Pippa Norris. New York: Oxford University Press, 1997.

Jackler, Rosalind. "Capital Gains: Governor Richards was the Center of Attention as the Nation's Governors Convened in Washington D.C." *Houston Post*, February 7, 1993, A35.

Jackson, Herb. "Whitman Parlayed Skill and Luck into Success, Ascendancy to EPA Only Appears Planned." *The Record*, December 21, 2000, A18. Lexis Nexis Academic Universe (accessed August 24, 2002).

Jamieson, Kathleen Hall. *Beyond the Double Bind: Women and Leadership.* New York: Oxford University Press, 1995.

———. "The 'Effeminate' Style." Pp. 67–89 in *Eloquence in an Electronic Age: The Transformation of Political Speechmaking.* New York: Oxford University Press, 1988.

———. "The Subversive Effects of a Focus on Strategy in News Coverage of Presidential Campaigns." Pp. 35–62 in *1–800–president: The Report of the Twentieth Century Fund Task Force on Television and the Campaign of 1992.* New York: Twentieth Century Fund Press, 1993.

"Jane Dee Hull." AP Candidate Bios. *The Associated Press Political Service.* October 1, 1998. Lexis Nexis Academic Universe (accessed October 20, 1998).

Jarboe, Jan. "Ann's Plans." *Texas Monthly* (July 1992): 78.

"Jess Jawin." *Texas Jewish Post* (January 23, 1992): 1+.

"Joan Finney." AP Candidate Bios. *The Associated Press Political Service.* Lexis Nexis Academic Universe (accessed October 20, 1998).

Johnston, Carolyn. *Sexual Power: Feminism and the Family in America.* Tuscaloosa: University of Alabama Press, 1992.

Jonsson, Patrik. "In Senate Bid, Dole Takes Shot at a New Glass Ceiling." *Christian Science Monitor*, February 22, 2002. Lexis Nexis Academic Universe (accessed August 16, 2002).

Kahn, Kim Fridkin. "Does Gender Make a Difference? An Experimental Examination of Sex Stereotypes and Press Patterns in Statewide Campaigns." *American Journal of Political Science* 38 (1994): 62–195.

Kahn, Kim Fridkin and Ann Gordon. "How Women Campaign for the U.S. Senate: Substance and Strategy." Pp. 59–76 in *Women, Media, and Politics*, edited by Pippa Norris. New York: Oxford University Press, 1997.

Kamlani, Ratu. "In Case She Wants Some Free Advice . . ." *Time* (March 1, 1999): 38–39.

Kaufman, Joanne and Barbara Kleban Mills. "While Nebraska Governor Kay Orr Makes Policy, Husband Bill, Her 'First Gentleman' Bakes Meat Loaf." *People Weekly* (December 12, 1988): 189+.

Kean, Tom. "Whitman Gets Rolling." *The Record*, April 20, 1997, O01. Lexis Nexis Academic Universe (accessed September 15, 1999).

Keeler, S. "The Illusion of Intimacy: Television and the Role of Candidate Personal Qualities in Voter Choice." *Public Opinion Quarterly* 51 (1987): 344–58.

Keerdoja, Eileen with Pamela Abramson. "Dixy Lee Ray is Still Speaking Out." *Newsweek* (June 8, 1981): 16.

Kelly, Mike. "Christie's Message." *The Record*, September 21, 1993, B01. Lexis Nexis Academic Universe (accessed August 29, 1999).

———. "Christie's New Gig." *The Record*, December 24, 2000, 01. Lexis Nexis Academic Universe (accessed August 24, 2002).

———. "Christie's Odd Tactics." *The Record*, July 11, 1993, O01. Lexis Nexis Academic Universe (accessed August 29, 1999).

———. "Go West Young Guv." *The Record*, August 30, 1994, D01. Lexis Nexis Academic Universe (accessed September 14, 1999).

———. "The Politics of Symbols." *The Record*, January 23, 1994, O01. Lexis Nexis Academic Universe (accessed September 14, 1999).

Kendall, Bridget. "The First Lady's Not for Turning?" *The Independent*, November 11, 1994. Lexis Nexis Academic Universe (accessed July 17, 2002).

Kennedy, Helen. "Gore's a Bore No More: Makeover Having its Effect." *New York Daily News*, January 19, 2000. Lexis Nexis Academic Universe (accessed August 1, 2002).

Kennedy, J. Michael. "The Cowboy and the Good Ol' Girl." *Los Angeles Times*, October 21, 1990, home edition, 12. Lexis Nexis Academic Universe (accessed April 28, 1999).

Kennedy, Mike. "'B-word' Used in Arsenal of Hate." *Kansas City Star*, January 6, 1995, metropolitan edition, A1. Lexis Nexis Academic Universe (accessed February 2, 1996).

Kennedy, Randy. "Richards Asks Texas to Unite." *The Daily Texan*, November 8, 1990, 1.

Keys to the Governor's Office. Brookline, Mass.: Barbara Lee Family Foundation, 2001.

Kiely, Eugene. "Both Born to Run; Whitman Accustomed to Being at Wheel." *The Record*, October 26, 1997, A01. Lexis Nexis Academic Universe (accessed June 27, 2002).

———. "Real Change is Whitman's Big Challenge; Will She Deliver on Promises?" *The Record*, November 7, 1993, A01. Lexis Nexis Academic Universe (accessed August 20, 1999).

———. "Whitman's Popularity Soaring; Poll: Job-Approval Rating 68%." *The Record*, October 24, 1994, A01. Lexis Nexis Academic Universe (accessed September 14, 1999).

Kiely, Kathy. "Hil Fiery in Rights Talk." *New York Daily News*, July 17, 1998, 30. Lexis Nexis Academic Universe (accessed November 21, 1999).

Kilday, Anne Marie. "Richards Gets Custom-Made Motorcycle." *Dallas Morning News*, May 16, 1992, 31A.

Kilday, Anne Marie and Terrence Stutz. "Richards Faces Tough Job as Governor, Lawmakers Say." *Dallas Morning News*, November 8, 1990, 23A.

Kimmel, Michael. *Manhood in America: A Cultural History*. New York: Free Press, 1996.

King, Wayne. "A Nemesis of Bradley Eyes Florio." *New York Times*, October 14, 1991, late edition, B1. Lexis Nexis Academic Universe (accessed August 29, 1999).

Kiousis, Spiro, Philemon Bantimaroudis, and Hyun Ban. "Candidate Image Attributes: Experiments on the Substantive Dimension of Second Level Agenda Setting." *Communication Research* 26 (1999): 414–28.

Klumpp, James F. and Thomas A. Hollihan. "Rhetorical Criticism as Moral Action." *Quarterly Journal of Speech* 75 (1989): 84–97.

Kolbert, Elizabeth. "The Republicans: The Tribute: A Wife Takes a Star Turn." *New York Times*, August 15, 1996. Lexis Nexis Academic Universe (accessed September 4, 2000).

Kornblut, Anne E. "Elections 2002: The National Battle GOP Victories; Bush's Outreach Bears Fruit." *Boston Globe*, November 6, 2002. Lexis Nexis Academic Universe (accessed November 14, 2002).

Kornbluth, Jesse. "Free Advice: Five Historians Comment on Hillary's Dilemma." *New Yorker* (January 30, 1995): 34.

Kosova, Weston and Michael Isikoff. "The Relentless Mrs. Dole: Is Liddy—Devout and Astute—Another Hillary." *Newsweek* (February 5, 1996): 30.

Kraemer, Richard H., Charldean Newell, and David F. Prindle. *Essentials of Texas Politics*. 6th ed. New York: West Publishing Company, 1995.

Kruh, Nancy. "From Dawn Till Dark, Richards Was on the Go." *Dallas Morning News*, January 16, 1991.

Lakoff, George and Mark Johnson. "Conceptual Metaphor in Everyday Language." Pp. 286–325 in *Philosophical Perspectives on Metaphor*, edited by Mark Johnson. Minneapolis: University of Minnesota Press, 1981.

Lanpher, Katherine. "Women Should Make Newt's Term Work for Them." *Dayton Daily News*, January 6, 1995, city edition, 11A. Lexis Nexis Academic Universe (accessed February 2, 1996).

Lawrence, Jill. "On the Road, Spouses Making Strides." *USA Today*, September 25, 1996, 4A.

Leibovich, Mark. "Liddy Dole in North Carolina. Hoping Her Roots Show." *Washington Post*, October 7, 2002. <washingtonpost.com> (accessed October 7, 2002).

Leiby, Richard. "TO B OR NOT TO B.; Reflections on a Word That Rhymes with Glitch." *Washington Post*, January 12, 1995, final edition, C1. Lexis Nexis Academic Universe (accessed February 2, 1996).

Lenz, Mary. "Richards Promises to 'Hit the Ground Running' in Austin." *Houston Post*, November 8, 1990, A1.

Lenz, Mary and Ken Herman. "Richards Tells 2 Members of Insurance Board to Quit." *Houston Post*, February 7, 1991, A1.

Leonard, Mary. "Role Models Are Few For Swift in New Office." *The Boston Globe*, February 18, 2001, A1. Lexis Nexis Academic Universe (accessed June 26, 2002).

Lewis, Neil A. "Back to College for an Image Makeover." *New York Times*, national edition, May 30, 1992, L9.

"Liddy's Walk." Editorial. *Houston Chronicle*, August 16, 1996. Lexis Nexis Academic Universe (accessed September 4, 2000).

"Listen with Hillary." *The Economist* (March 20, 1993): 26.

Loewenheim, Francis L. "Why not a (Hillary) Clinton vs. (Liddy) Dole Debate?" *Houston Chronicle*, September 1, 1996. Lexis Nexis Academic Universe (accessed September 4, 2000).

MacDonald, M. L. "Assertion Training for Women." Pp. 253–79 in *Social Skills Training*, edited by J.P. Curran and P.M. Monti. New York: Guilford, 1981.

"Male Candidates Tiptoe When Running Against Women." *The Daily Texan*, April 3, 1990, 1.

Mann, Judy. "For Elizabeth Dole, Time Will Tell." *Washington Post*, January 8, 1999. Lexis Nexis Academic Universe (accessed October 29, 1999).

Maraniss, David. "Richards Changing Face of Old-Boy Texas Politics; Key Appointees Include Women, Minorities." *Washington Post*, January 13, 1991, final edition, A3. Lexis Nexis Academic Universe (accessed April 28, 1999).

———. "Richards Seeks to Refocus on Issues; Rough Texas Democratic Campaign Leaves Image Questions." *Washington Post*, April 12, 1990, final edition, A6. Lexis Nexis Academic Universe (accessed April 28, 1999).

———. "The Texas Two-Step In the Race for Governor." *Washington Post*, October 22, 1990, final edition, B1. Lexis Nexis Academic Universe (accessed April 28, 1999).

Margolick, David. "Lake Lurleen Journal." *New York Times*, June 19, 1991, A16.

Martello, Thomas. "Whitman Tried by Abortion Issue; Walks Tricky Line within GOP." *The Record*, February 9, 1998, A03. Lexis Nexis Academic Universe (accessed October 11, 1999).

"Martha Layne Collins." AP Candidate Bios. *The Associated Press Political Service*. Lexis Nexis Academic Universe (accessed October 20, 1998).

Martin, Harold H. "'The Race of The Thousand Clowns,'" *The Saturday Evening Post* (May 1966): 25

Mathews, Tom with Paul S. Greenberg. "Washington: Lady with a Chain Saw." *Newsweek* (April 11, 1977): 45.

May, Elaine Tyler. *Homeward Bound: American Families in the Cold War Era*. New York: Basic Books, 1988.

Mayhead, Molly and Brenda DeVore Marshall, eds. *Navigating Boundaries: The Rhetoric of Women Governors*. Westport, Conn.: Praeger, 2000.

Mayhead, Molly and Brenda DeVore Marshall. *Women's Political Discourse*. Lanham, Md.: Rowman & Littlefield, forthcoming.

Mayo, Edith P. "The Influence and Power of First Ladies." *Chronicle of Higher Education*, September 15, 1993, A52.

Mayo, Edith P. and Denise D. Meringolo. *First Ladies: Political Role and Public Image.* Washington, D.C., Smithsonian Institution Press, 1994.

McAlpin, John P. "Whitman Offers Modest Proposals in Her Farewell Address." *The Associated Press State and Local Wire.* January 9, 2001. Lexis Nexis Academic Universe (accessed August 24, 2002).

McAneny, Leslie. "New First Lady Making Headway—On Her Own Terms." *The Gallup Poll Monthly* (February 1993): 2. Expanded Academic ASAP (accessed February 2, 1996).

McBrayer, Sharon. "Bob Dole Visits for Liddy." *News-Herald,* June 29, 2002. Lexis Nexis Academic Universe (accessed August 16, 2002).

McCarthy, Abigail. "ER as First Lady." Pp. 214–25 in *Without Precedent: The Life and Career of Eleanor Roosevelt,* edited by Joan Hoff-Wilson and Marjorie Lightman. Bloomington: Indiana University Press, 1984.

McGlen, Nancy E. and Karen O'Connor. *Women, Politics, and American Society.* 2d ed. Upper Saddle River, N.J.: Prentice Hall, 1998.

McLarin, Kimberly J. "The 1993 Elections: Woman in the News; An Outsider Wins Office: Christine Todd Whitman." *New York Times,* November 3, 1993, late edition, B6. Lexis Nexis Academic Universe (accessed August 29, 1999).

McMurdy, Deirdre. "The Political Wife: Hillary Clinton Redefines Her Role." *Maclean's* (July 20, 1992): 34.

McNeely, Dave. "Richards' Decision-Making Style Suits Governorship." *Austin American-Statesman,* December 27, 1990.

———. "Richards Record Stands a Far Cry from 'Feminist' Labeling." *Austin American-Statesman,* October 8, 1987.

McNichol, Dustan. "Warm Welcome Expected at Icy Inauguration, Safety Fears Cancel Parade, But Whitman Show Will Go On." *The Record,* January 18, 1994, A01. Lexis Nexis Academic Universe (accessed September 14, 1999).

"'Me for Ma,' Says Texas." *The Outlook* (September 3, 1924): 5.

Means, Marianne. "The Elizabeth Factor." *Denver Post,* October 10, 1996. Lexis Nexis Academic Universe (accessed September 4, 2000).

Merida, Kevin and Susan Schmidt. "The Candidate's Wife and Partner in Climb; Ascendant or Not Tuesday, Elizabeth Dole Rung Up a Win." *Washington Post,* November 2, 1996. Lexis Nexis Academic Universe (accessed September 4, 2000).

"The Merry Wives of Washington." *The Economist* (August 8, 1992): 26.

Meserve, Jeanne and Eileen O'Conner. "First Lady Responds to Allegations Claiming Right-Wing Conspiracy." *CNN Worldview,* January 27, 1998. Lexis Nexis Academic Universe (accessed February 9, 1998).

Meyer, Karl. "The President's Other Running Mate." *New York Times,* January 27, 1993, A22.

Miga, Andrew. "Convention '96; Look Out, Hillary; Liddy, not Bob, Steals the Show." *Boston Herald*, August 15, 1996. Lexis Nexis Academic Universe (accessed September 4, 2000).

Milbank, Dana. "Meet the Man Who Isn't Hillary; Rick Lazio, the Other New York Senate Candidate." *Washington Post*, October 7, 2000. Lexis Nexis Academic Universe (accessed December 28, 2000).

"Miriam Amanda Ferguson: Soon to Take Office as the First Woman Governor of Texas." *Current Opinion* (October 1924): 436.

Mitchell, Alison. "Elizabeth Dole Questions Clinton's Policies on Iraq and Serbia." *New York Times*, April 15, 1999. Lexis Nexis Academic Universe (accessed October 29, 1999).

Mooneyham, Scott. "Elizabeth Dole Kicks Off Campaign." *Associated Press*, February 23, 2002. Lexis Nexis Academic Universe (accessed August 16, 2002).

Moran, Thomas. "Whitman Hits the Road; GOP Challenger Launches Bus Tour of State." *The Record*, October 21, 1993, A12. Lexis Nexis Academic Universe (accessed August 29, 1999).

"More on the Presidential Crisis." *New York Times*, January 25, 1998, 1. Lexis Nexis Academic Universe (accessed February 9, 1998).

Morris, Julie. "Texas' Richards to Lead 15,000 to Her Inaugural." *USA Today*, January 14, 1991, final edition, 2A. Lexis Nexis Academic Universe (accessed April 28, 1999).

Morse, Rob. "Rhymes with Gingrich." *San Francisco Examiner*, January 5, 1995, fourth edition, A1. Lexis Nexis Academic Universe (accessed February 2, 1996).

Muir, Janette Kenner and Lisa M. Benitez. "Redefining the Role of the First Lady: The Rhetorical Style of Hillary Rodham Clinton." Pp. 139–58 in *The Clinton Presidency: Images, Issues, and Communication Strategies*, edited by Robert E. Denton, Jr. and Rachel L. Holloway. Westport, Conn.: Praeger, 1996.

Murphy, Eileen. "Hillary Slams Giuliani Homeless Sweeps." *abcnews.com*, December 1, 1999. <abcnews.go.com> (accessed December 2, 1999).

Nadel, Alan. *Containment Culture: American Narratives, Postmodernism, and the Atomic Age*. Durham, N.C.: Duke University Press, 1995.

Nagourney, Adam. "The Republicans Win Their Bet." *New York Times*, November 10, 2002. Lexis Nexis Academic Universe (accessed November 29, 2002).

"NC: Both Party Polls Show Dole Out Front Against Bowles." *The Bulletin's Frontrunner*, April 18, 2002. Lexis Nexis Academic Universe (accessed August 16, 2002).

Nelson, Lars–Erik. "Whitman Stars in the GOP's Fiscal Follies." Editorial. *New York Daily News*, March 26, 1997, 33. Lexis Nexis Academic Universe (accessed September 15, 1999).

"New York U.S. Senate." *New York Times*, July 7, 1999. <nytimes.com> (accessed July 9, 1999).

Norris, Michelle and Lisa McRee. "Hillary Clinton Plays Hardball." *Good Morning America*, January 26, 1998. Lexis Nexis Academic Universe (accessed February 9, 1998).

"North Carolina." *Washington Post*, November 7, 2002. Lexis Nexis Academic Universe (accessed November 14, 2002).

Northcott, Kaye. "Poll Says Governor's Race Even." *Fort Worth Star Telegram*, October 26, 1990, 7.

"Notebook." *The New Republic* (February 19, 1996): 10.

Nyhan, David. "This Texan is a Straight-Shooter." *Boston Sunday Globe*, October 1, 1989.

O'Beirne, Kate. "Nowhere Girl." *National Review* (July 28, 1997). <http://www.state.nj.us/governor/feature.htm> (accessed November 6, 1997).

O'Brien, Kathleen. "The Governor Exercises More than Authority, Behind the Pearls Lies a Player." *The Record*, November 26, 1994, A08. Lexis Nexis Academic Universe (accessed September 14, 1999).

O'Brien, Miles. "Campaign 2000: Is the Time Right for Madame President?" *CNN Sunday Morning*, January 10, 1999. Lexis Nexis Academic Universe (accessed December 30, 2000).

"On Political Courage, Witches, and History." *Ms* (November 1987): 84.

"On the Run with Ella." *Newsweek* (November 4, 1974): 21.

Orin, Deborah. "Politics as Usual: Prez Boosts Liddy." *New York Post*, February 28, 2002. Lexis Nexis Academic Universe (accessed August 16, 2002).

Osborn, Michael. "Archetypal Metaphor in Rhetoric: The Light–Dark Family." *Quarterly Journal of Speech* 53 (1967): 115–26.

Parry-Giles, Shawn. "Mediating Hillary Rodham Clinton: Television News Practices and Image–Making in the Postmodern Age." *Critical Studies in Media Communication* 17 (June 2000): 205–26.

Paulson, Michael. "Richards Leaves Them Wanting More in N.Y." *San Antonio Light*, July 19, 1992.

Pear, Robert. "First Lady Sets Aggressive Tone for Debate on Health–Care Plan." *New York Times*, May 27, 1993, A1.

Pederson, Daniel. "Richards: 'I Like to Make People Laugh,'" *Newsweek* (July 25, 1988): 22.

Peterson, Iver. "The 1994 Campaign: Whitman; Move Over. Rockefeller, G.O.P.'s Got A New Idol." *New York Times*, October 4, 1994, late edition, B5. Lexis Nexis Academic Universe (accessed August 20, 1999).

———. "On Politics; Think You've Seen Power In Trenton? Just Wait." *New York Times*, October 1, 1995, late edition, 13NJ: 2. Lexis Nexis Academic Universe (accessed August 20, 1999).

———. "Whitman's Right-Hand Woman in Trenton; Hazel F. Gluck, Lobbyist, Friend and Political Pro, Has No Office but Plenty of Power." *New York*

Times, January 7, 1994, late edition, B1. Lexis Nexis Academic Universe (accessed August 20, 1999).

"Petticoat Politics." *Collier's* (April 17, 1926): 19.

Phillips, Leslie and Patricia Edmonds. "Women in Congress: Fighting the Old Boy Network; Getting Voice Heard a Daily Balancing Act." *USA Today*, April 1, 1992, final edition, 1A. Lexis Nexis Academic Universe (accessed February 2, 1996).

Plummer, William and Anne Maier. "After Mudslinging Primary, Victor Ann Richards Sets her Sights on the Lone Star Statehouse." *People Weekly* (April 30, 1990): 85.

Pollitt, Katha. "The Male Media's Hillary Problem; First-Lady Bashing." *The Nation* (May 17, 1993): 657. Expanded Academic ASAP (October 27, 1995).

Port, Bob and Frank Lombardi. "Carpetbag Tag Didn't Halt Hil Steamroll." *New York Daily News*, November 8, 2000. Lexis Nexis Academic Universe (accessed December 28, 2000).

Porterfield, Billy. "Can Ann Richards Ignite Texas Women?" *Austin American-Statesman* March 19, 1990, 1–2.

Potok, Mark. "Richards in 'Race of Her Life' / Texas Gov Faces Tough Challenge." *USA Today*, October 17, 1994, final edition, 8A. Lexis Nexis Academic Universe (accessed April 28, 1999).

Potter, Karen. "Ann of 100 Days Finds Governor's Work is Never Done." *Fort Worth Star Telegram*, April 22, 1991, 10.

———. "Governor Accepts Gift for DPS Use." *Fort Worth Star Telegram*, May 16, 1992, 1+.

———. "Governor Wows 'em—Again." *Fort Worth Star Telegram*, July 14, 1992, 1+.

———. "Richards Clinging to Lead in Gubernatorial Dogfight." *Fort Worth Star Telegram*, November 7, 1990.

Potter, Karen and Joe Cutbirth. "Richards Vows 'New Texas' as She Takes Office." *Fort Worth Star Telegram*, January 16, 1991, 1+.

Potter, Karen and Kaye Northcott. "Slips of the Lip Trip Williams." *Fort Worth Star Telegram*, November 4, 1990, 1.

Preece, Harold. "Ma Ferguson Wins Again." *The Nation* (September 21, 1932): 255.

Pressley, Sue Anne. "Personal Touch Might Not Be Enough." *Washington Post*, October 4, 1994, final edition, A1. Lexis Nexis Academic Universe (accessed April 28, 1999).

Pribram, E. Dierdre. "Seduction, Control, & the Search for Authenticity: Madonna's *Truth or Dare*." Pp. 189–212 in *The Madonna Connection: Representational Politics, Subcultural Identities, and Cultural Theory*, edited by Cathy [Ramona Liera] Schwichtenberg. Boulder. Col.: Westview, 1993.

"Prime Time: Whitman Responds to Clinton with Brevity." *Asbury Park Press*, July 4, 1996. <http://www.state.nj.us/governor/primetim.htm> (November 30, 1999).

Proctor, David E., Roger C. Aden, and Phyllis Japp. "Gender/Issue Interaction in Political Identity Making: Nebraska's Woman vs. Woman Gubernatorial Campaign." *Central States Speech Journal* 39 (1988): 190–203.

Prodis, Julia. "Texas Governor's Race a Real Ripsnorter." *Los Angeles Times*, October 23, 1994, bulldog edition, A2. Lexis Nexis Academic Universe (accessed April 28, 1999).

Pryne, Eric. "Convention Doesn't Impress; Elizabeth Dole Does, Viewers Say." *Seattle Times*, August 15, 1996. Lexis Nexis Academic Universe (accessed September 4, 2000).

Pugh, Clifford. "'96 Campaign: Elizabeth Dole: Asset and Ally; Despite Problems of Her Husband's Campaign, She's a Hit." *Houston Chronicle*, October 29, 1996. Lexis Nexis Academic Universe (accessed September 4, 2000).

Pugh, Clifford and Mary Lenz. "Ann's People Flock to Austin for Celebration." *Houston Post*, January 16, 1991, A12.

Pulley, Brett. "The 1997 Elections: Profile—Born With Politics in Her Veins; Behind Whitman's Earnest Talk, a Fierce Spirit Lies." *New York Times*, October 29, 1997, late edition, B1. Lexis Nexis Academic Universe (accessed August 20, 1999).

———. "Woman in the News: Christine Todd Whitman; Just in Time, a Listener." *New York Times*, November 5, 1997, late edition, B7. Lexis Nexis Academic Universe (accessed August 20, 1999).

Purdum, Todd S. "Once Again in Arizona, Secretary of State is Suddenly Thrust into the Job of Governor." *New York Times*, September 5, 1997, late edition, A20.

Purnick, Joyce. "Gender Chasm for Hillary Clinton; Candidate Drew 60% of Women's Votes." *Milwaukee Journal Sentinel*, November 12, 2000. Lexis Nexis Academic Universe (accessed December 28, 2000).

"Quotes of the Day." *Chicago Tribune*, April 4, 1995, evening update edition, 2. Lexis Nexis Academic Universe (accessed October 20, 1998).

Ramsey, Ross. "She Whups Him!" *Times Herald*, November 7, 1990.

———. "Volume of Campaign Ads Increases but Will TV Viewers Turn It Down?" *Dallas Times Herald*, September 17, 1990.

Ransom, Harry. "Spirit of Texas." *Discovery* 10, no. 2 (1986): 5–9.

Ratcliffe, R. G. "Campaign '94; Governor; Gender Bias Worrisome Factor." *Houston Chronicle*, September 5, 1994, 2 star edition, A1. Lexis Nexis Academic Universe (accessed April 28, 1999).

———. "Few Fault Richards on Style, But Substance is Another Thing." *Houston Chronicle*, May 1, 1994, 2 star edition, A1. Lexis Nexis Academic Universe (accessed April 28, 1999).

————. "It's Governor Richards: Overwhelming Support of Women Keys Win." *Houston Chronicle*, November 7, 1990, 2 star edition, 1.

————. "Race Tight in Stretch, Poll Shows." *Houston Chronicle*, November 4, 1990.

————. "Richards Demands Shake-Up." *Houston Chronicle*, February 7, 1991, 1A.

————. "Richards Pushes for Whirlwind of Changes." *Houston Chronicle*, February 10, 1991, 1A.

————. "Richards and Williams in Dead Heat, Poll Finds." *Houston Chronicle*, October 26, 1990.

————. "Texas Governor's Race; Richards Stumps for Bubba's Vote." *Houston Chronicle*, November 4, 1994, 2 star edition, A1. Lexis Nexis Academic Universe (accessed April 28, 1999).

————. "Traveling a Bumpy Road Never Musses Richards." *Houston Chronicle*, January 3, 1993, 1A+.

Ratcliffe, R. G. and Clay Robison. "Richards, Bullock Pledge a 'New Texas.'" *Houston Chronicle*, January 16, 1991, 1A.

Ratcliffe, R. G. and Cindy Rugeley. "Win Hailed By Richards as Inspiring." *Houston Chronicle*, November 8, 1990.

Ratnesar, Romesh. "A Race of Her Own." *Time* (March 1, 1999): 28–40.

Rebovich, David P. "As America Assesses Whitman, Does New Jersey Win or Lose?" *New Jersey Lawyer*, February 6, 1995, 3. Lexis Nexis Academic Universe (accessed September 14, 1999).

————. "Governor's Race Tests Conventional Wisdom." *New Jersey Lawyer*, October 27, 1997, 3. Lexis Nexis Academic Universe (accessed September 15, 1999).

————. "McGreevey and Whitman Woo 'Working' Jerseyans." *New Jersey Lawyer*, June 23, 1997, 3. Lexis Nexis Academic Universe (accessed September 15, 1999).

————. "Picking Next Election: Don't Bet the House!" *New Jersey Lawyer*, November 23, 1998, 3. Lexis Nexis Academic Universe (accessed October 11, 1999).

————. "Report Card on Whitman; School's Still Out On Impact of Policies in First Two Years." *New Jersey Lawyer*, January 8, 1996, 3. Lexis Nexis Academic Universe (accessed September 15, 1999).

————. "Sen. Christie Whitman? No Foregone Conclusion." *New Jersey Lawyer*, March 1, 1999, 3. Lexis Nexis Academic Universe (accessed October 14, 1999).

Reed, Julia. "Running Against Hurricane 'W,' Scrambling for Dollars." *Newsweek* (July 12, 1999). Lexis Nexis Academic Universe (accessed January 7, 2001).

"Revise the Tank Cleanup." *The Record*, December 27, 1993, A14. Lexis Nexis Academic Universe (accessed August 20, 1999).

Richards, Ann W. "Governor's Report." February 2, 1992.

———. Inaugural Address. *House Journal* (January 15, 1991): 137–39.

———. Remarks. Cattle Raisers Association. March 29, 1993. Center for American History, University of Texas at Austin.

———. Remarks. Civil Rights Conference. December 16, 1992. Center for American History, University of Texas at Austin.

———. Remarks. Commencement Ceremonies of St. Edwards University. May 9, 1992. Center for American History, University of Texas at Austin.

———. Remarks. Conference on Women's History. June 3, 1994. Center for American History, University of Texas at Austin.

———. Remarks. East Texas State University Women's Enrichment Series. November 12, 1991. Center for American History, University of Texas at Austin.

———. Remarks. Executive State Agency Heads. April 24, 1991. Center for American History, University of Texas at Austin.

———. Remarks. Grand Prairie Chamber of Commerce Annual Awards Banquet. January 7, 1993. Center for American History, University of Texas at Austin.

———. Remarks. Higher Education Appointees. July 17, 1991. Center for American History, University of Texas at Austin.

———. Remarks. Houston Club Centennial Distinguished Speaker Series. January 27, 1994. Center for American History, University of Texas at Austin.

———. Remarks. Joint Session of the Legislature (State of State). *House Journal* (February 6, 1991): 275–83.

———. Remarks. Lubbock Eagle Scouts. November 11, 1991. Center for American History, University of Texas at Austin.

———. Remarks. Polk County Chamber of Commerce. March 5, 1992. Center for American History, University of Texas at Austin.

———. Remarks. Special Session of the Texas Legislature. July 15, 1991. Center for American History, University of Texas at Austin.

———. Remarks. Sweet Briar College. October 23, 1993. Center for American History, University of Texas at Austin.

———. Remarks. Texas Chamber of Commerce. February 10, 1994. Center for American History, University of Texas at Austin.

———. Remarks. Tribute to Sam Houston at Sam Houston State University. March 2, 1993. Center for American History, University of Texas at Austin.

Richards, I. A. *The Philosophy of Rhetoric*. London: Oxford University Press, 1936.

"Richards Named to Glamour List." *Dallas Morning News*, November 5, 1991, 22A.

"Richards Names Diverse Group." *Austin American-Statesman*, April 21, 1991, A16.

"Richards' Rivals, You Don't Say?" *New York Times*, March 11, 1990, late edition, sec. 4: 7. Lexis Nexis Academic Universe (accessed April 28, 1999).

Richmond, Kelly. "Whitman at Center Stage in Washington, Trenton Picked from Many Governors for CNN's Political Talk Show." *The Record*, January 29, 1994, A03. Lexis Nexis Academic Universe (accessed September 14, 1999).

Roberts, Roxanne. "House Mates: Loretta and Linda Sanchez are Congress's First Sister Act, They Work Well Together, The Question Is, Can They Live Together?" *Washington Post*, December 12, 2002. <www.washington post.com> (accessed December 12, 2002).

Robertson, Pamela. *Guilty Pleasures: Feminist Camp from Mae West to Madonna*. Durham, N.C.: Duke University Press, 1996.

Robison, Clay. "Richards to Take on State's Problems." *Houston Chronicle*, January 16, 1991.

Rohan, Virginia. "Governor Never Forgot She's a Politician." *The Record*, July 7, 1995, A06. Lexis Nexis Academic Universe (accessed September 14, 1999).

"Rollins Scandal Clouds Whitman's Victory." *The Record*, November 28, 1993, O03. Lexis Nexis Academic Universe (accessed August 20, 1999).

Romano, Jay. "A Day with Christine Whitman." *New York Times*, April 4, 1993, late edition, 13NJ: 1. Lexis Nexis Academic Universe (accessed August 29, 1999).

Rosellini, Lynn. "The Woman Who Could Beat Him." *U.S. News & World Report* (March 15, 1999). <www.usnews.com> (accessed July 18, 2001).

Rosenbaum, David E. "Many Questions Arise in Race for Helms Seat." *New York Times*, June 29, 2002. Lexis Nexis Academic Universe (accessed August 16, 2002).

Rosenberg, Debra and Michael Isikoff. "Forgive Us Our Revolution." *Newsweek* (September 20, 1999): 30.

Rosenberg, S.W. and P. McCafferty. "The Image and the Vote." *Public Opinion Quarterly* 51 (1987): 31–47.

Rossant, Colette. "A Visit with Vermont's Governor." *McCall's* (January 1988): 82.

Rowe, Kathleen. *The Unruly Woman: Gender and the Genres of Laughter*. Austin: University of Texas Press, 1995.

Rozen, Leah and Elinor J. Brecher. "Kentucky's New First Family Includes Another Beauty Queen—But Martha Layne Collins is the Governor." *People Weekly* (November 28, 1983): 59–60.

Ruddick, Sarah. "Maternal Thinking." *Feminist Studies* 6 (1980): 342–67.

Ruderman, Wendy. "Republicans Turn Out to Raise Money, Profiles at 'Governor's Gala.'" *The Associated Press*, September 26, 1998. Lexis Nexis Academic Universe (accessed October 11, 1999).

Ruess, Michelle. "Cutting Spending by Consensus; Whitman: I'll Ask Public's Advice." *The Record*, December 9, 1993, A03. Lexis Nexis Academic Universe (accessed August 20, 1999).

―――. "NOW Battles Division Within; An Opened Door Has Brought a Chill." *The Record*, October 25, 1994, A01. Lexis Nexis Academic Universe (accessed September 14, 1999).

Runnion, Marge. "Once a Refugee from Nazi Europe, Madeleine Kunin Takes Charge as Vermont's First Woman Governor." *People Weekly* (April 1, 1985): 105. Lexis Nexis Academic Universe (accessed October 20, 1998).

Russert, Tim. "Elizabeth Dole Discusses the Straw Poll Results from Iowa and Her Presidential Campaign." *Meet the Press*, August 15, 1999. Lexis Nexis Academic Universe (accessed December 30, 2000).

Safire, William. "Clemency Episode Just More Clinton Deceit." *Houston Chronicle*, September 14, 1999. Lexis Nexis Academic Universe (accessed December 29, 2000).

Saint-Amand, Pierre. "Terrorizing Marie Antoinette." *Critical Inquiry* 20 (1994): 379–400.

Salholz, Eloise with Karen Springen. "Are We in Kansas Anymore?" *Newsweek* (October 8, 1990): 34.

Salmore, Barbara G. and Stephen A. Salmore. *New Jersey Politics and Government: Suburban Politics Comes of Age*. Lincoln: University of Nebraska Press, 1993.

Sanderson, Bill. "Look Out Howard Stern! Whitman Show's Coming." *The Record*, March 6, 1994, A25. Lexis Nexis Academic Universe (accessed September 14, 1999).

Sanger, David. "Bush Campaigns for Mrs. Dole in North Carolina Race." *New York Times*, February 28, 2002. Lexis Nexis Academic Universe (accessed August 16, 2002).

Saxonhouse, Arlene W. "Introduction—Public and Private: The Paradigm's Power." Pp. 1–9 in *Stereotypes of Women in Power: Historical Perspectives and Revisionist Views*, edited by Barbara Garlick, Suzanne Dixon, and Pauline Allen. New York: Greenwood Press, 1992.

Scharrer, Gary. "The Richards Style." *El Paso Times*, November 17, 1991.

Schieffer, Bob. "Elizabeth Dole Discusses Straw Poll Results in Iowa and Her Presidential Campaign." *Face the Nation*, August 15, 1999. Lexis Nexis Academic Universe (accessed December 30, 2000).

Schmidt, William E. "Lincoln *Journal*: Nebraska's First Man Enjoys the Last Laughs." *New York Times*, October 21, 1988, late city final edition, A14.

Schneider, William. "First Lady's Unwavering Words Win Her Play of Week." *CNN*, September 8, 1995. Lexis Nexis Academic Universe (accessed February 20, 1996).

Schwichtenberg, Cathy [Ramona Liera], ed. *The Madonna Connection: Representational Politics, Subcultural Identities, and Cultural Theory*. Boulder, Col.: Westview Press, 1993.

"Second Time Around." *Time* (September 24, 1984): 31.

Sedgwick, John. "The Woman Behind That Unwavering Smile." *Newsweek* (August 19, 1996): 36.

Seelye, Katharine Q. "After Pepsi and Viagra, Dole Is Pushing Dole." *New York Times*, October 1, 2002. <www.newyorktimes.com> (accessed October 1, 2002).

Selby, Gardner. "Governor Hogs Spotlight." *Houston Post*, May 16, 1992.

————. "Richards Proclaims a 'New Texas.'" *Times Herald*, January 16, 1991, A1.

"Senate Race Dead Even." *abcnews.com*, March 29, 2000. <abcnews.go.com> (accessed March 29, 2000).

Shales, Tom. "Mrs. Dole's Political Oprah." *Washington Post*, August 15, 1996. Lexis Nexis Academic Universe (accessed September 4, 2000).

Sheeler, Kristina Horn. "Marginalizing Metaphors of the Feminine." Pp. 15–30 in *Navigating Boundaries: The Rhetoric of Women Governors*, edited by Molly Mayhead and Brenda DeVore Marshall. Westport, Conn.: Praeger, 2000.

Shipp, E.R. "Hillary and Rick: Safe, Bland and Dull." *New York Daily News*, October 29, 2000. Lexis Nexis Academic Universe (accessed December 28, 2000).

Siegal, Joel. "Hillary Rues Slip in Advice on Clemency." *New York Daily News*, September 11, 1999. Lexis Nexis Academic Universe (accessed December 29, 2000).

Siegel, Ralph. "Land Makes for a Governor's Best Legacy as Whitman Touts Open Space." *The Associated Press State & Local Wire*. January 20, 2001. Lexis Nexis Academic Universe (accessed June 26, 2002).

Simon, Roger. "Just Answer in a Whisper: Can Connie be Trusted?" *Baltimore Sun*, January 6, 1995, final edition, 2A. Lexis Nexis Academic Universe (accessed February 2, 1996).

Sirotu, Janet. "*McCall's* Goes to a Party: Derby Day Breakfast for 12,000!" *McCall's* (April 1987): 109.

Slater, Wayne. "Candidates Spar on Final Weekend." *Dallas Morning News*, November 4, 1990, 1A.

————. "Governor Outlines Activist State Agenda." *Dallas Morning News*, February 7, 1991, 1A.

————. "Richards Helps Women Raise Funds." *Dallas Morning News*, July 15, 1992.

————. "Richards Makes Mark on Office." *Dallas Morning News*, April 21, 1991, 1A+.

————. "Richards Pledges 'Sociological' Change." *Dallas Morning News*, November 8, 1990, 1A+.

————. "Richards' Popularity Puts Her in the Limelight Dawn to Dusk." *Dallas Morning News*, July 14, 1992, 1F+.

————. "Richards' Popularity Still High." *Dallas Morning News*, July 24, 1993, 33A.

————. "Richards Says Address Will Offer New Answer to Familiar Themes." *Dallas Morning News*, February 6, 1991, 1A+.

————. "Richards Still Popular in Poll." *Dallas Morning News*, February 20, 1993, 3A.

————. "Richards Takes Oath as Governor." *Dallas Morning News*, January 16, 1991, 1A.

Smith, Richard. "Richards Says She'll 'Hit the Ground Running.'" *Express News*, November 8, 1990.

Spy (February 1993): cover.

Starobin, Paul. "McCain's Men, Dole's Women." *National Journal* (September 4, 1999): 2510. Lexis Nexis Academic Universe (accessed January 7, 2001).

Stearney, Lynn M. "Feminism, Ecofeminism, and the Maternal Archetype: Motherhood as a Feminine Universal." *Communication Quarterly* 42 (1994): 145–59.

Steele, Scott. "A Man of Hope (Ark.)." *Maclean's* (November 16, 1992): 42–43.

Stengel, Richard. "Liddy Makes Perfect." *Time* (July 1, 1996): 30.

Stewart, Barbara. "In Person; Mrs. Whitman's First Lady." *New York Times*, November 12, 1995, late edition, 13NJ: 4. Lexis Nexis Academic Universe (accessed August 20, 1999).

Steyn, Mark. "I Was Wrong Again! Hurrah!" *Spectator* (November 9, 2002). Lexis Nexis Academic Universe (accessed November 29, 2002).

Stile, Charles. "Whitman Ending Era of Peaks and Valleys; A Look Back at Her Years as Governor." *The Record*, December 25, 2000, A1. Lexis Nexis Academic Universe (accessed 1 July 2002).

Stoeltje, Beverly. "It Makes a Good Story." *Discovery* 10, no. 2 (1986): 25–30.

Stokes, Elizabeth K. Phelps. "Your Business in Washington." *The Woman Citizen* (March 21, 1925): 8.

Sullivan, Andrew. "Sacred Cow." *New Republic* (June 22, 1992): 42.

Sullivan, Patricia A. and Carole Levin. "Women and Political Communication: From the Margins to the Center." Pp. 275–82 in *Political Rhetoric, Power, and Renaissance Women*, edited by Carole Levin and Patricia A. Sullivan. New York: State University of New York Press, 1995.

Sullivan, Patricia A. and Lynn H. Turner. *From the Margins to the Center: Contemporary Women and Political Communication*. Westport, Conn.: Praeger, 1996.

Suro, Roberto. "In Texas Race, Richards Reflects on Negativism." *New York Times*, May 6, 1990, late edition, 24. Lexis Nexis Academic Universe (accessed April 28, 1999).

————. "Texas Governor Proves Adept in Her First Year." *New York Times*, January 19, 1992.

"Surprises from Nation's Two Woman Governors." *U.S. News & World Report* (October 10, 1977): 45.

Sutton, Laurel A. "Bitches and Skankly Hobags: The Place of Women in Contemporary Slang." Pp. 560–72 in *Locating Power*, edited by Kira Hall, Mary Bucholtz, and Birch Moonwoman. Berkeley: Berkeley Women and Language Group, 1992.

"A Symbol at EPA; Whitman's Pro-choice but is She Pro Environment?" Editorial. *Pittsburgh Post Gazette*, December 27, 2000, A14. Lexis Nexis Academic Universe (accessed June 26, 2002).

Tannenbaum, P. H., B. S. Greenberg, and F. R. Silverman. "Candidate Images." Pp. 271–88 in *The Great Debates*, edited by S. Kraus. Bloomington: Indiana University Press, 1962.

Texas Monthly (October 1990): cover.

"Texas Tangled in 'Ma's' Apron-Strings." *The Literary Digest* (September 24, 1932): 11.

Thomas, Evan and Debra Rosenberg. "Hillary's Day in The Sun." *Newsweek* (March 1, 1999): 29.

Time (July 1, 1996): cover.

Time (July 1, 1996): 30–31 [Dole photo].

"The Titan of Texas." *Vogue* (August 1, 1991): 244.

Tolleson-Rinehart, Sue and Jeanie R. Stanley. *Claytie and the Lady: Ann Richards, Gender, and Politics in Texas*. Austin: University of Texas Press, 1994.

Tomasky, Michael. "Hillary's Turn." *New York Magazine* (March 30, 2000). <nymag.com> (accessed March 30, 2000).

Toner, Robin. "Bitter Race in Texas Ends with Richards as Democrats' Pick." *New York Times*, April 11, 1990, late edition, A:1. Lexis Nexis Academic Universe (accessed April 28, 1999).

"The 2002 Elections: South; North Carolina." *New York Times*, November 7, 2002. Lexis Nexis Academic Universe (accessed November 14, 2002).

Tyler, Patrick. "Hillary Clinton, in China, Details Abuse of Women." *New York Times*, September 6, 1995, A1. Lexis Nexis Academic Universe (accessed February 20, 1996).

Vekshin, Alison. "Whitman is Confirmed Unanimously; Heads to EPA Post Today; Defrancesco to Take Oath." *The Record*, January 31, 2001, A1. (accessed June 26, 2002).

"Vermont: Statehouse Stakes." *Newsweek* (October 29, 1984): 44.

"A Viable Candidate?" *Nightline*, September 13, 1999. <abcnews.go.com> (accessed September 15, 1999).

Vistica, Gregory. "Schroeder Hopes Navy Vitriol has Faded." *San Diego Union Tribune*, February 20, 1993. Lexis Nexis Academic Universe (accessed February 2, 1996).

Vulliamy, Ed. "White Hot Mama Fights a Texan Bush War." *The Observer* (October 2, 1994): 19. Lexis Nexis Academic Universe (accessed April 28, 1999).

Walsh, Kenneth T. "America's First (Working) Couple." *U.S. News & World Report* (May 10, 1993): 32. Expanded Academic ASAP (accessed February 2, 1996).

———. "Barbara Bush's Subtle and Significant Campaign Role." *U.S. News & World Report* (April 27, 1992): 36.

————. "Now, the First Chief Advocate." *U.S. News & World Report* (January 25, 1993): 46.

Walsh, Kenneth T. and Gloria Borger. "Psst, Bob Dole Beats His Wife." *U.S. News & World Report*, May 31, 1999. Lexis Nexis Academic Universe (accessed January 7, 2001).

Ward, Mike. "Crime Rates Are Down, But Are We Safer?" *Austin American-Statesman*, September 4, 1993, C1+.

Warren, Susan. "Defections by Republican Women Crucial to Richards' Victory." *Houston Chronicle*, November 8, 1990, 1A.

Weingarten, Paul. "Richards Takes Texas by Horns." *Chicago Tribune*, Center for American History, University of Texas at Austin.

Welch, William M. "'Rock Star' Dole Protects Lead in Key Senate Race." *USA Today*, July 1, 2002. Lexis Nexis Academic Universe (accessed August 16, 2002).

Wertheimer, Molly Meijer, ed. *Inventing a Voice: The Rhetoric of American First Ladies of the Twentieth Century*. Lanham, Md.: Rowman & Littlefield, 2004.

Whaley, C. Robert and George Antonelli. "The Birds and the Beasts: Woman as Animal." *Maledicta: International Journal of Verbal Aggression* 7 (1983): 219–29.

"What's in a Name?" *Time* (April 5, 1993): 15. Expanded Academic ASAP (accessed February 2, 1996).

"White New Jersey Governor Strongly Supports Affirmative Action Programs." *Jet* (December 25, 1995–January 1, 1996): 30. Lexis Nexis Academic Universe (accessed August 20, 1999).

Whitman, Christine Todd. "Breaking the Glass Ceiling." WESG Awards Luncheon. Washington, D.C. January 31, 1995. Governor's Office. Trenton, N.J.

————. Remarks. American Legion Girls State. Rider University. June 28, 1996. Governor's Office. Trenton, N.J.

————. Remarks. American Legion Girls State. Rider University. July 2, 1998. <http://www.state.nj.us/governor/girls98.htm> (accessed November 30, 1999).

————. Remarks. Annenberg School for Communication. University of Pennsylvania. Philadelphia. September 29, 1999. <http://www.state.nj.us/governor/annen.htm> (November 22, 1999).

————. Remarks. Budget Address. March 15, 1994. Trenton, N.J. Governor's Office. Trenton, N.J.

————. Remarks. Budget Address. January 23, 1995. Governor's Office. Trenton, N.J.

————. Remarks. Budget Address. January 29, 1996. Governor's Office. Trenton, N.J.

————. Remarks. The First State of the State Speech. January 10, 1995. Governor's Office. Trenton, N.J.

————. Remarks. General Assembly of the American Legion Jersey Boys State. Lawrenceville, N.J. June 22, 1995. Governor's Office. Trenton, N.J.

————. Remarks. Joint Session of the New Jersey Legislature Regarding the Fiscal Year 1998 State Budget. February 10, 1998. <http://www.state.nj.us/governor/ budget98.htm> (accessed July 29, 1999).

————. Remarks. National Council of Women of the United States. March 8, 1994. Governor's Office. Trenton, N.J.

————. Remarks. The 1999 CEO Summit. Waldorf Astoria Hotel. September 28, 1999. <http://www.state.nj.us/governor/ceosum.htm> (accessed November 29, 1999).

————. Remarks. Second Inaugural Address. Newark, N.J. January 20, 1998. <http://www.state.nj.us/governor/inaug98.htm> (accessed November 30, 1999).

————. Remarks. State of the State Address. January 2001. Governor's Office. Trenton, N.J.

————. Remarks. Town Hall. Los Angeles, Calif. September 10, 1998. <http://www.state.nj.us/governor/town.htm> (accessed November 30, 1999).

————. Remarks. Urban Summit Kickoff. Trenton, N.J. September 14, 1999. <http://www.state.nj.us/governor/urbsum.htm> (accessed November 30, 1999).

————. Remarks. Women in Government Luncheon. Masonic Temple. February 23, 1995. Governor's Office. Trenton, N.J.

————. "Unique Voices/Unique Service: Women Serving in the NJ Legislature." Trenton, N.J. September 12, 1995. Governor's Office. Trenton, N.J.

"Whitman for Governor." *The Record*, October 26, 1997, O02. Lexis Nexis Academic Universe (accessed September 15, 1999).

"Whitman Gets Nod from NOW." *United Press International.* August 9, 1993. Lexis Nexis Academic Universe (accessed August 29, 1999).

"Whitman Planning Party Average Jerseyan Can Afford." *The Record*, November 22, 1993, A03. Lexis Nexis Academic Universe (accessed August 20, 1999).

"Whitman's Big Hurdles are Still Ahead of Her." *The Record*, January 8, 1995, A24. Lexis Nexis Academic Universe (accessed September 14, 1999).

Whitman, Willson. "Can a Wife be Governor?" *Collier's* (September 5, 1925): 5.

Wilgoren, Jodi. "A Nominee with Vigor Gives Michigan Democrats Hope." *New York Times*, August 8, 2002. <www.nytimes.com> (accessed August 8, 2002).

Wilkie, Curtis. "Read Her Lips." *The Boston Globe*, October 25, 1992, 15. Lexis Nexis Academic Universe (accessed April 28, 1999).

Williams, Dennis A. with Michael Reese. "Can Dixy Rise Again?" *Newsweek* (July 14, 1980): 28.

"Williams Holds Commanding Lead Over Richards, Poll Shows." *San Antonio Express*, September 16, 1990.

Windel, Candace. "Texans Like Richards More and More." *Corpus Christi Caller Times*, May 4, 1992, A1.

Winfield, Betty Houchin. "'Madame President': Understanding a New Kind of First Lady." *Media Studies Journal* 8 (1994): 59–71.

Witt, April. "Next Md. First Lady No Junior Partner." *Washington Post*, November 9, 2002. <www.washingtonpost.com> (accessed November 9, 2002).

"Witty Richards Easily Wins Fans." *Austin American-Statesman*, July 20, 1988.

"Woman's Bigger Dent in Politics." *The Literary Digest* (November 22, 1924): 17.

"Women Who Won on November 4th." *The Woman Citizen* (November 15, 1924): 9.

Wood, Julia. *Gendered Lives: Communication, Gender, and Culture*. Belmont, Calif.: Wadsworth, 1994.

Woodbury, Richard. "Winds of Change Sweep the Lone Star State." *Time* (April 29, 1991): 32.

"The Write Stuff." *Texas Monthly* (April 1992): 108.

"Wyoming's Woman Candidate." *The Literary Digest* (November 1, 1924): 13.

Zaeske, Susan. "The 'Promiscuous Audience' Controversy and the Emergence of the Early Woman's Rights Movements." *The Quarterly Journal of Speech* 81 (1995): 191–207.

Zernike, Kat. "The 2002 Elections: North Carolina; Elizabeth Dole Easily Defeats Clinton Aide in Senate Bid." *New York Times*, November 6, 2002. Lexis Nexis Academic Universe (accessed November 14, 2002).

Zolper, Thomas. "Gubernatorial Rivals Stress Law and Order: After 4 Years, Whitman Has Tougher Image." *The Record*, October 5, 1997, A01. Lexis Nexis Academic Universe (accessed September 15, 1999).

———. "Whitman's Star Loses Heat, But Still Glows." *The Record*, November 23, 1997, A01. Lexis Nexis Academic Universe (accessed September 15, 1999).

Index

About the Authors

Karrin Vasby Anderson is Assistant Professor of Speech Communication at Colorado State University, where she teaches courses in political communication and directs the public speaking program. Her research on women in politics has appeared in journals such as *Rhetoric & Public Affairs*, *Communication and Critical/Cultural Studies*, and *Women's Studies in Communication*. In 2003, she received the Feminist Scholarship Award from the Organization for Research on Women and Communication.

Kristina Horn Sheeler is Assistant Professor of Communication Studies at Indiana University Purdue University Indianapolis (IUPUI) where she teaches courses in political communication, persuasion, and gender and communication. She has published in *Women's Studies in Communication* and written chapters on political women for *American Voices: An Encyclopedia of Contemporary Orators* and *Navigating Boundaries: The Rhetoric of Women Governors*.